AF777660

Child-Centered Family Therapy

WILEY SERIES IN COUPLES AND FAMILY DYNAMICS AND TREATMENT
Florence W. Kaslow, Series Editor

Treating the Changing Family: Handling Normative and Unusual Events
Michele Harway, Editor

In-Laws: A Guide to Extended-Family Therapy
by Gloria Call Horsley

Handbook of Relational Diagnosis and Dysfunctional Family Patterns
Florence W. Kaslow, Editor

Child-Centered Family Therapy
by Lucille L. Andreozzi

Strange Attractors: Chaos, Complexity, and the Art of Family Therapy
by Michael Bütz, William G. McCown, Linda L. Chamberlain

Infertility: Psychological Issues and Counseling Strategies
by Sandra R. Leiblum

CHILD-CENTERED FAMILY THERAPY

Lucille L. Andreozzi

John Wiley & Sons, Inc.

New York • Chichester • Brisbane • Toronto • Singapore • Weinheim

This text is printed on acid-free paper.

Copyright © 1996 by John Wiley & Sons, Inc.

All rights reserved. Published simultaneously in Canada.

Reproduction or translation of any part of this work beyond that permitted by Section 107 or 108 of the 1976 United States Copyright Act without the permission of the copyright owner is unlawful. Requests for permission or further information should be addressed to the Permissions Department, John Wiley & Sons, Inc., 605 Third Avenue, New York, NY 10158-0012.

This publication is designed to provide accurate and authoritative information in regard to the subject matter covered. It is sold with the understanding that the publisher is not engaged in rendering professional services. If legal, accounting, medical, psychological, or any other expert assistance is required, the services of a competent professional person should be sought.

Library of Congress Cataloging-in-Publication Data:

Andreozzi, Lucille L.
Child-centered family therapy / by Lucille L. Andreozzi.
p. cm. — (Wiley series in couples and family dynamics and treatment)
Includes bibliographical references and index.
ISBN 0-471-14858-X (cloth : alk. paper)
1. Family psychotherapy. 2. Child psychotherapy. I. Title. II. Series.
RC488.5.A525 1996
616.89'156—dc20 95-52822

Printed in the United States of America

10 9 8 7 6 5 4 3 2 1

To my son, Lyle Benjamin,
whose warmth and child's wonder
have shown me the way.

Foreword

IT IS AN HONOR AND PLEASURE to be asked to write the Foreword to this outstanding book and major contribution to family theory and practice. It is deeply gratifying and rewarding when a former student, and now valued colleague, breathes upon a theory that you have been working on for 30 years and brings it to life in her own special and original way. With skillful, experienced understanding of the psychological and behavioral world of children and the patterned, interactional life of families, Lucille Andreozzi guides us through the resolution of developmental crises and the process of family systems change. She successfully integrates child and family developmental theory into a practical, innovative, growth-oriented family model and provides many, effective methods and creative techniques for facilitating optimal child development and therapeutically-induced systems change. What is striking about this work is how cogently she depicts the dynamic interplay between self and system—the ways individuals, children and adults, influence systems and systems, in turn, shape individuals.

Three other important features of Lucille Andreozzi's work are worth noting: her sensitive treatment of and response to the developmental plight and potential of children; her emphasis on the important interaction of practice and research as an ongoing system of personal/professional development and feedback to the therapist that can be used to maximize and improve family therapy outcomes; and her deep commitment to the development of a child-centered family therapy practice model.

In this book, she integrates child and family development and incorporates children, the family system, the role of the therapist, the therapy process, and family research into a full cycle of influence and interaction that positively affect outcomes.

What makes reading Lucille Andreozzi's work so satisfying is how brilliantly she has charted a path for us to a complete family theory that therapists will be able to readily use. For all the great work done by the pioneering family therapist-thinkers, none in my opinion, offers a complete theory of the family and family practice. Lucille Andreozzi has opened the door to a vast subject that has been ignored largely because of the immensity and complexity of the task. The integration of child and family development and a developmental theory of the family are missing pieces in family therapy theory building. These are daunting tasks that few have dared to assume, and that Lucille Andreozzi has had the intellectual courage to undertake.

Family therapists, like Minuchin, Haley, Bowen, Satir, and Whitaker have invented stunning practice theories. But all of their "theories of family," to varying degrees, have been unequal to their theories of intervention. Gregory Bateson, a hero to many in the field, offered a pure theory of family process which others could run with. However, Bateson himself was skeptical about the wholesale application of his ideas by family therapists to clinical practice. Thus, the field has suffered for want of a more complete theory of the family that integrates a model of practical interventions with a pure theory of family process and development.

What would a more complete theory of the family and family therapy look like? It would be fully grounded in a philosophical base of a systems view of the world. Such a theory would formulate a set of theoretical postulates and human development principles broad enough to describe and explain the range of structures that evolve in different types of family systems. This theory would also propose a typology of family models or paradigms and relate these family system types to types and levels of intervention. It would identify and situate levels of assessment and intervention on a treatment continuum from prevention to early intervention to family crisis and therapy. A complete theory would also link concepts of here and now, face-to-face family relationships and overt behavior—the special provence of family therapy—both with these family system paradigms (family types) and with the interior worlds of individuals living in systems. It would integrate child and family development and view children as unique, individual entities who influence and are strongly influenced by the family in ways that reflect where each is developmentally. This theory would view children as central to family change, and child and family development as reciprocal, mutally dependent processes. A complete theory would also systematically apply systems concepts of change in a practice theory based on developed strategies and tools for intervening effectively in families that need help. This is quite a formidable and remarkable task!

Lucille Andreozzi presents a distinctly original work of unusual clarity and reach of mind. This book provides the therapist with a developmentally focused practice model and theory of child-centered family intervention and change. Keeping the developmental needs of vulnerable children clearly in focus, Lucille Andreozzi's work cuts through the dense, conceptual brush and underexplored terrain of child and family development, and goes a long way in setting us on the right path toward a unified theory of the family.

DAVID KANTOR

July 1996

Series Preface

Our ability to form strong interpersonal bonds with romantic partners, children, parents, siblings, and other relations is one of the key qualities that defines our humanity. These relationships shape who we are and what we become—they can be a source of great gratification, or tremendous pain. Yet, only in the mid-20th century did behavioral and social scientists really begin focusing on couples and family dynamics, and only in the past several decades have the theory and findings that emerged from those studies been used to develop effective therapeutic interventions for troubled couples and families.

We have made great progress in understanding the structure, function, and interactional patterns of couples and families—and have made tremendous strides in treatment. However, as we stand poised on the beginning of a new millennium, it seems quite clear that both intimate partnerships and family relationships are in a period of tremendous flux. Economic factors are changing work patterns, parenting responsibilities, and relational dynamics. Modern medicine has helped lengthen the life span, giving rise to the need for transgenerational caretaking. Cohabitation, divorce, and remarriage are quite commonplace, and these social changes make it necessary for us to rethink and broaden our definition of what constitutes a family.

Thus, it is no longer enough simply to embrace the concept of the family as a system. In order to understand and effectively treat the evolving family, our theoretical formulations and clinical interventions must be informed by an understanding of ethnicity, culture, religion, gender, sexual preference, family life cycle, socioeconomic status, education, physical and mental health, values, and belief systems.

The purpose of the *Wiley Series in Couples and Family Dynamics and Treatment* is to provide a forum for cutting-edge relational and family theory, practice, and research. Its scope is intended to be broad, diverse, and international, but all books published in this series share a common mission: to reflect on the past, offer state-of-the-art information on the present, and speculate on, as well as attempt to shape, the future of the field.

FLORENCE W. KASLOW
Florida Couples and Family Institute

Preface

CHANGES IN OUR SOCIETY are making family outreach, early intervention, and child-centered family therapy more crucial than ever. Certainly, the landscape and contours of our society are shifting. One of those shifts can be seen in the many forms that today's families take. It is a myth that the majority of children live in two-parent households. Too, there is the feminization of poverty, in which a rising number of those who are economically disenfranchised are women and children, combined with the growing numbers of the working poor.

Yet, it is not only poverty that creates difficulty or the disenfranchised who show signs of stress and crisis. Today's family system, regardless of the form it takes, its socioeconomic status, or geographic location, has much more laid on its doorstep. The family system is being asked to take on and absorb many more responsibilities, stretching family developmental limits in the face of dwindling social support, vanishing neighborhoods, and a fragile sense of community and connection.

Another shift, standing at the center of the need for the Child-Centered Family Therapy Model presented in this book, is the change in the types and onset of serious problems seen in children, combined with shifting orientations in health care. On an epidemiological level, we are becoming a more aggressive, violent, and anonymous society, with children having fewer constructive outlets available. The onset, chronicity, and severity of behavior problems is occurring with greater reported frequency and often at an earlier age. In our private practices and child guidance clinics, we are seeing increasing numbers of children who show antisocial, apathetic, or aggressive behavior—youths with an under-developed "conscience" or sense of responsibility and purpose. Disruptive behavior often masks accompanying, underlying depression. As we see more and more sad and angry children, without direction, who have lost or who have never been shown their worth or value, we also see overworked families at their wits end, who do not know what to do—families who would have benefitted immensely from short-term intervention at the earlier signs of distress. There are hosts of other families who have acted courageously and resourcefully in the face of a changing society and daunting environmental circumstances. These families have turned adversity into opportunity for family system growth. Combine these shifting family trends and childhood imperatives with the demands imposed by the new directives of managed care, and this effective short-term, three-tier Child-Centered Model of prevention, early intervention, and therapy becomes more crucially important to the therapist and family than ever.

Furthermore, while the catalog of prominent childhood disorders and family pathologies may vary according to the field's scientific attention and historical interests, the substance of this point remains true to date. Emphasis on family pathology overshadows coexistent growth-oriented, healthy family processes. The most "pathology dominated" family systems also contain "islands" of functional family process. Family systems do not unilaterally or uniformly display problems or disturbance across all family dimensions, as family assessment research in general and clinical practice and research on the Child-Centered Family Model have shown.

How a family handles ordinary daily events and activities reveals a great deal about family process. Even families in crisis, and the troubled, multiproblem family, must perform ordinary daily activities—feeding the cat, buying groceries, paying the heating bill—or the family ceases to be. Even in such families, where pathology is apparent, family strength, often well-hidden, is also present. Emphasis on pathology or counterproductive, problematic family patterns or strategies in our clinically-driven field of mental health service can obscure and divert recognition of and important change inroads available through the family's competencies and strengths. Once we, as therapists, identify these "secret," positive strengths, we will have the tools necessary to begin the process of family change. Child-Centered Family Therapy connects with the fundamental, healthy inclinations of the family, and the more morphogenetic or change-amplifying strategies of family systems. While family disturbance is clearly addressed, the Child-Centered Model builds on family competence and strength. By identifying fundamental family processes and dimensions, as well as the generic tasks that all families must perform if the family system is to grow and thrive, we find a common link and unified, developmentally focused understanding of family change that integrates prevention and early intervention into a single, growth-oriented systems model.

Prevention and early intervention are emphasized for two very important reasons. The first reason is obvious and self-evident and relates directly to the confirmed and reinforced crucial role that the family plays in shaping optimal child development. The guiding objective of the Child-Centered Model is to influence positive child development outcomes through positive family systems change. Another highly relevant reason pertains to the practice of child-centered family therapy. The overall systematic program of clinical practice and research on the Child-Centered Model empirically confirms the efficacy of the model across a range of treatment contexts, from prevention to family therapy. Assessed from both therapists' and families' perspectives and multiple evaluation vantage points (change indices), problem intensity and therapy outcomes (results on the clinical tier of the model), highlight that families facing serious presenting child problems improved after therapy. In addition, research on prevention and early intervention (the first two tiers of the model) indicate that family problems can be averted and family strengths can be solidified and reinforced through child-centered family practice. Approximately 500 families of young children who participated in a five-year community-based intervention program, focusing on intensive family outreach, reported positive child development and family system gains.

The Child-Centered Model first began as part of a five-year Rhode Island State Department of Education parent training and community outreach grant program aimed at families at risk. The purpose of the grant project was to develop an effective prevention and early intervention model that positively influenced parent-child relationships and improved the predicted outcomes of children at educational and emotional risk. The overall objective was to create family change by awakening within families self-reflective and self-corrective processes—to make families "family system experts"—a concept and process (principle) that will be illustrated throughout this book. In contrast to parent skill training programs, which focus on parenting skills as discrete and separate entities occurring outside whole-family process and provide educational interventions that are behavioral and prescriptive, the Child-Centered Model takes a decisively family system approach, a path quite different from parent training programs, that involves the integration of child and family development.

The Child-Centered Model has systematically researched "what works" in the lives of children. The model provides an effective, clinically and empirically derived, multilevel program of family change (techniques and activities) that address the needs of children, parents, and families across a range of perspectives: prevention, early intervention, and family therapy. In the Child-Centered Model all three orientations to family growth and change are termed "prevention"—primary, secondary, and tertiary. Prevention is consistently interwoven across intervention contexts, reflecting the model's central principle and abiding commitment to normalizing family process. The model firmly holds that:

- Growth-oriented as well as problematic patterns co-exist simultaneously in a family. Such change-generating patterns are the route to and the source of a family's sense of competence.
- Acts of intervention (early intervention and therapy) are simultaneously acts of prevention. The intent of intervention, to bring about positive problem resolution, is, at the same time, ultimately aimed at prevention: strengthening a family's capacity to effectively handle or avert future problems.

In the early stages of the model's development, a variety of family theories, modes of intervention, and methods of parent training and involvement were explored, evaluated, and researched. The research involved empirical analyses but also included talking directly and extensively with parents in their homes, neighborhoods, and communities. The questions posed revolved around the main theme and issue "Why were other parent programs (skill training alone) so poorly attended?" The answer families resoundingly gave reflected the following consensus: Parent skill training programs are not meaningful in terms of the real world of family experience. Parents explained that the "advice" and "prescriptions" skill training programs offered were "too nice and neat," too idealized and unrealistic, outside the realm of everyday experience. Parents wanted programs that made real, practical, and emotional connections in their lives; programs that did not simply fill their heads with all kinds of information that they forgot as soon as they left the parent group meeting or therapist's office. As parents expressed, skill training alone was not making a meaningful and lasting impact in their lives.

Dialogues and round-table discussions with families and community center staff, providing the best and most immediate sources of feedback, evaluation, and consumer research, along with systematic family needs assessments, reviews of prevailing models, and empirical outcome analyses, contributed to the Child-Centered Model's family system perspective. Careful analysis and review of parent-child programs and family process research, combined with the strong experiential statements parents expressed, led to the following four main conclusions:

1. Parenting "exercises" and activities, when separated from the full picture of family dynamics, leave parents "cold" and at a cognitive disadvantage. The learning that occurs is less effective because parenting exercises have low-task relevance for families. Parent-child re-education is treated as if it takes place in a vacuum.

For example, to instruct parents to practice communicating "I" messages to their children ("I am upset that you broke the cup."), instead of "you" messages ("You bad girl, look at what you did, look how upset you made me!"), was akin to giving parents a "band-aid" or superficial solution—a technique that may miss its mark because it is not fully grounded in the larger picture of family process. While "I" messages, which involve a parent taking ownership of his or her feelings and differentiating between the behavioral act and the child's worth, are significant improvements over blame-oriented "you" messages, parents expressed they often lacked the broader perspective. Parents explained that, in addition to needing to know *what* to do (the behavior change), they also needed to know *why* they were making the change and *how* to apply (generalize) newly acquired parenting skills across a range of family situations. Skill development, parent re-orientation, and knowledge of child development and the parent-child relationship need to be embedded in a fuller understanding of family process.

Parents also communicated the sense and experience that parenting and child development information, often provided in the form of "advice," was not sufficient for several other reasons:

2. The information, although practical, does not relate directly to day-to-day parent-child transactions and problems, nor do prescriptions mirror neighborhood, community, and family realities.
3. The advice parenting programs provide often seems "too tidy and perfect," portraying an idealized or fairy-tail version of family life: the way families ought to be and parents and children ought to behave.
4. Because the information is often communicated as "advice" and "instruction," even when the information is perceived as relevant, parents feel as if they do not own the knowledge personally but that the information is taught to them prescriptively.

As a result, rather than being internalized and integrated, the information remained largely external, foreign, and unassimilated.

If families are to change, and optimal child and family development is to take hold, then families should be engaged cognitively and affectively: learning, as the research on adult education has shown, requires a redirection. Family understanding and individual learning should begin not from the outside-in, where knowledge is transplanted from facilitator (therapist, social worker, child development specialist) to participant, but rather should be developed organically, from the inside-out. The family program and activities should begin with what parents already know, their personal and family life experience. Learning should originate with the self and progress outward to the next obvious intimate space—the family.

For genuine, sustained family change to take root and continue, the program and activities need to engage the whole person in heart and mind, capturing the collective imagination of the entire family. This challenge involves creating activities that engage families, parents, and children cognitively and affectively, and that accurately translate complex system theory into everyday, practical family awareness. Although parents never used the word "system," or spoke in the technical language of family therapy, they expressed the recognition that parent training programs lacked the system process of building knowledge from within. What was absent was knowledge grounded in a family foundation. The objective of the Child-Centered Model extends well beyond parent training and education, and involves the translation of family system principles into practical, relevant family activities and interventions.

The Child-Centered Model synthesizes and integrates major child development theories and human development principles of growth and change into a family systems framework. David Kantor's Structural Dynamic Theory (Kantor, 1980; Kantor & Lehr, 1986) forms the unifying foundation around which child development principles and a program of child-centered family interventions (techniques and activities) are layered and integrated. What was most striking to me about David Kantor's theory in 1975—a feature that continues to impress me to this day—is the breadth and depth of concepts and their natural affinity for a "marriage" with child development theory and principles of child-centered family practice. We can judge the merits and integrity of a scientific theory of the family by its fruitfulness and utility, its capacity to generate new theoretical offshoots and translate this knowledge into practical models of intervention and research. David Kantor's cutting edge Structural Dynamic Theory offers an ideal match or fit with child development and an evolving child-centered family practice. The Child-Centered Model adapts, applies, and extends structural dynamics to the domain (developmental imperatives) of children and the special circumstances of child-centered family therapy. A set of Child-Centered Activities have been designed and developed to stimulate family growth from within. The activities simultaneously elicit and highlight child and family development, build on family strengths, and nurture the individual's (adult and child) and family's capacity to act as informed system experts, explorers, and guides. Hence, the integration of child and family development, the development of Child-Centered Family Activities, and methods of assessment and intervention, plus David Kantor's Structural Dynamic Theory equals Child-Centered Structural Dynamic Therapy, the model presented in this book.

The Child-Centered Model began as a community-based program that focused on early intervention in families and children at risk. Gradually, the model expanded to include prevention and family therapy applications. The model started with parent/family groups. Through research and evaluation, home-based intervention, children's playgroups, and a toy lending family resource library were incorporated. Together, these components form the four main, interactive modules that the therapist can flexibly apply, according to the demands of the treatment setting, family system type, and presenting problem. These modules serve as the contexts for facilitating family growth and, therefore, are the equivalent of different perspectives on child and family development.

While the Child-Centered Model has shown positive, quantitative (statistical) family outcomes, there are also other tangible signs of family growth and change to consider. There are important qualitative measures of family changes that indicate that the program made a meaningful, psychological, and social difference in the lives of participating families. As the model grew, an expanding network of training and a system of education simultaneously developed, creating widening circles of community involvement and family change. In addition to positive program evaluations, some of the more palpable and tangible changes in the lives of participating families included many socioeconomically disadvantaged parents gaining access to college educations, some earning their high school equivalencies, and some obtaining careers in social service. The model communicated and set into motion a full cycle of community involvement and volunteerism. Many of the parents, who began as participants, became family educators and home-based teachers, who trained others in the model, enabling other families whose position they had once experienced to make positive changes. Some of the participants who entered the program as members of families at risk are now preschool teachers and directors of child development and social service centers. Other tangible gains involved observable improvement in children whose families participated, as indicated by preschool and classroom teacher evaluations.

Child-Centered Family Therapy combines child development and family process, creating a developmentally focused, family initiated, and therapeutically induced model of system change. Its activities and interventions are practical and behavioral. The activities are consciously designed to emphasize normalizing family process and to nurture, within families and individuals, a sense of self-reflection and a capacity to guide family development by understanding family process—naming what is taking place, and then constructing strategies of positive family change.

An overview and orientation to the Child-Centered Model, including core concepts and terms, are provided in Chapter 1. This chapter explores the theoretical roots of the model and the clinical links between child and family development in facilitating child-centered family change. In Chapter 2, parent-child relationships and family process are framed as patterns of access around salient child development tasks and family goals. This chapter provides a process vocabulary for recasting parent-child problems in a blame-free light and offers methods for charting developmental crises and assessing problem level or intensity. In Chapter 2, the role of the individual (adult and child) is drawn into the foreground and given center stage, immersed in a background of family influence and process. The emphasis is on the relationship between the psychological world of the individual, including children as emerging, developmental systems, and overt behavior. This chapter focuses on the "self" in the shifting, self-system gestalt of family interactions. Chapter 2 explores the intersection between the personal world (motivations and behaviors) of the individual and the family's transactional life.

Keeping the personal, psychological world of the individual clearly in mind, Chapter 3 moves to a system level view. This chapter integrates child and family development and describes and illustrates a multilevel view of family organization, development, assessment, intervention, and change. Chapter 3 explores the involvement of children in family therapy. The sphere of involvement and analysis grows increasingly broader and wider to incorporate the role and influence of the therapist and research on family practice as self-supervising systems. The aim of the Child-Centered Model is always growth-oriented, designing and facilitating positive developmental pathways, opportunities, and outcomes. The model applies this principle to all involved participants: the therapist, in terms of ways to improve efficacy through self-supervision; the research process as an ongoing, rich source of family analysis, an intimate feedback system allied to the therapy process; and the family as a capable, self-reflecting system engaged in all phases of developmental change, whether primarily self-generated with the guidance of the practitioner, or clinically induced through the interventions of the therapist. Chapters 2 and 3, together, create a transactional picture of a full cycle of influence that incorporates the individual and system.

Chapter 4 delves more deeply into the practice of child-centered family therapy, addressing pragmatic as well as conceptual issues. The chapter focuses on engaging children and families in therapy, preparing the room for the family, child-centered materials, presenting child problems and diagnostic categories, and the therapist's cognitive and emotional frames of reference. This chapter also examines the role of the therapist in structuring family change, introducing concepts and exploring issues related to professional development and self-supervision. Chapter 4 examines the impact and interplay of the therapist's technical mastery and evolving relationship skills. The broad outlines of a training model are presented, emphasizing the role of self-knowledge and professional skill in clinical practice. Chapter 5 examines primary prevention and early intervention, the first two tiers of the Child-Centered Model. This chapter focuses on the four modules for integrating child and family development: parent/family group, children's playgroup, home-based intervention, and the family resource lending library. The building blocks (components of the model) and role of the therapist are examined in these contexts. Chapter 5 explores the process and concept of families as informed system guides. This chapter describes and illustrates techniques and interventions directed toward facilitating family initiated and therapeutically guided systems change.

Chapter 6 provides an in-depth description, step-by-step plan, and applications of the five Child-Centered Family Activities, routes to system understanding and change. These activities are the Family Notebook Activity, the Family Photograph Activity, the Family Network Drawing, Living Sculpture, and Family Role Play. The overall aim of the activities and the model is explored and illustrated—creating family change through system awareness or families as system experts. The goal of the Child-Centered Model, through the special role of the therapist and cumulative effect and intent of its five Family Activities, is to provide families with cognitive, affective, and experiential knowledge about child development and family process. The model's activities are designed to strengthen a family's capacity to observe, reflect, evaluate, and generate new solutions: the foundation of systems change. When families learn about systems by first learning about themselves, when they can name the dynamics they see in family interactions and relationships, and when this knowledge strikes a balance between thought and feeling awareness, they are far better equipped to handle crisis. Families can become conscious creators, as opposed to helpless victims of an unowned family future. The activities presented in Chapter 6 have been purposely designed and developed to stir in families the self-reflective capacity to state, "We see what is going on. Do we want to continue this way or change?" The five Child-Centered Activities described in Chapter 6 provide families with new action-strategies (child development, parent-child, and system problem-solving skills), helping them to recognize and approach problems more effectively, and guiding them along a positive developmental path.

Chapter 7 explores the family therapy tier of the model. This chapter provides an in-depth overview and description of the therapy process, including assessment and treatment phases, sub-phases, and goals. To round out and complete the picture, Chapter 7 also focuses on the role of the therapist and presents a model of training, supervision, and self-development. A set of instruments, the Rainbow Forms (Kantor & Andreozzi, 1985), and their clinical application is described and illustrated. The Rainbow Forms are designed to help therapists formulate, focus, test, and refine their treatment plans. Family case illustrations are provided. Chapter 8 turns to the practice of Child-Centered Structural Dynamic Therapy, as shown in a range of family cases. In this chapter, four cases of crisis resolution drawn from child-centered family therapy practice are examined in detail. Each family vignette depicts and highlights a different family problem and developmental crisis, and illuminates a different key clinical concept of the model. Implicit within the therapy process involving each family is the conscious thought process of the Rainbow Forms.

I am writing this book to convey the excitement and wonder in child-centered family therapy and to communicate the importance of intervening early in the lives of vulnerable children. This book grows out of my deep commitment to the rights and needs of children and their precarious, often disqualified positions in troubled families. The emphasis is on intervening early, before family problems become entrenched and cause great emotional expense to parents and children alike. Helping families by strengthening system competencies ultimately helps children. Throughout my work and experience as a family therapist, I have been continually impressed by the uncomplicated honesty, courage, and power of children to move family systems forward. Their innocence is their objectivity. As spontaneous and innovative communicators, children are often the first to lead the family through the process of healing, and to increased states of health. Frequently, they are the first to pick up on and reflect family tension and distress, and the first to forgive. The Child-Centered Model presented in this book nests child development and parent-child relations within family process, and integrates child and family development into a growth-oriented family model. The model meets parents, children, and families at this developmental crossroads, making optimal use of the creative as well as crisis-borne moments of family change. When the therapist and family capitalize on the opportunities provided by these evolutions in the family structure, they can effect important turning points in family development.

LUCILLE L. ANDREOZZI

July 1996

Acknowledgments

THERE HAVE BEEN MANY strong influences in my life, both personal and professional, that have shaped my concept of family, my commitment to children, and my belief in the power of the systems perspective. When I consider the role of important people at decisive points in my life, I think of them in terms of interrelated, concentric circles, widening ripples of influence and important life-lessons. At the innermost center of the circle, and the most crucial shaper of this book, the person I want to acknowledge first is my 8-year-old son, Lyle, whose enthusiasm, energy, warmth, and spontaneity toward life's challenges have taught me volumes. His resilient, joyful, and adventurous spirit has shown me the real-life meaning of child development and the wonder of the world through children's eyes. I wish to acknowledge Lyle, and the many other children I have seen who have confided their life stories with trust and frank, uncomplicated honesty, freely and courageously sharing their innermost thoughts, feelings, and experiences.

Next, there are my parents and extended family, who showed me the intricacies of patterns of intimacy and relationships long before I ever picked up or read an academic text on family process or systems theory. Growing up in an extended family household, where generations of relatives and several nuclear families blended together in patterns of connection and autonomy, showed me the many, subtle nuances of human interaction: how family life continues and is expressed from many points of view and different, simultaneous developmental perspectives. There were many teachers, resources, and lessons to absorb. I wish to express my appreciation to my mother, Madeline, for her indomitable spirit and perseverance; my father, John, for his humor and objectivity in the face of adversities; my aunt, Dorothy Andreozzi, for her unconditional support; my grandmother, Gilda Pompa, for her practical wisdom; and my uncle, Dante Pompa, who taught me the invaluable lesson of human dignity and worth, and an abiding respect for individual differences. To all these life-mentors, I am deeply grateful for all they have shown me and for what I continue to learn by their examples.

I also wish to acknowledge several other very important people who helped shape my personal and professional views. I wish to thank Dr. Jack Wideman for his humanistic, empathic approach to clinical practice; Dr. Samuel P. Hunt for his many hours of clinical insight, understanding, and supervision in individual psychodynamic psychotherapy; and my friend Barbara Roberts, for her commitment to and concept of equality and social change. I also want to express my deep appreciation to Dr. David Kantor, who taught me the fundamentals and, perhaps more importantly, the heart of family therapy and effective practice; what it truly means to be a family therapist. I am grateful for his concept of family, as well as for his warm, enduring friendship. I also owe a great deal of gratitude and appreciation to Dr. David Faust, my dear friend and mentor, for our many conversations and his careful insights into issues of clinical assessment, human nature, and the predictable as well as unpredictable patterns of human behavior. He has always been there for me. I am deeply grateful for his warm and generous support and encouragement throughout the writing of this book and other important life projects.

I also want to acknowledge a number of other special people who contributed significantly to the process and preparation of this book. I owe an immense debt of gratitude to Linda Mahoney for her cheerful outlook and consistent, tireless efforts in the typing of this manuscript and tables, for extending herself, often working under the pressure of deadlines and numerous revisions; Jeanie Powell, who came through, stepping in at the eleventh hour to help with the technical production of graphics and figures; Kiersten Stevenson, who offered feedback and comments on the manuscript; Rosanna DiGregorio and Berta Jones, who worked with me many late evenings proofing the initial drafts of the text. I especially want to acknowledge and express my appreciation to Ryan McNulty, who assisted me with library research and worked beside me in the office for many hours and weekends, well beyond the call of duty, to complete this manuscript. I am extremely grateful for his care and attention to detail, his efficient organization, sense of humor and intelligence, and his support in the face of many crises, technical and otherwise. I also wish to thank Kelly Franklin, my editor at John Wiley & Sons, for her feedback, guidance, and support. Regardless of how busy she was, she always was there to answer all of my questions and offer generous amounts of encouragement and advice.

L.L.A.

Contents

CHAPTER 1

Child-Centered Structural Dynamic Therapy

Overview and Process

Jennifer, who is seven, is doing poorly in school. Her attitude and behavior have changed dramatically over the past 6 months. She is easily distracted, fails to follow directions, refuses help, and forgets things. Her behavior is also disruptive at home. She bites or pinches when she cannot get her way, engaging adult family members (especially her grandmother) in physical struggles. The family complains that she is rude and disrespectful, a "regular smart mouth," "7 going on 17." The family expresses, in words and behavioral imagery, feeling menaced and intimidated by her.

When the family enters the therapy room, they look as if they are physically embattled and under emotional siege. Anne, the mother, sits impassively, entrenched in disappointment. She looks weary and sad as she holds the couple's younger child, 18-month-old "Baby Noel," close on her lap. She explains how she feels "disappointed," "cheated," a "failure as a parent"; her resignation now often builds into sudden bursts of irritability and anger. She turns imploringly toward Jennifer, "Please, be a good girl for Mommy. Remember what I told you . . ." She stops short and then adds, "Oh, what's the use. Be a rotten kid. Go ahead. Show your stuff." Tom, her husband, sits opposite her, silent. His eyes are trained on Jennifer, and he is seething. Looking indirectly at his wife, his head turned to follow Jennifer's movements, he mumbles, "Men are as dumb and dense as mushrooms, hidden in the shadows in this family . . . what difference does it make?" Abandoning his thought in midsentence, in a low and irritated tone, he says, "Jennifer, causing trouble again? Don't you ever quit? Stop making such a racket!" Just then Margaret, Anne's mother, the maternal grandparent (included in therapy because she watches the children for extended periods due to recent changes in Anne's and Tom's busy work schedules), pipes in, "This child is too much. She eats with her fingers. She defies me terribly. Yesterday she smeared toothpaste all over the bathroom mirror and floor. When I told her to clean it up she bit me. This child is disobedient, willful, and an impossible terror."

"Stop criticizing her," Anne snaps, "In your eyes Jennifer can't do anything right. You're on her back too much, like a big Harpy bird, picking on her all the time. Always criticizing and complaining. You and I never agree on anything." As the adults talk, Jennifer races from one family member to another, beseeching them with questions and distracting interruptions.

Tempers flair and the conflict escalates as family members push one another's emotional triggers and interpersonal buttons, revealing the heart of the family's image-struggle. Anne continues, half imploring, half sniping at her mother, "You worry about the wrong things. Material things. How clean the house is; how neat Jenny's homework papers look; did she eat every morsel of food on her plate. But you forget her as a person. What about emotional food! Don't you ever wonder if you've made a mistake and hurt someone's feelings? I know I do."

Margaret responds in a well-defended voice, "No, I never feel guilty. I can't remember when I thought I was wrong. I've never felt guilty over anything I've done." Anne, looking utterly astonished, hurls back the blow of a precise insight, "That's so cold. Then you're stone-cold perfect and living in a dream world of absolute denial." Margaret winces; she falls back against her chair as if she had just been punched. Then, rising to her feet in indignation, she announces, "I am a kind person. I see myself as a giver. I always put myself last. I give sometimes until there is nothing left of me . . . to give."

Both women, Anne and Margaret, mother and daughter, have wounded each other with their words. They have struck deep blows, resonating cords at the center of emotionally charged interpersonal images, views of self and family, important statements about identity and worth. A family knows these images and their power implicitly. Moments later, both women are in tears, sorry for the line they have transgressed and also relieved that the conflict is out in the open.

Crisis Resolution: The Family's Symbolic and Systemic Life

The key to crisis resolution, behavior change, and positive family development revolves around understanding and identifying the expectations, behaviors, and intentions associated with these potent interpersonal images. These images are constructed out of the patterned experience and interaction of everyday family life: the ways we are *seen* and *known, ignored* or *forgotten.* We can also think of these interpersonal images, the internalized views that we carry around inside us, as stories with a structure, intimate interpersonal identity expressed on two levels: the symbolic or psychological and the systemic or behavioral. The symbolic or psychological speaks to the level of personal imagery and self-concept, the "individual inside the family" and the "family inside the individual." The "systemic" speaks to pure family process, how members interact, and the level at which family patterns shape individual behavior. Both the family's behavioral and symbolic life are essential elements to consider in crisis resolution.

The individual's psychological interpretation of self and internalized view of family, combined with the family's preferred and learned behavior patterns—the intersection where past and present meet in decisive ways for child and family development—create the stories that families bring to therapy. These vivid image-scenes and image-vulnerabilities of self-in-relation to others and others vis-à-vis self form the crucial puzzle pieces that contribute to and explain the family crisis. The extent to which the pieces do not fit—the degree to which these images (the physical and psychological voices and identities of family members) are vying to be seen and straining to be heard—equals the intensity of the family conflict. Families and children show therapists these "image-worries" and "image-wonders" (image-scenes) through what they tell us (what they can or cannot express, will or will not say) and how they behave (what they do or do not do, will or will not try).

The preceding scenario sheds light on these behavioral guides and interpersonal imagery. There is "Baby Noel," who is perceived as the family's "gift"; Anne, who views herself as a failed parent and also expresses her "adult-child's disappointment" toward a parent she perceives as emotionally cold and critical; and Margaret (grandmother) who views herself, in contrast, as an inexhaustive, relentless giver and supplier of nurturance. There is also Tom, the husband, who views men, and by inference, himself, curiously as "mushrooms"; senseless, inert, insignificant things. His seemingly offhanded comment and unusual metaphor is a revealing one. Tom seems to be saying that men, as a social category of experience, are inconsequential in the family. He feels dwarfed, overshadowed, powerless, and without real influence. And, finally, there is Jennifer, who is caught in the structure of a three-way developmental struggle, the scapegoat on whose head each member casts his or her own family aspersions: "Please . . . Mommy," "causing trouble again," "terror," "rotten kid," who is dared to "show your stuff." Jennifer's evolving interpersonal image, expressed in her behavior, is that of an agitator and deflector; she interrupts (intrudes) and is ultimately blamed, rebuked, and rejected.

The developmental nature of the family problem is also apparent in this scenario. The conflict reflects crises occurring on multiple levels: current family interactions, recurrent relationship patterns (generational histories), child development, and family development. The scenario illustrates the crucial role and fundamental quality of a family's relationship images and symbols, and the influence such imagery exerts on behavior and family structure. Jennifer is caught in a three-way interpersonal struggle; her child development stage both captures and provides the convenient content for a recurrent, reawakened family developmental struggle. The scenario emphasizes the interplay of child and family development in a presenting child problem. Four interactive perspectives and interrelated structures are considered in Child-Centered Family Therapy:

1. The current child development task or dilemma at risk or in crisis.
2. The intersection of child and family development, specifically the influence of current family process (organization and structure) on the problem.
3. The contributions of each family member on psychological and behavioral grounds to the problem-process and current crisis.
4. The quality and cumulative impact of prior child and family developmental stages on the family.

Accordingly, child development or, more precisely, "child development stages" are viewed as important "structures" that shed light on crisis resolution and the process of family change.

Child-Centered Structural Dynamic Therapy

Child-Centered Structural Dynamic Therapy is a developmentally focused model and method of family therapy. Child-Centered Structural Dynamic Therapy integrates child and family system development into a comprehensive framework of family assessment, intervention, and change. The model is organized into three tiers or levels: prevention, early intervention, and therapy (crisis intervention). Because the model is grounded in a normative view of family process, the concept of prevention is interwoven throughout all three levels. In addition, a supralevel is built into the model that permeates all three practice-levels and acts as a process guide to effective therapy: The therapist can use this structure to evaluate the progress and efficacy of therapy. This method provides ongoing self-supervision for personal and professional development.

By providing a stage-specific, developmentally focused framework the model offers the therapist a comprehensive program of interventions, techniques, and practical activities to promote positive child-centered family change. Because the model is primarily process oriented, transforming child development and family system theory and concepts into an integrated, systematic program of self-guided and therapeutically induced family change, the therapist can create time-limited, individualized treatment plans and also test the effectiveness and validity of the therapy process, making appropriate changes when indicated. The therapist can flexibly apply the concepts, the model's "building blocks" and techniques, to fit the special circumstances (developmental stage, system type, problem dynamics) of the family and treatment setting.

The structure of the Child-Centered Model has evolved out of David Kantor's classic theory of structural dynamics (Kantor, 1980; Kantor & Lehr, 1986). In this model, Kantor's theory forms a unifying foundation and framework around which child development theory and principles of growth and change have been layered and integrated. Kantor's concepts of family process have been melded and adapted to fit the context of children in therapy; and child-centered activities (family-guided and therapeutically induced, developmentally focused techniques) have been developed (Andreozzi, 1977, 1978, 1979a, 1979b, 1979c, 1979d, 1988) that translate and transfer Kantor's family theory into the domains of children, parent-child relations, and child-centered practice. Hence, child development, child-centered activities, and a program of developmentally focused family interventions, plus Kantor's structural dynamic theory equal Child-Centered Structural Dynamic Therapy.

In *Inside the Family* (Kantor & Lehr, 1986), David Kantor presents an incisive, comprehensive five-component framework of family process. The breadth and depth of the concepts make Kantor's model ideally suited for the integration of child development and provide a rich foundation for generating child-centered family practice. Kantor's components include family subsystems, a typology of family systems, access dimensions (space, time, and energy), interpersonal goals (power/efficacy, nurturance/intimacy, and meaning/identity), and family player parts. Together, family access dimensions and interpersonal goals (components 3 and 4) form multiple, branching pathways of evaluation and description on a six-dimensional social space grid that conceptualizes family interaction. Child-Centered Structural Dynamic Therapy represents the translation and adaptation of Kantor's family process framework to integrate child development and family development. The child development concepts of space, time, and energy and developmental tasks of children are interwoven with family system concepts of development, yielding a comprehensive model of assessment, treatment, and positive change. In this way, parent-child conflicts and presenting child problems are reformulated as developmental crises.

In 1980, David Kantor introduced an innovative, breakthrough concept in the family therapy field: the *critical identity image.* This concept forms the central, organizing principle of structural dynamics, and, hence, the centerpiece concept of Child-Centered Structural Dynamic Therapy. Kantor's critical identity image concept, a special, emotionally intense form of interpersonal imagery (discussed later in this chapter), effectively links individual, couple, and family therapy. The Kantor concept and accompanying phases of structural dynamics have been adapted to fit the developmental needs of children in the context of child-centered therapy. To date, structural dynamics has focused almost exclusively on couple and family therapy, concentrating primarily on the adult world of experience. The Child-Centered Model presented in this book reflects an evolving program of research and practice (Andreozzi, 1976, 1977, 1978, 1979d, 1979e, 1980, 1985a, 1988, 1993a, 1993b) and the first application to children. The child-centered research and practice described in this book have built pragmatically from one phase to the next. Each stage has formed a successive bridge, with more refined links, between an empirical understanding of the family and experimental outcomes, including the assessment of family change. The research also has been interactive and twofold (descriptive and evaluative) in examining the intersection between child development, parent-child relations, and family process. Clinical research on child-centered practice, the model presented in this book, has focused on issues of system assessment (the interplay of child and family development), family measurement, and outcome interpretation (the relationship of process events to therapy outcomes).

When we distill Child-Centered Structural Dynamics to its essence, the therapy involves a threefold process. First, the therapist identifies the intersection of child and family development, the developmental structure in crisis. This involves tracing and integrating child and family development on two interactive levels—cross-sectional development (Child-Centered Structural Dynamic Therapy's unique concept of current family organization) and longitudinal development (historical development, the interplay of stages of development over time). Next, the therapist locates and pinpoints the key elements of the current conflict. The therapist assesses a number of interrelated features of the current conflict pattern including child-development-oriented dimensions of family process. Each family member's transactional role is evaluated for its part in the recurrent problem pattern. The therapist puts these pieces (the transactional part of each family member) together to form, metaphorically speaking, a "behavioral sentence" that encapsulates and expresses the essence of the family problem. This behavioral sentence is, in effect, synonymous with the "systemic hypothesis" (which structures should change) and conveys the developmental crisis.

Next, the therapist makes preliminary changes (positive inroads) in behaviors, while looking for and confirming the motivators or interactional scripts that guide the family's mismatched, problem behaviors and maintain the developmental conflict. Here, the therapist identifies critical identity images, what Kantor terms "salient memory pictures" of important relationship moments. When the therapist locates and identifies the exact nature and structure of these images—the positive behavioral intent and psychological expectations associated with these images, for child and adult alike—the work of restructuring and developmental progress begins. Families are offered a blame-free view of the problem; the positive aspects of family behavior are affirmed instead of denied. A negative and entrenched blame-oriented viewpoint is replaced with a positive one.

Parent-child and marital conflicts are recast as misguided, mismatched, and misunderstood behaviors (interpersonal strategies) that family members have been using to gain access and recognition.

In his epilogue to *Inside the Family* (Kantor & Lehr, 1986), David Kantor provides the theoretical foundation and springboard for child-centered practice:

> *When two people live together for any length of time, they evolve a conjoint image hierarchy in addition to preserving and expanding their own individual meanings and images. . . . When a child is added to an ongoing system, a disruption of ongoing distance regulation strategies is inevitable. Suddenly new rhythmic patterns must be negotiated between child and parents, and parent and parent in a triadic relationship requiring the formation of new distance regulation patterns . . . for the baby is the image bearer as well as a "receiver of images." (pp. 248–249)*

Now add to this formative triad the appearance and interaction of other children, each as an image bearer and receiver, and the emergence and overlapping of successive child development stages, with each evoking its own family system imagery and symbolic as well as behavioral meaning, and the stage is set for the Child-Centered Structural Dynamic Family Therapy Model presented in this book.

Developmental Intersections

Child-Centered Structural Dynamic Therapy, when situated in the landscape of family therapies, shares in a common systems perspective. A number of overarching system principles and fundamental assumptions about problem onset, ideation, etiology, and change guide Child-Centered Structural Dynamic Therapy. These assumptive givens cut across diverse family therapies to create a consensual view that is recognized as family therapy. As a profession and practice, family therapy draws its special status and strengths not only from its integrative systems framework, but from its unique perspective on change. After all, systems theory has been around far longer than family therapy and is no stranger to psychology and psychotherapy in general. Instead, and more importantly, we enjoy a phenomenological distinction. It is the richness and complexity of our understanding of a relational world that holds the excitement and intrigue. We focus on different phenomena—interpersonal relationships and how disruptions and crises in these relationships, occurring along a family's developmental course, are linked to individual and family distress.

However, while we focus primarily on relationship phenomena, we must also consider the individual in the family. Thinking about individuals in the family means more than considering the family's transactional life, and the roles that individuals play in it. It is more encompassing than that, focusing on the intersection, interplay, and conflict between the developmental courses of individual members and the family's overall development. In no other system context, and in no other stage along the family life cycle continuum, is the impact of developmental crises so palpably seen and poignantly felt than in the lives of children and during the early stages of family systems (when individual and family needs, tasks, desires and expectations, for one reason or another, collide or clash). The emotional costs to parents and children, in terms of lost opportunities and relationships gone awry, can be immense and profound. Ironically, however, when the emphasis shifts to the level of individual and family development, the bridge between child and family in therapy, problems are recast in a more normal light. They are seen as normal crises, efforts along the road toward growth and change. As part of a larger picture of family development, these problems can be more readily anticipated, prevented, and forestalled.

Child-Centered Structural Dynamic Therapy differs from other forms of family therapy in several prominent ways. The model is developmentally focused and provides a comprehensive stage theory of therapy and an integrated child and family developmental framework of intervention. The model consciously incorporates concepts and methods that treat "the individual inside the system" and the "system inside the individual." When we are working with the concrete world of children, the content of child development combined with the process of family development, it requires attention to the place where the worlds of individual experience and system dynamics meet.

Child-Centered Structural Dynamics provides a family process vocabulary, set of techniques, and activities for describing and successfully treating family dynamics at the individual-system interaction level, sensitive to the age-appropriate developmental readiness of children. The model focuses specifically on the borders between inner and outer worlds of experience, where self and system, child and family, connect in the observable world of interaction. Child-Centered Structural Dynamic Therapy is patently child focused. It incorporates children in family therapy and consciously builds the therapy process around them and their developmental needs. Child-Centered Structural Dynamic Therapy addresses three long-standing tensions and, hence, three levels of family change in the field of family therapy.

Three Levels of Family Change

Three dynamic, long-standing tensions, sources of growth and change, stand at the center of family therapy. Framed in the form of three salient dimensions or dilemmas, they are:

1. The individual-family system interface question.
2. The integration of child and family development.
3. The role of children in family therapy, child versus family treatme ,
   and the development of child-centered system models.

Individual-Family System Interaction

The first issue speaks to the individual-system interface question, or the tension in the dilemma of integrating individual and family system paradigms. The development of models that combine both perspectives requires concepts and techniques that simultaneously balance attention to the family and the individuals within it, viewing the family as a special kind of social group. This has proven to be a thorny issue for family therapy, explaining why we have shied away so much from the dilemma. For example, there is much to decide. We need to make decisions about what to look at; how to organize our knowledge and understanding of system change. Systems are multidimensional and configural. We need to determine which family dimensions to emphasize, which levels we are to chart, and why.

Family change can be viewed on different levels and from different vantage points inside and outside the family system. We can look at the whole family system. Next, we must decide what comprises the "whole family system." So a second set of choice-points arise. For example, we can look only at the family unit level or at different subsystems—marital, parental, parent-child. These considerations raise other practical and conceptual issues of family treatment; we must decide how to weigh, value, and evaluate the different individual experiences of family members. We need to decide how to interpret events and therapy outcomes when, for example, there are different views of change on different system levels in the same family. In essence, when we follow a system perspective, we must set the boundaries and limits of our conceptual and practical configural analysis. We can study the whole system, all the levels within the system, including individuals and their subsystems. Or, we can focus on some smaller set of salient subsystems. Ultimately, we are confronted with the links between individual and family, and the important necessity of an organizing principle that unites our understanding of the individual, the family, and individual and family development.

Integrating Child and Family Development

The second issue revolves around what we actually know about system development. We can ask, "What guides or models do we have as practitioners to help combine child development and system development, individual and family change, into an organized overall picture—a comprehensive framework for integrating and blending developmental crises, experienced on multiple system levels and multiple system fronts, in the same family?" The practice of family therapy and systems models of change have successfully dissolved the artificial boundary between the individual and his or her social context. The systems perspective has effectively blurred the distinction between "inner" and "outer" physical, psychological, and metaphoric space, and has shown us how what we experience as "real" depends on the interdependence and influence of inner and outer worlds—the interaction of internal and external events.

These events crisscross each other in ways that make the family, and the people within it, act almost like an "extracerebral mind," to adopt the classic analogy drawn by Minuchin (1974). There is "mind" and then "Mind"; in effect, there is the personal world of family members and the family's enveloping influence. Transactions and behavior can better be understood in context, and context ultimately involves the interplay of person and environment. Experience is determined by interaction with our environment. Environments equal contexts, the powerful shapers of our behavior, thoughts, and perceptions of ourselves and others. The individuals within families form the extracerebral sources of the mind, influencing the roles we choose or are compelled to play in the family. Yet, the personal worlds of family members and family system interaction present different pathways of conceptual understanding and clinical access as well as additional, crucial boundaries for the workers in the field of family therapy to open and explore. A major critical issue in family therapy, the topic and focus of this book, involves the interplay between individual and system, the juncture where personal, interpersonal, and family worlds meet in developmentally decisive ways for the vulnerable child.

The Role of Children in Family Therapy

The issue of development ultimately leads us back to children and the third issue, which focuses directly on children or, even more practically, on the place or role of children in family therapy. Children are uncanny statement makers. They are ingenious nonverbal and verbal communicators. They are frank and honest and courageous, and they are often the first to "spill the family beans" and break the spell of family secrets. When they are not included in family therapy sessions, something invaluable is lost. This has led Carl Whitaker, in speaking on the importance and utility of children in family therapy, to say of children, especially 2-year-olds, that if a family did not have one it might be a good idea to ask them to go out and borrow one. Children say and do revealing things with remarkable symbolic and verbal economy. They are a powerful and integral part of the family's overall healing process. Sometimes, it is children who, undauntingly, start the journey, leading the way for others.

Yet, despite the firm recognition, in theory, that children are central to family life and integral to family interaction, there is a tendency to leave them out or not to include them in family therapy as often as they should be. There is, as a result of this, a dearth of information and literature on children in the process of family therapy. Thus, there is the strong impression that children are not typically seen in family therapy, and are often excluded from it, for one reason or another: because they are distracting; because they require too much attention; or because family therapists believe, quite frankly, that children should see specially trained therapists in individual sessions. Hence, we arrive at the third dynamic, long-standing tension, what McDermott and Char (1974) originally termed the "undeclared war between child and family therapy," a tension that surfaced in the 1970s and still persists today.

In this, we face the myth about our practices as well as our commitment to children in family therapy. As Korner and Brown (1990) write, calling attention to the duration and extent of this oversight and problem:

> *The strange "paradox" of excluding children from family psychotherapy while at the same time espousing a commitment to treat the whole family was first observed by Ackerman (1970) and later by Block (1976), both of whom found it to be a common occurrence, even among experienced and dedicated family therapists. Yet, only recently has recognition been given to the issue of including children in family therapy . . . and the neglect of children's individual needs, which may be fostered by exclusionary practices. . . . Moreover, there is no research to define the scope and nature of this practice. (p. 420)*

These concerns, offered in the form of both caveats and challenges to the field of family therapy, are echoed by a number of other well-known family clinicians, including Combrinck-Graham (1991); Benson, Schindler-Zimmerman, and Martin (1991); Masten (1979); Szapocznik, Kurtines, Santisteban, and Rio (1990); and Zilbach (1989).

Children are important shapers of a family's destiny. They are powerful emotional barometers who give great insight into the family's ideals about intimacy and its struggles with it. Since intimacy is the "stuff" of therapy, then children are integral to it, and the grist of family developmental process can be best and most tangibly seen and discovered in the interplay of generations of parents and children in the family. As Combrinck-Graham and Kerns (1989) eloquently illustrate: "The culture of the young family dominated by centripetal forces is ideal for the development and reworking of sensuality and the capacity for intimacy. Doing so will provide a grounding in family relatedness and a basis for healthy intimacy in future relationships of all family members" (p. 89), for parents and children alike.

We need only look to the early pioneering of Ackerman (1966), Haley (1962, 1963, 1970, 1971a, 1971b, 1972, 1973a, 1973b, 1976), and Minuchin (1970, 1974), the field's luminaries, who dramatically illustrated how a presenting-child's problems can be diagnosed, reframed, and successfully treated as symptoms or signs of wider system distress. Similarly, case after case in the work of Fraiberg, Adelson, and Shapiro (1975), Guerin (1976), and Zilbach, Bergel, and Gass (1972), show how treating a child's symptoms and problems in the family system is more effective and efficient than treating the child alone. What our clinical practice and family system interaction research have consistently shown is that the child responds symbolically and often somatically to family distress; that a child's symptoms often are a barometer of wider family tension and instability; and that a child's troubling behavior often evolves to deflect deeper or more threatening marital or family conflict.

The collective science and art of family therapy have shown that a child's symptoms improve more readily when treated inside the family system, and that even when children are not presenting, they enrich the therapeutic atmosphere immensely and often accelerate the process toward growth and change and healing. The belief that childhood symptoms are best treated inside the family system and as a part of the wider family is integral to the historical roots of the field. The pioneering, cutting edge of family therapy focused on two simultaneous groups: one, the families of schizophrenics, concentrating on major mental illness; and the other, nonpsychotic delinquent children.

Child-Centered Family System Assessment

The young child's family system offers a rich store of insight and information on the family's capacity to grow and change. Perhaps in no other family developmental stage do we, as family therapists and theorists, have such an ample opportunity to witness and understand rapid, complex, multidimensional family developmental system transformations. The birth (entrance) and development (age-appropriate psychosocial changes) of the child, perhaps more than any other developmental challenge, require dramatic shifts and transactional quantum leaps forward on the part of the family system. The demands of a child, induced on one level simply because the child is there, alive, and must be cared for and included and, on another level, because the family must accommodate to a new, hitherto unknown quality of family functioning, evokes a powerful impact on the family. The family is now tacitly forced or consciously compelled to work out new transactional patterns: to divide labor and face the intensely personal issues of what it means to be a child and a parent, to be a husband and wife, mother and father.

The birth and development of a child is far from a simple, self-contained event involving a clear-cut set of responsibilities; it holds rich possibilities and unforeseen transactional offshoots. The impact of a child on a family, as evidenced in clinical practice, has the power to upset or enhance the family's world. If the developmental stages involved in raising young children offers the family therapist and social scientist any kind of understanding, it is the elegant economy of assessment.

Children can bring out the best and worst in families. They are often the litmus test of a family's transgenerational sufficiency, strength of a couple's marriage, and degree or capacity of the family to weather developmental tasks and system transformations without undue crises. A parent-child interaction or observable interchange between husband and wife is an excellent instant "process sample" of a family's intergenerational history and a revealing predictor of the family's future. Children are the crucible through which ghosts of relationships past symbolically emerge. They also offer, in the demands their individual developmental needs make on the family system, the potential for positive, increased family functioning, flexibility, and constructive change beneficial to all family members. However, the reviews of family therapy efficacy (Alexander, Holtzworth-Munroe, & Jameson, 1994; Gurman & Kniskern, 1991; Gurman, Kniskern, & Pinsof, 1986; Hahlweg & Markman, 1988; Hazelrigg, Cooper, & Borduin, 1987; Shadish et al., 1993) reveal the paucity of family therapy research on young children. Except for a small number of symptom-focused childhood diagnostic categories, broadband groupings of "externalizing" and "internalizing" behaviors (most notably conduct disorder and autism), and the associated effectiveness of parent management training models (Estrada & Pinsof, 1995), relatively little cohesive research exists on the effects and efficacy of family therapy with children. Several reasons, some more obvious than others, account for this oversight.

Foremost, the kaleidoscopic rapidity with which children manifest and outgrow problems, often accounting for transient symptoms, is partially responsible. Often, problem behavior in children straightens out over time, and because the problem does not persist, families are less likely to seek professional help. From a different vantage point, well-meaning professionals can further support this line of reasoning when they dismiss a child's quasi-problematic behavior (a budding preventive, early-intervention sign) as normal behavior, discouraging the family's intuitions that something might be going wrong. Important enrichment opportunities are lost when preproblem family concerns are prematurely glossed over or "swept under the rug" for time to "heal." The developmental course of childhood (the amazing ways children quickly change), coupled with the pat explanation that the child will "outgrow" the problem, sometimes join forces to aid in masking the beginnings of real conflict, keeping families, well before the onset of crisis, from seeking early intervention.

There is also the issue of the study of childhood developmental psychopathology itself. Children, as a group, have been understudied compared with the clinical and research attention devoted to adult psychopathology or emotional disturbance. For example, the development and refinement of diagnostic classification systems of childhood disorders have lagged behind their adult counterparts. A primary reason relates to the issue of "continuity" versus "discontinuity" (Lerner & Tubman, 1989) around the etiology, course, and presentation of disorders: Do childhood disorders evolve into adult disorders of the same kind? For example, do depressed children become depressed adults? Does oppositional defiant disorder progress to conduct disorder in adolescence and antisocial personality and behavior in adulthood? The continuity-discontinuity question highlights the problems encountered in developmental research, accounting for the secondary attention given to childhood disorders. As Hersen and Last (1990) point out:

Research is warranted, not only documenting the tie between child and adult behavioral disturbances, but also the familial and environmental antecedents of psychological malfunctioning. This is a priority if we are to progress beyond the level of the description and classification of problems to an understanding of developmental processes and preventative factors. (p. 7)

Another factor contributing to dilemmas around access to the clinical world of families of young children is the challenge of interweaving the delicate balance between the needs of the family and the developmentally poignant needs of the very young child in distress. This poses a troublesome theoretical problem for family therapies based on general systems theory in which the system is focal and the individual is deemphasized. Children in family therapy raise strong ethical issues. The family system, indeed, is critical. However, the child's cry for help in the telling statement of his or her symptoms, combined with the child's vulnerable family status, cannot be ignored. This is especially true when a child develops noxious or precocious behaviors. In the case of the predelinquent child or parentified child, the child's inflated status, abuse of power, and inveigling manipulations are even more compelling signs of the child's ultimately helpless vulnerability in a runaway family system. It is imperative to weigh equally the child's individual needs as well as clinical efforts designed to achieve system-level change. The real child in crisis should never be sacrificed for the technical elegance of systems interventions. This is a blunt but necessary statement.

In 1981, Lynn Hoffman described the family therapist as a special kind of behavioral scientist who, in charting the impact of larger "relationship configurations" on the "variable weather" of the human "soul," works much like a social systems "meteorologist." In her important contribution to family therapy, by shifting the site of pathology from the individual self to the social group, Hoffman gives an example of schizophrenia:

To say "This is a schizophrenic," that is, a person with a supposed mental disorder—makes as much sense as to state, "This is a rainy day." The so-called schizophrenic can just as well be described as a manifestation of larger weather systems in human affairs. (p. 10)

The message in Hoffman's analogy is a timeless and transtheoretical one for family therapy. Its inclusion here is not meant to call into question the supposed nature or existence of mental illness or to dispute the growing trends in brain-behavior research that currently support biochemical and neurophysiological views of schizophrenia and other major mental disorders (Carlson, 1991; Gaebel & Pietzcher, 1987; Miller, 1989). Nor does it pertain to schizophrenia, per se, or where our treatment emphasis is best placed. Current consensus and clinical wisdom support a combination of psychopharmacology and psychosocial treatments for schizophrenics that include social skills training and psychoeducation, as well as individual and family therapy. This broader more comprehensive approach, in contrast to the use of medications alone, has proved to significantly reduce the frequency of relapse rates of schizophrenics, which, once again, highlights the importance of family involvement as well as attention to the family system context (Goldstein & Miklowitz, 1995; Hersen & Last, 1990; Wynne, 1993).

But we might be speaking about any of the major mood, anxiety, or conduct disorders of childhood, from depression, attention deficit disorder, social phobia, and separation anxiety, to conduct disorders such as oppositional defiance or antisocial personality, the referred problems, clusters of traditionally diagnosed psychiatric symptoms. In short, we might be speaking of the typical childhood or child-centered problems we find in family therapy practice that family therapists often call by different names. Hoffman's obvious point is that the human being is invariably context dependent.

As mental health professionals, regardless of our orientation, we must, to some extent, pay attention to the presence, impact, and nature of these large, moving "weather systems" surrounding and influencing the symptom and symptom-bearer. It does not matter whether we favor biochemical views or system models; whether we emphasize a child's symptoms as arising more as processes within the child or as arising out of family interactions, we need to consider the system. Whether our therapy methods propose that change occurs as a result of presenting problem-centered, technique-based interventions (the "pragmatic" approach), or we favor a relationship-based intervention, in which the child's real presenting problem is believed to be initially hidden (the "aesthetic" approach) and is viewed as disguised marital distress, we must consider individual-system interaction. Even if we choose to treat the child alone, as some child therapists do, we must consider context.

Child-Centered Structural Dynamic Therapy meets parents, children, and families at this developmental crossroads. The model finds and makes optimal use of the creative and crisis-borne moments of family change that avail themselves to clinicians and family alike at important turning points in family development. Child-Centered Structural Dynamic Therapy provides methods and a model for integrating the points of view of children and parents and the reality (structure and interaction) of the family as a whole. The model addresses the needs of families and children along the continuum of family change, from prevention to family crisis and instability.

Family Crises and Family Structure: A Broadly Sketched Overview of Child-Centered Structural Dynamic Therapy

In Child-Centered Structural Dynamic Therapy, a crisis is viewed as a temporary disruption in structural laws (Kantor, 1980) governing the family system. In itself, a crisis is seen as a normal developmental event, an episode in family development that can lead to system elaboration, evolution, and growth. The resolution of crises is the basis for the formation of new structures, the prelude and necessary ingredient to change. In this way, crises are viewed as integral parts of development. We can understand development in a family system to be a series of structural changes or transformations that are the end product and resolution of these crises.

In this light, crises take on new meaning. They now become part of a natural growth experience and cycle in family development, and an opportunity or turning point that sometimes, along the way, can take on extraordinary meaning. Whether the family system moves on or gets bogged down and mired in crisis largely depends on the meaning that crisis raises for the family. To understand the connotation of "crisis" in Child-Centered Structural Dynamic Therapy is to understand the model's specific application of three system concepts from the Kantor theory of structural dynamics: *formal structures, content structures,* and the cornerstone concept, *critical identity image.*

Together, these concepts create the conceptual framework and practice method of child-centered family change. Each concept will be briefly illustrated and described to provide a broadly sketched overview of the therapy. In a later section of this chapter, these three key concepts will be discussed in greater detail and nested within the wider network of related terms that make up the foundation and practical tools of Child-Centered Structural Dynamic Therapy. The place to begin, and the central introductory concept to illustrate, is the notion of structure. The extent to which a family moves on developmentally or experiences conflict depends largely on the meaning a given crisis has for the family on the level of family structural organization, or what Kantor (1980) terms formal structures and content structures. Each concept takes on special, additional meaning when applied in the context of child-centered therapy.

Formal Structures and Content Structures

Critical to the practice of Child-Centered Structural Dynamics are the concepts of "formal" and "content" structures. Unlike system theory which focuses on formal structures, changing family patterns at the transactional level, Child-Centered Structural Dynamic Therapy considers both formal or interactional, pattern level structures of the family and content and theme. We can think of formal structures as the "form" or "map" of an interaction and content structures as the subjective details that color (particularize) an interaction. Whether we are looking at a "slice" or "sample" of current family transactional patterns or taking a longitudinal view of family development, each perspective contains both formal and content structures for the therapist's consideration. In this light, child development takes on new meaning. There are formal "child development structures" and content "child development structures."

For example, there is the form or process of parent-child interaction—the sequence of moves or dynamics of the parent-child relationship. There is also the "child development" content around which transactions take place and a parent-child relationship builds (e.g., parent and child may repeatedly engage in mutually opposing behavior around tasks of independence and declared autonomy). In this light, we find child development structures embedded in both form and content in a family's wider transactions, structures that the therapist can chart and assess. On the broadest level, formal family structures are:

- Patterns, the sequence or series of actions that make up a typical family transaction.

Over time, transactions build into predictable patterns. The therapist in focusing on "formal structures," is considering pure process. The following example illustrates a formal structure.

Consider a family of four, two parents and two children. The wife initiates a conversation with her husband around a routine family task, an issue that is important to her. Her husband, distracted or uninterested, reluctantly participates, joining her half-heartedly. As his wife moves toward him, seeking access, he moves away, disengaging from her. Soon the couple begins to argue. The children, hearing their parents' raised voices and sensing the tension build, start to squabble. The children's behavior turns the attention away from the couple's rising disagreement, focusing their attention on the children's misbehavior. The husband leaves the interaction as the wife attends to the children.

On the other hand, content structures imbue formal patterns with detail, nuance, and meaning. Content structures particularize family transactions, making family patterns distinct and recognizable as belonging to a given family. A content structure takes into account:

- Recurrent themes.
- Mood states.
- Personal meanings that individuals bring to the transaction (formal structure).

For example, the couple may engage in patterns (formal structures) around themes of money, or shared resources and responsibilities that, in turn, raise in each member of the couple personal issues around abandonment, support, and commitment. System therapies have typically ignored intrapsychic content, or the personal psychology of self, viewing personal internal states (self) as the primary domain of individual psychotherapy. Systems theory is more concerned with formal structures, with patterns of behaviors. Content structures evoke memories, subjective meanings, and consideration of individual feedback states which are largely inferential and non-observable. Content structures in the context of family development also involve themes and the relationship among themes as family members interact and relate. Themes and the relationship among themes involve history which, in turn, is associated with linear models of causality. Family systems therapists favor circular causality.

A family developmental theory must rely on content and history. Child-Centered Structural Dynamic Therapy starts with the assumption that it is essential to understand families and the ways that they deal with crisis in terms of formal (transactional) structures and content structures, specifically, the family's child development structures. Horizontal time, or transgenerational and personal history are combined with the vertical "here and now" of family process, interactions, and functions. This is accomplished through the central organizing principle and key explanatory systems construct, the Kantor critical identity image concept (1980), which joins individual, couple, and system development, providing the conceptual vehicle for designing practical methods of child-centered family change. The notion of "critical identity image" calls on content as well as formal structures of a family's life in the context of child-centered therapy in a special way.

Critical Identity Images: A Brief Definition and Illustration in the Context of Child-Centered Family Therapy Process

Imagery gives substance to subjective meaning and adds a realistic cast or dimension to abstract thought. Images are the currency of human communication, a common telegraphic and symbolic shorthand language we all share. The rainbow is a symbol of hope; the sun, a symbol of warmth; the egg, a sign of fertility and renewal; dark clouds, a sign of a storm ahead. The concept of image as mental act or representation, how the mind comes to know the world, has a long multifaceted tradition and philosophical history in psychology and psychotherapy. The concept of mind or consciousness and the role of imagery as internal representation or mental act is integral to our theories of knowledge, language, and cognition. Images are the symbolic language of the mind. Through acts of creation, a mixture of the objective and subjective, in dynamic interaction with the environment, we transform and interpret our experience. Images provide invaluable insight and access to the phenomenology of self, an individual's self-concept, and view or window on the world, including the family.

Guided imagery and image-work have a rich history of practice and application in individual, dyadic therapy. From Jungian imagery of individuation, to the emotive and reconstructive therapies and the use of mental imagery, to experiential mind-body imagery, visualization and centering movements in the transformation of negative self-image, to imagery as a metaphor for health, psychotherapy interventions using imagery and guided image-work have been shown to offer a potent route to emotional reintegration, healing, and behavior change. This process of self-knowledge and system-knowledge—the self inside the family and the family inside the self—leads us once again to the intersection of child and family development, the crossroads where family therapy as an evolving science stands. This juncture has strong implications for children in family therapy.

In 1980, David Kantor introduced the breakthrough critical identity image concept, which refers to a distinct or special type of image. As Kantor describes, these images are distinguished from other less potent forms of imagery by the depth of their intensity and their persistence or tenacious influence on relationships. Drawing on Kantor's work, we find critical identity images as internalized memory pictures of crucial transactional scenes in an individual's life. They merge content and process. Central to the Kantor critical identity image concept is the notion of distance regulation. Distance regulation expresses, in actual and symbolic space, the pattern of family relationships: the movement of individuals toward and away from each other (formal structures). Critical identity images are, therefore, cogent visual relationship statements. Content structures add the dimension of theme, mood, nuance, emotional intensity, and personal history. They are the behavioral scripts or interactional blueprints we call on and that function to guide and structure our relationships with intimate others. Content structures form the recurrent themes or issues at stake in an interaction.

Critical identity images are evolving identity structures on personal and collective family fronts that have added dimensionality and a distinct and special form of meaning and application in the context of Child-Centered Family Therapy. Although they do not stop in childhood, these images undoubtedly and unmistakably start there. This is what the work of structural dynamic therapy with children is all about. A child's "me and you in the world" images are just beginning to form. Children are filling in these blueprints, working to figure out the details in the here and now of their real family world, in that intimate space we call family. Their images grow and change and increase in intensity and complexity as cognitive and other abilities mature.

Figure 1.1 shows the effects of the interplay of horizontal and vertical time on evolving child, parent-child, and family critical identity imagery and interaction. In this figure, we see past family history (the personal childhood family histories and experiences of each parent) influence current child development, family structure, and interaction. As Figure 1.1 depicts, children are immersed in family process and are active observers, absorbers, and participators in the interpersonal world that the family creates.

Children's ways of expressing these images are decidedly different from those of adults and, therefore, access to and understanding of the systemic nature of these images is arrived at through different routes in child-centered therapy. Although children, as intuitive system experts of their own evolving family experience, are conscious of these images, they do not identify (label) them as adults do. Instead, they offer the content and transactional change-possibilities associated with these intense images (internalized relationship scenes) through behavioral reenactments

Figure 1.1
Evolving Critical Identity Images

and brief comments or observations. Children can act out their evolving views of self, the parent-child relationship, and family. Their behavior is the system message and map, the life lessons the family is teaching and children are absorbing. Or they can tell the therapist, directly or implicitly opening the door on their image-worries and image-wonders, through a strategically timed phrase. For example, Justin, a 9-year-old who has grown up too quickly on the mean streets of a violent neighborhood and within a troubled family, announces himself as "Stone Crusher"; Elise, who is 7, the source of nervous and disingenuous overprotection in a family of adult members desperate to avoid each other, stuns her family when she wonders, "Everyone pays attention to me, but no one pays attention to anyone else"; Billy, aged 4, whom we will meet in later chapters of this book, murmurs "greedy love." Children's evolving imagery of self-vis-à-vis family and family vis-à-vis self are the equivalent of the compressed, precise, concrete images we find in imagistic poems.

Critical identity images are salient visualized, transactional scenarios that lay out the blueprints for taking on familiar roles and create the unfinished relationship areas children carry through into adulthood as they seek positive resolution and better outcomes. There are perhaps four or five major foundational "identity image scenarios" that color, structure, guide, and predict future relationships as well as explain the mood, content, themes, and transactional patterns we see recurring in crises and relationship struggles. Clinical research and practice strongly suggest that the individual will develop and recall internalized transactional scenes that profoundly affect an individual's current and future relationships. Those crucial identity image scenes include rejection, shame, betrayal, and abandonment.

The excitement about Child-Centered Structural Dynamic Therapy for families is mirrored in the spontaneity that denotes "children." With simple, uncomplicated, intuitive clarity, they freely offer their images. They are rich image makers and creative image bearers. They have ready and quick access to imagery, expressing it to therapists and families alike, in many playful and imaginative ways. Invaluable helpers, often the first to break family silences, children show us the way.

Critical Identity Images, Developmental Crises, and Child-Centered Structural Dynamic Therapy: Five Routes to Family Change

In Child-Centered Structural Dynamic Therapy, crises are viewed as a normal developmental occurrence. Developmental crises evoke critical identity images. How a family handles a developmental crisis depends on the quality, content, and intensity of the collective critical identity images that arise and are at stake in a developmental transition. A family can resolve the developmental crisis in one of five ways. It can choose to make one of several kinds of developmental changes:

1. The family directly addresses the crisis and resolves the problem.
2. The family assesses its current developmental limits (resources) and temporarily delays dealing with the problem.
3. Drawing on collective family identity and a sense of system solidarity, in a healthy, protective response to the crisis, the family assumes joint, collaborative responsibility with the community and outside world.
4. The family denies and locates the problem outside the family system.
5. The family denies and internalizes the problem in the form of recurrent family crises and unresolved conflicts.

Taking the more growth-oriented road, the family may work to acquire new structures and increase family structural complexity and efficiency. The family clarifies its rules, evolving new conscious system strategies for more effective and efficient ways of reaching its goals. By doing so, the family brings into focus a clearer understanding of its model for living.

Another choice the family may make is to temporarily set aside, not deny, its critical identity struggle, to deal with an immediate and more pressing concern. This can be a healthy, protective mechanism. The family is not ignoring the deeper critical identity struggles; instead, it is consciously deciding to delay dealing with these struggles to ensure system viability. A healthy family system effectively recognizes its problem-solving limits.

The family may choose another consolidating route and, in a different kind of healthy, protective maneuver, locate the problem source partly outside the family. In this growth-oriented form of externalizing the conflict, the family adopts collaborative responsibility relative to the outside world. Deciding to localize and view the problem as emanating outside the physical and symbolic borders of the family can serve as a beneficial strategy under certain circumstances. Instead of rifts or divisive splitting from within, the family can choose to rally around beliefs in itself and its members, promoting system growth and viability as it strengthens and deepens a collective sense of identity. In contradiction to external feedback, when the outside world impinges on the family, there are a number of situations in which a family's sustained belief in itself, is enabling. The most obvious situation involves instances of discrimination and prejudice in which minority families are treated stereotypically. To reject or seriously question the stereotype can steady a family system and induce growth from within.

An example of externalizing may include a school intervention, when parents are called for a consultation to discuss their child's academic or social status. The family and the school choose a position of collateral responsibility. The family can choose to temper the school's evaluation, viewing it as a function of the discrepancies between the school's and their model of reality or worldview. In doing so, the parents do not take on the onus, but rather support their view of their child, mediated by parental accountability and adequate family reality testing. The family then successfully averts either blame or labeling of the child, themselves, or the school. This effective use of shared information can serve as a wake-up call for both parents and educators. These are the three divergent, positive routes a family can take at decisive developmental turning points.

Yet, the family can also make less favorable choices around conflict resolution and travel down more destructive, emotional paths. Adopting a counterproductive form of externalizing, the family can project the conflict onto the outside world, creating an "us" against "them" mentality and stance. In this instance, the family denies and deflects the problem in a developmental strategy that amounts to psuedo-growth. The family can become a well defended and entrenched camp, looking outside rather than inside for explanations for the crisis. In this instance, the family appears to move on developmentally; however, the crisis remains, unresolved and ever present, like a low-grade fever just below the surface. This kind of developmental choice parallels the individual who blames others for his or her misfortunes and essentially lives an unexamined life.

The family may show another form of denial. Instead of turning its gaze outward to externalize the problem, blaming an agent or aspect of the outside world, the family can gloss over the crisis, burying its developmental rifts in family silence. Or, the family can devolve into ritualized cycles of unresolved and unfocused conflict. Ironically, however, in its efforts to avoid the real issues at stake in the developmental crisis, the family never argues over the true conflict but chooses less threatening issues around which to vent frustrations. This family is a veiled and oblique group of communicators who cloak real conflicts in trivial disputes, chronic criticisms, and an uncanny ability to concentrate on the unimportant; the family remains oblivious to the most crucial issues threatening child and family development.

For example, the family may go to great lengths to argue over whose turn it is to "do the laundry" or complain vehemently over specks of lint on the living room carpet, while denying the emotional pain or serious problems of a family member or the reality based anxiety involved in preparing for an upcoming family court date over child custody or the adequacy of parental supervision. Here, the family is literally stalled in chronic denial and indecision and resembles a system in which "anger turns on itself." These are the two unfortunate paths families can follow in their system efforts to resolve developmental crises. Through therapy and early intervention, these chronic, counterproductive meanings and methods of crisis resolution can be averted. Families can discover the growth opportunities of crisis and develop growth-oriented strategies compatible with positive child and family development.

The Family's Influence on the Child and the Child's Influence on the Family: The Theoretical Roots of Child-Centered Structural Dynamic Therapy

Wondering about the mind's perplexing responses to trauma and emotional betrayal is as primeval as the study of human nature itself, and as fundamental as Homer's mythical portrayal of courage and self-determination in the *Odyssey.* Why one person survives and another collapses in the face of ordinary and extraordinary disasters (e.g., divorce, family illness, war, rape, violent assault) continues to intrigue us. From Maya Angelou's (1969) *I Know Why the Caged Bird Sings,* to Faulkner's (1931) *The Sound and the Fury,* to Arnold's (1990) *Childhood Stress,* to Hersen and Last's (1990) developmental perspectives on the origins, course, and contexts of childhood psychopathology, artists, poets, and novelists, on the one hand, and social scientists, on the other, have been working to unravel the mysteries and predictable laws of human change, crisis, and survival.

We are fascinated with the prospect of explaining ourselves to ourselves, of depicting and understanding the "how" as well as "why" of human events, both tragic and triumphant. For example, we want to know why some thrive in less than optimal environments while others, born into more favorable environments and enriched circumstances, may choose destructive paths. "What causes one person to be resilient while another is vulnerable?" and "What makes one family grow stronger and another fall apart?" are questions that draw attention to two dynamic recurrent themes and alternating approaches to our understanding of human development and change. These include the nomothetic perspective (the lawfulness of human behavior) and the idiographic (individual differences) perspective, or in family therapy, the developmental intersections of individual and system.

From Angelou to Arnold, children have always been central to our social and emotional consciousness. Thinking about children leads us inevitably, one way or the other, to thinking about families. Families and children, taken together, equal development. We are now faced with a second set of important issues regarding developmental laws and different developmental outcomes. Framed in the form of questions: What makes one family flourish and grow and another family, faced with the same problem, flounder or disintegrate? Why do some members of the same family do better than others? Why does one child succeed and another fail? What can we say about these different outcomes? Once more, we find ourselves drawn back to the criss-crossing links and overlapping paths of individual and family development, the topic and theme of this book.

One current creative tension at the center of family therapy as a profession and developing science is the extent to which we choose to shift and move toward traditional mental health practices, including adapting and using traditional psychiatric diagnostic categories (*Diagnostic and Statistical Manual of Mental Disorders* [DSM-IV],™ American Psychiatric Association, 1994) with its attention primarily on the individual. Or, do we choose to preserve our autonomy and remain on the periphery of the larger mental health system? As we stand at the center or inner circle of the mental health field, we simultaneously stand on the field's fringe, creatively working to combine individual and systems level assessments. Regardless of where we stand on the relevance and compatibility of traditional diagnostic categories (nomenclature) with family systems assessment and concepts, family therapists must come to some practical position on blending and incorporating individual and family development. Whether we favor integration as Denton (1990) and Horton and Retzlaff (1991) urge, whether we look toward synthesis and a more moderate stance, as Anderson (1994) recommends, with family therapy enjoying the best of both worlds, or whether we favor Hardy's (1994) challenge of holding the line on our strong system stance as system purists, seeing everything only through family system lenses, we must reach some consensus.

Individuals live in systems and systems live in individuals and each affects the other. We have known this fact for years. It is so self-evident as almost to have become an incontrovertible psychological truism. We know this from our lives and from our experiences, first as children living in families and then as parents nurturing our own children. Therapists who practice individual psychotherapy know this in their symbolic reference to the "child" and "family" inside us. For family therapists this basic "developmental premise" (psychological axiom) is virtually a given, a necessary assumption raised almost to the level of scientific principle or family system law.

When we take a panoramic view of the body of comprehensive knowledge of families—what we know about parent-child relations, child development, and the family—we almost invariably find that we can approach this issue from two opposite and yet interrelated, or complementary, vantage points. We can start at either of two ends of a common line of access leading to a basic understanding: the crucial role that the family plays in developing psychological health as well as psychological problems in children. The origins of this consistent and incontrovertible finding, like those of the family therapy movement itself, are richly diverse and interdisciplinary, cutting across professional orientations, lines of research, and perspectives on the family.

At one end point of this common path or continuum, several access routes converge. One is child development and, therefore, child oriented. It looks at the ways the family affects the child's growth and development. Here, the child stands in the foreground and is the central concern. Another access route involves the study of family interaction and whole family process. In this instance, the family stands in the foreground and the child becomes a part-process and one of a number of roles explored within the family. The difference between these two access routes is a matter of emphasis and focus. A third body of information, insight, and research into the family's influence on young children derives from early intervention, which primarily targets the psychoeducational and socioemotional development of the child. Again, the child's needs are tantamount and the family is viewed in the context of its capabilities for promoting his or her psychological and educational growth and achievement. These avenues of access form the strands of knowledge that comprise one end point and one access route into the family. Each of the three strands of child-oriented knowledge and child development theory are relevant to the practice of Child-Centered Structural Dynamic Therapy in prevention, early intervention, and family crisis contexts (see Figure 1.2).

Figure 1.2
Diverse Disciplines and Empirical Sources: A Common Understanding of the Impact of the Family on the Child

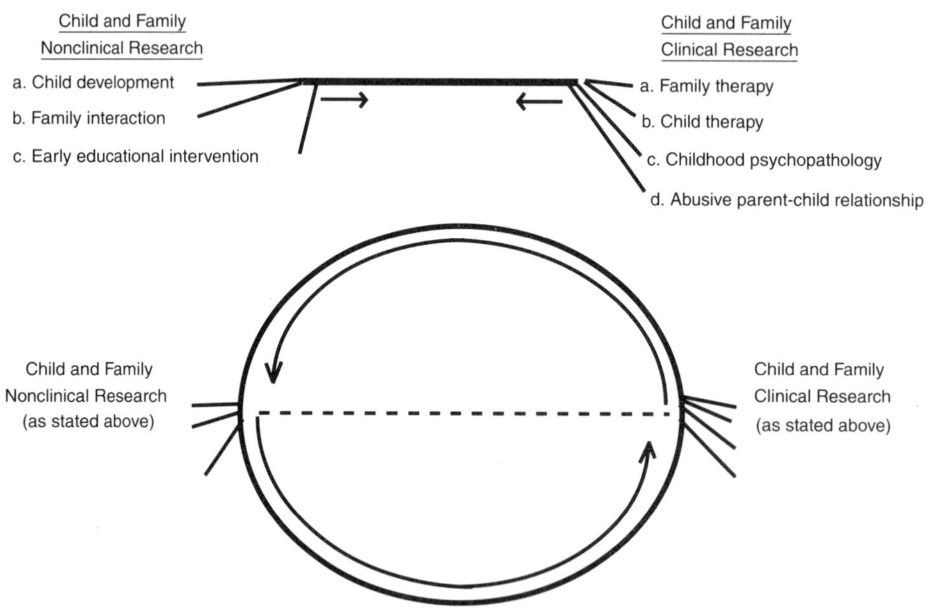

Note: These two diverse empirical access routes, like two ends of a line, if drawn together come full circle to support a common understanding about the impact of family systems on the well-being of children.

Child Development and Early Intervention

Turning first to a child-centered view and the role of the family for promoting optimal child development and positive mental health, the evidence gathered in just the past 30 years is virtually unanimous. One strong fundamental principle of development is that parents and children exert powerful reciprocal influences on one another. We also know that parent-child relationships may start out looking largely asymmetrical with parents as responsible adult caregivers assuming and providing the lion's share of nurturance, protection, and guidance to the child. However, almost from the beginning of the parent-child relationship, this balance slowly and eventually shifts as children take on a more active role of influence and participation in the family as well as in the quality and structuring of the parent-child relationship. Almost from the first moments of life, parent-child relationships take on their special fluidity, rhythm, and interpersonal meanings. Infants, we know, are highly sociable and their world is an active and interpersonal one (Brazelton, 1992; Sander, 1980; Stern, 1985).

We can say then, as a general rule of thumb, that parent-child relations are mutually interdependent and transactional. These relationships are also nested subsystems, dynamic relational patterns of predictable experience, embedded in the wider family context and larger patterned development of the family system. In this way, parent-child relationships have a life of their own and also are affected, shaped, and molded by the needs and the demands of the larger family system.

While we have identified common phases in the developing parent-child relationship, and there certainly are common denominators of parent-child relationships across different children in the same family, each relationship also has its own unique, idiosyncratic, and distinct interpersonal features. This speaks to the particular dynamic process created by a particular parent with a particular child. Although we have been told that we should love all our children, we may like one better than another. We may have a natural affinity to one and find ourself in conflict with another. This has partly to do with the parent and partly to do with the child, and involves basic issues of attraction and common identity or perceived identification.

In addition to the highly idiosyncratic content or "chemistry" of any parent-child relationship, there are also other factors. These relationships, ensconced in broader family developmental tasks, also go through stages, turn corners in decisive ways, sometimes raising their own crucial problems. Particular children in the family may encounter difficulties at successive developmental stages, or the same child, along with our relationship with that child, changes because the child, who has been successful in the present developmental stage, has trouble adapting to the tasks of a new phase.

Some children are slow to warm up and others are more exuberant. Sometimes the tasks and processes of bonding and attachment with one child are easier than with another. Some children are fierce in declaring their independence, boldly announcing their boundaries, whereas other children are more compliant, allowing parental influence to guide with greater latitude, joining parent and child in a cooperative venture. Sometimes the dynamics of testing and working out autonomy and the child's boundaries of independence are rockier for us with one child than another. Sometimes it also depends whether the child is a boy or a girl and how the stage-specific task interacts with our conceptions of gender.

Children are evolving their own internalized behavioral guides and interpersonal views of themselves and us, as parents, and the family. When children learn language, they are freed from the here and now boundaries of physical acts and activities and enter the world of symbolic representation. Words are used to symbolize objects, events, and feelings. Relationships patterns in the family are internalized and, through the creative act of mental representation (as will be shown in Table 1.1), relationship ideas as well as relationship possibilities emerge and take hold. Fundamental conceptions of "self" (self-concept) and family (group identity) are forming out of children's experience and immersion in the concrete world of images and symbolic play. Children are continuously creating and constructing these images on physical, psychological, cognitive, and interpersonal grounds. At the same time, children generate evocations in parents' dormant and often unspoken image-vulnerabilities around important child development tasks and themes and the associated demands of an evolving parent-child relationship. The point is that these images are in process—in formation—and thus are more changeable than for adults. The child's core self-concept and growing sense of identity involve a dynamic process of ongoing change, formation, and flux. Parents, too, to a somewhat lesser extent, are also forming, revising, reshaping, and reconstructing these images in the context of their own and the family's development.

Shared and Nonshared Family Environments

Even though parents believe they are imparting similar values, attitudes, and standards to their children and provide them with generally similar experiences, what can actually affect their children most is what each child experiences uniquely, not what they share with their siblings. Children negotiate two simultaneous levels of experience, traveling back and forth and interweaving two simultaneous family worlds: one of shared environmental events and the other of their unique responses to environmental events.

Plomin and Daniels (1987) put the question to an emperical test: "Why are children raised in the same family environment often so different?" They

Table 1.1
Charting Normal Development

I
0–12/12–18 Months
Trust versus Mistrust
Sensorimotor Learning

A somatic sense of emotional and physical well-being; trust in a reliable, consistent world of events and people; responsive (sensitively attuned), predictable relationships; practical, action-oriented cognitive and social intelligence and sensorimotor experience: "I want to be touched, talked to, played with, cuddled, and held. I want to feel safe, secure, and protected—that the world is a dependable place."*

0–12 Months

Socioemotional/ Cognitive	Communication/Language: Spoken (Expressive) Understood (Receptive)	Physical Development/ Self-Mastery
Smiles indiscriminantly to human face (3 months).*	Cries to express physical and emotional needs (e.g., wants to be fed, changed, cuddled, talked to).	Holds head erect for lengthy periods (3 months).
Smiles to engage others; genuine, frequent social smiling; (3 months).	Experiments with own voice (speech sounds).	Turns over (5 months).
Displays intersubjectivity: awareness of the rhythms and tempo of relationships; actively engages, responds to, and maintains interaction (relationship) with parent.**	Localizes (turns toward) source of sound (ear-eye coordination).	Follows movement of objects; stares at movement of own hand and fingers (sustained hand regard); visually guided reaching (eye-hand coordination; 3–6 months).
Responds to (reflects) emotions of others (e.g., cries when other babies cry in distress; responds differentially to tones of voice: angry, happy, sad).	Strong association of parent's voice, appearance (presence) with the "good feeling" of being comforted.	Sits unaided (5–8 months).
Actively contributes to (coordination of action, behavior, emotion) patterns of intimacy; shows attachment.	Engages in vocalizing "duet"; imitates and vocalizes in response to being engaged by another's vocalizations (adult's or child's).	Crawls, scoots (6–9 months).
Getting and holding the attention of another (particularly parent).	Explores consequences of sounds objects make; banging objects (toys) on different surfaces (e.g., crib slats, floor, blanket, own body).	Transfers (passes) object from one hand to the other.
		Pulls self to standing position; cruises (8–11 months).
		Grasps objects with thumb and finger (pincer grasp).

(Continued)

Table 1.1 (*Continued*)

Socioemotional/ Cognitive	Communication/Language: Spoken (Expressive) Understood (Receptive)	Physical Development/ Self-Mastery
Pleasure at affectionate interplay (e.g., exchanges smiles and sounds with others; imitates facial expressions).	Play and preoccupation with making sounds (prelude to speech).	Climbs 6-inch units including stairs (7–11 months).
Gradual narrowing of focus on family; selective smiling; reactions of hesitation and wariness to unfamiliar faces ("stranger anxiety"; 9 months).	First words understood (e.g., "mommy," "daddy," "bye-bye"; 7–9 months).	Batting, banging, releasing objects; gradual shift from practicing of motor skill to interest in physical properties of objects (8–12 months).
Curiosity over the physical attributes of objects and the sound qualities of speech/words (9 months).	Receptive vocabulary of about a dozen words by age 1.	Drinks from cup; holds cup with two hands (12 months).
Explores the effects of actions on objects (e.g., dropping or throwing toy).		Walks with or without assistance (12–14 months).
Explores own body (e.g., hands, fingers, feet, toes).		Significant transition: locomotion and independent exploration of the environment increases dramatically.
Responds to and imitates simple directions (e.g., "Wave bye-bye"; "Roll the ball"; 9–12 months).		
Repetition of actions and activity as a means of learning (e.g., repeatedly drops block or spoon from highchair).		
Simple problem-solving (e.g., pushes one object aside to reach another).		
Beginning of intentional acts to attain goal.		

Table 1.1 (*Continued*)

12–18 Months

Socioemotional	Cognitive	Communication/ Language: Spoken (Exressive) Understood (Receptive)	Physical Development/ Self-Mastery
Deepening bonds of attachment. Uses adult as resource; first requests for help (e.g., "milk," "cookie"). Watches (studies) older sibling(s) playing alone or with friends. Primarily on the responsive end of sibling interaction (rivalry); begins to object strenuously to sibling's aggressive behavior. Shows pride in accomplishments. Interested in all behaviors of parent(s), especially in reaction to self/child (8–14 months). Beginning of independence; uses own name, possessives (e.g., "mine"); says "no" by resisting simple directives; asserts self, testing wills. Begins to differentiate self from objects and invest objects and people with some permanence in time and space.	Fascination with collections of small objects (e.g., filling and emptying containers, kitchen drawers). Practicing fine motor skills (e.g., turns knobs). Discovers the characteristics of objects and how things work (e.g., slide, roll, bounce). Fascination with function and motion (e.g., swinging cabinet doors, jack-in-the-box). Explores relationship of parts-to-wholes by putting things together and taking things apart. Concept of causation is egocentric; nothing happens except as a result of the child's own wishes (subjective causation). Begins to engage in make believe and role play behavior. Actively seeks novelty and acts to produce new, unexpected, interesting results.	Responds to own name. Looks toward other family members when they are addressed. Complies with simple requests (e.g., "Give me the ball"; "Go get"; "Find"; "Show me"; "Let's go."). First word(s) spoken (about 16 months). Understands simple warnings (e.g., "no," "don't touch" by about 14 months). Understands simple phrases with key words (e.g., "Open the door"; "Get the ball"). Follows request to bring familiar object (toy) to adult.	Walking. Climbing 12-inch units (stairs). Holds and handles small objects (preparation for later, more refined writing skills). Signs of interest in scribbling. Looking, gazing, staring at objects and people. Throwing, dropping objects; feeling each object's surfaces; mouthing and chewing on objects (exploratory skills, 14 months). Swinging (opening and closing) hinged objects; stacking; knocking down; switching lights on and off (practicing skills, digital finger skills). "Riding" small four-wheeled wagons.

(*Continued*)

Table 1.1 (*Continued*)

II
18–24/24–36 months
Autonomy versus Doubt and Shame
Sensorimotor Learning Evolves into Intuitive Thinking

An emerging sense of physical and psychological identity and growing confidence in self-mastery and independence (ability to effectively exert control over bodily movements) versus doubt in own capabilities and the shame that accompanies "being seen" in disapproving (critical) ways by those the child is attached to, depends on, and turns to for help. A period of practical, action-oriented problem solving: "I want to know I can do, explore, experiment, make mistakes. Sometimes I step cautiously; sometimes, too boldly. I want to hold on and also let go of myself (arms, legs, muscles, words, thoughts, feelings). I want to know my freedom and limits."

18–24 Months

Socioemotional	Cognitive	Communication/ Language: Spoken (Exressive) Understood (Receptive)	Physical Development/ Self-Mastery
Focus shifts from interest in physical properties of objects to events, interactions, and interpersonal experience. Getting and holding adult's attention increases. Expresses positive (affectionate) and negative (anger, annoyance) emotions toward adults and children (siblings). Engages and directs adults in activities. Exhibits fantasy behavior on an interpersonal basis (24 months).	Begins to manipulate (represent) objects mentally (images). Uses objects for imaginative play, constructing scenes with dolls, animal figures, etc. More reflective, less impulsive problem solving. Achievement of object permanence: ability to represent an absent object internally and to act "as if" it continues to exist when outside of physical view (transition skill, 24 months).	Understands prepositions, negatives, and plurals. Receptive vocabulary expands to several hundred words by age 2. Spoken language expands from words and telescoped phrases ("some," "more") to simple sentences by age 2. Understands and expresses many words and major grammatical forms by age 2. Responds correctly to "where" questions when the question is accompanied by gesture(s).	Runs. Plays with four-wheeled objects, straddling them and walking them along. Builds a tower of 3 blocks. Uses a spoon. Turns storybook pages 2 or 3 at a time. Drinks from cup, one hand, unassisted. Walks up and down stairs (hand held). Throws small ball. Picks up toys from floor without falling. Paints with whole arm movement. Basic control of the body practically complete.

Table 1.1 (*Continued*)

24–36 Months

Socioemotional	Cognitive	Language/ Communication	Physical Development/ Self-Mastery
Emergence of true social interest, including gradual decline in negativism.	Knowledge and curiosity about motion (paths of moving objects).	Speaking.	Scribbles.
Increasing emotional control.	Awareness of simple cause and effect and chains of events enough to anticipate outcomes (consequences).	Uses small sentences or a few words and sentence fragments; joins vocabulary words together in two-word phrases.	Rides a small tricycle.
Increasingly conversational.	Primarily egocentric (sees things from own point of view).	Majority of language acquired.	Jumps in place, two feet together.
Emerging social interest in peers.	Moral reasoning revolves around reference to external, physical events or objects. External physical source of motivation is obedience or perceived punishment from powerful authority figures. Act is judged right or wrong whether it is or is not associated with punishment (negative consequences); complies (makes simple moral "choices") around avoiding punishment in favor of rewards (toy, cookie, praise); first stage of preconventional moral reasoning.	Asks "what" and "where" questions.	Turns book pages singly.
Child's temperament and emerging personality becomes clearer, more reliable.		Makes negative statements (e.g., "Can't open it.")	Holds crayon or marker between thumb and finger, not fist.
Curiosity and exploration of body functions.		Shows frustration at not being understood.	Makes circular, vertical, and horizontal strokes.
Continued expansion of imaginative role play.		Points to (identifies) pictures of common objects when they are named.	Paints with some wrist activity.
Plays alone and with parent(s).		Enjoys listening to simple storybooks.	Kicks ball.
Plays near other children, joining in briefly.			Uses spoon.
Defends own possessions.			Puts coat on and takes coat off with some assistance.
Begins to play house, imitates adult actions and family roles.			Opens door by turning knob.

(Continued)

Table 1.1 (*Continued*)

Socioemotional	Cognitive	Language/ Communication	Physical Development/ Self-Mastery
	Begins to understand functional concepts of familiar objects (e.g., that a cup is used for drinking) and part-whole concepts (e.g., parts of the body). Creates products (e.g., puzzles, block tower; first drawing by age 3). Selects and looks at picture books, names pictured objects, and identifies several objects within one picture. Matches and relates associated objects meaningfully (e.g., given plate, spoon, and block, puts plate and spoon together). Recognizes self in mirror, saying "baby," or own name. Can talk briefly about what he or she is doing. Shifts emphasis from working problems out in action to working problems out in mind.		

Table 1.1 (*Continued*)

III
3–6/7 years
Initiative versus Guilt
Preoperational Problem-Solving

A sense of self-assertion, worth, initiative; moving freely in interaction with the environment without feelings of guilt or the restrictive ties of overly binding attachments (enmeshed relationship loyalties). The child's world expands to peers, neighborhood, school. The child is predominantly an egocentric thinker relying heavily on perception-dependent problem-solving strategies; what the child sees (senses to be true) is what the child believes: an intuitive and subjective (how events seem to the eye) thinker versus a logical (rules or principles governing events) thinker. The child's thoughts, feelings, and wishes are at the center of "explanations" of events (cause and effect, function, and interpersonal relationships): "Now that I have words, control over my body, and can move freely and confidently, I want to try things, explore new people and relationships without fear of losing my parents' love and approval. I want to know what it is (means) to be a girl-person, a boy-person; I want to know how to 'be' a person (values, sense of right and wrong)."

Socioemotional	Cognitive	Language	Physical Development/ Self-Mastery
Mutually responsive and adaptive to the speech and social cues of children and adults (sociocentric). Shares with others; prosocial behavior (seen as early as 2 years). Altruistic and empathic behavior (seen as early as 2 years) toward adults and children. Uses adults as resources after first determining that a task is too difficult. Leads and follows peers (not seen until 3 years).	Ability to notice small details and accurately observe discrepancies. Ability to anticipate consequences. Ability to put self in another person's place. Concept of a "justice structure"(fair play) is expanded: external physical events are paired with self-needs or those of a significant other to justify behavior; makes moral decisions on the basis of self-interest–guided fair play (e.g., trading toys or equal shares of food); second stage of preconventional moral reasoning.	Asks "why," "when" and "how" questions, requiring simple answers (3–5 years). Understands sequence of events when clearly and simply explained (e.g., "first A," "next B," "then C"). Recounts content of a story but may misinterpret facts or confuse details (3–5 years). Increased, expanded concept of function (e.g., names and associates object with its use; "Tricycles are for riding").	Throws and catches a ball (3–4 years). Copies circle (3–4 years); squares (4–5 years); triangles (5–6 years). Cuts along a line (3–4 years). Draws a person with 2 to 6 recognizable parts (e.g., head, arms, legs, hands, feet); 4–5 years. Cuts food with knife (4–5 years). Knows first and last name; own street and town (4–5 years). Cuts out simple shapes (5–6 years).

(Continued)

Table 1.1 (*Continued*)

Socioemotional	Cognitive	Language	Physical Development/ Self-Mastery
Expresses affection and annoyance to peers as well as adults (communicating sense of self-confidence and inter personal comfort).	Ability to make interesting associations (creativity).	Begins to understand and express time and can talk about the past; uses past tense (3–4 years). Time concepts expand; can talk about yesterday or last week ("a long time ago"), today, and what will happen tomorrow (4–5 years).	Colors within lines (5–6 years).
Growing pride in personal accomplishments.	Arbitrary methods (criteria) for sorting, classifying objects/things (e.g., "This block and frog go together because they are both green"; "This teddy bear and pillow go together because they are things to hug").	Understands size comparison (e.g., "small," "smaller," "smallest"); 3–4 years.	Pastes and glues appropriately (5–6 years).
Begins dramatic play, acting out whole image scenes, stories, and relationships (e.g., "play house," "pretend to be mommy").	Plans and carries out activities with other children (organizing skill).	Understands and carries out a series of 2 or more simple related directions (3–4 years); follows 3 unrelated directions in proper order (4–5 years).	Uses paints, scissors (5–6 years).
Cooperative play (group decision making, teamwork) and competitive play (games) with peers (5–6 years).	Ability to concentrate on a task while simultaneously keeping track of what is going on around child (dual focus); about 3 years of age.	Understands "let's pretend" (3–4 years).	Dresses self and ties shoes (5–6 years).
Can take appropriate turns in a conversation or game (5–6 years).	Draws simple picture; names and briefly explains this picture (3–4 years).	Refers to self using pronoun "I" or "me" (3–4 years).	Skips on alternate feet; jumps rope (5–6 years).
Curiosity about birth, reproduction, gender roles, sex differences (e.g., "How are boys and girls made differently?").	Relatively short attention span (3–4 years).	Word play; creates own rhymes; makes up own words (4–5 years).	Adult grasp of pencil; handedness well-established (5–6 years).
Gender identity.	Relates (associates) clock time with daily events/ schedule.	Talks about causality by using "because" and "so" (4–5 years).	
Self-concept is forming.			

Table 1.1 (*Continued*)

Socioemotional	Cognitive	Language	Physical Development/ Self-Mastery
	Begins to understand sentences that express time concepts (e.g., "We are going to the park tomorrow"); 3–4 years. A more accurate use of time concepts: past (yesterday) and future (tomorrow) by 5–6 years. Relates story from picture book with reasonable accuracy (5–6 years). Sorts/classifies objects by single characteristic (size, shape, color); 5–6 years.	Incorporates verbal directions and "self talk" (running verbal commentary) into play activities. Intuitive child (2 years) uses language to "think aloud"; in preoperational problem-solving, communicative language increases as monologues decrease (7 years).	

(Continued)

Table 1.1 (*Continued*)

IV
7–12 Years
Industry versus Inadequacy/Inferiority
Concrete, Practical Intelligence

The child, immersed in wider spheres of social interaction and equipped with greater cognitive maturity and physical competence, focuses on acquiring, testing, and practicing life tasks and skills: learning the requisite competencies for being a successful adult in society. If a child learns these skills well (what to do and how to do it), than he or she will develop a sense of industry, purpose, confidence, and self-esteem: "I want to know I can be effective, competent, appreciated, and exert positive influence. I want my accomplishments to be appreciated, noticed, and rewarded. I want to feel smart and important in the world, and valued by those I care about and who care for me."

Socioemotional	Cognitive	Competencies/ Self-Mastery
Increasingly broader (more objective) view of events and things, including a growing appreciation of how others see things (different view points).	Can focus now on 2 or more attributes of an object simultaneously.	Focuses on school achievement/activities.
Chooses own friends.	Order objects or events according to size, weight, height, or sequence (e.g., a story: beginning, middle, and end).	Acquires fundamental academic competencies and skills.
Understands and respects rules (purpose and function).	Ability to conserve: recognizes that quality (amount) of an object's properties stay constant (remain the same) despite changes in shape or position (e.g., 3 ounces of milk is still 3 ounces of milk whether in a wide or tall glass).	Develops interest in sports, athletics, recreational activities.
Friendships revolve around concepts of intimacy (shared experiences) and loyalties (keeping confidences).	Focus on transformation (process) in addition to static states (instead of "A" or "B"; A-B).	Explores talents and competencies (e.g., music, gymnastics, dance, etc.).
Peer group influence is stronger.	Can reverse a process; how objects can regain initial states (e.g., ice melts and can be refrozen).	Develops a sense of self-achievement through mastery.
Development of conscience.		

Table 1.1 (*Continued*)

Socioemotional	Cognitive	Competencies/ Self-Mastery
	Classification capacity increases: ability to relate parts to parts as well as parts to whole, (e.g., all the round candies are M&M's; 10 candies are green M&M's, 8 candies are orange M&M's).	
	Thought process is bound by reality; events have concrete, real existence; sees little difference between child's own thoughts and feelings and "what is"; equates perceived reality with actual reality.	
	Behaviors (moral "choices") are right if the behavior meets with approval. Social approval (self-image; perception of others that child is a "good person") is a prime motivator over physical rewards; first stage of conventional moral reasoning.	
	Gradually moral decisions shift and expand to a sense of or need for objective order; a world governed by adherence to rules (e.g., rules of a game, "fair play" in sports); second stage of conventional moral reasoning.	
	Reasoning is tied to particular situations and objects; cannot generalize and abstract across contexts.	

(Continued)

Table 1.1 (*Continued*)

V **12 Years–Adolescence** **Identity versus Role Confusion** **Formal, Logical Problem Solving**
The child now faces the crisis of integration (selfhood). This can be a naturally stormy and tumultuous process. Body, mind, self, and interpersonal relationships are undergoing rapid and significant transformations, placing the adolescent on the brink of adult responsibility. The result can be a stronger sense of identity or a lack of direction and meaning that persists beyond the normal bounds of this developmental stage.

Social	Cognitive	Physical Development
Preoccupation with self, own feelings and thoughts (adolescent egocentrism). A crisis of identity: the adolescent asks "Who am I?"; society and family ask "What role will you assume (adopt) in society?" Reappraisal of life values and self-attributes and worth. Formulation of beliefs, attitudes, and ideals (a personal and social ideology); role plus role-defining ideology.	Capacity to think abstractly and hypothetically (if A, then B). Moral reasoning reflects growing critical social and intellectual awareness; obligation of people to society and society to people (social contract) for a common good. Moral standards and social principles are questioned and challenged; evolving personal framework of self/social conduct beginning of postconventional stage of moral reasoning.	Emergence of secondary sexual characteristics. Emergence of sex drive and new bodily sensations.

*Ages associated with developmental milestones and the emergence of competencies are approximations and vary within a normal range that considers individual differences.
** Parent(s) or primary caregiver.

identified three determining and interactive factors that may account for similarities and differences between children raised in the same family: biology, and what they termed "shared" and "nonshared" environmental effects. The first is simple, straightforward, and not very surprising. It speaks to genetics and individual disposition and how much the variability and differences are accounted for by biological factors. The two remaining factors call attention to the fact that some environmental events influence children uniquely, whereas other elements of shared environments affect all the children in a similar way. It is just such nonshared environmental events and experiences, symbolic or real, that get parents and children into trouble with each other and put the child's and family's developmental needs at cross-purposes. Clinical practice and research strongly support the observation that when nonshared environmental events or unique experiences are ignored, invalidated, or are misunderstood in the family this leads to, and often accounts for, a child showing symptoms, and a child's symptoms bursting on the family scene, sending the entire family into developmental crisis and system instability.

The family system, on a higher and broader level, is also working through the collective energies of its members toward developing a set of family ideals and a common family identity. This provides the seeds as well as the incentive for growth and crisis. Crisis can be both enabling and disruptive to a family and its members. Families can find themselves in crisis instability at any of the turning points in family development when the family's guiding purpose is shaken from within and the challenge of change reverberates on all system levels. Some families struggle to work out and fill in the details of intimacy as they encounter the challenges and difficulties created by raising an infant. Other families thrive on this closeness, sailing onto the next family developmental task. Some families find letting go difficult and have confusion over these choice points, struggling with the demands and declarations of their toddlers, and later their adolescents, surrounding issues of independence and the rites of protest and passage.

When we fit Kantor's theory of structural dynamics and its developmental framework within the exciting and yet broadly predictable ebb and flow of child developmental stages, the match is a natural fit and the rationale and logic underlying the Child-Centered Model are unmistakable. It makes many of the child-centered as well as family problems that we see as family therapists clear and more comprehensible. Identity struggles or normal developmental crises are best understood and treated at the juncture where individual, child, and family development meet, coalesce, and sometimes collide. Table 1.1 shows the progression of child development stages, describing the milestones and tasks associated with the child's unfolding psychosocial, cognitive, linguistic, self-help, and personal mastery skills. The table depicts, in highly condensed form, what to expect and anticipate from children of different developmental levels. This table is designed and organized to create a dynamic, unfolding picture of child development. It represents the integration of Piaget's (1963; Piaget & Inhelder, 1956) theory of cognitive development, Vygotsky's (1978) conceptions of the origins of social intelligence and language development, Erikson's (1963) theory of psychosocial/psychosexual development, and Kohlberg's (1981, 1984) and Gilligan's (1982) models of moral reasoning. Table 1.1 also reflects a decidedly systems perspective combined with a view of development derived from infant research on early attachment theory and the family and the concept of intersubjectivity or the symmetry of the parent-child relationship and interaction. Table 1.1 incorporates object-relations research in conjunction with the child's expanding capacity for mental representation and symbolic thought, particularly in relation to play.

In the spirit of systems thinking and commitment to a transactional view of development, Table 1.1 emphasizes the social nature of learning, that development occurs in the context of reciprocal interaction, a fluid reciprocity between individual (child) and environment (family). In charting normal development, Table 1.1 conveys the organic nature of development—the simultaneous emergence and overlap of competencies and abilities within and across stages, including the gray areas or transitional periods between child development stages. For example, in keeping with an interactional or prosocial frame, categories of cognitive and socioemotional development are merged and treated as one whole source of experience for the infant. Gradually, as Table 1.1 illustrates, as the child develops and the self becomes more fully formed, a set of stable and predictable developmental structures, the cognitive and socioemotional categories of growth and learning are differentiated (treated separately). While there is a wealth of information and perspectives on child development, Table 1.1 focuses on those milestones, skills, competencies, and behaviors most likely to be seen in the therapy setting and elicited by therapy materials (e.g., blocks, books, puppets, dolls, playhouse). Table 1.1, organized with the therapist in mind, focuses on child development filtered through the actual experience of children in therapy, their conversations and play in the therapy room. When integrated with family development focal tasks and dilemmas (examined and illustrated in Chapter 3), Table 1.1 can function as a useful guide to the therapist in designing developmentally focused child-centered interventions.

When we work with Child-Centered Structural Dynamic Therapy and view the family's problems through this framework, it is analogous to being engaged in a continuous process of tracking and charting child and family structures, of identifying and tracing multidimensional developmental events in the family and their points of contact (compatible blending) as well as conflict and tension with the emerging identity and developmental needs of children. This process requires a changing gestalt, a moving and shifting back and forth between parts to whole, and whole to parts, in which the puzzle pieces of family structure and individual identity (critical identity images) and competing identity claims (family members' positive values and self-assertions) are discovered, distilled, and crystallized into the single, central, collective family critical identity image at the heart of the family's current crisis and instability. This collective critical identity image constructed out of the puzzle pieces of individual, interpersonal, and family unit experience provides the therapist's blueprint for child-centered system change, as Chapters 5 through 8 will illustrate.

Parent-Child Relationship Styles

While some aspects of any parent-child relationship are idiosyncratic and unique, and while some relationship difficulties parents and children get into are partly a function of the varying and different demands of successive developmental stages, studies of child development and parent-child relationships have also shown that some parenting styles are more effective and beneficial to children than others. Fishler, Sperling, and Carr (1990), in their retrospective examination of the quality of adult relatedness, found that the capacity to enjoy and to relate to others both socially and intimately was directly related to the quality and style of the parent-child relationship experienced throughout childhood and adolescence. Object-relations research has focused extensively on the quality of the parent-child relationship, on object representation, and on the degree of optimal functioning expressed in parent-child transactions.

Researchers have examined parent-child interactional styles as a function of child developmental stages in parents' and children's present lives as well as through the retrospective lens of adult experience, or the quality of "relatedness" adults display and its association with earlier parent-child relations. The key factors that have been identified include perceived warmth, empathic understanding, and emotional accessibility of the parent to the child. Lerner, Lerner, and colleagues (1986), in the Pennsylvania Early Adolescent Transitions Study (PEATS), a short-term longitudinal research project, demonstrated the developmental contextual model, or the relationship between parental patterns and levels of adjustment in children. Their longitudinal research highlights the impact of the environment on positive as well as negative developmental outcomes. Talwar, Nitz, and Lerner (1990) also found that a poor fit between parent and child in mood and approach-withdrawal patterns at the end of sixth grade was associated in the seventh grade with low teacher-rated academic and social competence and negative peer relations. We will see, in Chapter 2, that approach-withdrawal patterns express mismatched or discordant relationship patterns in family access strategies and goals.

Similarly, researchers who explored parents' capacity to understand and correctly identify the emotional state and developmental needs of their children found that this capacity was significantly and directly associated with the quality of security and attachment that the children felt and expressed (Fonagy, Steele, Steele, Moran, & Higgitt, 1991). Along similar lines, Stevenson-Hinde (1990) also confirmed the overlapping connections between parent-child attachment issues and the family's working out of attachment dilemmas at the system's developmental level.

Regarding the role of the quality of parenting in terms of the overall developmental outcome of the child, research and clinical studies of abusive parenting styles (Azar, 1991; Azar, Barnes, & Twentyman, 1988; Azar & Siegel, 1990; Burgess & Conger, 1978) speak directly, although implicitly, to the power of the Kantor critical identity image concept as an explanatory principle. Work with both healthy and abusive parent-child relationships convincingly shows, in case after case that, underneath most abusive parent-child relationships, there is a misunderstanding about the developmental needs and expectations for children combined with misplaced self-reference. Abusive parents often have unrealistically high expectations, demanding more than their children are capable of, based on their age-appropriate behavior and stage-specific development.

Research on abusive parent-child relationships has found that parents often overpersonalize the child's behavior, attributing more negative than positive motivations to the child. They tend to read more into the behavior, seeing the child often as a "little adult." For example, a child's boisterous laughter and sounds of glee are interpreted by the parent not as expressions of joy and exuberance but as the child's intentions to frustrate, annoy, or irritate the parent. The uninformed or abusive parent often sees a child's messy room, crumpling and tossing of paper, or the repeated building up and knocking down of a block tower not as expressions of play but as purposeful misbehavior and may retaliate aggressively.

Parents' misunderstandings about children's capabilities partly flow from an inaccurate picture of child development and reflect the differences between the cognitive and emotional lives of adults and children. Clinicians know too well that child development information alone is not enough to help these parents. In such parent-child struggles, the parent's tendency to overpersonalize the meaning and intent of the child's behavior (which can often have disastrous, if not deadly effects) stems also from the parent's deeply felt, unspoken, and unresolved critical identity images. Abusive parents often experienced family abuse themselves during childhood. In this way, transgenerational insufficiencies, the denied or disqualified affirmations of self and others (the blueprints of family relationships gone awry) are perpetuated, passed down from one generation to the next, played out over and over again without resolution.

CHILDREN AT PSYCHOLOGICAL AND EDUCATIONAL RISK

The impact of the family and access to an understanding of the parent-child relationship has also grown from a third line of child-oriented research and practice. This knowledge base and practice-orientation strongly supports and reinforces the preventive and early intervention tiers (levels) of the Child-Centered Model. Almost three decades of systematic early intervention, originating in the 1960s and continuing today, have focused on the child at educational and psychological risk. These programs, exemplified by Head Start, have been aimed at improving or enhancing the cognitive and socioemotional development of young children at risk, focusing primarily on families living in poverty and other disenfranchising social conditions. In the early 1960s, when social science and social philosophy consciously merged, the term *human ecology,* as a method of social intervention, evolved with a threefold aim:

1. To develop intervention strategies for improving the cognitive and language skills of young children at educational risk that would be ecologically compatible with the child's learning environment.
2. To enrich vulnerable or at-risk family learning environments.
3. To strengthen the parent-child relationship and the parent's link to the child as the child's primary teacher of life skills.

From the pioneering work of Bronfenbrenner (1974, 1975, 1976, 1977), Chilman (1973), Horowitz and Paden (1973), Levenstein (1970), and Schaeffer (1972) and the findings of Anthony and Koupernik (1974), Anthony, Koupernik, and Chiland (1978), Lamb (1977), Clarke-Stewart (1977, 1978), Lewis and Rosenblum (1979), and Belsky (1981), to the current mandate and priorities of Head Start (B. Smith, personal communication, September 1994), three decades of early intervention evaluation, insight, and wisdom underscore the crucial importance of family involvement and family self-directed strengths. The most successful programs, in terms of sustained gains for the child, have been those programs that placed greatest emphasis on involving parents and also focused on the overall health and integrity of the family system. In contrast, those programs that only involved the child, strategically targeted the mother and child, or mother alone have not proven as effective and successful. Today's family system, regardless of the form it takes, its socioeconomic status or geographic location—rural, urban, or suburban—has much more laid on its doorstep. The family system is being asked to take on and absorb many more responsibilities, stretching family developmental limits in the face of vanishing neighborhoods, dwindling social support, and a fragile sense of community and connection. Therefore, the need for community-based family support and social policies that ensure the integrity of the family is more important than ever (Barnard, Morrisset, & Spieker, 1993; Weissbourd, 1993; Zigler, Hopper, & Hall, 1993).

In the arena of school achievement, the family reigns supreme, and the family's influence is primary and profound. Early intervention programs found that their strategies worked best when they considered the whole family, creating strategies that were synergistic and thoughtfully matched to the individual families that the programs served. Those programs that took a decidedly systems approach reaped surprising benefits and unanticipated gains that spread well beyond the target child. When the educational program moved beyond the cognitive and into the interpersonal worlds of the families, children began to teach other children in the family, creating patterns of both horizontal and vertical knowledge diffusion, in which older siblings taught younger siblings and parents began to feel more optimistic about their own educational opportunities. In this way, information, education, and emotional support traveled up and down and back and forth throughout all levels and subsystems within the family. Parents' self-esteem was raised and they, in turn, sought jobs and job training, believing now that change was possible. They began to envision a better future for themselves and for their families.

These programs worked best when they connected with a family's immanent sense of identity and purpose. It is not enough simply to arm a child technologically with a specific set of cognitive skills necessary for academic achievement and economic survival in our highly advanced technological society. What families and children at risk needed then, and need even more urgently today, are programs that go well beyond child development and early intervention, per se. What is needed are programs that bridge families' identity and sense of affirmation, and involve and capture their imagination. This central principle underlies all three tiers of the Child-Centered Model and guides the purpose and objective of its methods, techniques, and activities.

FAMILY CRISIS AND HUMAN VULNERABILITY

With the exception of a brief foray into difficult or abusive parent-child relationships, we have explored and traveled down one path or access route regarding the family, involving child development, early intervention, and family interaction. At the other end point of this common continuum, shown in Figure 1.2, there is another access route or entry into our understanding of family process. This view focuses on troubled families and children. The view is essentially a clinical route, focusing on disruptions in normal family development and process, which combines substantive knowledge from both child and family therapy. One clinical route is primarily child-centered and considers the origins of human vulnerability and, by inference, the question of human resilience and strength, a central, underlying principle of the Child-Centered Model. This has led us once again to models of predicted outcomes that cross the child's developmental status or current condition (good or poor) with the quality of the family environment (good or poor), producing interactional frameworks for predicting and understanding child development outcomes.

Research in the areas of developmental delays and vulnerability exemplified by the work of Sameroff (1975, 1993; Sameroff & Seifer, 1990) and echoed by many others, including Anthony (1980) and Wertheim (1973, 1975a, 1975b, 1978), crystallizes this long-standing viewpoint: that the family has a persistent and indelible influence on its members and that its members, in turn, shape family destiny. For example, developmental delays in children are modified and ameliorated by the quality of the family environment. Such developmental models highlight the interplay of the child's individual differences (constitutional factors) and family process. High-risk children raised in optimal, emotionally responsive environments have been found, on average, to perform much better on a wider range of skills and psychosocial functioning than similar children raised in emotionally unstable environments.

Family systems research has also provided us with a rich, multidimensional perspective. One major and compelling strength of the systems perspective is that it has brought intensely into focus and into the forefront the phenomonology of children inside the family, and of the family's effects on the child, including the development, treatment, and resolution of presenting-child symptoms. For example, in our transgenerational approaches we have merged the here and now of family transaction with the child inside us or our early internalized families. Interactional views, with emphasis on how all the puzzle pieces of family transactions fit together to form whole family processes, have shed considerable light on the child's actual behavior while growing and developing in an evolving family system. Family therapy's beginnings and many of its early breakthroughs are associated with its explorations into the world of troubled families and symptomatic children. What our clinical work has consistently shown is that the child responds symbolically and often somatically to family distress; that a child's symptoms often are a barometer of wider family tension and instability; and that a child's troubling behavior often evolves to deflect deeper or more threatening marital or family conflict.

Child-Centered Structural Dynamic Therapy: An In-Depth View

Earlier in this chapter, three fundamental concepts drawn from the Kantor theory of structural dynamics were described and illustrated in the context of child development: formal structures, content structures, and critical identity image. These concepts form the pivotal center around which a larger network of terms in the Kantor theory of structural dynamics revolve and around which child-centered clinical concepts and techniques for working with children in family therapy (Andreozzi, 1977, 1978, 1979a, 1979b, 1979c, 1979d, 1979e, 1988, 1993a) have been developed. We can think of these concepts as the core of the model: The nucleus or genetic material from which family behavior and interaction flow. We can also think of the Kantor concepts in a specific way, as they are melded and shaped to fit child-centered family practice and integrated with child development. In this light, while there is considerable fidelity to a complete description of concepts and terms as Kantor has defined them, the overarching frame—the crucible—through which the network of terms has passed, has been the decided world of children and practical considerations of child-centered therapy.

The first term in Kantor's theory of structural dynamics focuses on the critical identity image concept. Critical identity images are stories with a structure. These images reflect each family member's "system-map" or "family story," deeply felt and experienced from his or her personal viewpoint; hence, they bear the stamp of each family member's identity, child and adult alike. Critical identity images represent the interpersonal set of instructions we carry around inside us based on the crucial life lessons families teach in both subtle and obvious ways. Critical identity images comprise our unique family stories about decisive relationships: the guides that inform our behavior and that we consciously or unwittingly follow when shaping our intimate relationships.

For children, however, these relational maps are usually behavioral statements about self and the family in the here and now that are strongly developmental in nature. Child development tasks and crises color their stories, and the level of detail and articulation is a function of the child's developmental maturity. Yet, regardless of the child's cognitive skill or facility with language (verbal expression), these image scenarios and stories provide rich telegraphic or shorthand statements that the child communicates and that the therapist can read and the family can come to know and understand. The crucial feature of Kantor's critical identity image concept is that it is a "story with structure."

In therapy, as in other intimate conversations, individuals organize their thoughts and feelings into cohesive and coherent stories or statements about important experiences. In describing an experience, usually about the self-in-relation to others and others-in-relation to self, a selective process or "selective memory" takes place. Some details are emphasized while other details are minimized, reinterpreted, or totally forgotten. Just as the process of psychotherapy is one of integration during which an individual discovers or realizes an explanation of traumatic events now compatible with a positive sense of identity, the ultimate goal of family therapy and child-centered therapy is the evolution of a family view that integrates the personal explanations of its members, a common "story" (explanation) with a structure that incorporates and values the separate identities of its members, parents and children, alike.

The stories we tell each other and ourselves about crucial events or experiences in our lives have a sequence or flow (beginning, middle, and end) and a gestalt, an overall "feel" or tone. Each element, sequence (parts-to-wholes) and gestalt (whole) speaks to a different aspect of systems theory. Each person's story is, in essence, an explanation, an attempt to understand what happened or is happening around important events and relationships in our lives. In this way, stories are important explanations to self and others and, in turn, reflect a personal developmental theory of how events and circumstances (e.g., the current problem) evolved.

When we witness (weigh and consider) a family's story, including its children, we are delving into two aspects of creativity and crisis implications for our work as therapists. There is the structure of the story, the who, what, where, when, and how of the event, relationship, or conflict. Too, there is the deeper metalevel message or import of events, the emotional content of the story, what it means to each participant (owner of the story and part of the family experience). Two individuals can interpret the same sequence of events in vastly different ways. In this light, we arrive at two interactive levels of a story: its process or sequence, which is systemic and represents the transactional footsteps we follow (as event A leads to event B and event B leads to event C) in a family interaction; and also the subjective mood or feeling each family member brings to "an event" or observed structure of interaction (overt behavior). This is the individual and idiosyncratic aspect of each family member's perspective on shared events.

Adults can recount highly detailed, elaborate scenes of betrayal, rejection, indignity, and abandonment. For example, an adult family member (parent) may relate (recall) a father who berated a mother in the presence of a helpless onlooking child (self). The structure on the level of family process (repetitive problem transactions) may have taken the form of an overbearing and aggressive father who initiated confrontations with an intimidated mother who acquiesced, as a bewildered child, impotent to help, looked on. The child (adult currently relating the story) may have felt in those instances (interactions) rage against a brutal father, scorn, embarrassment, or pity for a humiliated mother, and guilt and shame (self-recrimination) at the child's (self's) inability to intervene. The emotional frame in which a story is cast, its mood and subjective meaning, conveys a great deal about the systems psychology (internalized family) of the storyteller.

However, unlike the adult's fully formed cognitive and affective capacities to analyze and self-reflect, a child offers image stories that are inchoate and fluid and, as clinical experience with children shows, akin to the two-word metaphors or primary thought process of a poem. Children's image-scenes are much more rudimentary, similar to the muted and blurred edges of impressionist paintings. Sometimes the therapist cannot ask children directly about their stories but instead must access these scenes indirectly through humor, fantasy, and play-guided techniques, as will be shown in Chapters 4 and 7. The structure of a child's story is often synonymous with the structure of the child's behavior or behavior problem. Yet, while children and adults relate these critical stories differently and give them quite different textures, both children and adults tell or enact a developmentally focused story on two levels: process or transactional (family interactions), and content or self-psychology.

Here is where the interior world of self or personal worlds of individuals (personal subsystem level) connect with the family system in observable interaction, the family's developmental here and now. Much in the way we weave strands of thread together to make a fabric pattern, or join puzzle pieces to create a complete picture, the therapist and family integrate these image-stories into a cohesive "family critical identity image scenario": a ritualized scene of family conflict that expresses the family's current developmental crisis. What is unique and decidedly systemic about critical identity images and Child-Centered Structural Dynamics is the continuous emphasis on the tracking of structural change. The therapist always keeps a watchful eye on structure at several levels. This leads us to two related concepts introduced by Kantor that provide a link between inner and outer worlds of experience, a bridge between individual and system: "formal" and "content" structures.

As Kantor describes, critical identity images of family members express formal structures (recurrent patterns or styles of relating) and content structures (recurrent themes, conflicts) around important interactions (family domains). The issues at stake may be quite different between parents and children, husbands and wives, and indeed, concepts of "formal" and "content" structures are applied differently with children. However, the therapist must consider both levels to understand the contribution of each family member's behavior to the current family conflict. For example, when the husband feels rejected around themes of sexual or emotional intimacy (content), he withdraws (behavior). When the wife feels rejected around sexual or emotional intimacy (content), she entreats, appeases, or pursues (behavior). Or, when a particularly vigorous child strikes out to test the limits of self-mastery and exploration while performing the childhood tasks of independence and industry (content), the parent, feeling anxious, moves in too close, emotionally and physically overprotecting the child (behavior). Over time, if repeated enough, these interactions rise to the level of a recurrent pattern. The scripts for these patterns flow from critical identity images, system stories with a developmental structure. For children, the genetic form and content of these relationship scenes are evolving, still being shaped, in accordance with the child's age- and stage-specific readiness. For the parent or adult, the genetic material, while still being acted on in the present family context, emanates from important childhood family lessons in human relationships. These image scenes figure crucially in the current structure of family organization.

Critical identity images simultaneously express and contain what Child-Centered Structural Dynamics Therapy terms "competing identity claims," Kantor's (1980) companion concept. Competing identity claims, as Kantor defines, are the positive values, beliefs, and intentions underlying family members' behaviors (strategies). When working with children, these are the positive reality assertions we find when we turn a critical identity image scene around and name the implicit interpersonal goal and/or personal claim contained in it. Critical identity claims reflect what is at stake in the family conflict and developmental struggle. Another way we can think about and identify these positive assertions (critical identity claims) and their family "purpose" (function) in the developmental crisis is to focus on the symptom(s). We can ask ourselves, "What is the meaning of this child's symptoms?" or more precisely, "What important dimensions or aspect of family transactions would be lost if the symptom(s) or symptomatic behavior were to disappear?" "What important family process dimension or relationship is the symptom protecting?" Therefore, a critical identity image, on individual and systems levels, has two important parts: one shows the crisis or conflict (where the family is developmentally stuck); the other expresses the positive goals and expectations of the family and members within it, often the family's best, well-kept positive "secret."

An additional feature of critical identity images, which makes them decidedly systemic and structural, involves the emphasis Kantor's (1980; Kantor & Lehr, 1986) theory of structural dynamics places on "distance regulation," or approach-withdrawal styles, patterns of joining and separation in families. Distance regulation expresses the quality and organization of the family's emotional life. It is what we see in visual-spatial terms when we first meet a family, the organized way they introduce themselves to the therapist. It is also what family members communicate in the structured stories of their most salient critical identity scenes. Figure 1.3 depicts five families discussed in the book. Each spatial sketch, or "family system snapshot," conveys a highly condensed and potent relationship statement about "who" each family "is" and what family members feel about each other.

When we integrate child development into our understanding of critical identity images, we can think of these images as evolving object relations, internalized transactional relationship pictures of crucial scenes expressed in visual-spatial form. Critical identity images merge content and process. Central to the critical identity image is the concept of distance regulation. Distance regulation expresses, through actual and symbolic space, the pattern of family relationships: the movement of individuals toward and away from each other (formal structures). Enmeshment and estrangement are examples from family therapy that illustrate well-known patterns of family distance and distancing. Critical identity images are, therefore, visual relationship statements that contain and vividly illustrate both content and formal structures, the current transactional life and emotional patterns of an evolving family system. Content structures add the dimension of theme, mood, nuance, emotional intensity, and personal history. Critical identity images convey important information to the therapist. Through image exploration and the staging of change, families can sense and recognize the potent influence and positive developmental potential of these images. This leads us to another set of concepts or branch of interconnected terms in Kantor's theory of structural dynamics and the Child-Centered Structural Dynamic Therapy Model—the model's developmental view of family organization.

Figure 1.3
Visual-Spatial Relationship Statements That Express the Patterned Emotional and Structural Lives of Five Families

Family Organization

In Child-Centered Structural Dynamic Therapy, the concept of structure is applied in multiple ways, as Table 1.2 indicates. This table provides a list of the model's key terms followed by a brief definition in both systems and everyday language; Kantor's structural dynamic concepts are translated and integrated with child development theory in preparation for a full explication of the Child-Centered Model and the practice of child-centered therapy.

Having begun our overview at the innermost center or core concept of critical identity image (Kantor, 1980), we will now move systematically outward, proceeding first to the definition and illustration of structure as it pertains to the family—specifically, current family organization.

Child-Centered Structural Dynamic Therapy integrates, plans for, assesses, and views family change on two interactive levels and from two perspectives: current family organization and the quality of the family's developmental history, including the tasks and intersecting stages of child development. As Table 1.2 indicates, current family development and, hence, the signs of family conflict (the problem the family brings to therapy) are occurring simultaneously on four family organizational levels (Kantor, 1980): meaning, action, pattern, and model. A normal developmental crisis is seen as an identity struggle taking place on all four levels of the family system. Meaning structures, in this context, refer to:

- The family's shared store of images and meanings about individuals, relationships, and the family itself, as a group. This involves fundamental images and imagery about what it means to be a parent, a child, a person, and a family.

For example, a family's meaning structures may involve graphic images: "We are a family under attack"; "We are a strong family"; "We are a family that rallies around just causes." Or, a family can express its group image and sense of identity by stating, "We are a socially active family who usually participates in community activities. The community sees us as involved and committed. If we do not take part in our neighborhood's efforts to keep the neighborhood safe, then what will the community think of us? Will we be living up to our family image?"

A family's action structures describe:

- Day-to-day practical actions and family activities; family member behaviors.

For example, Mother gets everyone up in the morning and sees that no one is late; Father walks the dog and drives the children to school. A family's

Table 1.2
Related Terms in Child-Centered Structural Dynamic Therapy

Term	Definition
Family crisis	A normal developmental event or occurrence.
Critical identity image	A highly emotionally charged image of self-in-relation to others and others vis-à-vis self that influences and guides the dynamics of intimate relationships of spouses and children. Developmentally focused "relationship ideas"; the mental representations of important relationship lessons—"image-worries" and "image-wonders" that children communicate through the language of their behavior and symbolic play.
Competing identity claims	The positive intentions and expectations underlying an individual's negative or unproductive behavior; what a person seeks to affirm and communicate in an interaction that others do not recognize or see; the positive intention of a child's negative behavior and healthy "underside" of a child's symptom (s).
Distance regulation	A visual-spatial relationship statement. The patterns of closeness and distance, joining and separating among family members; how individuals move toward and move away from one another; evolving patterns of parent-child bonding and attachment, independence, and autonomy. Takes into account all three types of distance: physical, psychological, and social.
Family type	Family worldview, life paradigm; preferred style and orientation for relating interpersonally and for interacting with the outside world. One of three "models" (open, closed, random) associated with a different parent-child dynamic, style of parenting, problem-solving, concept and experience of "being a child."
Closed family system	Fixed space, structured time, evenly modulated energy styles; reserved affect, hierarchical power (authority), values tradition; authoritative parenting styles; parents set clear rules and limits for children.
Open family system	Flexible space, variable time and energy expression; openly demonstrates affect, consensual power; a balance between individual and collective family identity (meaning); parent and child negotiate rules; rules vary according to context.

Table 1.2 (*Continued*)

Random family system	Erratic space, idiosyncratic time and energy styles; passionate affect, highly individualistic; self takes precedence over family group identity; laissez-faire parenting style; rules are arbitrary.
Core purpose	A family's guiding group image; central purpose and meaning; the family's plans for the future; guides child development; sets a value (valence) on the purpose, worth, place, and priority of children and their relationship to the family's group identity and future.
Homeostatic ideal	How the family responds to sameness and difference as well as signs of disturbance in the family system. The family's model for how to change as well as how to remain the same (stable); the measure and latitude of the family's tolerance of children's behavior and individual differences.
Formal structures	Family patterns; the sequence of transactions among family members that characterize typical family interaction; parent-child relationship patterns.
Content structures	The recurrent themes, mood states, personal meanings that motivate behaviors; the personal histories, needs, expectations, and desires associated with family patterns; the "content" around which the parent-child conflict (problem-pattern) arises; usually associated with dilemmas related to child development, stage-related tasks.
Longitudinal development	The integration of family life cycle stages and stages of child development.
Current family development	A cross-sectional view of family organization on four interactive levels: meaning, model, action, pattern; corresponding "child development" and "parent-child structures" are present (available for assessment) at each level.
Meaning structures	The family's store of images; symbolic life; what the family selectively talks about and notices on a day-to-day basis; the family's image of "childhood"; what it means "to be a child" and "to be a parent." One level of family organization and development.
Model structures	The family's rule book and compass for guiding family life and interaction. The family's problem-solving strategies, including the "ought to's " and "should's" of parenting and child development. The family's concept of "child" and "childhood." One level of family organization and development.

(Continued)

Table 1.2 (*Continued*)

Action structures	The actions and activities of everyday life; basic tasks; what the family does to keep the family going; caregiving, instrumental, and expressive tasks and parental responsibilities. One level of family organization and development.
Pattern structures	The family's characteristic strategies and sequences. Actions build to form family patterns; predictable family behavior. The characteristic patterns of the parent-child relationship and the family's developmental (current and historical) orientation to children. One level of family organization and development.
Family access dimensions	The physical, psychological, and social pathways (mediums) of space, time, and energy that family members use to gain access to one another integrated with child development concepts (the child's conception of space, time, cause and effect, function, and children's temperament/energy styles) and family process; a framework for identifying parent-child patterns and problems.
Family interaction domains	The domains/goals of affect (nurturance/intimacy), power (efficacy, competence, mastery, learning), and meaning (identity, purpose) integrated with unfolding child development stages and tasks of trust, independence, initiative, and industry.
Psychopolitics	Psychopolitics bridges the psychic (psychological) and systemic (transactional); the juncture where the interior world of self is expressed in overt family behavior and interaction; individual-system interplay; where the personal world of self (motivation, cognition, emotion, biology) meets the observable world of family interaction. Considers the reciprocal relationship and influence of child and family development.
Four family parts	Four transactional roles or behavioral options family members can choose, learn, or feel compelled to play: mover, follower, opposer, bystander. All four parts coincide with child development stage-specific tasks associated with healthy cognitive and socioemotional growth.
Mover	The individual who gets things started; initiates the interaction; leads; corresponds to the child's need to develop independence, initiative, and autonomy. One of four transactional options in family interaction.

Table 1.2 (*Continued*)

Follower	Supports the mover and the goals of the interaction. Supports; enables others; validates; corresponds to the child's need to develop trust, compliance, and cooperative behavior. One of four transactional options in family interaction.
Challenger/Opposer	Changes the direction of an interaction. Challenges the mover and attempts to redefine the purpose of the interaction; corresponds to the child's need to develop autonomy, independent judgment, and self-assertion. One of four transactional options in family interaction.
Bystander	Offers thoughtful impartial observations and evaluations of what is taking place; the family's or group's "conscience" and "system consciousness"; the group's observing ego; corresponds to the child's need to develop critical powers of observation and self-reflection; the capacity to analyze and form an objective overview. One of four transactional options in family interaction.
Psychopolitical configurations	Family transactional roles or parts combine and settle into predictable interactional sequences; what family members come to expect from self and others; who does "what" and "when" in an interaction.
Ritual impasse	Recurrent, episodic playing out of the family crisis; child and family development at cross-purposes.

actions build into predictable patterns of family organization. Family patterns are composed of and evolve into preferred roles and interactional player parts. A pattern structure, in this context, refers to:

- An interactional sequence; a discrete set (series) of transactional moves with a definite beginning, middle, and end; the sequence aspect to the family's "story with a structure"; in effect, the family's behavioral sentence.

For example, Mother typically initiates family projects (cleaning out the garage, an instrumental task) and family recreational activities (picnics, trips to the beach; nurturance and intimacy); the children join in and follow her lead; Father, however, challenges either by criticizing or disparaging the plan, or by withdrawing into his work, in effect, opposing the family's group plan and growing sense of collective purpose (shared experience).

Model structures, in this context, refer to:

- The implicit, tacitly held, deeply felt "guides" that the family develops, and individuals contribute and use to direct the family and keep it on course; the family's guiding compass and conscious collective identity.

The family's model level of organization is a cumulative one that combines and integrates foundational images (meanings), actions, and patterns into what a family comes to experience as its collective or core purpose. Here we find its behavioral and conceptual guides—the family's "rule book" that implicitly tells members what to expect, anticipate, and hold as ideals. For example, a family may ask, "Are we a family that cares about each other and values each other's opinions? Is it one of our ideals, that we can fairly and openly agree to disagree?" Or a family may wonder, reminding members, "Does being married mean that money and family resources as well as family responsibilities are shared? Are we a family that pools our money?" Here, as is often the case in real family transactions, meanings overlap between family group image and the images held up as ideals for specific family relationships.

In the example illustrating pattern structures, the mother's (wife's) concept of family may involve a high degree of togetherness (affect domain): "A family that is emotionally close spends a great deal of time together." On the other hand, the father's (husband's) model, guiding his interactions, may involve a concept of family quite different from his wife's model structure. He may prefer a qualitatively different degree of physical and metaphoric space, patterns of joining and separation (coming together and being apart). The husband may prefer less family time in favor of greater "private time" and individual pursuits. He may also differ with regard to the family domain he typically emphasizes. He may derive meaning and value from competence (tasks of mastery and skill), whereas his wife draws worth and a sense of identity from the family affect domain. Both spouses are, therefore, operating from different models—different rhythms of intimacy, access, and individuation. The children, who are absorbing those lessons, stand in the middle, observing and experiencing both models. During family development, models can either meld (fit, match, coordinate) and "agree" or they can clash (compete, conflict) and "disagree." When models clash, we find developmental crisis. At the root of family crisis, critical identity images, reflecting meaning, action, pattern, and model levels of family organization, are in conflict and the family's identity is in jeopardy.

Signs of Crisis and Predictable Problem Patterns

There are two main outward signs or features of a family crisis. One involves a temporary collapse of the family's problem-solving, decision-making capabilities—a disruption in events occurring at the pattern level of family organization. The other observable sign of crisis is the constriction and rigidification of family behavior at the action level of family organization and process—a gravitation, for the right or wrong reasons, on the part of family members toward stuck and/or stereotypic behaviors.

This leads us to the intersection of two clusters of concepts in Kantor's theory of structural dynamics and their implications for Child-Centered Therapy: family organization and player parts. Less visible features of the crisis are found in the meaning and model levels of family organization. The family conflict or struggle begins at the least complex level of organization—the meaning or foundation level of the family where, as Kantor conceptualizes, it is fueled by competing critical identity images—and continues upward throughout all family system levels, as critical identity claims (positive values) vie for recognition, until the conflict reaches the highest, most complex model level. At this point, model instabilities in the form of competing ideals for the shaping of the collective identity, a common core family purpose, will surface and, one way or the other, will or will not be resolved. Family crisis means crossroads, turning points, growth. It also means choices, implicitly made or explicitly stated. These choices make a difference. Crisis, therefore, equals identity struggle.

Hence, we have moved outward in increasingly wider arcs of family involvement and understanding. We began with critical identity image, its positive assertions (critical identity claims), and the notion of distance regulation expressed in the structured developmental story of crisis the family tells (reenacts in unresolved problem patterns). Model and meaning structures are the conceptual levels, points on a family organizational continuum, from which and to which, observable behavior and family patterns begin and return in full cycle. The behaviors of individual family members that contribute to the conflict are termed in Child-Centered Structural Dynamic Therapy, a term Kantor identifies in his theory of structural dynamics, as "psychopolitical configurations": the transactional parts (psychopolitics) we see in observable interaction sequences. Equipped with the conceptual knowledge of the family's model and meaning levels of organization, psychopolitical configurations (defined in Table 1.2) are the behavioral place where the therapist's developmentally focused interventions begin. Psychopolitical configurations and associated player parts have special, developmentally crucial implications for children and child-centered assessment, as will be shown in Chapter 2. The "ritual impasse," again highlighted in Table 1.2, holds the crisis dynamic; it communicates the content and structural essentials of the family's recurrent, episodic problem. A ritual impasse, a term coined by Kantor, is the sequence of behavioral transactions in a family that "cause problems" because the interaction is never satisfactorily brought to closure (resolved). These are the fundamental terms and foundational focus of Child-Centered Structural Dynamic Therapy.

Standing back to examine the model on a broader level, we can think of family organization in Child-Centered Structural Dynamic Therapy as follows: The family's model structures are its paradigm for living, its window on the world, and view from its "front porch." It is the sum and substance of the family's cognitive and experiential group identity. Embedded within a family's model of organization are its instructional guides; the life lessons it communicates including its rules for parenting. Model structures tell us a great deal about the family's problem-solving strategies and "guides" for development. Model structures steer the family's course in two ways: through the family's core purpose (collective identity and goals) and through the family's checkpoints or rules for handling/responding to difference (homeostatic ideal). A child's symptoms and problem behavior signal disturbance, and a family, depending on its ideals of sameness and tolerance for difference will respond in dramatically different ways. The way the family processes disturbance (e.g., developmental crises or a symptomatic child's behavior) reflects the family's system type. The Kantor system typology includes open, closed, and random family types. Each type carries strong implications for how the therapist joins with the family, including the tempo or rhythm of therapy process compatible with the family's concept of change, as will be shown in Chapters 2, 5, 7, and 8.

Closed family systems favor fixed space, structured time, and evenly modulated physical and interpersonal energy styles. Open family system types are more variable and fluid in these family domains. Random family systems are erratic and highly individualistic. The Kantor Four Player Model, consisting of four transactional options—mover, follower, opposer, bystander (defined in Table 1.2)—draws our attention back, once again, to the individual, the locus or juncture where self and system meet in observable, concrete ways. Therefore, having begun with the individual, the smallest unit, we shift back and forth (between self and system) to grasp a comprehensive developmental view of child-centered problems.

Stepping back farther to gain a wider, long-range perspective, we can also involve the therapist, applying the four levels of organization—meaning, model, action, and pattern—to the practice of effective therapy and the role of the therapist. This draws into the picture the fourth, supralevel of the model that provides "process feedback" to the therapist in the form of the Child-Centered Structural Dynamic Therapy's model of personal and professional development and self-supervision. Here, we encounter the therapy process unfolding at two simultaneous levels or double description. There are the effects and effectiveness of therapy as organized techniques and skills. There is also the relational level, or therapy as an intimate process in which the therapist stands as an evolving self. In this light, the therapist's model structures or level of organization represents the therapist's "model of living" which contains such salient personal and professional features as his or her "model of change." The action and pattern levels of practice reflect the therapist's technique (technical aspects of therapy and technical skills). The therapist's meaning level of organization, in turn, contains his or her own store of critical identity images and, accordingly, the potential for these unfinished puzzle pieces either to interfere with therapy or to be used in wise and well-informed ways. In effect, consistent with its strong developmental focus, Child-Centered Structural Dynamic Therapy invites therapists to mold, modify, and continue to refine their own evolving model of practice.

Individual and Family Developmental Interplay

Family therapy and the systems perspective have effectively dissolved the artificial boundary and distinction between individual and environment and shown us a context-dependent world. Behavior is best understood when it is judged in the context of wider transactional patterns. Still, there are other crucial boundaries to dissolve, beyond individual and environment or self in social context, as well as other ways of viewing and dissolving this artificial dichotomy. There are other practical and conceptual territories to explore in family practice. There are additional pathways of understanding to open and different conceptual tools to apply—lenses through which to view and recast the individual-system context. Putting it another way, there are both different forms (formal structures) and content (content structures) that express and reveal interchange across this permeable boundary.

Child-Centered Structural Dynamic Therapy dissolves two artificial and important, hitherto overlooked, boundaries. One involves the technical and conceptual focus of the field and has to do with content versus formal structures in the family. In fact, this is not so much a boundary issue as a "missing piece" in some aspects of family therapy theory building. Systems therapists, by virtue of the way they see the world, routinely ignore content, viewing it as the primary domain of psychic life, individual therapy, and linear history. They favor formal structures or the transactional life of the family. Family therapists are especially attuned to patterns and the structural present of the family's life. In contrast, Child-Centered Structural Dynamic Therapy strategically and consciously makes use of content and formal structures and has developed systematic methods and tools for integrating both, especially in work with families and children. The model consciously considers and concentrates attention on the transactional juncture between the inner world and interior life of individuals and the outer world of family process, the intersection where self and system merge in the observable world of family transactions. A major critical issue in family therapy, the topic and focus of this book, involves the interplay between individual and system, the juncture where personal, interpersonal, and family domains connect in developmentally decisive ways for the vulnerable child.

The other important boundary dissolved through the Child-Centered Structural Dynamic Model is the one between child and family development, an issue of crucial and imperative importance given the many pressures on families today and the many troubled children who search for purpose and meaning and guidance from what often seems like an impervious and child-indifferent society. To say that the child is influenced by family development and that the family is influenced, in turn, by child development may, on the face of it, seem obvious. We talk about children and the importance of the family a great deal in our society, and the family is the centerpiece of all family therapy work. Certainly, the concept is an only too familiar theme or refrain throughout the social and behavioral sciences. These developmental principles have been raised to the level of "assumptive givens" and form the diffuse developmental frame of reference in which therapists work. But, being the social systems "meteorologists" that we are, with our eye on those large, moving "weather systems in human affairs" (Hoffman, 1981), we need, once again, to ask the question: "What do we actually know about family development?"; "What models do we have that systematically merge, integrate, and blend child and family development, and provide clinical, creative, and process opportunities on this level?"

Family development has not received the kind and quality of consistent attention that it deserves in the field. While family therapists think in terms of "child development" and "family development," while fundamentals of child and family development implicitly guide therapy, forming a backdrop of human development principles, child and family development rarely, if ever, form explicit or integrated models. Family therapy as a developing field requires integrated models of child and family development. Child-Centered Structural Dynamic Therapy meets parents, children, and families at this developmental crossroads, making optimal use of the creative and crisis-borne moments of family change—growth opportunities that avail themselves to clinicians and family alike. Through the organizing principle of the Kantor critical identity image concept, Child-Centered Structural Dynamic Therapy provides methods and a model for integrating the perspectives of children and parents and the family as a whole along the continuum of family change, from prevention to family crisis and instability.

Child-Centered Structural Dynamic Family Therapy is an effective model because it brings together into a single, guiding, cohesive structural image, the individual and collective identity claims, developmental needs, and expectations of family members, and the family as a whole. Once the clinician has identified the central, single most critical identity image, composed of the puzzle pieces of the family and individuals in it, tracked and followed the reverberations of this multidimensional structural image across all four organizational levels of the family—meaning, model, action, pattern—the therapist can use the experiential information to help the family move beyond its current developmental crisis and system impasse.

From our uses of metaphor, myth, narrative, and ritual in therapy, to the story as precursor and the in-depth case study or single case designs, to encompassing group-level views and models of family change, we, as family therapists, need to continuously move back and forth between all three perspectives. We need to balance and alternate attention to all three levels of knowledge, all three types of experience, and all three kinds of information about families. We can synthesize this information into a dynamic and cohesive whole that considers the family and the individuals in it, individual families or individual family differences, and families as a group or the concept of family as a developing system over time. The Child-Centered Structural Dynamic Model combines assessment and treatment of all three types of knowledge. The model provides the therapist with a framework for shifting back and forth between levels and a means of synthesizing multiple levels of information into a developmental picture.

The field of family therapy has generated a dazzling array of theoretical orientations, methods, models, and techniques to treat marital and family distress. Research efforts, increased in direct proportion to the proliferation of therapy methods and techniques, as well as in response to the growing awareness that full descriptions of the ways in which these methods and techniques actually work, are required to understand them completely. These research efforts, directed largely toward the assessment of therapy outcomes and explication of the therapy process, have yielded considerable empirical support for both the effects and effectiveness of marital and family therapy, issues of critical importance to both practitioners and consumers of family therapy.

The intellectual history of family therapy tells its own system story leading full cycle to the central role of children and highlights the next, natural step: the importance of developmentally focused child-centered therapy. The known world of family therapy research has grown from rough-hewn terrain to detailed empirical landscapes. The developmental crises of family therapy, when viewed as a developing science and profession, can be grouped into a series of successive growth cycles (Andreozzi, 1993b). Empirical research and practice have progressed from the pioneering exploratory research of early family therapy as a developing method and social science, when as Haley (1978), Wynne (1983), and others characterize, family therapist and researcher were of the same ilk, fundamentally one. In the pioneering stage of family therapy, the first growth cycle, research focused on broad issues: What is this "thing" called family therapy and how does it work? Broad "what" questions about family process formed the empirical framework for the field's foundation years. In the early 1970s through the late 1980s, the field, like every developing science seeking recognition from neighboring disciplines, entered a consolidating and legitimizing phase, the second and third growth cycles, the controlled-comparative and controlled-competitive research.

In this stage of development, the field of family therapy, as a discipline, distinct science, and treatment-paradigm, was working diligently to prove its efficacy and unique perspective as a profession. By the early to mid-1980s, an empirical baseline was established for the efficacy of family therapy. In the late 1980s and 1990s, the field's fourth growth cycle, empirical research has now focused on refinement, synthesis, and integration across therapy schools; in effect, an emphasis on broader theory-building and theory-testing issues. The evolution and efficacy of family therapy as a treatment modality and distinct social science view of human problems and change have been approached in the 1990s through two complementary paths: The first involves the testing, articulation, and confirmation of well-defined whole theories (structural modeling), a route just beginning to emerge in family research, although it has been widely adopted in psychology for a number of years. The second empirical path is a meta-analytic one that summarizes and examines the magnitude of therapy outcomes (effect sizes) across large, diverse groups of studies.

The impact of clinical research (its results, the questions posed, the strategies used) and the impact of therapy (events inside the therapy hour) are, in many respects, interdependent and related, reflecting a relationship of mutual influence (Andreozzi, 1985a, 1985d, 1985e, 1993a, 1993b; Kantor & Andreozzi, 1985). However, while accumulated empirical research and meta-analyses of the general efficacy of family therapy confirm family therapy's positive treatment claims, this collective clinical research often raises more questions than it answers. A striking observation is the virtual absence of outcome research on the treatment of presenting-child problems with family therapy, an issue of crucial importance given the rising trends in childhood behavior problems and the growing recognition of the need for prevention and early intervention.

The challenges that face family therapy as a developing field, and family therapists as social interventionists, echo the question of T.S. Eliot's (1962) Prufrock, who wonders, "Do I dare disturb the universe?" Often the task of capturing and understanding the complicated and complex events in any given therapy hour are similar to trying "to squeeze the universe into a ball" and "roll it toward some overwhelming question"; in this case it is one involving children and the efficacy of family therapy, issues with the promise of many "visions and revisions."

CHAPTER 2

Structural Dynamic Therapy with Children

Parents and Children, Family Dimensions, and Transactional Roles

CHILD-CENTERED STRUCTURAL DYNAMIC THERAPY is an effective, efficient, and flexible model for facilitating change in families and children across a range of contexts, problem types, and levels of problem intensity. The strength of the Child-Centered Model flows from the model itself, its malleability and multileveled structure. The model is used in family practice and in research, and can be used by the therapist to monitor progress on multiple levels, a check and balance for the therapist's professional efficacy and self-supervision, as well as an invaluable self-exploration. The model's strength also derives from the very nature of the family system, the process, organization, and structural life of families raising children. The Child-Centered Structural Dynamic Model is ideally suited and highly compatible with families in the formative stages of family development for a variety of important reasons.

This chapter focuses on four of the five building blocks of the Child-Centered Structural Dynamic Model, drawn from the Kantor theory of structural dynamics and applied to child-centered family practice, highlighting the compatible links between the model and work with children in the broadest way. Later chapters are devoted to an explication of the various uses of the Child-Centered Structural Dynamic Model and its corresponding Child-Centered Activities and techniques, from prevention to crisis.

A Normalizing View of Process: Family Problems in Context

Child-Centered Structural Dynamic Therapy derives from a comprehensive model of normal family process and interaction set forth by Kantor in the mid-1970s. The model is not pathology driven or pathology focused. Crisis is viewed, for example, as a normal occurrence in a family's life, a developmental necessity of growth and a precursor to change. In this light, rigid or counterproductive family strategies are viewed as ironic displacements, and a child's symptoms as originally benign or healthy attempts to cope that now have become ineffective and problematic for the child and family. As David Kantor illustrates in *Inside the Family* (Kantor & Lehr, 1986), and as clinical research on the Child-Centered Model (Andreozzi, 1978, 1979d, 1980, 1985a, 1988, 1993a, 1993b) confirms, even troubled and chaotic family systems devote portions of their time to ordinary family process and interaction. Troubled families are not in crisis and chaos all the time.

Emphasis on "what's right" instead of "what's wrong" is often the first step in staging change in a multiproblem and disenfranchised family such as the Brimmers, who will be introduced in this chapter. Families experiencing moderate crisis and instability do not experience instability across the board, or in every context of their interactional life, which partly accounts for some of the complicated dilemmas the field faces around outcome interpretation and measures of change. These dilemmas extend to the problems and tasks associated with the construction of family unit assessment instruments that delineate a valid multilevel picture of family functioning. These measures must reflect high degrees of clinical specificity (accurate identification of disturbance) and clinical sensitivity (accurate identification of healthy family functioning)—important requirements that will be examined in later chapters.

When we approach the task and challenge of constructing a family-level view or single, composite measure of outcome (Andreozzi, 1985a, 1985b, 1985c), we invariably face a number of crucial theoretical and practical considerations that relate directly to the notion of "system." For example, there is the conceptual question and related pragmatic (computational) issue of "how to" construct an effective and accurate family unit view of outcome and change that best combines the separate or distinct viewpoints (behavioral and perceptual changes) of individuals in the family and also reflects the family's change process as a whole. Conceptual decisions influence computational choices, and both decisions have philosophical implications for understanding systems and outcome interpretation.

A family unit view or composite measure of change may not be best expressed as an additive one. If we adhere to the principle that a system is more than the sum of its parts, then an additive view of family change simply does not hold. To add up mother's and father's and the children's perspectives (scores) does not adequately reflect system totality. If we average the individuals' viewpoints, we also lose a vital dimension. An averaged outcome is a homogenized view of family unit change. Important differences can be camouflaged in the process.

Two families may reflect the same average measure of change but, underneath it all, may represent qualitatively different kinds of change. One family member's extraordinary progress among family members who made minimal progress may express the same average change (score) as a family in which all members made small gains. The average scores of these two families are not equal, highlighting the problems inherent in family-level assessment. Similarly, there is the well-known dilemma involved in outcome interpretation in which we find families showing normal functioning on, for example, five out of seven subscores on family assessment devices. This makes it difficult to create global statements about family dysfunction. The problem also highlights and sensitizes us to the finding that families in crisis do not show disruption in all family dimensions or across all assessment criteria.

Structural dynamic therapy with children is strongly rooted in a normative view of family process, interaction, growth, and change. To understand structural dynamic therapy with children is to first understand the content, goals, and implications of Kantor's descriptive framework of family process, which focuses on the family's structural present, the individual within the family system, as self and social actor, and the ways in which both converge, and then adapt this understanding to the context of child-centered family practice.

The Kantor model emphasizes the observable, concrete interactional world of the family, a family's action and pattern levels, interweaving strategic knowledge of its structural present with inner experience, or the phenomenological life and events of individuals in the family. This is where content and process, or formal structures merge in the meaning and model levels of family organization.

The model involves five interactive building blocks that, working in synchrony, explain family process and crisis, both growth-oriented and disruptive or problematic. Crisis is explored as a leap toward increased system growth and complexity, as well as system breakdown and rigidity. Five interactive parts, the building blocks of family process, drawn from Kantor's structural dynamics and integrated with child development, contextualized to meet the demands and exigencies of Child-Centered Family Therapy, are integrated into a dynamic view of the family. The five building blocks are:

1. Family subsystems.
2. Access dimensions (space, time, and energy).
3. Family and personal goals (nurturance, competence, and identity).

4. Family player parts.
5. Family system types (open, closed, and random).

This chapter focuses on the first four building blocks, while Chapter 3 completes the fifth building block, family system types. The first building block, well known to family therapists, considers the network of family subsystems (family unit, interpersonal, and personal) and their interrelationships. The second building block involves family and marital transactions, key family processes on critical family access dimensions and goals.

Family Transactions on a Six-Dimensional Social Space Grid

The second and third building blocks are especially intriguing due to the ideal match that they provide in child development, the life tasks and needs of children, and the dynamic interchange of parent-child relationships, both enabling and problematic. Family interaction is conceptualized by Kantor as occurring on a six-dimensional social space grid. Figure 2.1 depicts my diagrammatic interpretation and visual representation of Kantor's six-dimensional social space grid. Three dimensions are access pathways to goals that family members seek on personal, interpersonal, and family system grounds. Access dimensions are observable and quantifiable dimensions of the family environment: physical aspects of family members' experience, including the need for safety and participation, through the mediums (pathways) of space, time, and energy.

The three remaining dimensions (what Kantor has termed "communicational domains of social interaction") represent the qualitative and conceptual aspects of family members' experience. These dimensions are the qualitative means through which family members' needs for specific life goals are thematically actualized. Individuals and families continuously seek access to space, time, and energy for themselves and from others to gain the conceptual and qualitative common life goals of affect (emotional expression, nurturance, and intimacy), power (constructive efficacy, personal autonomy, freedom, and decision making), and meaning or identity (a sense of connection, destination, and collective purpose). Out of developmental necessity, children are active navigators of space, time, and energy, exploring each quite differently than adults. Power, affect, and meaning are also very important goals of young children, the basic fabric of selfhood and framework for their conceptions of reality and identity. In this way, the family is leading a double, child-oriented and system-oriented developmental life: organizing family process and interaction while creating a physical, psychological, and social environment for children to grow and learn.

Figure 2.1
Dimensions on the Family Social Space Grid

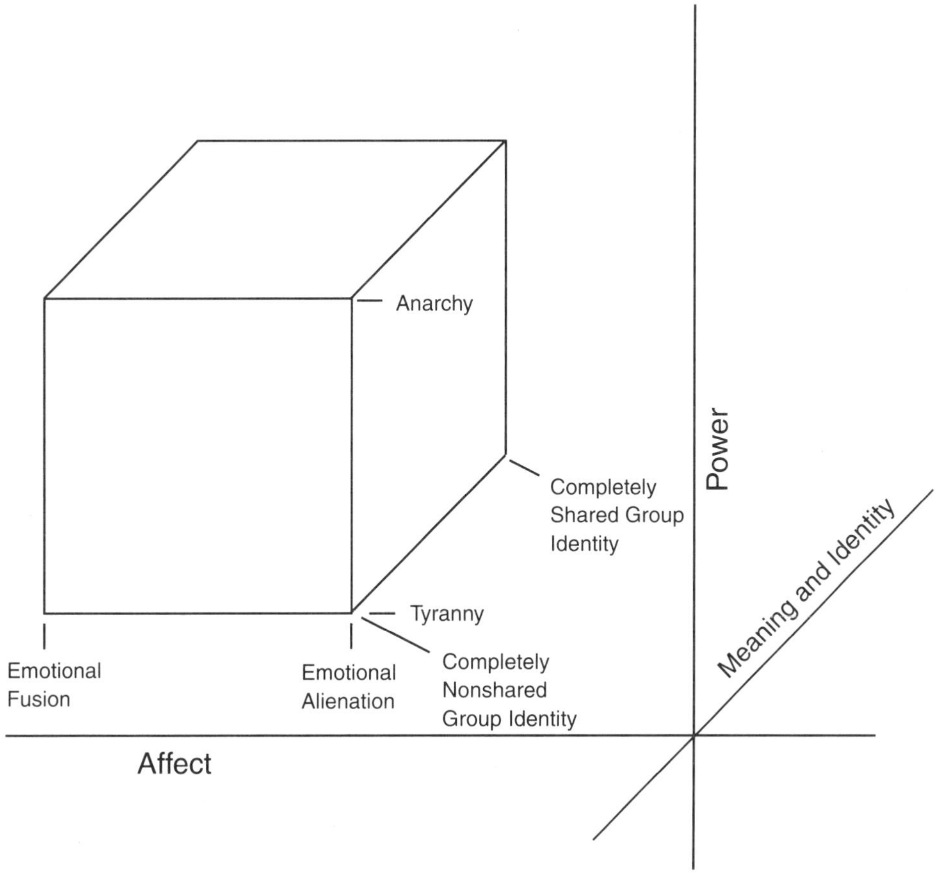

- Power = learning, mastery, constructive efficacy, social influence.
- Affect = nurturance and intimacy.
- Meaning = collective identity.

Note: The dimensions are considered on three levels: personal, interpersonal and family unit.

The family's social space, its transactional patterns along its social field—the movements of people, events, objects, ideas, and transactions within the family—is best envisioned symbolically as a six-dimensional cube in which parents, children, and family interact. As Kantor emphasizes, distance regulation is the central, mediating concept uniting all six dimensions (space, time, and energy, power, affect, and meaning) of family process. How the family organizes and expresses physical and metaphoric space is the substance of family life and family patterns. In everyday family interaction, distance regulations translate into visual relationship statements. For example, in a family photograph, a daughter may stand closer to her mother, the son, closer to the father. This visually expresses physical and emotional patterns of joining and alliance. The family may state, "We're a close family," but a photograph may indicate a theme of subtle alliances and estrangements not in their awareness on a day-to-day basis. Similarly, a family may develop patterns of access and distance around themes. Some families have ready access to nurturance and intimacy. Other families are close around competence, offering family members clear and immediate access to the experience of power and personal influence. These visual relationship statements are where the therapist is focused in terms of actions and patterns, and the themes that imbue individual and family actions with meanings. Distance regulation within the family's interior social space is expressed in the patterned continuity and flow of interaction along all three pathways on the social space grid, including how parents and children and husbands and wives join and separate, cooperate or compete, around specific goals. Access dimensions connect with goals at all three family interfaces: personal, interpersonal, and system.

NURTURANCE AND INTIMACY

In envisioning the family's social space as a six-dimensional grid or interpersonal matrix of transactional intersections, events associated with emotional expression are represented laterally. These transactions involve intimacy and nurturance in both social and personal realms on a positive to negative continuum, moving toward or away on a horizontal plane, ranging from emotional fusion to emotional alienation among family members. The lateral, positive to negative pole of this dimension provides a quantifiable research dimension for assessing changes in intimacy and nurturance as an expression within the family and also the therapy process. When we think of "intimacy" (the process of emotional closeness) and "nurturance" (the process of providing guidance and support), the image we associate this interaction with is a level field of equality; hence Kantor's conceptualization of "lateral moves."

POWER DIFFERENCES

The concept of "power" raises a range of associations, many of them pejorative and unfavorable. Power relations in the therapy process have engendered considerable attention, discussion, and controversy. Some hotly contested debates have centered around the unequal power differential operating within the client-therapist relationship and therapy process itself, as well as the role gender may play; hence a "feminist" or "gender-sensitive" or gender-specific view of therapy process and outcome in which gender is explored as a social category of experience. Such questions concerning the uses and misuses of power are familiar themes in the psychotherapy literature that self-reflect on our practices.

To a greater extent, family therapy, strongly guided by nontraditional Batesonian views of epistemology, has seriously called into question the legitimacy of the notion and metaphor of power, and proposed alternative, pattern-oriented notions such as consensus and dissensus as explanatory devices (Flemons, 1989) for human interaction. The point here, however, beyond the acknowledgment of these controversies around constructivist thought, is "what is in a name, anyway?" Regardless of what we call it, how we name it, what words we use to dress the idea up or down, power relations exist, are here to stay, and are palpably felt in families. In Child-Centered Structural Dynamic Therapy, power means influence, family and self-efficacy, competency, and a sense of "moving" and being "moved" or persuaded by others.

Power events within the family are depicted vertically. These transactions are voluntary and conative, involving constructive personal, interpersonal, and family efficacy. Power relations are a family's ability and capacity to get things accomplished: its learning, striving, and mastery spheres of activity. This dimension focuses on the freedom versus restraint of family members' physical mobility in social relations. Power regulates who or what will move freely or who or what will be constrained by whom and under what conditions. The exercise of guidance and constructive influence (the positive aspect of power) or coercion (the negative aspect of power) have strong implications for child development and a child's sense of competence, identity, self-concept, and efficacy.

Power differences are virtual facts of life in parent-child relations. They are striking features and potential sources of tension and conflict in a family. Children are, by their physical size, cognitive and socioemotional immaturity, social status, and family position, much smaller, as well as more vulnerable and developmentally unprepared. The parent's world looks larger and often overwhelming from a child's-eye view in the parent-child relationship. This is not to say that children are totally without power or influence; they exert relative amounts of both. They are active effectors and influence family transactions in decisive ways. Sometimes a child wields inordinate, developmentally inappropriate power, a burdensome influence that results from the paradoxical effects of having too much license without the reassurance of clear rules, guidance, and caring restraints. Unlike the situation of unsupervised children, most children's "power" or personal self-efficacy is limited, circumscribed, and inexperienced. Their expression and experience of personal influence primarily derives from observation and family enactments, vicarious learning and incorporation of behaviors, and relationship dynamics modeled in and by the family.

Children are continuously seeking, absorbing, and constructing models of behavior in interpersonal relationships. The strong and compelling influence of this type of vicarious learning, first identified by Bandura (1977, 1986) and shown across numerous empirical studies of children and the relationship of modeling to behavior and self efficacy, is that learning is cognitive and affective, taking place steadily within the child, often without external signs. During a family crisis, these models of behavior and interpersonal strategy become visible signs of what the family has unknowingly been teaching all along, with implications for both the repetition of learned helplessness as well as learned aggression often noted in children and families.

This power difference also helps parents guide their children. Often the power differential gets out of hand when either parent or child has too much power, resulting in unbridled license in which the child needs caring and firm limits. At the opposite extreme, power can get out of hand when there is oppressive control in which the child's spirit is stifled in the name of arbitrary and blind obedience. The power dimension is quantifiable and ranges from anarchy to complete tyranny.

Meaning and Identity

Returning to the family's transactional patterns along pathways of access, the meaning dimension on this social space cube is viewed as the family's depth dimension. This is a rich and multifaceted sphere of activity in the family's developmental life. The family's meaning dimension is particularly crucial for children who, through the concrete operations and interactions of everyday family events, are cultivating, revising, and continuously reshaping their identities.

The family's meaning dimension communicates the depth of a family's foundational life. This dimension signifies and expresses who and what the family is, its integrity, collective identity, immanent purpose, felt participation and sense of belonging. Ultimately, a family's meaning is shown through its self-knowledge, the ways it chooses to express itself, the ways it organizes ideas about the world, and the degree, depth, and latitude of system understanding it displays and offers its members. The family's meaning dimension reflects the family's continuity and identity as a living entity by its ongoing transmission of ideas about the family and its place in the world.

Maps of Experience

Children learn who they can and cannot become, who they will and will not be within the family. Each family develops its own "map" of the exterior culture. This map communicates to family members, particularly to eager and avidly curious children, the ways in which the exterior culture resembles and differs from the interior family, as well as those people and items (events, objects, and experiences) that are safe or worthwhile for family members and those that are not.

In doing its mapping, a family seeks to recognize, label, and identify what is outside the family space to guide family members' transactions within and across family borders. The family identifies what is safe and familiar and what is dangerous and off-limits on physical, social, and psychological grounds. The family creates cognitive and affective maps for its members with strong implications for the learning styles children will adopt. In this way, all items of experience are checked and tested against the family map. The map, too, is tested by experience and often altered by it, as the relationships between interior and exterior family events develop, fluctuate, and change over time. A family map expresses one view of cross-sectional as well as longitudinal system development.

Families can readily depict these maps, representing them graphically, and these maps can serve as both self-guides to the family and also process and pre-post measures of family change as will be shown in Chapters 5 and 6 through the Family Network Drawing Activity. Using this technique (Andreozzi, 1977, 1978, 1979a, 1988), developed in the Child-Centered Model for enrichment and early intervention, enables families to visualize these maps in order to explore concretely what their family consists of, how it distinguishes what is inside and outside the family, and to identify the quality of connection between people and relationships.

Another concept related to a family's meaning dimension is its core or central purpose. A family's core purpose contains its system ideals and goals. These are model structures. They are not necessarily the family's moral values but rather the patterns, rules, and preferred transactional styles a family develops to reach its goals. In a family crisis, one feature of a family's breakdown in structural laws involves its guides for problem solving. These interactional guides represent that group of strategies at the pattern level of family organization that family systems develop and then call on in crisis situations. They consist of the family's decision-making, problem-solving and crisis-resolution capabilities. These strategies are what a family does when it experiences and encounters frustration; obstacles from the outside world that interfere with the family's routine strategies for reaching its goals, or when competition over the definitions and priorities of these goals, and the means of achieving these goals, develops from within the family system. The family's conscious, yet implicit, group purpose conveys to its members, most notably its children, a collective sense of "us," who we are and what we believe in as a family, and our place in the culture and community through the ways the family responds to "sameness" and "difference" in family organization.

Consider the predicament of a child who is usually well behaved, whose behavior is usually seen and treated in one particular way in the family. In response to or provoked by a newly emergent family developmental crisis, the child may shift to problematic and troubling behavior. The once familiar child now turns a decisively different corner on the social space grid, seemingly overnight as the family might see it—becoming a "stranger" inside the family—and is ushered presumptively or unwittingly into a corridor of experience reserved in the family for "difference" or, in more unfortunate situations, "deviance."

The experiences of children who gradually, or suddenly, show signs of distress and troubling behavior are often similar to the shifting, uncertain, and precarious positions experienced by a visitor who tries to become part of a family's world. Visitors who seek access to a family's interpersonal world experience a period of prenegotiation as they stand on the family's periphery and outermost borders, awaiting permission to enter the family's more intimate and central environment. This interpersonal dance of prenegotiation and perusal by the family is an experience well known to therapists during the rapport-building and engagement process of therapy. A family member who occupies this marginal social space, a corridor that is neither inside or outside the family, is often labeled an "outsider." Symptomatic children are similarly relegated to this symbolic and ambivalent transactional experience of pseudointimacy and perfunctory nurturance in the family. Depending on a family's meaning and the interpretation of "sameness" and "difference" in the family map, a child can easily become the "bad child" if relegated to a category of family experience that makes the child's identity and behavior suddenly more unlike than like the family. This can set in motion various levels of negative and conflictual parent-child interactions that, when escalated, lead to mutual frustration and unhappiness.

Even clear-cut medical conditions or constitutional factors are not always as fixed or immutable as they seem but are often affected by family process and development. The family has been shown to exert powerful influence over many constitutionally determined cognitive, behavioral, and medical childhood conditions. Something even as individual and ostensibly inherent as a child's temperament (Chess & Thomas, 1986; Thomas & Chess, 1977) has been shown to be modified or shaped by the family system.

The question of constitutional factors raises intriguing questions that draw the individual-family system connection into clear focus. Regardless of which side of the nature-nurture fence we find ourselves on, whether we are more individually oriented, seeing some disorders as purely or primarily biochemical, residing in the individual, and therefore, best treated that way, or whether we believe in systems concepts of distress, placing most of the responsibility of change on contextual intervention, most therapists, even individually oriented clinicians outside of family therapy, agree that constitutional factors alone do not produce family unhappiness.

The family's perceptions, expectations, attitudes, beliefs, and behavioral responses to the notions of "illness," "difference," and of "having an ill child," the nature and quality of the family's viability, competence, complexity, and flexibility, can intensify or ameliorate the problem, viewing it as a crisis or turning crisis into challenge and family adaptation and change. Once a child is born into a family, constitutional factors blur into contextual and transactional ones. Psyche, soma, and society—the intimate interpersonal worlds of the family—unite in interaction, for good or ill, and family patterns are created. But, as reason and empirical research show, a child's constitutional nature, while undoubtedly influencing family dynamics and family development, can never completely account for all the family's problems. Often the appearance of congenital disorders or constitutional differences in one child or the appearance of a child's physical disability can provide an only too easily and readily available dustbin into which a family can sweep, discard, localize, and accumulate all its losses, failures, and relationship doubts.

Family crisis does not necessarily crystallize around the disturbing behavior of a particular child, but instead the crisis can be brought about by the advent and thematic significance of the tasks and transactions—the dilemmas raised by a specific developmental stage, itself, such as independence and attachment—that emerge on the family's interpersonal scene. The family raising children must cope simultaneously with the demands and imperatives of child and family development. At each of Kantor's four levels of family organization (meaning, model, action, pattern) are corresponding parent-child structures and child development levels of organization, embedded in family interaction, that the Child-Centered Family Therapy Model considers. Difficulties around themes associated with particular child development stages can resonate throughout all four levels of family organization—meaning, model, action, and pattern—with a potential for crisis and instability reverberating throughout.

The Relationship of Meaning and Model Structures to Critical Identity Images in Child-Centered Family Practice

The family's meaning dimension is reflected in its meaning and model levels of family organization. At the highest and most complex level, the model level of family organization, we find the family's group identity. This is what the family values, deems safe and worthwhile, labels as purposeful; it is their worldview and set of expectations for members. At the most fundamental level—a family's meaning structures—we find the family's imagistic and symbolic life. Family meaning, here, is expressed in the activities of everyday family life: what family members typically talk about, like to do, and selectively notice about themselves, the world, and others around them. Both meaning and model structures, derived from the meaning and model levels of family development and organization, are more inferential than visible.

The following example shows both model and meaning structures on the family, parent-child, and child development levels. We know we have discovered a model or meaning structure when families act as if we have hit a raw nerve. We know we have touched on both when we are "wrong" about a family and misread its identity. A family will let us know, as members try to tell us who they are and talk us out of a wrong impression:

The Bliss family prizes physical appearance. The family looks as though they just stepped out of House Beautiful or a fashion magazine. Their house is filled with carefully displayed antiques and reproduction art. Talk of "beauty" and "good looks" are frequent in conversations. The first and most important aspect of a person or an environment they notice is physical attractiveness and aesthetic appeal. They often sound like ruthless critics. These are the family's meaning structures, what they emphasize, their values and focus, what the family selectively notices. If a relative makes an impromptu comment about the "family portrait," ("My God, what a family of 'posers' you guys are!"), the entire family takes offense. They exclaim, "That's not us." The reason, they explain, is that while they frankly like pretty things, they are not "ostentatious and vain." Their particular model structure rejects vanity for vanity's sake and accepts luxury only in the context of earned, hard work.

In a family crisis, signs are visibly observed in the family's patterns of action, specifically its repetitive problem patterns and strategies. The crisis is also reflexively felt in the family's meaning dimension. This happens in two ways: The family experiences model instability as its group identity is challenged and shaken. Simultaneously, at the family's foundation, its core set of meaning structures and critical identity images are elicited and seriously called into question as they vie for affirmation and recognition. Both critical identity images and competing identity claims influence family transactions. As Kantor describes, critical identity images are highly, emotionally charged vivid memories and transactions that guide individual relationships. Critical identity claims reflect positive, affirming intentions and expectations of the self-in-relation to others. This concept takes on special meaning when applied in the context of the Child-Centered Family Therapy Model. We can think of these claims as expressing the positive underside of negative behaviors and interpersonal strategies. A child may threaten to "run away from home" to signal the need for recognition of his or her growing autonomy.

Or a child, when hurt emotionally, may become reticent, withdrawing within him- or herself as a means of declaring the need for private space. This emotional turning inward may result from the hope, indeed misguided belief, learned from adult role models (parents) that "if I play possum, coy, or hard to get, then you [the person who cares for the child] will pursue me"; the logic goes: "the extent to which you [parent] entreat, cajole, or solicit me [child] is the extent to which I am important to you, a measure of my self-worth." The child may also have learned (absorbed and observed) the emotionally expensive lesson of communication hide-and-seek or "telepathy intimacy": "If you love me, then you know what I feel without me having to say a word. Being close means reading each other's minds." Indications of critical identity images, and competing identity claims, as they emerge in crisis situations, are revealed through a family's recurrent strategies, around specific issues and their repetitive themes. Like a cat trying to catch its tail, these recurring patterns show the family running in circles and getting nowhere, while trying unsuccessfully to resolve their problems. Consider the following two examples.

A wife and mother may be continuously acting on critical identity images colored by a mood of urgency and transactional theme of abandonment. Just as with her childhood family, she seeks access to parents who leave her cold emotionally. As she moves toward them, seeking connection and a sense of belonging, they move away, preoccupied and unavailable. In her relationship with her spouse, as she seeks access, he pulls away. In response to his distancing, she intensifies her moves toward him, which in turn, ironically, because of his critical identity puzzle piece, causes him to move farther and farther away until the inevitable and unintended happens: The husband shuts down emotionally and she again experiences abandonment.

Her image is one of protecting herself, trying to appease her spouse and experience authentic intimacy; her reality claim, to be valued and appreciated by her husband; the critical and ironic outcome is that her image is invalidated, her claims are not seen, and she experiences alienation instead of the intimacy and nurturing she seeks.

A conflicted relationship between father and son revolves around a similar theme. After several attempts to entreat or in some way get his father's attention, the little boy, who is quickly running out of choices, anxiously begins to tease. His teasing provokes the father, causing the father to move farther away, rejecting the little boy and the emotional father-son connection he desires. The boy's teasing behavior arises from his evolving critical identity image with a father who appears emotionally constrained and unavailable. If we turn the child's teasing behavior inside out, as is often the best way to explore the child's reality claims, then the affirmation is the little boy's desire to try anything, to draw his father's attention to him, to be close.

Out of developmental necessity, families evolve strategies—purposive, goal-directed behavior patterns—for seeking access to safety. In addition, these strategies prompt them to seek participation in the advancement of crucial life goals that are relevant both to the self and to the family. Strategies and themes, therefore, naturally develop around crucial goals and each family member learns to play a predictable part. Children who are participators in this continuous process of family development, collaborators in the family's group identity, who are also negotiating important childhood milestones of self-development, learn almost by osmosis to play their parts well. Infants cry on cue when parents' arguments begin to escalate. They may cry to interrupt a tense or threatening silence in a therapy hour. The family's meaning dimension is the "mind" of the family's experience. What is measurable in the meaning dimension is the degree to which a family's meaning and group identity is shared or not shared. Again, from a child's point of view, this echoes the crucial weight and important developmental role attributed, for example, to the impact of "nonshared family environmental events" on the child's sense of identity, belonging, and behavioral outcome.

Questions Posed to the Family's Collective Mind: A Source of Family System Awareness

Space is location. Time is sequence. Energy is vitality and intensity. Power is efficacious, constructive efficacy, autonomy, the capacity to make one's own decisions. Affect is perceived nurturance, the giving and acceptance of support, a sense of intimacy and felt connection and attachment. Meaning is equated with intentionality, a sense of purpose and destination. Identity connotes integrity, a sense of integration, a blending of the unique and special with common features that are shared. Each of the family dimensions in this framework branches out on multiple levels, connecting in some way with every other dimension on the social space grid, with simultaneous implications for the family, the family's interpersonal or interactional life, and the personal worlds of self. This model is about selfhood and system integrity, communication, and change.

At every juncture of this social space grid of family development, parallel as well as interactive child development activities are taking place. At each intersection, we find coexisting and simultaneous child developmental dimensions, dilemmas, and tasks. Depending on where the therapist encounters the family, whether in the developmental context of prevention, early stages of intervention, or in full system instability, each interface and dimension on the social space grid offers the therapist its own set of systemic questions to ask and answer. When engaged in enrichment work with families, the therapist can pose these questions directly to the family to evoke and strengthen system awareness. If the family is in crisis, the therapist can use these questions to frame observational understanding of the family's transactions and the thematic features of its developmental crisis, as well as to guide and design family system interventions. In either case, the six-dimensional social space grid with its convergence of dimensions and goals, family members' quests for self and family expressions, access to important personal and family relationships, provides a ready synthesis of child and family development, an integrated framework for understanding children and child-centered problems.

For example, the therapist can craft questions or experiential techniques that highlight the family's use of space in conjunction with the child's developmentally determined concepts of space; the family's organization of and orientation toward time with the child's conceptions of time and sequence; or the family's management and utilization of its energies with the child's perspective on and expression of energy, behavioral styles or interacting and relating, or what we can think of as "temperament." This applies equally to the goal dimensions in the realm of the child's developmental tasks and the family's expectations around issues of power, or mastery and learning; affect or socioemotional growth and nurturance; and identity or a sense of self, self-esteem, and achievement, as Figure 2.2 illustrates.

Figure 2.2 depicts, in visual form, the conceptual integration of critical child development stages with Kantor's six-dimensional social space grid. Child-Centered Structural Dynamic Therapy nests child development within the family's social space and transactional patterns of family

Figure 2.2
Parent-Child Relations and Child Development on the Family Social Space Grid

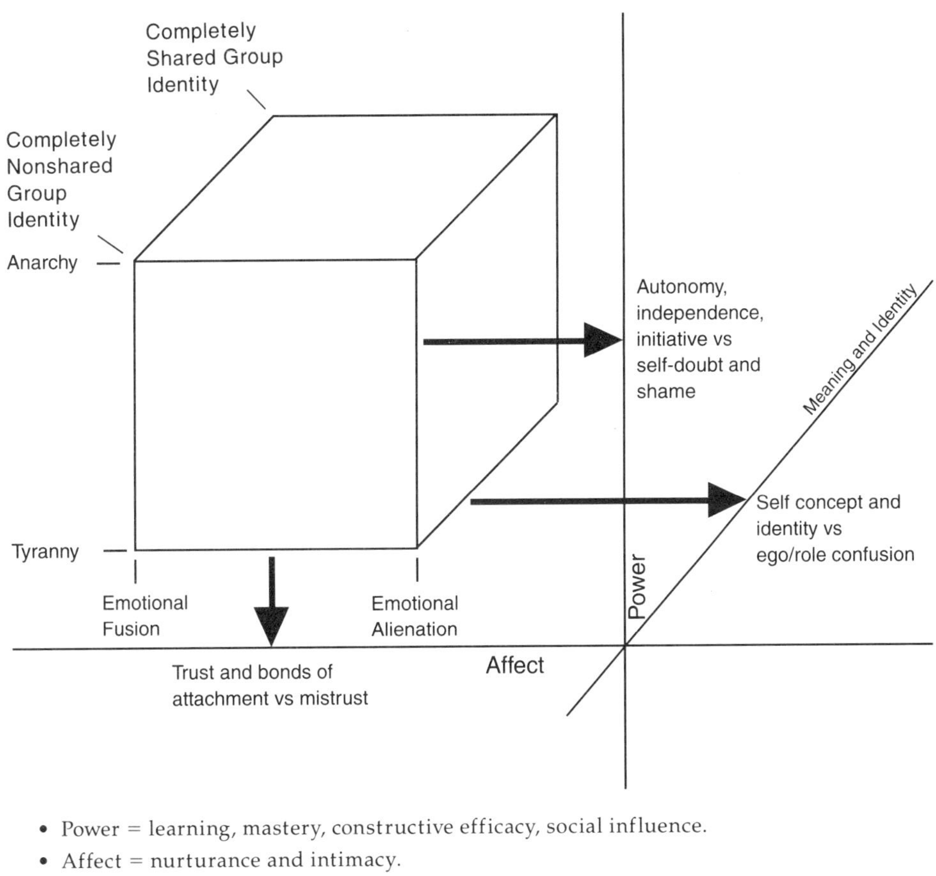

- Power = learning, mastery, constructive efficacy, social influence.
- Affect = nurturance and intimacy.
- Meaning = collective identity.

Note: The dimensions are considered on three levels: personal, interpersonal, and family unit. Each dimension contains parallel and interactive child development tasks.

development. It specifically focuses on and explores the intersection between human development and family development.

The following possibilities arise around this common developmental theme. Beginning with the smallest unit, the individual, the chain of events and interrelationships can unfold in several ways: Each child is endowed with a particular disposition, temperament, and set of "personality proclivities." Immediately, the environment nurtures or impedes these endowments, shaping the child in important ways. Parents, similarly, come to parent-child relationships with their own strengths, temperaments, interpersonal styles, and histories, which they learned and experienced in their childhood families. Parents and children create the family's emergent structural present, and the family's structural present, reciprocally, acts on them, creating opportunities for growth and variation or arrested and thwarted development and system restraint. The inner world an individual family member experiences, crosses over into the family world, and the family world affects and influences individual development. Inner and outer experiences shift as personal and interpersonal worlds intersect and evolve.

Within this transactional ebb and flow of family life, children grow, and the parent-child relationship changes. Children are bound by developmental laws to negotiate successive, stage-specific developmental milestones. Children are born with a developmental imperative to fulfill a series of age-appropriate tasks. They grow according to an orderly, predictable developmental timetable. These stages unfold epigenetically, building one on the other in successive stages of complexity and depth, as exemplified by Piaget's (1963) stage theory on childhood cognition, Erickson's (1963) model of psychosocial development, Vygotsky's (1978) social theory of language and cognition, and Kohlberg's (1981, 1984) and Gilligan's (1982) stage theories of the child's moral development.

Periodically, the premises of stage theories, regardless of their content, have been challenged. Some criticisms and questions in the areas of children's development have involved, for example, the invariant nature of the developmental sequence of stages, the timetable of unfolding, and the fixed, indelible effects of early experience—notably in the realms of gender identity and self-concept formation. Bandura (1986), for example, favors a more fluid and evolving, less age- and stage-defined model of human development. Such a developmental orientation emphasizes a continuously revised and molded sense of self and self-efficacy, viewing an individual's manifest skills and competencies, child or adult, as reflecting many combined self-efficacies, and experiences of adequacy and competence across contexts. Proponents of this position hold that stage theories are too blanket or universal in their assessments of children. However, when child development stage theory is combined with family systems principles—notably the supreme and central role assigned to "context," as in the Child-Centered

Model—the concerns over static or crystallized views of children, their behavioral outcomes derived from stage theories, dissolve.

Charting Developmental Crises and Assessing Problem Level or Intensity

The Child-Centered Model embraces three levels of family crisis and identifies assessment criteria associated with each level of problem intensity or severity. The levels are decidedly developmental in focus and increase in degree of system involvement. They are:

Level 1. Problem is interpersonally localized, temporary, developmental-stage and family subsystem specific.

Level 2. Child development stage/tasks and critical identity image crisis converge in a conflict involving multiple subsystems.

Level 3. Chronic, deep-rooted critical identity image struggles surface around recurrent child development stages/tasks, reflecting pervasive systemwide distress and cycles (history) of transgenerational insufficiencies (parenting inadequacies).

Using the Child-Centered Structural Dynamic Model, developmental crises can be charted as shown in Figure 2.3, which depicts the interrelationship of Levels 1, 2, and 3, outlining broad assessment considerations. This figure shows in its gradually increasing shaded areas, from one level to the next, the shifting and expanding nature of presenting-child problems and their identification, moving, for example, from localized and context-specific, or mild problems (Level 1) to multifaceted, moderate-serious problems, still localized but somewhat more extensive family involvement (Level 2), to serious-intense, widespread disturbance, reflecting greater areas of system distress and chronic involvement (Level 3). Families who fall into Level 3 show the most complexity and overlap in relationships and in family patterns that repeat themselves in historically destructive ways. It is as if the family has lost its eyes and ears, conscience and sensibilities and, in ways painful to family and self, blindly and without thinking, continues to enact destructive relationships.

In Level 1, a particular parent may be having difficulty with a particular child in a particular developmental stage. This parent-child relationship may be, under most circumstances, quite rich and varied and robust. The problem may simply arise as a result of the child's and parent's temporary difficulty with a challenging developmental task. This relationship and ripple of instability may surface in a family system structure that is developmentally strong and viable, equipped to handle the momentary lapse and

Figure 2.3
Assessing Problem Intensity: Extent of the Problem Pattern and Developmental Conflict

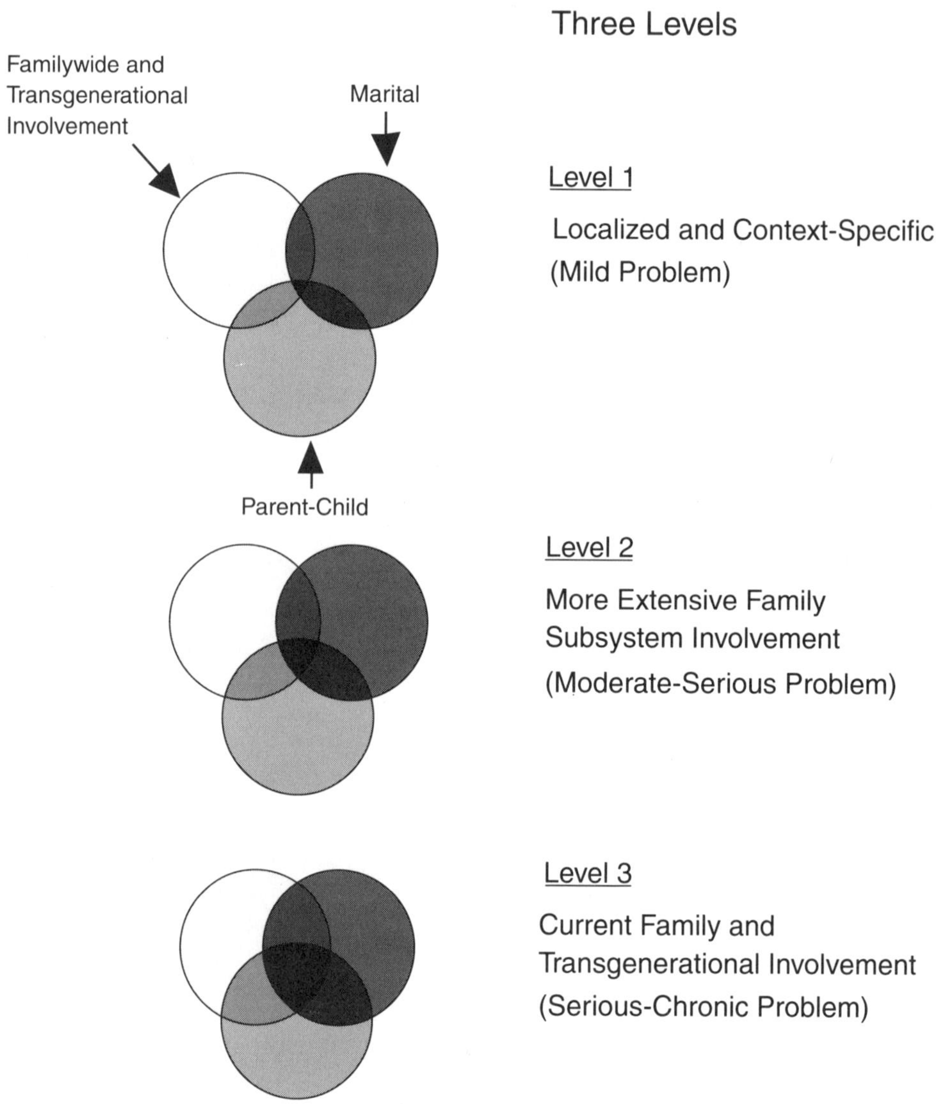

Note:

- Critical identity image conflict induces family crisis.
- The greater number of subsystems involved, the greater the conflict:

  Parent-Child

  Parent-Child + Marital

  Parent-Child + Marital + Current Family and/or Transgenerational Family of Origin Involvement instability. This comprises Level 1 of the assessment of problem intensity and severity. The following family illustration describes a Level 1 problem:

Becky is almost 7 years old and is beginning first grade. She is the youngest of three children, including her older sister who is 10, and her brother who is 13. Her brother and sister excel in school. The family is ambitious. Both parents, Ellen and Jay, work outside the home; Ellen, especially, has "big dreams" for her children, hoping that they will extend and fulfill her unfinished expectations and interrupted goals. Ellen was forced, due to the death of her father and family financial problems, to drop out of college just months before finishing.

Reluctantly, Ellen and Jay agreed that Becky should repeat kindergarten at her teacher's recommendation. The extra year of kindergarten was advised to give Becky the time and gradual transition period to improve her skills and increase in developmental readiness. The plan, however, did not seem to have worked as Ellen and Jay had expected. Becky did not have even the rudimentary readiness for reading and was academically well behind classmates, something that troubled and embarrassed her parents.

At a school consultation, initiated by Becky's first-grade teacher, the parents listen to how unprepared Becky is. The problem is not that the child is incapable. She was assessed by the school psychologist and found to be quite intelligent. Becky does not comply. Her parents feel that they have failed. To remedy the problem and begin to build academic skills, the school developed a set of goals involving Becky's parents. Most of the "homework" and skill-building exercises fall to Ellen, Becky's mother. The more Ellen pushes, the more Becky does not comply. To get her to complete one workbook sheet seems to take hours. When Becky's mother becomes frustrated, she becomes authoritarian and rigid, which causes Becky to withdraw and flit anxiously from task to task or, when most anxious and afraid to fail, to act "silly."

After several weeks of family therapy early intervention, the school reported a remarkable improvement in Becky's attitude, confidence, and skill. The emergent parent-child conflict, stimulated by the school's "alert," mobilized the family. The family was able to respond and adapt, showing its underlying sound and fundamentally strong structure. Through therapy, the parents relaxed their expectations and began to view each child as different. Ellen differentiated her image of success from her daughter's competencies, academic style, and temperament. Ellen also understood (claimed) her own unfulfilled ambitions; her husband's support and validation of her life losses grew; and the couple's marriage was strengthened. As Ellen no longer needed to prove her worth as a dedicated parent or live through her daughter, Becky began to bloom.

This family's problems reflect a temporary developmental impasse. The problem revolves around several misunderstandings regarding age-appropriate developmental skills and misplaced or unduly high expectations for the child. The crisis swirls mainly around Becky and her mother and is localized in the dynamics of their relationship. The critical identity image conflict arises between Becky's efforts at self-assertion and efficacy (autonomy) and her mother's counterbalanced efforts to show her competence as a parent and instructor of her child. The emergent crisis was a nascent one. The image-conflict was in its early stages and the parent-child relationship was embedded in a supportive and effective family system (healthy marriage and extended family relationships). The image-exploration and image-clarification was relatively straightforward and circumscribed. The therapy focused on facilitating positive child development, imparting effective parenting strategies and skills, and the cognitive-affective (emotional) components associated with Becky's experience and attempts to affirm herself as a competent child and her mother's efforts to be seen as a caring, valued, and important influence in her daughter's life. Specific attention was directed at disentangling personal images and establishing clear boundaries: Ellen's need to differentiate Becky's identity from her own and separate Becky's burgeoning interests from her own belated ambition and thwarted drive.

However, if a parent-child relationship, threatened by the access and goals raised by a child's rocky encounter with a developmental stage, occurs within wider family instability, or coincides with the family's critical identity struggles with similar family developmental issues, then the parent-child relationship and child are at a greater risk. This forms Level 2. Consider the following family:

The Nazarians, Walter and Meg and their two children, Heather, 5, and Benjamin, 8, are locked in a four-way struggle. The couple's marriage is unstable and, although the couple had the two children together, they had never made a genuine commitment. Both partners were still attached and influenced by their respective extended families. To complicate the struggle, Walter, the husband, had been injured in a car accident, crippling one leg, leaving him at the time unable to resume work as a photographer, further reducing his status in the family and worth in his wife's eyes. While the ambivalence and struggle of separating and joining, intimacy and autonomy have been smoldering for years, after Walter's car accident, the crisis intensified.

Not knowing what to do, unable to "name" the conflict, each parent draws a child into the emotional fray. Inappropriate cross-generational alliances are created: mother with son against father, father with daughter against mother. Each triangle contains its own potent critical identity image struggle. The warring triangles in the family keep the question of intimacy and independence safely at bay and the family in ritual impasse.

The children began to develop symptoms—behavior problems at school and at home. Heather began to act derisive toward her mother, precocious and coquettish toward her father, and sad and withdrawn at preschool. Benjamin bullies children at school. Cycles of arguments, never reaching conclusions, erupt increasingly in the family as the children are drawn in or, knowing their parts, enter the transaction on cue. During an early phase of therapy, the family described that the house has become "bedlam"; mother and son sat together and daughter and father sat together, squared off apart and against each other, a visual relationship statement and expression.

Therapy focused on forming appropriate generational lines, improving the couple's intimacy and sexual relationship, and relieving of the children's symptoms, including creating a child's role and childhood place for Heather and Benjamin in the family.

Critical identity images and the interplay of the children's current developmental stage with the parents' childhood developmental vulnerabilities were also explored.

The Nazarians' crisis, precipitated by the image of loss created by the car accident, had been smoldering like a low-grade fever in the family for years; it extended beyond a parent-child issue to include marital and current extended family relationship involvement and interference.

Shifting to deeper, more pervasive and widespread systemic involvement, a family may have difficulty with all or most of its children, or the family may be particularly vulnerable and predisposed to conflict around a particular developmental issue that comes up each time any child approaches that stage or developmental task. For example, some families have difficulty with "independence" regardless of who expresses it or how it is expressed. Other families have difficulty around intimacy, emotional access, and commitment or availability of members to each other. These developmental tasks resonate throughout the family, surfacing and resurfacing in signal fashion, reminding the family that it has unresolved or unfinished family developmental issues. This constitutes Level 3 in the assessment of problem severity and intensity in which disturbance is deep-rooted, often transgenerational, affecting the current family system in intensive and pervasive ways, implicating all or most family subsystem functions and family roles, including marital, parental, parent-child, and personal. The Brimmers, a multiproblem family, vividly illustrates Level 3:

The Brimmers call themselves the "Tons of Fun." The family is headed by Gail, the mother, who is 47. There are seven children ranging in age from 12 to 22. All of the family are overweight. It seems that they wrap themselves around and away from each other through food. Over the years, the family has become a kind of revolving door of "exits" and "reentrances" with most of the children at one time or another leaving for foster care only to return home again. The mother, overwhelmed with bouts of chronic depression, cannot cope with all that "horseplay, explosive energy, and disrespect."

The family has been through many social welfare agencies, mental health programs, and intervention plans. They now find themselves once again in crisis at an outpatient pediatric unit in a large general hospital. They say they feel like veterans at this, experts in the knowledge of predictable cycles of stability and crisis, coping and chaos. However, while being able to predict it, "seeing the train wreck coming" once more for the "Tons of Fun," as Larry the oldest son put it, they feel helpless to change the pattern. The train wreck is coming at them and they feel they cannot stop it; there is nothing that they can do about it.

The question around which the current crisis swirls is whether or not John, the youngest child, should be sent home to live with the family while he recuperates from surgery. The courts and social workers are undecided. John, who is 12 years old, is at the center of this developmental story. He has just had heart surgery, and his weight problem poses a definite health risk. Should he be returned home? Will he heal there? Is the family an emotional risk? Or could it be a safe holding environment for him?

The myth and subtext behind the story are that John's father had died during Gail's pregnancy with John, who was born 2 months after his father's funeral. Today John sits together with his worried family. He rarely and reluctantly speaks. He resists offering an opinion about where he wants or wishes to live, foster family or home. He says he does not care. On the front of his T-shirt, the words "It's my life" are printed in big bold black letters; on the reverse side, "Truth or Dare."

Everyone in the family has said that they love John and want and need him home. They also have said that they are sick and tired of strangers always butting into their family business, poking and prodding at them, telling them what to do. They feel like a family without borders or walls or, on the worst days, like a family living in a fishbowl. John is theirs and theirs alone, so they want him home with them where he belongs. Yet, prior to this session, at least four out of the seven family members had telephoned me individually, offering their own private piece of sometimes contradictory information. Gail, the mother, in our first telephone contact (as if issuing me a battle cry or challenge to be discovered), said "I'll tell you some things but not everything. There's a line I draw, a line I won't pass and a secret I will never tell, not to anyone, no matter what!" This week the excitement that has gripped the family, the story they were so anxious to open with was what Benny, John's 18-year-old brother, had done. Racing down the stairs in the dark to answer the doorbell, he had somehow stepped on and killed the family cat . . .

This family had chronic difficulty with the psychological independence of all of the children. The Brimmers, gripped around a central, unnamed image of "deep loss," demanded emotional fusion. As is often the situation, this kind of engulfment of members creates intense loneliness and a sense of isolation. The Brimmer family had a long and complicated transactional and relationship history built on the recurring relationship images of loss, betrayal, and emotional insufficiencies. The narrative of their family growth is complex and will be fully explored in Chapter 8.

The physical, emotional, and symbolic journeys of children within the family can act as catalysts for family change, either in the direction of growth or crisis and instability. In the tangible and concrete world of daily family life and transactions, it is often the child, not the developmental stage, who becomes caught up in the family struggle. What Child-Centered Structural Dynamic Therapy focuses on is the point of convergence, where the child and parents, and the family's critical identity images contribute to developmental impasse, preventing family growth, and producing family instability.

Using the family and parent-child access-to-goals pathways, illustrated in Figure 2.2, as a guiding framework, the Child-Centered Model tracks presenting-child symptoms and parent-child problems along family dimensions on two levels: from the child's point of view and the family system's point of view. The following is a sampling of questions drawn from the comprehensive framework of technique-guided questions, facilitative change-oriented interventions, and system activities explained fully in Chapter 6. These questions arise from the dimensions on this social space grid and illustrate the variations, flexibility, and wide range of application to children.

Space as Access

Some sample questions for clinical and empirical consideration, developed (Andreozzi, 1977, 1978, 1979b, 1988) to facilitate child-centered intervention and family awareness, include:

- What are the patterns of closeness and distance or separation that this family allows between family members and the family and the wider community?
- How close can one family member get to another family member, physically, psychologically, and emotionally?
- Which relationships or subsystems enjoy greater access; which subsystems are restrained or limited in movement?
- What lines are drawn about asking questions, and in what contexts?
- Are certain topics taboo and others not? If so, what are these topics? Can the family talk about ideas or facts but not about feelings? Can they talk about feelings but not about sex? Can they ask about family secrets?
- Is there a safe place for each family member in the family? And is there a safe place for the family in the wider community?
- How free are family members to enter another family member's room without knocking? Can they interrupt a family conversation, or are family doors, symbolically, always locked and interruptions forbidden, and discouraged? Do all family members show mutual respect?
- Are doors and interpersonal boundaries too open so that family members feel that there are no private spaces? Are there too few reassuring boundaries or demarcations, either physical or emotional?
- How far can each venture into another person's private thoughts or feelings?
- Is a designated, claimed place allotted to each family member regardless of age?
- Is there a common meeting ground or location for family members to congregate?
- Are physical and psychological boundaries between family members and family experiences flexible or fixed, clear or ambiguous?
- Does the family provide a "space" and "special place" for children?

TIME AS ACCESS

The clinician can organize similar questions and observations around time. A subset of a broader group of questions devised (Andreozzi, 1977, 1978, 1979b, 1988) to heighten child-centered system awareness, include:

- How is time orientation experienced in the family? How is time experienced on personal, interpersonal, and family unit levels?
- What is the family's sense of its history, lores, myths? What is the family's orientation to the past? What is its concept of "today" and its view of the family's future?
- Do family members participate in a common or shared sense of time? Or are family members idiosyncratic and clashing in their perspectives, priorities, and uses of time?
- Do family members' time schedules blend and coincide or conflict?
- Is there "time" for children in the family?

ENERGY AS ACCESS

The therapist can approach the integration of child and family development through family energy dimension questions such as:

- What is the family's ideal or optimal measure and use of energy?
- What is the family's energy norm, the demonstrable, degree of exuberance that is permitted or tolerated?
- What does it feel like inside this family?
- How much energy can this family absorb?
- What is the family's amount of energy reserve?
- What is the family's threshold?
- How vigorous and intense are family members with each other?
- Is the family's energy expression calm and modulated, depleted, or chaotic?
- What happens when the child's temperament (calm or vigorous style) is at odds (mismatched) with parents' energy styles and concepts of the "good" or "well-behaved" child?

This set of questions (therapeutic guides) is specifically constructed (Andreozzi, 1977, 1978, 1979b, 1988) to draw attention to the decisive, yet tacit ways family systems shape "personality." For example, the questions connect "temperament" with the "environment," a point worth further clarification. Young children are physical by development. Children pound, swing and kick their legs, put things in their mouth, bite, poke, and use their bodies in vigorous ways to experiment and explore the world around them. When parents misread this energy and respond aggressively, the neutral exploration of children and childhood can shift course and travel down more violent and interpersonally destructive paths. Children's energies often need to be actively channeled and constructively redirected by parents. Very young children can be distracted from one activity to engage in another, more productive one. Children benefit from thoughtful structure—a challenge that can be difficult for an overworked parent who is poorly equipped emotionally.

Distraught or emotionally conflicted parents, who overpersonalize a child's behavior, explode in anger (physical or verbal aggression), and lash out at the child with arbitrary and destructive criticism, not only teach a transactional lesson in the force and power of intimidation, but also a lesson in shame, rejection, and rage. A curious excitement, emotional arousal, and release may also accompany aggressive confrontations. The child may be torn between feeling frightened and repelled by aggression, while simultaneously being impressed or mesmerized by the sheer command, power, and vivid impact that the angry adult exerts on the child and family environment.

When reduced to their essence, a large number of the parent-child problems encountered in early intervention and family therapy involve "discipline" and methods of "behavior control." When parents resort to frequent physical punishment and combine aggression with discipline, they are ultimately providing children lessons in usurped (the child's) and excessive (parent's) power. These lessons involve the coercive influence of a more formidable human being (the adult) over a vulnerable human being (the child). Family patterns of intimacy, problem solving, and impulse control are at the heart of learned cycles of aggression. Impulse control is, in part, learned and, in part, tied to the notion of "temperament"; in this instance, the level and intensity of energy-expression.

To intervene early in a family's life, when parent-child conflicts and the child's behavior problems are nascent, can save a family from greater future distress. To become a warm, accepted, empathic observer in the family's own physical and social space, before the onset of more difficult problems that continue over longer periods and take root further down the road, can spare great emotional expense to parent, family, and child. In the intimate conversations with families of early intervention and therapy, and even prevention, common themes frequently expressed are family and individual scenes of psychological and actual aggression: subtle nuances as well as overt scenes that show some form of symbolic or actual violence against body, mind, relationships, and the human spirit as the self is denied important access and affirmation in relation to others (not being known, seen, found, and heard by those we care about and assume care about us). What research on the Child-Centered Early Intervention tier of the model has shown, in family and child development follow-up, is that through sensitively timed use of the Family Activities described in Chapter 6, family and parent-child relationships can be significantly enhanced and family abuse can be prevented.

When positive parental and family influence take hold in the early infant-toddler-preschool years, this family influence can more effectively mediate peer group influence. When a child feels secure in the family and has empathic, guiding parents to turn toward, as opposed to a troubled family to turn away from, the peer group influence will be there, but its influence may not be as negative or as great. The grade-school child, and later the adolescent, can filter peer influence through the grounding, internalized sense of security, self-confidence and self-trust, with a capacity to make good decisions that the family has communicated all along. Parents cannot accompany their children every minute, standing beside the child to guide and influence every decision and protect against every peer group dare or temptation, but an internalized structure of a responsive parent-child relationship and the transactional image of a parent who trusts the child's judgment and affirms the child's competence and autonomy "to do the right thing," can be there to guide the adolescent. Primary prevention, the foundation of such transactional imagery, begins in infancy, toddlerhood, and the preschool years.

REACHING THE FAMILY GOALS OF NURTURANCE, INTIMACY, EFFICACY, MEANING, AND IDENTITY

An additional set of questions, drawn from the Child-Centered Model and method, arise from consideration of family and personal goals. Some of the more salient questions (Andreozzi, 1977, 1978, 1979b, 1988) that make up the three-tier application of the Child-Centered Model, include the following:

- What are the family's collective and individual concepts of power?
- How do family members exert personal and interpersonal influence?
- Can this family get things accomplished?
- Can this family make decisions with little difficulty?
- Who generally holds the substantive power regarding decisions about the children?
- Who routinely exerts the most influence in the problem-solving process? Under what conditions and in what context and around what themes does each family member, to some age-appropriate extent, have a sense of felt influence and participation in the family?
- How does the family envision its group purpose? What are its aspirations? What are its ideals in terms of family transactions?

- How does the family want members to behave?
- What are the shared goals for adults and for children?
- What is the place for children and the child's world in the family's collective priorities and sense of purpose and destination?
- Are the opinions and observations of children valued and heard? Is there a place in the family for the psychological voices and perspectives of children?
- When and how often should certain events occur?
- What is and should be valued from the past? What does the family collectively and individually envision for the future?
- Are there appropriate and protective generational delineations?

As this sample of questions illustrates, access dimensions connect with goals on a threefold level: personal, interpersonal, and family system. As Chapters 5, 6, 7, and 8 will show, the quality and quantity of information that the therapist gathers from these important family dimensions as a question-guided technique enables the therapist to create structural interventions that simultaneously integrate child and family development, while giving priority to the imperatives of a child's symptoms and the incorporation of children in the family therapy process. Access dimensions connect with goal dimensions to form a matrix of potential parent-child interfaces, a range of combinations of avenues of intersection among dimensions. The Child-Centered Model considers the family's preferred transactional style around these six dimensions. The model emphasizes and explores the relationship of three contexts within the family: the individual and personal world of child and parent, the parental and marital relationship, and the family's development as a whole.

Shame, Guilt, and Self-Blame in Developmental Family Process: Parent-Child Relations at System Interface

The Child-Centered Structural Dynamic Model of family process integrates child and family development, and effectively recasts parent-child problems, framing them as process-conflicts or competing goals—well-intentioned personal and interpersonal aims gone awry. While a certain degree of guilt can precipitate self-reflection and change, excessive guilt and blame of self or others are counterproductive and stultifying.

One of the major stumbling blocks in initial consultations with parents and children, an issue that must be identified and dealt with immediately and sensitively, is the unacknowledged and disguised power of shame. Shame exerts a palpable charge, agitating, clouding and creating interference in the therapy hour. Shame distracts from and obfuscates the real work of problem resolution. Guilt and blame (either directed toward the self or to others) are closely allied emotions and cognitions, the process of self-doubt and recrimination too familiar to parents engulfed in a difficult or confusing parent-child relationship.

Guilt, self-doubt, and blame often mask deeper shame. While guilt is about "doing" or regret over past real, imagined, or exaggerated relationship transgressions, shame is about "being" who we are in our entirety. Shame is about selfhood and the broken bonds of attachment, emerging out of the felt experience of having failed, disappointed, or angered someone singularly important to us whom we depend on, or whose approval we fervently seek, as is the case with a child and parent.

Shame is a powerful emotion, central in a variety of parent-child critical identity struggles. Shame involves the participation of others, the prerequisite of relationship or attachment. It is the outgrowth of primary bonds, a "being seen" by a cold critical eye in the context of intimate awareness. Power differences are also a part of the dynamics of shame. Family process, therefore, has the potential for engendering intimate opportunities for both the emergence and concealment of shame.

Block-Lewis (1987) vividly described and highlighted the role of shame in symptom formation. The phenomenology of shame as an experience and emotion and motive are rarely, if ever, considered in psychotherapy, and its varied signs and signals to the therapist often go unnoticed. Behavioral rigidity, obstinence, anger, body posture, facial expressions, an averted gaze, as well as failure to return to therapy may all be subtle indications of unacknowledged or unrecognized shame.

Some family systems are, because of their preferred system model type, incubators of the emotion and interpersonal experience of shame. Shame cuts both ways. While we typically think of parents as wielding greater power and, therefore, more capable of creating intentional or unintentional interpersonal moments of shame in children (certainly this is often the case with abusive parents), shame travels both ways. Parents can often feel "shamed" by their ineffectual efforts with their children. Or, they may have experienced recurrent shaming in their families of origin, bringing to the family's "emergent structural present" the familiar, unproductive, unfulfilling strategies of their earlier parent-child relationships.

While the therapist's ultimate focus in working with critical identity images is centered on a family's structural here and now, these images have their roots in critically important memories. It is not uncommon to hear a parent talk about how, in certain instances, a parent feels a role reversal in which he or she feels like the child and experiences the child as if the youngster were the parent. If the therapy process were honed down to absolute essentials, technical elegance aside, the one interpersonal phrase that would best describe most therapy would be one in which participants, especially in families, *want in some way to be "found," to be seen and known and heard as they really are, and how they wish or want to be.* Shame is a crucial obstacle to this change process. A sense of guilt or family shame and embarrassment is sometimes the first hurdle to overcome in working with families with symptomatic children. In stressing the power of the family systems approach, French (1977) wrote nearly two decades ago that such a view ultimately frees "parents of symptomatic children" from "a mind-boggling list of accusations" toward the view that all members of the system are "involved in the creation, maintenance, and modification of all family patterns, adaptive and maladaptive, without scapegoating" (p. 28).

A Process Vocabulary for Recasting Parent-Child Problems

A theory of family process, like any scientific theory, is best measured in terms of its fruitfulness and utility. When we apply Kantor's theory of structural dynamics, translating and transferring its concepts to the domain of child-centered family therapy practice, we arrive at a "process vocabulary" for recasting parent-child problems in more neutral, descriptive, and "forgiving" language. A child who is exuberant in a quiet, sedate family can be recast as a mismatch between energy styles. The behavior of a child who prefers purposeful and idiosyncratic patterns of exploration and play, living in a family who prefers order and more circumscribed exploration, can be reconceptualized, for example, as expressing a mismatch in orientation to problem solving and use of space. Or, an adolescent who flamboyantly tests and challenges the fabric of family structure in an acting-out search for identity and autonomy can be recognized and viewed more objectively. Parents can be encouraged to see their adolescent's behavior less as a personal affront or as deliberate defiance.

Reconceptualizations of parent-child conflicts or, on the other hand, parent-child growth opportunities, along with accompanying technique-guided interventions, emerge at all junctures on the six-dimensional social space grid, as Chapters 5 through 8 will show. For example, at the affect and power interface, there are issues of belonging and place. Consider the pride and emotional closeness a child experiences when parents allow the child to do his or her first grown-up thing, such as sitting up in the front seat with Dad while younger brother and sisters sit in the back seat of the car. On the other hand, scenes of missed affect-power arise when parents, for instance, do not acknowledge the child's increasing status and autonomy in the family.

At the affect and meaning intersection, there are issues and potential struggles over which things to do, which activities are valuable and important, and to what extent family members should be involved in these activities, including whether a family member's lifestyle is acceptable. A child seeks security and validation through parental approval. The child who proudly holds up a drawing beams when a parent acknowledges the work. On the other hand, a parent who discourages a child from certain activities (e.g., a little boy's avid interest in playing house, or an adolescent's dream to be a dancer or visual artist) is challenging the child in the area of affect and meaning.

The power-meaning juncture evokes situations that bring into sharp focus the individual's rights versus the family system's rights. This crossroads often comprises the thinking, rule-governed, ideological battleground of a family where passionately held points of view and hotly contested opinions compete, vying for attention, acceptance, and family approval. Parents' differences in child-rearing practices and beliefs, as well as their views of child development and a child's role and place in the family, reveal one such crucial ideological battleground and are sources of marital distress and alienation.

For example, parents can be deeply divided around discipline. Differences over the right way to discipline a child strike deep cords in parents, usually, around the power-meaning juncture. The more obvious power struggle between husbands and wives can overshadow a deeper identity issue at stake, involving, among other things, what it means to each parent to be a child. Conflicts over models of discipline are, underneath it all, often critical identity image disagreements on what it means to be a "good person" and how to raise a "good child."

For example, sometimes when parents ask a child to comply with a request such as "Please pick your clothes up off the floor" or "Help me set the table," and the child is busy coloring or building a block city, the youngster may ignore or balk at the parent's request. Parents can become impatient and frustrated. In an ideal world, we might wish the child to comply immediately; children often do not. Instead they continue to play. If the parent postpones the chore until the child has finished the play activity, compliance is more likely. What is at stake here is not only the child's deep absorption in play, the work of childhood, but the parent's equally important recognition of the child's worth as a family member.

At the energy-affect intersection arise compatible matches or conflicts in the expression of energy and emotion. For example, when children are delighted, they often are loud and exuberant. The emotional excitement and enthusiasm they are conveying through their shouts of glee can be misinterpreted by a tired or unaware parent as "uncalled for" noise. The energy-meaning intersection thematically highlights what the family, and individuals within the family value. It equals the energetic "push" or motivational intensity or meanings that influence family and family member actions and activities. This junction of family process and interactions reveals a family's preferred symbols or icons, such as the Bible or Koran, report cards and school achievement, or travel memorabilia. Parent-child conflicts can surface around a parent's disapproval of how a child spends time. For example, a parent may complain: "All Billy thinks about is his rock collection"; "Sara is always glued in front of the television screen"; or "Peter spends far too much time playing with his toy cars instead of reading storybooks."

Child and Adult Family Player Parts

Child-Centered Structural Dynamic Therapy views family process and the potential problems that may arise as the interplay of the family's transactional here and now and the imprint and cumulative impact of the family's developmental history. Repetitive interactions around variations in central family themes build and recycle into broader patterns. Smaller and more discrete sequences of interaction evolve into larger "organized wholes." Family patterns, rhythms, and rituals of joining (moving toward) and separation (moving away) reveal a family's structure. In this light, we can think of family patterns as visual relationship statements, a behavioral sentence that summarizes and expresses the current character of family interaction. Family interactions reveal important information about a family's emotional life. The bridge between individual and family development, the link that unites the personal interior world of the individual, adult and child, and the transactional world of the family, is individual behavior viewed in context.

The fourth building block and integral part-process of the Child-Centered Model (family player parts) draws on the Kantor Four Player Model. In the Child-Centered Model's application, the family's psychopolitical configurations are viewed, and extended to integrate three interrelated levels of interaction and change: child development, parent-child relationship structures, and the family system. *Psychopolitical configurations* is a term that Kantor has developed to convey how the individual behaviors and personal puzzle pieces of family members, their player parts, combine to form predictable transactional styles and interactions. Accordingly, individual motivation, cognition, behavior, and choice (decisions) are viewed as context dependent, embedded within a social field theory of personality development.

The Child-Centered Model focuses on the contributions of individual family members' overt behaviors, the part these behaviors play in overall family interactional sequences, combined with stage-related knowledge, the behaviors and transactional parts that children need and must play as emerging, individual developmental systems. When the unfolding child development tasks shown in Table 1.1, are integrated with the various combination possibilities offered within the Kantor Four Player Model, we are provided with a ready and effective framework for describing and analyzing family process as well as designing system-based strategies for facilitating optimal child development within families.

Of the five building blocks of family process, the integration of child development with Kantor's Four Player Model brings us closest to individuals and their personal psychological contributions to family interaction. Exploring the personal or "person" inside family process places the spotlight on the individual-system intersection from alternative vantage points: that of the individual and the individual's transactional context. Here, the zoom lens of family analysis and understanding focuses directly and consciously on individuals showing their reciprocity and involvement in family transactions on multiple levels. In addition, in considering the individual, per se, the Child-Centered Structural Dynamic Model, viewed through the Kantor Four Player Model lens, draws us closest to individuals and their personal contributions, while simultaneously providing us with a clearly available conceptual and empirical framework for attending and responding to individuals in systems. In the context of child-centered therapy, this allows us to forge links between child and family developmental outcomes, an underdeveloped aspect of family theory and therapy.

THE DEVELOPMENTAL INTERPLAY OF PERSONAL AND FAMILY STRATEGIES: FREEDOM VERSUS CONSTRAINT

The Child-Centered Model explores individual puzzle pieces of behavior at interplay with other individuals within the family. In doing so, the model highlights each adult's and child's development of personal strategies in relation to family strategies and vice versa. The emphasis is on the ways in which individuals shape systems and systems shape individuals, calling into play themes of freedom and constraint, patterns of autonomy and conformity These patterns carry strong implications for the quality and direction of parent-child relationships, as well as the developmental needs and outcomes of children.

The Kantor Four Player Model identifies the personal roles and transactional parts (interactional options) of mover, follower, opposer, and bystander. Before illustrating each of the four parts in everyday life, the obvious question arises: What does the term psychopolitical mean and how is it being used in the context of child-centered therapy? Kantor introduced the term in 1975 to convey how the psychological and personal worlds of the individual influence and are expressed in family transactions, specifically the interactional choices a family member can or cannot make. These parts or transactional roles are simply the ways individuals behave in relation to others—the transactional parts that are available to them and the parts they eventually learn to play in the family. The four family parts form transactional sequences, each part having its enabling and problematic or counterproductive forms. The parts are fluid, dynamic, and evolving.

Viewed from the individual-system juncture, the role that the individual expresses and contributes to family patterns represents the learned parts individuals have chosen or are compelled to play. For the therapist, these parts can be thought of, and envisioned, as similar to punctuation marks in a family's transaction sentences, highlighting beginnings, pauses, redirections, exclamations, and endings in an interactional sequence. Any family member can play any part, and the same individual can play several parts in any one family sequence. The shifting and fluid nature of all four parts is experienced and expressed, drawing meaning from the overall transactional picture, what parts mean as a system-whole. These parts, far from static and fixed, communicate system totality. An example, drawn from everyday family life, illustrates the interplay of parts:

- When the father says, "Let's go for a ride in the car," he is acting as the *mover.*
- When the mother says, "That sounds like a good idea. I'm all for it," she is acting as the *follower.*
- When their son says, "No, let's stay home and play Nintendo," he is acting as an *opposer.*
- When their daughter chimes in, "We always go for rides like clockwork every Sunday. Or, we end up playing video games, why can't we come up with something new and exciting to do," she is acting as the *bystander.*

A second example revolving around children illustrates how the parts can mesh together in any subsystem or transactional context:

- Four boys are playing outside in a yard; two are brothers, and two are neighbor boys. In a corner of the yard, three girls are playing, including a younger sister.
- The younger brother says, "Hey, let's go and sneak up on the girls and scare them away." He acts as the *mover,* the one who proposes the start of this sequence.
- One boy says, "Yeah, and we can use this rubber spider. Will they scream!" He swings the spider in the air. This boy is acting as a *follower* to the other boy's initial move. His support moves the interaction forward, keeping it on course in a mischievous direction.
- Another boy says, "No. I've got a better idea. Let's run up and grab their toys and get them to chase us!" He makes a face like "Evil Shredder" and roars sinisterly. By introducing a new plan, the boy *opposes* or challenges the move, shifting the interaction away from the first idea in

another direction. [An *opposer* does not always oppose. An opposer acts often to turn the sequence in a different direction.]

- Just at that moment, the older brother interrupts, "If you scare the girls, you'll be in big trouble. Remember what Mom said." He is acting as a *bystander,* the observing ego of the group.

The psychopolitical aspect of a family's social field represents its judgments, choices, decisions, and actions. The family, like any social group, evolves patterns and rules or guides for "compliance" (conformity) and "self-assertion" (disagreement and self-expression): whether an individual wants to live in ways compatible with, or disapproved by, the family. The tension created and generated by this variance, either growth-oriented or pathogenic, is fundamental to the development of self consciousness (self vis-à-vis others and the environment) and system consciousness (the environment and others vis-à-vis self). David Kantor originated the term "psychopolitics" to denote the thematic area of family process in which family members try simultaneously to cope with the demands of the family and its interpersonal relationships and personal autonomy—individuals' right to be themselves.

One aspect of this individual-system developmental perspective emphasizes the self-in-relation to others from the point of view and direction of the individual. The other aspect of this reciprocal development emphasizes "others" or system-in-relation to the self. Once again, when we draw together both aspects of this reciprocal viewpoint, the self vis-à-vis the family and the family vis-à-vis the self, we create a transactional picture of a full cycle of influence that incorporates the individual, here viewed descriptively as the focal point of analysis.

In this way, the therapist first pinpoints the subsystem juncture, the location and level at which the transactional sequence is occurring, including the familiar or predictable parts that family members take. The therapist identifies which subsystems are involved in a sequence. Consider the following interaction possibilities that the therapist addresses in identifying the interaction level and dynamics:

- Is the problem transaction between the child (personal subsystem) in relation to one parent (personal subsystem)?
- Is the interaction between the individual (adult or child) and the family group?
- Is the transaction centered around the child (individual) and a particular interpersonal subsystem, such as parental or sibling?
- Is the issue broader than the particulars of two personalities, extending to more general subsystem functioning? Is the interplay between interpersonal subsystems, tensions around parental versus marital roles?

- Is the problem between an interpersonal subsystem (marital) and the family?
- Is the dynamic around an individual family member (adult or child) and the outside world?
- Is the problem transaction between the couple (interpersonal subsystem) and the wider community, for example the child's school?
- Is the dynamic around the family, the various worlds within it (personal, interpersonal) and the outside world, for example, neighborhood and community?

The therapist observes the sequence of moves, how the parts unfold, followed by the details of who plays what role, how often, and when in the interaction. The process is similar to following the sequence of events in the preceding two examples.

There is the personal psychology of the individual, the mix of cognitive, affective, and physiological processes, views of relationships, social interaction and the self in the world of experience that guide and motivate behavior. There are also unarticulated, unclaimed, and unnamed forms of experience that influence behavior, causing people to act in ways that are foreign and confusing, and that feel more compelled than consciously and intentionally chosen. There is the psychological and interior world of the individual and subjective experience, a view that brings us closest to the motivational guides influencing behavior. The group will of the family in the form of "guideposts" of established rules also influences (permits or disallows) autonomy and self-expression. The interplay and development of personal and family transactional strategies is especially poignant for children who are experimenting with independence and identity. Child-Centered Structural Dynamic Therapy works to raise preconscious experience to the level of self-awareness and system-awareness and employs the conscious, well-informed use of self (personal) and system (family) knowledge and understanding, on all three levels of the model, from prevention and early intervention to families in crisis.

The bridge between personal and interior, the motivations and behaviors of the child as a developing self, and the systemic and transactional, expressed in overt family interactional sequences and combinations of sequences, forms the principal point of access to parent-child relationship imagery. It is important for the therapist to locate and identify the type of motivator (personal, interpersonal, family unit) that an individual's social action and transactional move (decision) are primarily based on. This helps to define and situate the individual's contribution (actions) in relation to others' contributions (actions) in the family sequence. It gives meaning to the transactional part the individual is playing in the overall family scenario.

We can think of family parts as similar to family photographs, snapshots of family members alone and in relation to others, that epitomize that person in the family and that person's relationship to the family. We can also think of them as temporary freeze frames or "stills," akin to when a film or a videotape is put on "pause" to fix and hold the image, bringing it into sharper focus. After looking at all of these individual social acts and array of psychopolitical parts, following the videotape film analogy one step further, what the therapist or family practitioner does next is to shift from "pause" to "play" and let the images come alive in the form of a moving scenario or transactional sequence that tells something revealing about the family and the individuals in it. The use of family photographs as a research and clinical tool as well as enrichment method, will be fully explained in Chapters 6 through 8 on the Three-Tier Child-Centered Model.

FOUR TRANSACTIONAL OPTIONS

The Kantor Four Player Model includes mover, follower, opposer, and bystander. The term bystander is an intriguing, multifaceted concept that takes on enriched and amplified meaning in the context of children and the Child-Centered Model's Family Activities, techniques, and assessment method as will be illustrated throughout this book. Each part works in concert with all others and derives its meaning in context. Because the Kantor Four Player Model is rooted in overt behavior (face-to-face family transactions), the relationship between parts can be charted and mapped spatially, as shown in Figure 2.4. Figure 2.4 depicts my conceptual representation, in visual form (schemas), of the relational aspects of Kantor's Four Player Model. For example, the mover in a family sequence is usually geographically, psychologically, and interpersonally at the center of the action. The mover defines the space in which the action or activity takes place. A family system's comovers—its followers, opposers, and bystanders—influence the significance of the mover's initiating action. Comovers determine who will and who will not be allowed to play the prime mover part. The follower, in turn, moves in support of the center of the action, validating the mover, or promotes and supports the moves of others. The follower also moves toward the center of the action and joins the mover. As Figure 2.4 shows, the bystander observes on the periphery of the interaction, staying out of the direct action, serving a vital reflective part in the family. The important consciousness-raising features of the Child-Centered Model's application of this family system role will be explored in greater detail later in this section and Chapters 5 through 8.

While the mover is central to the action, defining it, the power of the mover's part is subject to comovers' responses. Kantor's family analysis has shown that a measure of a family's psychological and interpersonal wealth

Figure 2.4
Four Family Roles: Visual-Spatial Transactional Moves

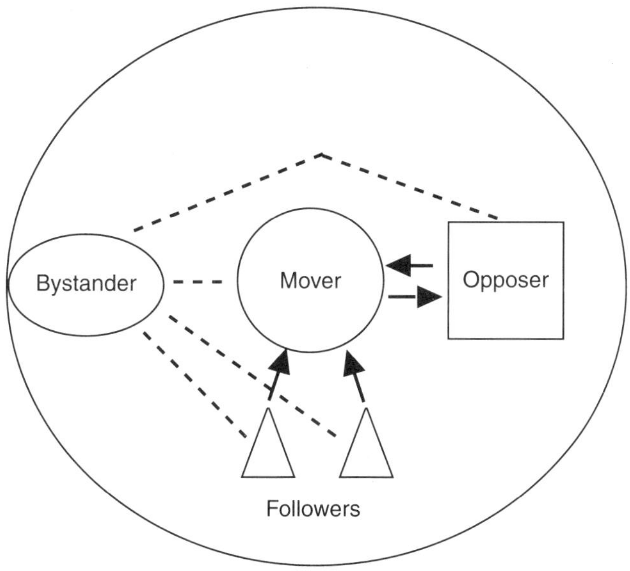

Transactional Field
Boundary of Family Interaction Sequence

Note: An individual can play one or a combination of parts in a given interaction.

is determined by the richness of its thematic content and the complexity of its social strategies. As shown in Kantor's research (Kantor & Lehr, 1986), further confirmed by child-centered research and practice (Andreozzi, 1985a, 1993a, 1993b), the mover is of primary importance in determining the family system's thematic richness.

A family's thematic richness, its conceptual and practical resourcefulness, is best expressed in the diversity, depth, and breadth of its subgoals. Which of these subgoals materializes in family interactions is largely a result of the direction in which a mover proposes to lead the family, defining the "destination" to be sought within any given family interaction. For example, is the mover attempting to initiate actions in the family's affect, power, or meaning domains? What is the mover in search of and what is the mover's intended destination or outcome? Without the support and movement of family coresponders, however, a mover's actions are disqualified and a family moves nowhere. A mover's actions cannot progress without family participation. Once an action is initiated, and a family scenario or sequence of interactions is under way, family members have a choice or may feel compelled to play one of several comoving options. Followers must support the mover for the action to continue. A family without movers cannot initiate. This is a family that essentially cannot get anything started or completed. Similarly, a family without followers also cannot progress, or move forward cooperatively. To support means to follow another's lead.

Multiproblem families such as the Brimmers, introduced in this chapter, usually show disordered, disrupted, and disqualified mover and follower functions, combined with ineffectual opposers and often a complete absence of system-conscious observers. The mover is a prototypic leader; the follower is a prototypic ally or joiner. The aim of the family therapist is to locate the direction of energy flow in the sequence of interactions, and identify the family's distance regulation around goals of affect, power, and meaning. The person, mover, who initially seeks to gain access to one of these family target dimensions establishes the context, both thematic and actual, for other family members' responses. The mover, in essence, sets the stage. The follower role is multidimensional as well, having both enriching and disruptive influences on family interaction. On the enabling side, the capacity to validate others by granting them support helps determine which family members' destinations, the goals and the means of reaching these goals, will dominate and which will be ignored, underdeveloped, or disqualified. Without a broad range of strategies available to the mover, the mover, as in families in crisis, can get locked into reenactments of stereotypic and rigid mover roles.

On the other hand, the opposer challenges or blocks the action of the mover, pulling away from the center. The opposer is moving in an opposite direction. In terms of distance regulation, the opposer is moving away, distancing him- or herself from the mover, center of the action, and direction of the family interaction. The opposer is initially a reactor who is attempting to shift the center of influence, redefining the direction and destination of the mover as well as the context of the family sequence and interaction. The opposer can be represented as moving away, pulling away from the center of the family transaction.

The opposer also serves a vital function in the family. Opposers challenge the family's actions in terms of specific goals and have the capacity to redefine the thematic and actual context of the family interaction. Opposers create opportunities for comovers, as family members express their positions either on the side of the mover or opposer. Ideally, the opposer sets limits on the energies and directions of the mover. The opposer functions to check and balance the family system by entering into a "dialogue" with the mover for developing strategies that are productive for the family as a whole. A family without opposers is a family that is out of control, unable to check and redefine its limits. This can take the form of tyranny or anarchy and chaos. A family of movers and opposers without access to followers is a family that will remain deadlocked in its opposition, recycling its disagreements and repeating chronic, angry, distancing moves.

The bystander role serves a crucial multidimensional function. Pursuing our spatial analogy, we can envision the bystander as observing on the periphery of the interaction. This participant-observer is an astute watcher, witness, and interpreter of family transactions, a role with the critical dual purpose of qualifying and checking the viability of a family's strategies and correcting them if they become ineffective. The term *bystander* on the surface, may create a misimpression, suggesting a passive part or minimal influence in the course and outcome of family interaction. The bystander role, however, is vital and active, central to family growth and change. The main function of this transactional puzzle piece is to communicate and accurately reflect the meanings and images inherent in family social interaction and, as such, to create or reawaken system consciousness, reminding the family when it is veering off course from its group purpose and ideals.

The family member who takes this part is an emotional and strategic mediator who, by providing an impartial, objective overview of interaction and family events, stimulates system consciousness. In the Child-Centered Model, this role serves a function similar to a Greek chorus, acting as the family's memory, its thematic refrain, and its wise, neutral arbitrator. As a well-informed observer and interpreter of family events and transactions, the bystander encourages family members to reexamine the meanings they feel are guiding and justifying their actions. This astute participant-observer and reflector of system consciousness has the threshold task of communicating major aspects of a family's meaning dimension by sensitizing and awakening in family members' others parts crucial system consciousness.

Each of the three parts—mover, follower, and opposer—additionally carries the bystander as a secondary function in the nature and expression of these psychopolitical parts. As family members express each role, they are not only enacting the role but are also interpreting and observing the effects on the family system and the family's reaction to their behavior. All three parts, mover, opposer, and follower, involve an awareness of interaction. Family members' assessment of their own behavior in the presence of this impartial arbitrator who grasps the "whole picture" (transactional overview) can remind family members to think about what they are doing and what they are saying and how it is affecting others and the family. An example will illustrate this point:

A little girl, Amy, comes home from school. She throws down her book bag, and without taking her coat off, runs straight to find Puddles, the family dog. Just at that moment her father gives her a series of orders and instructions. He asks her to take off her coat, put her lunch box in the kitchen, and pick her book bag up off the floor where she dropped it in a rush. The child, intent on petting the dog, ignores her father's requests. A man who likes order, he becomes annoyed. He begins to criticize his daughter. He complains to his wife that their daughter is "lazy" and "undisciplined." All the father can see at the moment is the little girl's misbehavior. Her mother, who sees the child's behavior more fully and knows Amy better, says to her husband, "She wants to pet the dog. She hasn't seen Puddles all day. It is important to Amy to do this. She is an affectionate little girl and she is especially attached to the dog. You know that." The mother is reminding the father of what is personally meaningful to Amy (an important child's image of self).

In the preceding scenario, mother identifies the personal intention and developmental imperative guiding Amy's behavior. Her deftly timed comments enlarge her husband's perspective. In this way, an astute interpreter of family process can tell the family when it is getting offtrack, asking the family to stop and take notice of what is happening. Ironically, the bystander can do this simply by his or her presence.

In itself, the act of witnessing is often experienced as a palpable force felt by others in the family sequence. Family members may feel uneasy in the presence of a silent observer because they do not know the observer's viewpoint. Think about uneasy pauses or silences that go on too long in a conversation or the influence that a silent member has on a group. The self-reflective, system consciousness capacity is crucial for any group, especially the family. In an enabling situation, this capacity is the principal source of potential change available to the family. In some instances, when the family member who embodies the family's "group conscience" leaves, family members can either feel betrayed, deprived of guidance and interpretation, or liberated from a watchful eye.

In other instances, when the family member who acts as the "organizer" and "interpreter" of family experience leaves the family interaction in premature and unanticipated ways, his or her absence can linger, leaving an afterimage of his or her watchful, and variously experienced and interpreted, presence. This happens, for example, when a family member dies, leaving unresolved personal and family myth and imagery. For example, this is the situation for the Brimmers, especially for their 12-year-old son, John, who lives in the shadow of the afterimage of his father. This strategic mediator of family events and witness of family experience, present or absent, can either comfort those he or she watches by communicating to them that they are known and valued, or oppress them by withholding his or her personal feelings and thoughts on the family. This silent witness can also convey that family members are known, but not valued.

The influence and interpretive power of this sensitive "family system observer" flows from the individual's capacity to maintain objectivity. It is important to emphasize that the bystander, while commenting on and interpreting family events and transactional roles vis-à-vis each other, stands apart, impartial, on the periphery of the social interaction. The bystander, in effect, stays out of the direct interaction, making no alliances with the mover, opposers, or followers, at least in relation to their three-way interaction. From this vantage point, the individual can offer comments, and feedback, and opportunities for self-evaluation and change to the family interaction. Once this participant-observer, watching on the sidelines and providing guidance by his or her impartial influence, decides to give up this vantage point or is directly drawn into the interaction, the role is transformed. The family member now leaves this impartial, reflective bystander position and has the choice of taking one of the other three parts, or combinations of these parts. This family member may now enter as either a follower or an opposer in the social interaction. Or the family member may choose to leave the social field altogether, to act as a mover in a new action sequence and thematic context.

This system consciousness capacity is what the therapist, in the areas of prevention and early intervention, seeks to nurture and support in the family. As they stay on the periphery of a given family interaction, these participant-observers can, from their unique sideline vantage point of the bystander role, act much like journalists, news commentators, or even therapists, calling attention to the family's transactions, communicating the degree of effectiveness of these moves. Families, who use the system consciousness methods of increasing family awareness and the five Child-Centered Activities described in Chapters 5 through 8, can begin to consciously guide family change and growth from within.

The therapist, acting as emotional mediator and systems guide to the family in crisis, strives to reawaken this capacity in families, when family patterns have rigidified and family parts have become stereotypic and ritualized. The prevention and early intervention methods and techniques in the Three-Tier Child-Centered Model presented in Chapters 5 through 8 revolve primarily around eliciting and enhancing the bystander role: the system's self-correcting capacity in families, the couple, and parent-child relationships. Additionally, the clinician can use the self-correcting and self-corrective bystander function as an active and interactive research tool to guide, monitor, and evaluate ongoing, process-oriented, session-by-session family system change.

Charting the Influence and Impact of Child and Adult Transactional Parts

All four parts serve their specific purposes in family transactions. Each part has its enabling and problematic or disqualifying effects in family sequences. These transactional roles take place in everyday life, as shown in the "Sunday afternoon drive in the car" scenario and the "rubber spider incident" shown earlier. The puzzle pieces of these parts also explain problem interactions in families. Similarly, when family sequences become predictable and are grouped together into larger family sequences, when "current" and "historical" in a family's interactional life come together, merging past and present, patterns can be discerned that highlight a family's repetitive, unresolved problems. An assessment of the quality, frequency, and adaptability of these roles in a family, including the parts each family member typically plays in and across contexts, can strengthen a family and prevent problems, serve as a means of early intervention, and provide the therapist with a psychosocial framework for organizing effective means of intervening in disrupted family patterns.

As research and clinical practice on the Child-Centered Structural Dynamic Model (Andreozzi, 1978, 1979d, 1985a, 1988, 1993a, 1993b) has shown, the Kantor Four Player Model can be extended to child development, per se. Each stage in a child's development carries with it the ascendance and practice of one of these four roles. Children need to practice their autonomy, their capacity to initiate. They similarly need to develop skills and facility in following, supporting, in being cooperative and compliant. They also need to learn how to exercise their rights to defend, to challenge, to offer a different viewpoint and have that viewpoint respected and heard. Additionally, children need to explore their capacity to observe, comment, self-reflect and interpret events around them and events or states occurring within themselves. Children need to develop "careful eyes," "careful ears," and a "careful mind." These skills are more than cognitive; they are life skills. They need to feel that they are credible witnesses, participants, influencers, and valued and worthwhile interpreters of environmental events, especially within their family.

Figure 2.5 shows the integration of child development with the Kantor Four Player Model in the Child-Centered Model. When we combine Figure 2.4 with Figure 2.5, we can see how the therapist has a twofold task. The first is to spatially organize, chart, and map the family's player part transactions, the direction and destination or distance regulation of the four player parts, including who plays them and when in the family sequence. The next step is for the clinician to superimpose another transparency, namely, one that shows how children navigate and express these roles differently according to development and age, and how these differences arise as a result of how children grow, unfold, and learn.

The follower is an important role in parent-child relationships. Parents who sensitively and astutely follow their children's developmental and interactional leads, the initiating cues of their infants and toddlers, promote better developmental outcomes, the optimal blend of autonomy and voluntary compliance. When such parents are followers to their children's developmental imperatives, they create more harmonious, interpersonally flexible and varied parent-child relationships.

Figure 2.5
Child Development and the Emergence of The Four Family Parts: Parent-Child Transactions

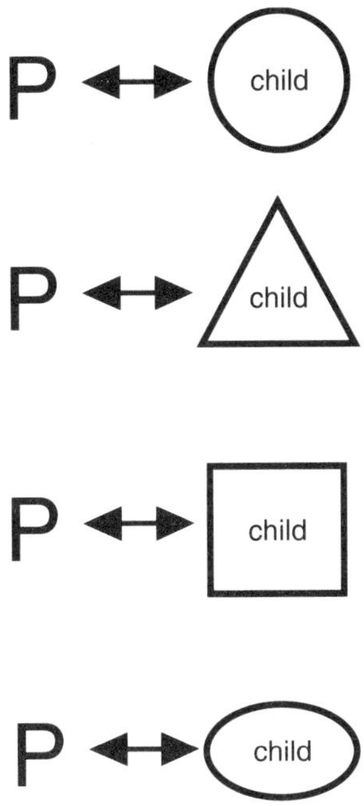

1. A validated mover
   Child initiates and is followed, affirmed by parent.

2. A compliant follower
   Child cooperates and parent supports the child's compliance.

3. An appreciated challenger
   Child declares independence and parent recognizes and allows the difference.

4. A respected observer and commentator of family events
   Child offers perceptions and interpretations and parent values the child's feelings/thoughts.

Note: The ascendance of all four transactional parts coincides with age-appropriate child development tasks: trust, independence/autonomy, initiative, industry, identity/self-concept. While one transactional part predominates per stage, all other parts are also present.

Mover and challenger roles are equally important to the parent-child relationship and optimal child development. Children need to feel that their voices, wishes, and requests, are heard and seriously considered. Self-initiated thought and behavior is rooted in a fundamental trust in one's own judgments. As children experiment with their "initiating moves" within the safe, nurturing, emotional space of the parent-child relationship, their self-esteem and sense of identity strengthen. The nagging self-doubt and worry over independent judgments ("Do I have the right to make my own decisions?") of emotionally insecure and overtly dependent children are often the outgrowth of a parent-child relationship that discouraged, disparaged, or thwarted autonomy and self-assertion.

Similarly, a strong and resilient sense of self is rooted in children's capacity and quality of experience as a challenger, one who offers an alternate and autonomous viewpoint, free of the undue fear of parental disapproval. In many ways, the extent to which the child can safely regulate and express opposition in the parent-child relationship (i.e., the child's feelings and behavior are acknowledged, channeled, and effectively contained) is related directly to the development of positive impulse control and effective anger management and coping techniques. Ultimately, the child's facility and practice of all three roles—mover, follower, and challenger—creates and reinforces the child's capacity to self-reflect, to be an astute interpreter of psychological, social, and family events. The capacity to read internal states and emotions such as "feeling sad" or "angry" is directly related to the capacity for self-initiated change. The parent-child relationship is an important learning environment that can either instill or discourage self-discovery, enhance or limit self-understanding.

The family parts work transactionally. They are not meant to be viewed as disparate and disjointed behaviors. Instead, these four parts form a broader picture, each having its place and capacity to move forward a family's interactional sequence. The mover, as we saw, begins the interaction, defining it. Family members as responders or comovers, have in any given family sequence, three transactional options: follower, opposer, or impartial arbiter/observer of family events. If a relationship is to continue, all four options must take place. One part can be played by any number of participant players. The parts played by each family member can be discerned by exploring the direction and destination of family members' actions. *Destination* connotes the psychological intention and interpersonal intent of an action (an individual's behavior) on a transaction's outcome.

The first indication of a family's psychopolitical configuration is seen in the order or sequence individuals act. The therapist assesses the following: What is the tempo, sequence, and unfolding of the events? Does the mother initiate, do the children follow, while father opposes? Does the mother begin, one child follow, another child oppose while the father looks on, not saying a word? The second feature involves identifying when, in what situations and contexts, and with what frequency and flexibility family members play predictable parts. Consider the following:

Does the father almost always act as the mover with mother acting as the follower around "limit setting," which their son then opposes? Or does the child try to initiate contact (emotional access) with the father only to be ignored (blocked) by the father who opposes the affectionate connection; with the father, in turn, being criticized (opposed) for his coldness by his wife? Here, the child is a thwarted or ineffective mover and the father who should have followed his son's moves toward nurturance, responds as an ineffective opposer who is then opposed by his wife. How rigid and entrenched is this sequence? To what extent does the thwarted mover (son), failed follower and opposer (father), and intervening, ineffective opposer (mother) pattern carry beyond themes of nurturance? Does this sequence replay itself when, for example, the son shows his "mastery" and learning? How widespread and frequent is the pattern? And can family members vary their parts, having access to all four behaviors or transactional moves?

The third important feature in analyzing a family's psychopolitical configurations, and relating this information to child development, is to pinpoint in which access dimension or sphere (space, time, energy) and toward what goals (affect, meaning, and power) the particular transactional part or move is directed. This was illustrated in the preceding example.

Patterns of sequences develop in every family as individual family members play predictable parts or combinations of some parts more than others. Typically, one person plays one part in one sphere and another part in another sphere. Mother may be the principal mover in areas of affect and power; father may be the principal mover in areas of meaning or defining the family's core purpose and ideals. The therapist charts the family's transactional moves and identifies the family's preferred psychopolitical configuration. The therapist synthesizes this process view (map or blueprint of the problem pattern) with knowledge of the problem domain or thematic content around which the conflict revolves. Embedded within and also superimposed on this system understanding is the identification and integration of the child development task primarily at risk.

Four Family Illustrations Drawn from Child-Centered Practice

In this chapter, we see in the "Sunday afternoon drive in the car" and the "rubber spider incident," the transactional nature of these family parts in everyday life. However, we also are shown various counterproductive and problematic enactments: personal, interpersonal, and family strategies that have somehow missed their mark. The following four illustrations, drawn from Child-Centered Structural Dynamic Therapy, show what happens when family members' moves do not mesh, as well as when the parts played by family members, including their personal meanings, go misinterpreted and misunderstood:

Lila Stone is a tall, slender strawberry blond in her mid-30s. She is elegant and poised. She says tearfully, tissues crumpled in one hand, "My whole life is wrong. I feel terrified and out of control and I don't know why. How did it all get to this point?" She sounds intense and at the same time demoralized. Her husband, Ted, somewhere in his mid to late 40s, is also tall and strikingly handsome. He looks oblivious at times, plaintive at others, as if in search of some magical answer that might miraculously appear out of the air. His round, sullen boyish face makes him seem much younger than Lila, and because of this, overshadowed by her. He sits impassively, silent.

Below the surface resignation, there are flashes of anger between them, mostly unspoken. Anger emerges from Ted in quick, furtive, darting glances, and anger is there in the edges of his body, seen in the way he folds his arms against his chest. For Lila, the anger is all in the subtle and well-controlled tone of her voice. The Stones have been married for nine years. Three feet of rigid space separate the couple in the small room. Lila declares that "there is no passion left between us any more." Ted, in response, shrugs his shoulders, mumbling something about "and whose fault is that any way?" It appears to hurt for the Stones even to look at each other.

In the center of the room stands their 6-year-old child, Keith. He has dressed himself in layers of mismatched clothing: brown cowboy boots, red pants, a yellow belt, purple striped shirt, green Ninja Turtle suspenders, a tall black top hat he has made out of construction paper, and an orange insulated winter vest too warm for the summer day. He is a figure of brightly clashing exuberant color. Turning away suddenly from his parents, his back toward them, he leaps up in the air. He jumps up and down several times, landing with his legs spread wide apart, feet rooted as if to take a firm hold. Brandishing what looks like an imaginary whip in one hand, and making a small menacing fist with the other, there is a smile of triumphant glee on his face as he says, "I am the ringmaster. Ruler of the universe! I will save her from that old man . . ."

In the Stone family, Lila and Ted remain covert opposers, keeping their opposition hidden—a part that Keith, their 6-year-old son, readily assumes in a developmentally inappropriate way. As we follow the Stone family through the initial phases of therapy, we will find that Keith emerges as a thwarted or ineffectual *manifest mover* (Kantor & Lehr, 1986). In the midst of marital conflict, the Stones struggle with indecisiveness and confusion over the tasks of parental limit setting. Keith wields inordinant and uncomfortable power as both a developmentally unprepared and disqualified manifest mover, trying to bring out a system decision, and a bystander whose behavioral comments are not heard; Keith loses his child's status.

A manifest mover differs from a mover in several ways. A manifest mover, who may be overt or covert, may never actually play the mover part. Yet the manifest mover is the player who ultimately functions as the primary negotiator of a system's access dimensions and goals. In the brief but epitomizing opening scene of the Stone family in their first therapy session, Keith inappropriately emerges as the family's primary distance regulator, the organizer and definer of the family's social space and context. Keith is the center of energy and action, directing his parents' attention even in the form of perceived helplessness. His behavior determines the direction and outcome of family interactions, at least at this point in the Stone's family development.

Next there are the Greens. The Green family, consisting of Tara, a single mother, her two children, Billy, aged 5, and Tanya, almost 4, and their maternal grandmother, Florence, whom they live with, provides another example of emergent, discordant, player parts:

Tara Green is in her early 20s. She is a thin, pale, nervous-looking woman with waist-length, thick black wavy hair. As she walks cautiously into the room, two wan and fragile-looking children trail behind her: Billy, who is about 5 and shows signs of some neurological problems, and Tanya, who is barely 4. Tara's mother, Florence Perkins, the maternal grandparent—a robust, ruddy-looking woman—follows behind her daughter and the children. The children stand sandwiched between the women.

Tara is a single mother working hard to make ends meet. She is in a vocational training program studying to be a court stenographer. She has been divorced barely one year and is living back home with her mother and the children in a small, two-bedroom urban apartment.

Her marriage was tumultuous, filled with her husband Brandon's drugs and violence and what felt to her like "empty sex." Both of them were teenage parents, wrestling prematurely with the problems of intimacy and responsibility. Tara urgently blurts out, in our second session, "I don't know how to describe it. The guilt I feel is so big that if I let it go, if I let it out, it would fill this entire room and there would be no space, no room left for anything else . . ." Her hands cover her eyes, rubbing them. She leans forward, her dark hair falling, covering her face so there is even less of her to be seen. The grandmother suddenly interrupts, "I'm so concerned. There is a story going around in our neighborhood that the women next door beats her kids. I don't mean to change the subject but isn't there something we can do, we should do? How can people do such things to their own flesh and blood!"

The children, well-behaved, sit quietly together, listening. They are almost too well-behaved and there seems to be no motion or energy within or between them. However, sometimes Billy tries to speak. His speech is hard to understand, partly because of his age, partly because he speaks softly and lisps. The children sit close together, their arms almost joined. Each time Billy tries to speak, Tanya, his sister, (like a Greek chorus) begins, barely audibly, to clap. The sound is so soft, and the gesture of her hands so slight, that it could be easily missed. But it is also distinctly there, accompanying every one of Billy's faltering and halting efforts. It is as if she is trying to italicize, to draw attention to the purpose and meaning of his actions in some important way. Her almost imperceptible gesture on behalf of the brother that she loves is both brave and faint, wanting and at the same time not wanting to be heard.

In this family therapy excerpt, we see that Tara begins to act as a mover as she initiates conversation, drawing and defining the action-center and context when she begins to talk about the guilt and anxiety that fill her. However, her mother's brief but potent interruption overshadows Tara's move, shifting the focus of conversation away, in a different direction. The grandmother's interruption, thus, works as a strategic distance regulator, with the effect of acting as an opposer to her daughter's action.

Also, in the Green family the children play important, yet disqualified participant-observer roles. As Billy tries to speak, to offer comments on the family, his opinion of his experience and what he sees from his child's view, he, like his sister Tanya, is disqualified; his whispered comments go unnoticed.

Similarly, in this brief scenario, Tanya shifts and enacts two psychopolitical parts. First, she moves to support her brother, a caring follower to his plight. This is seen in her gesture—the way children often communicate these psychopolitical strategies—as she subtly and quietly claps. In doing so, her actions serve a twofold, multidimensional purpose. She both follows her brother, supporting him and, along with him, comments on how the family organizes itself and the places it accords for its members.

The Gladshores exemplify disrupted opposer-follower family patterns:

The Gladshore family, Candy and Ed and their three children, arrive late, exasperated, and out of breath. Angelica, aged 6½, prances into the room first. Her parents are visibly upset and embarrassed. On the way into the room, Angelica has broken free of her mother's hand, managing to pinch and kick her, while yelling by way of introduction, "Here's my mother, the idiot. She hates me!" Angelica now spins around, running back to her father who is holding the hand of Sarah, Angelica's 3-year-old sister.

Candy, the mother, is in her late 20s and looks beleaguered by it all; she blurts out, "See, she's such a terror. We're having so much trouble with her everywhere, at home and at school. She's a thickhead with me. Nothing I do works. But just watch, you'll see how she minds for him," pointing to her husband Ed, also in his late 20s, who says, "That's because I treat her right." Candy, who is just about ready to explode and is visibly struggling to regain her composure, adds, "I've got one good and one bad kid. And who knows about this one?" She nods towards the 9-month-old infant she is holding in her arms.

Candy has returned to work full time at the phone company, in the customer service department, doing her best to try to help the family make ends meet. She works days; Ed works nights as a printer for a local newspaper. Before the last baby was born, the couple belonged to a small rock band that would perform at local clubs. Ed played drums while Candy sang. Barely settled in the room, first Candy and then Ed rattle off a laundry list of complaints: "There's no time for us anymore. There's no time to get anything done. Everything is unmade or undone in our house"; "The kids just have too much energy. They go nonstop, especially Angelica, and she knows, especially when I'm tired, how to get to me"; "Everything feels like a tug-of-war, a battle between us, and then between us and the kids, and it goes round and round." Candy adds, "I think I need Prozac or Valium or something . . ." Ed says, "No drugs!" Then he adds, "What's happening to our family, anyway?"

In the Gladshore family, as Candy and Ed (the parents) bicker and reveal their thinly disguised marital tensions around separate as well as collective images of lost freedom in the service of this "thing" that they now call "family," the children act as comovers. Angelica acts as opposer to her mother. Ed, joining with Angelica, follows, in his own way opposing his wife. Sara, Angelica's younger sister, sides with her father, supporting him by her following behavior. The baby punctuates the family transactions and events by crying on cue, calling for attention and simultaneously corrective measures. As a signaler of family distress, the baby is a behavioral interpreter of family interaction.

Considerable attention, time, and space have been devoted to the family's player parts because of their importance in the Child-Centered Structural Dynamic Model. Player parts bridge personal meanings of individuals and family social transactions and overt behavior. By making critical identity images visible in ritualized transactional roles, player parts form the conceptual, empirical, and clinical links that often define and characterize a family in developmental crisis.

Player parts or roles are concrete, observable, and behavioral. In this way, the roles form the substantive basis for charting family change and awakening and eliciting family system consciousness. At this observable juncture, the therapist enters, and the first level of exploration and analysis of family process begins. The conceptions of both abstract family process and concrete family strategies begin at the level of how individuals behave and respond toward each other. This is the observable world of family process. Player parts begin as "acts" that, when assembled into a dynamic family interaction—a system gestalt—reveal a family's psychopolitical configuration.

In the Child-Centered Structural Dynamic Model, the individual is viewed as an independent entity and seen as intimately interdependent with the environment and the individuals with whom he or she relates. Personal autonomy is seen as influenced by social context. No psychopolitical part can be known or recognized in isolation. Rather, the intent (personal meaning) and behavioral efficacy of each part is determined according to the overall effect on and context of the family sequence. An individual's transactional part modifies and is changed by the family sequence, and by other family members playing their parts.

A family's sequence of interactions and overall psychopolitical configurations are analogous to a shifting self-system experience. Directions and destinations in family sequences often fluidly shift orientation and change, altering family members' options and available transactional parts in crucial, unanticipated ways. At the level of individual act and social action is the place where family therapist observation begins. In this model, an act in family process is viewed as a complex behavioral event, within which the individual is an active agent with degrees of freedom, selectivity, creativity, and innovation mediating between external influences and the overt behavior of individuals. The bridges between experience and behavior are "personal meanings," the images (critical, positive, and negative) that the individual holds and values of self, other, and the world around him or her. Once committed, the individual's social actions become part of the family's environment, where they provide a new input stimulus for all participants in the family social field. In a family interactional sequence, feedback processes take place at various levels of experience for all players in the course of each action.

Interactional sequences build into repetitive patterns, some effective and others troublesome. One of the more remarkable aspects of family process is the tendency for family members to play particular parts. Correspondingly, an individual's stereotypic behaviors—highly ritualized and predictable parts family members play—are drawn from two major interacting sources of experience within the family. One is "personal preferences" as influenced by the individual's internal biopsychosocial state. This is synonymous with the psychology of self, the signaling of private needs, impulses, meanings, and images. The other source is the individual's experience within the family from which the individual learns what part he or she is or is not allowed to play, is or is not required to play, is or is not permitted to explore.

Kantor's Four Player Model provides a rich, useful, and effective tool for analyzing single family interactional sequences. It also provides a method or mode of synthesis when applied to a larger number of sequences, highlighting "historical context" as well as "current family structural dynamics," serving as an important indicator of the individual's personal attitude toward the family. When the therapist and family grasp underlying repetitive patterns, what is available is an epitomized, compressed view of the family's transactional identity. It is similar to what Kantor (1980) calls the family's "unique signature."

All three transactional perspectives (actor, interactor, and catalyst) as well as the four player parts, influence the positive developmental integrity and outcome of children. For example, when parents intensely differ in their child-rearing ideologies (worldviews), the results can be traumatic for the child who is vulnerable and developmentally unprepared, an immature participant in the family. Couples can often contain, deny, or dismiss their child-rearing differences, virtually unaware of their deep ideological rifts, while they remain as a couple. However, once a child is born and begins to grow within the family, the couple's relationship bifurcates, by necessity branching into two overlapping and separate functions: marital and parental roles. At this point, as parents begin to care for the child, parental differences may be articulated, graphically exposed, surfacing either to be resolved by the couple or to divide the couple in deeply felt and unstated ways.

Blending Marital and Parental Parts

Differences on the family's meaning and model levels of family organization in terms of the child's development and parent-child relations that have lain dormant in the couple's marital dynamics around access and goal dimensions can now emerge in the form of strong, overt disagreements on the family's action and pattern levels of family organization. For example, if intimacy was a problem for the couple before, with spouses having limited or insufficient access to each other for one reason or another, problems with intimacy can intensify once a child is drawn into and becomes part of a new family triad or triangle.

Shifting between parental and marital roles, devising and blending the optimal balance between both, is a difficult and artful process that can bring out a family systems's strengths or its problems and limitations. Just as the family system can bring out the best and worst in its members, developmental transitions—stages in the family's life cycle when the family is required to make structural changes and to rise to the challenge of new system complexity—can serve as a litmus test of the family's viability. The onset of a new developmental transition often highlights a family system's structural depth and breadth, thematic richness, strategic complexity, and resourcefulness. Developmental turning points specifically evoke a family system's quality and experience in the areas of problem-solving and decision-making strategies. A developmental transition, with the challenges inherent in successive developmental stages both of the family and the child, places families at a crossroads where developmental crisis, a normal occurrence, can either initiate family growth-oriented changes, or problems and distress. The family can choose to work out new ways, or it can stagnate, mired in ritualized psychopolitics and repetitive, unproductive patterns.

Playing the double role of parent and spouse is a complex, precarious juggling act. Families today are under great stress, both structurally and sociologically. To say that families are under considerably more stress today is not to paint a bleak, but rather a realistic picture of shifting society and family life. The courage, tenacity, and ingenuity of the many families seen in therapy, some whose lives have formed the research fabric of this book, point to an encouraging outlook. It is not the increasing demands that are a family's undoing. Instead, as therapists have seen, and families have repeatedly emphasized, it is when these demands are paired with isolation, feelings of family loneliness, and a genuine unavailability of social support and resources, that families face real and greater risk. Families just reflect, and are responding to, a broader national existential angst, feeling alone in an indifferent, anonymous world, offering too few moments of real human connection and intimacy. In the midst of hectic daily schedules, the playful exploration of childhood may be lost for both parent and child alike. Some families, devoid of available resource networks and social support, have all they can do to meet the everyday demands of family activities, the things that need and must be accomplished if the family is to survive and function on the most practical daily levels.

Children, in the nature of the family's requisite provision of protection and safety, make large demands on the system's resources—its space, time, and energy; its nurturance, competency, and core meaning; and as catalysts, they often reveal underlying system instability as well as personal or parental vulnerabilities or insufficiencies in these areas. In effect, important lost moments in the family's "structural present," patterns of parent-child relations, become tomorrow's memories—the emergent critical identity images that adult children bring to their own marriages, families, and parent-child relationships.

There are many personal and family narratives of missed or squandered transactional opportunities, misguided relationship turning points, lost interpersonal moments, the many varied versions and revisions of the common theme and story of parents and children in search of each other. We need only to survey hours of clinical conversations to recognize that (as a matter of course, human economy, and averted emotional suffering), it makes good empirical, clinical, sociological, and intuitive sense to intervene early. Early intervention includes supporting the adaptive processes in families along the continuum from prevention to crisis. When we consider the unproductive, ineffectual, lost or unseen good intentions of parents and children alike, and the emotional cost to all parties involved, including community and society, then prevention and early intervention—before family crisis rises to full-scale instability—become not a mental health luxury, but an ethical imperative.

In the next two chapters, the other essential building blocks, those processes and concepts that complete the overview of the Child-Centered Structural Dynamic Model are described. The focus enlarges to a system level, an integrated view of child and family development, critical identity images, crisis, and change. The sphere of involvement and analysis grows increasingly broader and wider to encompass the influence of therapist and research on family practice as self-supervising systems. The aim of the Child-Centered Model is always growth-oriented, designing and facilitating positive developmental pathways, opportunities, and outcomes. The model applies this principle to all involved participants: the therapist, in terms of ways to improve efficacy through self-supervision; the research process as an ongoing, rich source of family analysis, an intimate feedback system allied to the therapy process; and the family as a capable self-reflecting system engaged in all phases of developmental change, whether primarily self-generated with the guidance of the practitioner, or clinically induced through the interventions of the therapist.

CHAPTER 3

Critical Identity Images

Family Typology, Development, Crisis, and Change

In Chapter 2, the individual was drawn into the foreground and given center stage immersed in a background of family influence. The family member, child and adult, was shown to be a potent social factor, interactor, and catalyst in family transactions. We saw how the individual learns parts or predictable roles, has an array of behavioral choices in the flow of an interaction, and makes crucial psychopolitically guided decisions that move interactions forward in intended and also unexpected directions. Sometimes individuals' roles, or parts, become hollow, rigid, and stereotypical in crisis and problematic situations. In viable development and family systems, however, individuals experience greater degrees of personal influence and freedom in their transactional parts and the behavioral roles available to them. In the preceding chapter, we focused on the shifting and oscillating influences of self consciousness and system consciousness, the dynamic interplay of personal and family worlds of experience. At this crossroads, the critical identity image work of Child-Centered Structural Dynamic Therapy and enrichment begins.

The overview of the trilevel model is still incomplete. All of the building blocks have not been assembled and examined, and the flexibility that they provide the practitioner has not been fully explored. In this chapter, we complete the picture. Keeping the personal world of the individual clearly in mind, we now move to a system-level view. Moving upward through the orbits of subsystem interaction, feedback, and information-exchange in the family, we look at the family as a whole. We consider next the family's preferred system type and best suited mode of growth and change. The integration of child and family development is shown. Principles of family crisis and intervention are illustrated.

Three System Types

The fifth interactive building block, or "area" in the map of family process, available to the therapist using the Child-Centered Structural Dynamic Model focuses on the Kantor system typology's three major types of family systems: open, closed, and random. All three forms represent ideal, descriptive system types; differences in their structural arrangements, strategic styles, and homeostatic ideals account for their preferred distance regulations around family access dimensions and goal dimensions described in Chapter 2. In the Child-Centered Model of family process, the idea of space, actual and symbolic (social and psychological), is central. Distance regulations are visual and psychological expressions, powerful statements about a family's relationships. The labels "open," "closed," and "random" are meant descriptively, not evaluatively. No greater emphasis in the direction of assumed family mental health is associated with any of the three system types. All three system types work, and are efficient. Each model has its own ideal as well as its counterproductive form. In essence, no one model is prone to problems more than any other. Just as we find open, closed, and random healthy family types, we also encounter open, closed, and random family systems in crisis and distress.

Despite the typical associations we bring to value-laden words such as open, closed, and random, along with our culture's tacitly held assumption that "being open," for example, is more functional or attractive, than "being closed," these terms, in the language of the Child-Centered Structural Dynamic Model, do not carry the same cultural or societal connotations. In the language of the model, the terms open, closed, and random are intended to be value-free and to convey cultural relativity and a sensitivity to family system differences. The terms provide the practitioner with a useful typology of how families evolve and develop preferred structures (forms), and how they regulate daily family process in relation to internal and external demands and exigencies of the environment. In some circumstances, a closed system is the most efficient and preferable type. Consider, for example, the family struggling to maintain its system integrity and protective, positive influence and guidance over its children growing up in dangerous neighborhoods: the chaotic, anonymous, or violent—often peer- or gang-dominated—urban and suburban landscapes populating many regions of our country.

In identifying the "homeostatic ideal" for regulating development and process in each system type, we recognize and are provided with valuable information about the method of facilitating change most compatible with each system type encountered anywhere along the trilevel model, from prevention, to early intervention, to crisis. When we apply the Kantor system typology to Child-Centered Structural Dynamic Therapy, we can group system types according to observable differences in three areas: the family's core purpose, homeostatic ideal, and system vocabulary in terms of child development, parent-child relationship styles, and presenting-child problems. The descriptive features of each system type, taken together, emphasize and make known to the practitioner the family's favored pattern of continuous growth, synthesis, and predictable style of handling and responding to internal as well as external events, information, stimuli, and disturbance. In this way, each system type defines different methods of access that the family practitioner can use to engage the family, as well as offers the practitioner an array of interventions that are "system-type specific."

When the family's preferred system type is identified and its preferred structure is clarified, the practitioner can use this knowledge to accommodate his or her therapeutic style and tempo while creating precise interventions that zero in on the most crucial family system structures in need of positive perturbation and change. The idea of accommodating the practitioner's style touches on the therapist's evolving professional identity and personal profile (the wise and well-informed use of self is described and illustrated in Chapters 4 and 7). We have gotten ahead of ourselves in explicating the building blocks and processes of the model. It is enough to state that the therapist, both as a trained professional and evolving self, who is an emergent expression of his or her own family and social experiences, combines the ongoing process of self-supervision and self-monitoring, crucial ingredients in the Child-Centered Model.

Returning to the broader, overall purpose and description of the Kantor system typology in the context of the Child-Centered Family Therapy Model, several important points should be made. In identifying key system features and, hence, a map of family structure, the typology provides the therapist with working knowledge, including specific strategies and alternate plans of family change.

Family Structural Arrangements

A family's system type focuses on its structural arrangements. As Kantor notes, "structural arrangements" refer to how the family chooses to maintain its boundaries. Different boundary styles, both within and across system borders, evoke and are equivalent to the development of different ways of regulating distance, organizing relationships, and influencing interactions. Each system type contains within it simultaneous attention to both change-resistant, or morphostatic strategies, and change-amplifying or morphogenetic strategies. These patterns have been variously referred to as "positive" and "negative." However, the use of these terms can be misleading, suggesting an evaluative meaning. These labels are purely descriptive. Both positive and negative feedback cycles of development in families are important. From a pragmatic or evaluative point of view, both feedback loops have their positive and negative counterparts and consequences. There are times when a family system should stabilize and self-correct to maintain and protect current structure, just as there are times when resisting change can result in stagnation. Similarly, morphogenetic patterns, or change-amplifying feedback processes can work against system viability and integrity as too much continuous variety and shifting process can threaten continuity and stability.

Taken together, morphostatic and morphogenetic processes create an evolving family system framework. Each system type, therefore, provides the therapist and the family, itself, with a different distance regulation plan, a visual expression of family relationships, and preferred style of interaction to examine and consider. In keeping with its underlying normative and normalizing theme of family process and development, the Child-Centered Model provides the family practitioner and the family with the crucial information of change-resistant patterns, and problematic features of the family system, with a recognition of positive change-oriented patterns, often less overt, yet available to the family.

When adapted to the context of Child-Centered Family Therapy and the developmental needs and imperatives of children, the Kantor system typology permits the therapist and family a two-way view and reciprocal blend of knowledge, a view from within combined with a view of the family across system borders, in transaction with the outside world. This reciprocal viewpoint continuously charts and evaluates the family's behavior in context, taking into account several different vantage points in a variety of important ways. One perspective involves the alternating focus and synthesis of change-resistant (morphostatic) and growth-oriented (morphogenetic) aspects in the family, or the system's internal structural arrangements as shown in each family type. When we think about structures within families, or their structural maps, we inevitably return to, and must concern ourselves with lines of demarcation, boundaries, and the organization of system parts into larger configurations. A family's structural arrangements comprise all the orbits of influence, interactions, and relationships known as "family dynamics." This is a view of the family from within, the equivalent of shining an intense spotlight to illuminate the family's internal structural dynamics.

Consider a common presenting problem and also the common family structure of an acting-out adolescent in which the mother is overinvolved and the father is underinvolved. When the therapist succeeds in separating mother and son, and strengthens and reestablishes a bond between husband and wife around the issues of parental authority, the therapist is creating a clearer generational alignment and boundary, or a "new family structure." This is the way I am using the term structural arrangements in family practice.

The Child-Centered Model's application of the Kantor system typology extends the view of family in still another direction. Viewing the family as embedded in the larger community and societal circumstances, taking a distinctively social view of family growth and development, the framework for understanding, assessing, and designing compatible intervention strategies for the three respective system types, also emphasizes the family's preferred and predictable transactional patterns with the outside world. Each of the three family types, open, closed, and random, displays different adaptive and maladaptive "distance regulation profiles" vis-à-vis the wider community. Each type of system, in turn, regulates information, events, and communications across its system borders in distinctively different ways.

For example, the closed family system type is associated with the longest prenegotiation or "warm-up" period in its decision to grant access to outsiders, including community and social institutions. On a purely descriptive level, the closed family system establishes protective family borders and carefully assesses the outside world and its influence. The closed family system's cognitive style is analytic and sometimes skeptical, needing concrete proof that the world outside or outsider in question (therapist) merits admission to the family's intimate world. We can think of the closed family system's cognitive and affective style as analogous to the psychological temperament and social orientation of the "slow-to-warm-up" child. Similarly, the closed family system establishes clear guidelines, or rules that check the flow of information across family boundaries. In this way, the closed family system's orientation to experience, novelty, and cultural information affects the child's map of experience and ultimately, the child's learning, problem-solving style, and concept of creativity.

Open and random family system types also have distinct orientations toward the outside world, community-family reciprocal access information exchange, and influence. The borders and boundaries that surround the open family system are more permeable and easier to access than those of the closed family system. Information flows more freely across family-community borders. The merit and validity of the information offered by the exterior culture is determined consensually. Children have a larger role in the family's decision to consider and include outsiders and outside experience. The open family system's "receptivity" to novelty can influence children's cognitive orientation and interpersonal approach to new experiences. The open family system nurtures children who are active explorers of the environment. The random family system is the most idiosyncratic, prizing individual expression. The random family system encourages divergent thinking and the child as a "free spirit" and active experimenter of ideas, thoughts, concepts, and feelings. Creative children flourish in random systems.

Here, again, at the family unit's wider community intersection, we recognize descriptively different orientations and preferred strategies developed by each of the three system types. We also find distinctively different stability-oriented and change-oriented patterns that distinguish open, closed, and random system types. Change-resistant and change-receptive or growth-oriented strategies at the family unit-community crossroads not only tell us a great deal about the family's perceived relationship and participation in the community, but also have implications for the therapist's selection of the best method of engagement and the most appropriate and conducive therapist style for awakening the family's imagination and commitment to the therapy process.

To this point, we have focused on a cross-sectional view of family development. We have looked at the coexistence and coalescence of patterns of stability and change in the family's developmental continuity. The three types of family systems discussed (open, closed, and random) have emphasized the therapist's integration and identification of the family system's stability-maintaining strategies, both problematic and productive, in conjunction with the family's potential for change, or the positive features of family process. However, the trilevel Child-Centered Structural Dynamic Model accommodates another perspective on the evolutionary potential of the family system.

As a family grows and matures, its structures are frequently challenged, torn down, tested, and built up again. Structural change is an inherent function of family development, part of its natural progression and change over time. This represents the second or longitudinal view of family process, development, and change, an abundant source of assessment information and insight into current pathways of family change. To thrive and grow, a family must permit change to occur. Without it, a family and its members stagnate. In favoring a fluid and flexible view of family structure over a fixed and static model, each family system type, like the concept of "personality types," never completely fulfills or approximates a pure type in practice.

Just as aspects of an individual's personality and self-concept are consistent across situations while other aspects vary and are context dependent, a family's preferred system type may vary across contexts. When we decipher a family's preferred structural arrangement, we inevitably discover a predominant rather than a pure type. We can expect, for example, that a family who is predominantly open in the majority of its overt transactional instances and patterns may also display, less frequently and in limited contexts, random or closed patterns as well. One task of the family practitioner is to establish the predominant system type that best exemplifies the family's behavior in the majority of circumstances and conditions. Identifying the family's preferred distance regulation model serves as a compass, guiding the clinician in fixing the location, pinpointing the best, most appropriate level and mode of intervention, and the therapist relationship position most suited to facilitate change. The Kantor system typology (referred to in this book as the three family system types) carries within it inherent diagnostic and assessment categories, important information for promoting child and family development.

Open, Closed, and Random Family Systems

Each system type identifies what we can think of as a distinct family style: open, closed, or random. While every family typically evolves a unique configuration of patterns, strategies, player parts, and rules and often blends aspects of each pure type, most families tend toward and prefer one or another of the three forms. All three forms are "good" and "workable." Each has its own successful, as well as unsuccessful variety, as will be shown in Chapters 4 through 8.

When we think of these system types and their relationship to one another, we can envision them on a continuum, which is purely descriptive rather than evaluative. As a visualized representation or schemata, I have found the continuum a useful organizing tool in training, supervision, and practice in several ways. Each system type itself moves along a continuum, from the expression of typical, successful forms of the model to stereotypic, unsuccessful, structurally "stuck" or problematic versions of the system type, when the family is experiencing either model instability or breakdown in a struggle over preferred system types. One of the primary uses of the continuum—the vantage point it gives us—is the relative position indicating where the family falls on the successful-unsuccessful scale in terms of its current expression of its chosen or preferred distance regulation system type. Is the family a successful or unsuccessful open type? Is the family a successful or unsuccessful closed type? Or, is the family a successful or unsuccessful random type?

Another application of the continuum considers all three system types together on three family dimensions. One effective decision aid useful in discerning a family's type grows out of thinking about and then assessing the family along three continua or tiers of transactions. Figure 3.1 represents my interpretation of Kantor's system typology and outlines a series of clinical decisions in the assessment process. As Figure 3.1 shows, the practitioner can formulate a correct, working identification of the family's type by placing the family along four parallel but interrelated transactions and then integrating this information into a dynamic statement about the family's predominant type. This series of continua highlights the decisive ways in which systems differ and illustrates how the system typologies' criteria (Kantor & Lehr, 1986) can be usefully applied, plotting where each falls on each of three dimensions of family interaction and development:

1. Core purpose.
2. Homeostatic ideal of stability and change.
3. System goals.

The first continuum marks how family types differ in the way they define their respective core purposes. The second continuum focuses on differences in homeostatic ideals. The third descriptive continuum relates how each system type defines its goals in each of the major family dimensions (access and target areas), framing them in different family "vocabularies" or transactional language. The fourth continuum, which is evaluative in contrast to the preceding descriptive series, situates and assesses the relative success or efficacy of the system type for the family in its present development.

Figure 3.1
Identifying the Family's Preferred System Type

1. CORE PURPOSE

Closed Family	Open Family	Random Family
Tradition (strong group unity)	Adaptation (consensual)	Exploration (strong sense of personal autonomy; individualistic)

2. HOMEOSTATIC IDEAL

Closed Family	Open Family	Random Family
Mainly constancy (constancy-maintaining family patterns)	Blends constancy and variety (constancy-maintaining and variety generating patterns)	Mainly variety (novelty-generating patterns)

3. ACCESS PATTERNS AND TRANSACTIONAL GOALS: EXPRESSING AFFECT, POWER, AND MEANING

Closed Family	Open Family	Random Family
Favors rationality Reserved affect Strong family loyalty Rules are fixed	Favors debate and dialogue Open emotional expression, family loyalty, and individual expression equally encouraged Rules are flexible (context dependent)	Favors individual autonomy Effusive affect Rules determined experimentally Individual loyalty

4. ASSESSING THE EFFECTIVENESS OF A FAMILY'S PREFERRED TYPE

Closed Open Random	Closed Open Random	Closed Open Random
Workable? Effective? Successful?	Problematic? Signs of conflict? Instability?	Crisis-level? System instability? Model breakdown in structural laws?

On the broadest level, Kantor's three family types can be recognized and distinguished as follows: The closed family system shows a stable structure. Fixed space, regular time, and steady energy are relied on as reference points for order and change. In the open family system, order and change are expected to result from the interactions of relatively stable, evolving family structures. Movable space, variable time, and flexible energy styles serve as this system's reference points. The random family system thrives on and prefers unstable or fluid structures. Dispersed space, irregular time, and fluctuating energy are experienced not as reference points for order and change in this system type; instead, they function as territorial guideposts to members' individuation, autonomy, and relationship styles.

When we are discovering a system's type, we are dealing in highly condensed and simplified descriptions that cannot approximate the complexity and real variety of the families we see in practice. This qualification duly noted, the closed family system can be characterized as valuing tradition, the open family system as keeping a watchful eye on the balancing of individual and family rights or the importance of consensus, and the random family system as extolling personal freedom, invention, and the individuality of its members. A family's preferences for one of these system types can be observed through the family's overt behavior, including the ways they manage feelings (the degree to which feelings are openly shared or kept private), meanings (the blend of individualistic and collectivistic ideals or individual and shared values and belief systems), and power (a sense of autonomy and competency, and the degree to which authority is fixed, relative, or idiosyncratic).

Closed family systems are convergent systems that build family life around a stable center or "hub." In this way, they are "centripetal" systems, directing or moving the family's activities, including information, experience, events, goals, and interactions, toward a common center. Open family systems, while still being centripetal, are more consensual. They move activities and events toward the center, but their center is less concentrated. The concentric cycles of their preferred patterns are looser, more dispersed, and flexible, spreading over more physical as well as metaphoric space. In an open system, family members' sense of meaning and belonging derives from the negotiation of different points of view: Feelings are openly shared rather than kept private and authority issues are flexibly negotiated. Parents and children occupy positions of relative power or influence at different times and in different contexts. Disagreement or opposition of children to parental directives or guidance, or of one spouse to the other, is openly voiced, even encouraged, as long as loyalty to the family's blend of individualistic and collective ideals is maintained.

The random family system falls more along the individualistic end of the continuum. It is a family of not one, but many simultaneous centers.

The random family system is more "centrifugal" than "centripetal," or more spread out, moving family members, activities, information, and events outward in diverse and idiosyncratic directions. For example, in random systems, individuals' meanings tend to be determined by personal ideals and high tolerance for individualistic goals. The subjugation of individual preferences or beliefs for the sake of the collective needs of the family is not preferred. Similarly, feelings among family members tend to be expressed passionately and more spontaneously. Authority relations between parents and children are determined more experimentally, with individual initiative usually prevailing over family role and status. Of all three types, the random family system tends to be most sensitive to and encouraging of individual potential.

In the closed family system, individual and collective meanings are expected to be similar or to converge. This family type tends to generate and perpetuate its values and beliefs through a reliance on rationality, tradition, and traditional symbols. Feelings, as we might expect, are kept more private and, when expressed, reflect a sense of earnestness and sincerity. Ideals and strong value-systems are integral to the centrally oriented closed family system type. Accordingly, strong loyalty to the family is expected and elicited, the implicit and expressed assumption being that individual needs are, under most circumstances, subordinate to the collective needs of the family. In a similar vein, authority relations are hierarchical, with parents in control and opposition from children discouraged.

Consider, for example, "play," the important work of childhood. All three system types, encourage, organize, and respond to play in distinctly different ways. The closed family system requires orderly sequence and rule-governed play, ideal for the grade school child who is cognitively ready for and attuned to the structure of games and the notion of fair play. The open family system permits greater latitude and interchange between parent-child roles. Play is the active world of exploration. The random family system, with its spontaneity and interpersonal experimentation, often creates the most playful atmosphere of all three family system types. Embedded within the broad sketch of system response to play is the variance of individual differences (e.g., a random child in a closed family system or a closed child in a random family system) combined with each family system type's response to the child's developmental stage and task. We can see, in the brief descriptions of all three system types, both the potential strengths and problems or trouble spots that may emerge for different family types as they negotiate different child developmental stages, an issue that will be explored in depth, through full case illustrations, throughout the book, particularly in Chapters 5, 6, and 8.

When we look at Figure 3.2, which shows milestone child development stages superimposed on the descriptive continuum of Kantor's family "system types," translating child development subtext, as well as the tasks and

Figure 3.2
Parent-Child Relations and Family System Types

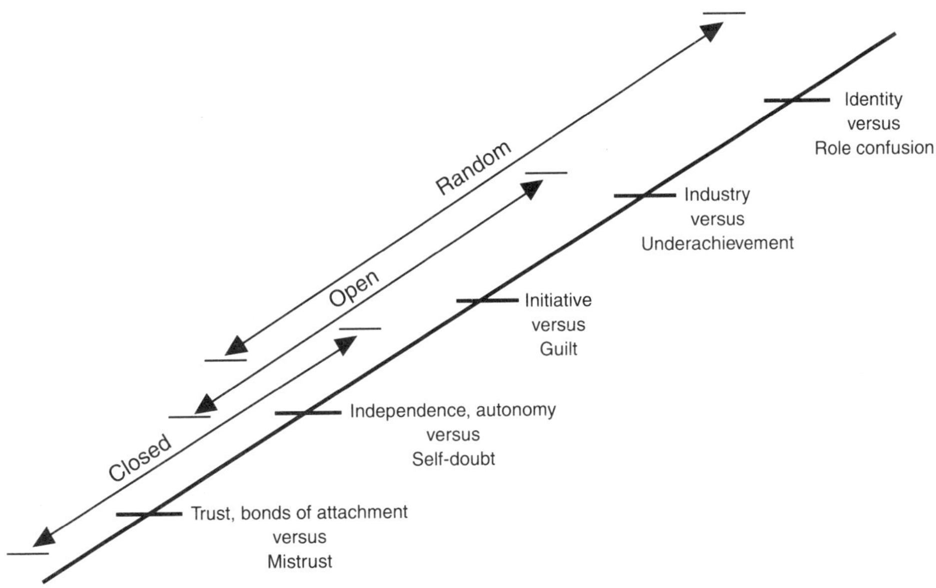

- The closed family system, with its strong family loyalty, nurtures intimacy and bonds of attachment.
- The open family system, with its consensus and dialogue, nurtures independence and autonomy.
- The random family system, with its emphasis on experimentation, nurtures the child's sense of personal industry and initiative.

developmental challenges children face as they mature and grow, we begin to see how each family type handles these tasks, developmental turning points, and the potential disruptions, as well as the differing potentials for growth that each family has to offer. Knowledge of the family system's preferred type serves the practitioner, child development specialist, family therapist, and family, as a primary entry point, a relative position of information and access that can guide and facilitate change. In this way, either family initiated or therapeutically induced change derives not from one view of the family, but from consideration of the family as it shows itself in three descriptive forms. Figures 3.1 and 3.2 present useful decision aids and assessment methods developed to guide the therapist in the Child-Centered Family Therapy Model.

In viewing these three family system types as simplifications of ideal types, the Child-Centered Structural Dynamic Model expects to find within predominant open, closed, and random family system types, other features as well. Families may cross over at times from open to closed, closed to open, closed to random, random to open and so forth, depending on contexts, themes, and the nature of developmental tasks. This is an important point, as will be shown in later chapters. After the therapist and family have determined its preferred distance regulation system type, the most opportune moments for real family change may come in those unexpected instances when families, knowing what they usually prefer to do, choose to do something differently. Returning, once again, to the series of continua, each of the first three continua reflects an important way in which "system types" differ and, therefore, can be identified. Now we can take a closer look at the three main features of how family types differ.

CORE PURPOSE

Each system type defines its core purpose differently. The closed family system, for example, seeks the most stability, relying strongly on the certainties of tradition. The open family system strives for adaptation, which it accomplishes through dialogue and consensus, a give-and-take of openly expressed points of view. The random family system, in contrast, prefers exploration with a reliance on intuition. The core purpose continuum, therefore, runs from tradition to adaptation to exploration as Figure 3.1 shows.

HOMEOSTATIC IDEAL

Each system type also has a different homeostatic ideal. The closed family system mainly relies on negative feedback or constancy-maintaining loops. Strict conformity to traditional norms is rewarded or approved, and typically, signs of deviance are reprimanded, punished, negatively sanctioned, or strongly discouraged. Difference is often interpreted as deviance in this system. The open family system, however, seeks to create a balance between negative and positive feedback patterns of change and stability. In this family system type, while deviance is seriously discouraged and punished, some latitude surrounds the family's discussion, interpretation, and response to deviant behavior. Divergence from the family's collective purpose is a topic open to discussion. Family rules around family infractions or the handling of emergent difference are, in contrast to the closed system, more context dependent.

Whereas the closed family system type tends, primarily, to maintain an absolutist stance around rule-governed behaviors, the open family system reflects a sense of adaptation around order and its expectations of family members. The open family system couches this message in words and actions that permit a more relativistic stance around family members' divergence from family rules or collective identity. Personal autonomy usually wins if the rights of the self digress from the rights and needs of the family and the family's core purpose is not threatened substantially. The open family system offers members greater degrees of freedom and evaluates challenges to the family in terms of the defining details and demands of situations. The open family system has clear rules and responses around the handling of signs of deviance or difference; it also rewards initiative and novelty.

The random family system relies more on positive feedback or variety-stimulating patterns. In the random family system, novelty is particularly encouraged. As shown in Figure 3.1, the "homeostatic ideal" continuum runs from the closed system on one end (preferring constancy-maintaining patterns and feedback loops) to the open family system, falling approximately in the middle (favoring a blend of constancy-maintaining and variety-stimulating feedback patterns) to the random family system, falling on the other end (preferring mainly novelty-generating feedback patterns).

There are several ways in which the knowledge of system type is beneficial and useful to the practitioner devoted to finding ways to stimulate and structure family change. Each system type, as Figures 3.1 and 3.2 depict, embodies a different style or self-corrective response to disturbance and preferred developmental ideal. To decipher where a family falls on these interrelated continua is to provide the therapist with a strong advantage—the ability to match treatment plans to family system type. In using this system knowledge to make clinical decisions and anticipate client-family responses to intervention methods, recognizing that some techniques and kinds of activities will be more effectively and favorably received in some families but not others, makes the therapy process more precise, elegant, and reflexively responsive, saving both time and emotional cost for both family and practitioner.

Families tend to intuitively sense and recognize their preferred type. For example, in the areas of prevention and early intervention, when families are gathered in family groups, when there are three families together and each represents one version of the three system types, families are quick to observe similarities and differences, as well as what they do and do not have in common with other families. When families have learned about themselves (by using the child-centered techniques presented in later chapters), focusing on the six family access and target dimensions, they have been shown to readily identify their system types. Families recognize exactly what each type is and they can differentiate themselves clearly. Sometimes, the initial route to family understanding, the family's knowledge about itself, comes by determining what the family is not.

Families can recognize themselves in other families. Often the most striking awarenesses come when a family meets another family unlike itself. When an open and a closed family meet, when a closed and random family meet, or when an open and random family meet, regardless of the combination of encountered types, families observe differences, which often emerge quite graphically through children's play. When children of different family types play together, family rules become apparent, even without naming them. If we want to know a family's system type, make its invisible rules visible, and identify its homeostatic ideals, we ask children of different families to play together and invite their parents to converse and participate. Parenting differences will become clear very soon, as parents voice their opinions, intervene, facilitate, guide, and interrupt the children's play. Examples of this rich incisive, qualitatively revealing type of family observation and assessment will be discussed extensively in Chapters 4 through 8 on the three-tier Child-Centered Model.

Similar Goals, Different Vocabularies

Although families of all three system types pursue the same goals or dimensions of affect, power, and meaning, each system type defines its goals within each of the major dimensions using different words. Each family develops its own emotional alphabet, so to speak, expressing its goals in ways that are compatible with its core purpose and homeostatic ideal. All three family system types sound, talk, converse, communicate, and interact differently. However, underneath their different vocabularies and voices—the different words they choose to attach to concepts—they are all in search of affect or nurturance, a sense of intimacy, power, or efficacy and competency, and meaning or validation and a sense of belonging. Yet, each family system type sees these dimensions, defines their goals, and governs activity within them in different ways, determined largely by the family's chosen core purpose and homeostatic ideals.

In the closed family system, meaning emerges and is maintained through reliance on reason, tradition, and traditional symbols. Closed family systems talk with reverence of time-honored ways. Their affect is earnest but not effusive, modulated, marked by control of public displays of emotion. A sense of strong loyalty guides this family system type. Power relations are organized vertically, rules are clear, and opposition is discouraged.

In the open family system, meaning flows from a commitment to the appreciation of different points of view and the process of dialogue, argument, and the healthy interchange of ideas. Authenticity is expected in a blend or balance between individual rights and the family's rights, personal experience, and family expectation. Affect is expressed openly and shared with less reserve. While challenges to the family system and members within it are voiced, even encouraged, loyalty to both the family's individualistic and collectivistic ideals is still expected and held as a central family value. Unlike the closed family system, power relations are lateral. Universal participation, and access to the world of family influence and interpersonal relations, is expected.

In the random family system, meaning and reasoning—the family's cognitive style—tends to be governed by personal inspiration and ideals. Paradox, ambiguity, creativity, symbolism, experimentation, and innovation prevail as the preferred modes of expression. Affect tends to be passionate, intense, and immediate. Power is also determined and expressed more experimentally than in the other system types. Personal influence and ability predominate as means or modes of moving the family system forward or inciting it to act. As Kantor (1980) describes, "The random style is extravagant in paying tribute to potentiality." If we were to associate a cognitive style with each of the system types, then we would attribute convergent thinking (the tendency toward order and closure) to the closed family system, consensus through debate and dialogue to the open family system, and divergent forms of thinking to the random family system. In Chapters 4 through 8, we will encounter, in greater detail, each of these three family system types, their purposes, problems, and ideals, as seen in full-length case studies drawn from the areas of prevention, early intervention, and clinical application.

Integrating Child and Family Development: A Multilevel View

The Child-Centered Structural Dynamic Model traces, maps, and integrates family, parent-child relations, and child development from two perspectives. Development means several things in this model. There is the child's and family's developmental course to consider in two interactive ways:

1. Cross-sectional development.
2. Longitudinal development.

One view involves a cross-section of development, including both the child's and the family's structural present. Another perspective is the history, cumulative knowledge and effect of the child's, as well as the family's, experiences within earlier developmental stages. Taking a family's and a child's history is akin to a combined genogram, extending beyond the interconnections among people and relationships in the family tree, to include consideration of the quality and connection among developmental stages. Developmental stages represent relational structures that are as crucial as the generational networks that give form to the family tree. The emphasis on prior stages is not necessarily for the purpose of gathering linear history, although when we are evaluating a child's symptoms, linear history is illuminating. When a symptomatic or presenting child is involved in family therapy, it is almost an ethical necessity to take a comprehensive developmental history of the child. This linear history is important for several reasons. The first relates to what we know about "critical time periods" in child development: An overlooked or missed opportunity to provide a child with critical educational or special services, especially early stimulation for diagnosed developmental delays, may have unfortunate lifelong effects on the individual's development. Early intervention, combined with enriched or "repaired" family environments, is associated with optimal outcomes, resulting in the fullest realization of a child's potential.

Another reason relates to what we know about the onset, course, and treatment of major childhood disorders. We know that some disorders can reflect disguised physical problems, and that untreated chronic low-grade illnesses can intensify a child's psychological and behavioral symptoms. Similarly, certain forms of conduct disorder and attention deficit disorder, inattentive and hyperactive-impulsive types, can be associated with or exacerbated by certain medical conditions. Therefore, it is imperative to ask important historical questions that address physical development, patterns of illness, and the child's general health. Information gained about the child's and family's negotiation of preceding developmental eras is used to shed light on the family's and child's "developmental present." Cross-sectional and longitudinal views of the family's development coalesce in the family's transactional here and now.

In the Child-Centered Structural Dynamic Model, cross-sectional development takes on two meanings. Cross-sectional development is considered from both the child's and family's perspective. Regardless of where we meet the family in its life cycle, when we fit Kantor's concept of family organization to child-centered practice, there are four simultaneous levels of family organization that need consideration; they have strong implications for child development (i.e., child development structures and the evolving structures of the parent-child relationship):

1. Meaning level.
2. Action level.
3. Pattern level.
4. Model level.

Two of these levels, pattern and action, are observable—identified in overt, everyday family behavior and transactions. The meaning and model levels are inferred from the observable aspects of family organization, or the family's and parent-child's action and pattern structures. Regardless of what the family presents, whether the family is engaged in preventive or intervention-based change, we take into account all four simultaneous levels. These four levels are usefully envisioned in a cutaway, three-dimensional, layered view of current family organization.

It may be helpful to illustrate this point further using a visual diagram. Think of family development, in this context, as layers of complexity built one on the other. Now think of child development and the parent-child relationship as embedded within each level; each level coincides with and corresponds to a "parent-child" and "child development" structure. To capture family development from this perspective requires taking a sectional view of all four levels simultaneously. What this reveals, what the therapist or family practitioner is looking for, is the quality, variety, or transactional richness of the family as we find it in the present.

Figure 3.3 depicts the integration of child development, parent-child structures, child-centered family therapy, and Kantor's (1980) concept and visual model of family organization. A corresponding child development and parent-child structure is identified and associated with each level of family organization, providing the clinician with a child-centered model of assessment and intervention.

Family Organization

The four levels of family organization are interrelated. Yet, each level is distinct from others. Knowledge of each level and all four levels together facilitates a comprehensive understanding and assessment of change. As Figure 3.3

Figure 3.3
Charting Child Development and Parent-Child Structures, Current Levels of Family Organization: A Developmental View

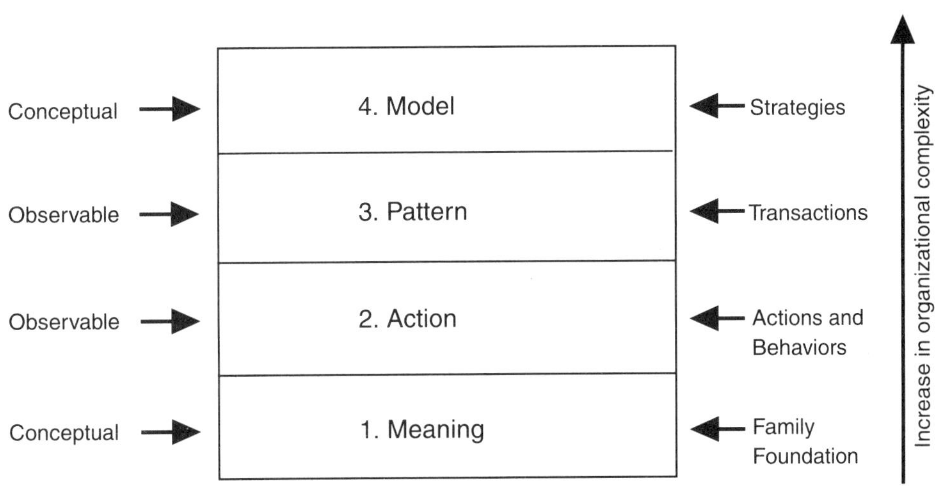

- Four simultaneous levels of family organization that reflect the family's current state of development.
- Child development and parent-child structures are present (available for assessment) at each level.
- All four levels are present (available for assessment) at each stage of the family life cycle.
- The foundation level of family development reflects the individual (images, myths, lores, personal histories).

illustrates, the four levels represent ascending levels of organizational complexity. In the three-dimensional view depicted, we see that the action and pattern levels fall in the center, and are framed or sandwiched between the meaning level, or the most fundamental level of family organization, and the model level, or the highest and most abstract level of family organization. We have used the words "meaning" and "model" before, as well as the terms "action" and "pattern," but what are their specific definitions in the context of family development and Child-Centered Family Therapy?

Starting at the base or bottom level of the diagram, we encounter the family's meaning structures. This level of organization represents the family's foundation, or the personal meanings each individual brings to and acquires in the system: members' histories, myths and lores, personal image hierarchies, symbols and icons. The form of family development, expressed at the organizational level of meaning structures, consists of the things the family routinely talks about, remembers, and selectively notices. At this level, we find corresponding and decisively important child development and parent-child relationship structures. Here, for example, we encounter a family's tacitly held, potent images and imagery of childhood, what it means to be a child, from both the vantage point of the developing child and the parent's childhood experience. At the meaning level, there are also images of what a child "is" and what a parent "is"; an image of how children grow and a visualization of an evolving parent-child relationship.

For example, one family may associate the notion of parent with the image of teacher; another family may associate the image of parent with the image of protector; still another family may equate parent with the image of disciplinarian. The family's meaning level of organization is akin to its stream of consciousness in graphic form. Here, we also find images about the concept of "child." One family may view children as delicate plants or flowers to nurture; another family may view children as wild spirits, creatures with unruly emotions and impulses to tame. These images, the sources of potential crisis or optimal development, are formed and are present in the minds of parents and family before children are born.

Moving upward to the next action level of organization, we find the family's preferred behavioral repertoire, or what comprises the practical and instrumental activities, the action structures of daily family life. Just as the family's meaning structures represent its developmental life at a symbolic (image) level, reflecting the content and perceptual priorities of its collective system's consciousness, a family's action structures correspond to the family's pragmatic developmental life, or its practical organization and efficiency around instrumental activities, including actions such as driving children to school, washing the dishes, feeding the cat, and doing the laundry.

As Figure 3.3 shows, the family develops corresponding parent-child and child development structures at the action level of organization. There are the routine instrumental acts and activities around which the parent-child relationship revolves—basic caregiving and supervisory functions that facilitate social and educational opportunities for the child. Parent-child interactions revolve around the basic tasks of child care (food, shelter, safety, physical health, and well-being). Parents and children are also joined around life-skill activities: the child's evolving competence in athletics, music, art, or academic achievement. There are also expressive tasks, actions, and activities that nurture both parent and child. For example, a father and daughter may read together, and a mother and son may go on naturewalks. Parent-child problems can arise in the three areas of caregiving, instrumental, and expressive tasks. Parent-child daily activities build into larger, repetitive patterns.

At the next level, as the figure shows, we discern a family's current developmental organization in the form of its transactional patterns. Family activities or actions at the preceding lower level now coalesce into broader and more complex patterns, or what we call the family's "strategic structures." A family's strategic structures represent its preferred strategies and sequences—its habituated behaviors on a transactional level, what the family typically does—including its activation of predictable psychopolitical configurations around recurrent themes.

Take, for example, the Stone family, Lila and Ted and their 6-year-old son, Keith, introduced in Chapter 2. The following excerpt from a session in therapy highlights a typically problematic transactional sequence around the key issue of food, a theme that has reverberating, multifaceted meaning for them.

In response to my question, "When does the problem get most out of hand?" the family unravels the following scenario:

When Keith comes home from school, he runs straight to the refrigerator. When Ted is home, he scolds Keith, chastising the child for "letting all the cold air out" as Keith searches inside the refrigerator for something good to eat. Keith ignores his father's orders and grows visibly rebellious and defiant. Ted responds by vigorously pulling Keith away from the refrigerator door, slamming it shut before Keith has chosen a snack. Next, a boxing match of fisticuffs ensues between father and son. The noise of the scuffle draws in Lila, who enters the kitchen, yelling furiously at Ted, "What are you doing to the child?" as she pulls them apart and comforts Keith. Ted skulks off, humiliated and silent. Mother and son are now alone, together. Lila surreptitiously hands Keith a cookie she has stashed away for him in direct opposition to Ted's nonindulgence, what Keith happily refers to as "Mommy's treasure trove."

This pattern is cycled in myriad ways appearing and reappearing in the Stone family. Food is a withheld and secretly offered sustenance in this family on many real and symbolic levels: it represents developmental, unmet needs and conflicts permeating each of the four family organizational levels and corresponding structures.

The top level of family organization, the family's model structures, represents the most complex level of family organization. This uppermost developmental level combines and integrates elements from the three lower levels to form the system's ideals and goals, that, taken together, define the family's guiding core purpose. For example, a family might say, "In our family, we really value honesty. We expect it of each other." Such a statement about the family expresses part of the family's core purpose. Also contained within a family's model structures are its preferred ways of, and ideals for, regulating conflicts. For example, the same family who described itself as "valuing honesty" might add, "We are blunt and direct with each other. We say what's on our mind. When we sense a problem, we talk about it right away. We like to think of ourselves as handling our problems directly. We get things right out in the open."

At this level of family organization, we also find models of parenting, the rules and belief systems that guide child development. Here, at the model level of organization, we find the family's concept of children and blueprints for the parent-child relationship. In fact, as the intimate conversations with families in therapy indicate, each child development task and stage evokes its own model structure. For example, there is a different model structure for "trust," "autonomy," "industry," and "initiative." Whereas meaning structures on parent-child developmental levels evoke graphic, emotionally charged imagery, model structures evoke ideal concepts and plans. At the model level of family organization, we find a family's concept of the good child and good parent, optimal child development, and ideals of the parent-child relationship.

Developmental Assessment

In Figure 3.3, we are shown a sectional (or lateral) inside view of system development that highlights the dynamics of parent-child relationships and child-centered problems from the level of model or ideal to the level of action or overt behavior. The notion that arises as we consider this diagram is that the view of system development in the Child-Centered Model is decidedly structural. What the therapist or family practitioner, using the model, typically does is to continuously chart, map, identify, remap, trace, and revise structures—the interplay of present, past, and emergent structures. Families are seen as evolving systems, and the therapist keeps his or her eye always on the family's developmental structural present and the child's transactional place or role in it. The past is considered mainly in terms of its developmental imprint on the family's current transactional style (structural arrangements), its influence on what is happening now in the family. The concept of development used in the Child-Centered Structural Dynamic Model builds on the assessment of complexity in systems. The process of assessing family development is analogous to learning about the experiential history and current life stage of a tree by studying the tree's external form, its height, breadth, and sturdiness, as well as by examining a cross-sectional, or internal, view of its concentric rings, its age from the center emanating outward.

When families of children are engaged in prevention or intervention, they bring this multilevel developmental structural complexity to the process of change. In addition to the age and developmental status of the presenting child, this family level view of development must be considered. *All child developmental stages intersect this developmental complexity, or here and now, of the family.* We look at families in three ways and combine this information into a multilevel perspective on the family, an assessment that captures both the contemporaneity and continuity of family and child development over time. When we interact with the family, what we see in family transactions reflects the family's current developmental present expressed in emergent, observable structures, its multilevel developmental complexity.

We must also consider the more traditional view of family development, specifically the family life cycle, and the task of pinpointing a family's location on this evolving life-stage system. Given the varied forms of family and the evolving nature of family systems in our society, the life-stage progression is not as straightforward as it used to be. Couples who have had former marriages may renegotiate earlier stages in family development when they remarry, while they are simultaneously confronting a broader range of child development stages. For example, the couple that remarries, blending their respective families, decides to have a baby. In this situation, we have two family developments almost superimposed, or integrated, one upon the other. Or, even more accurately, we are looking at three family systems: one headed by the wife, the children she has brought to the marriage, and that family's developmental history and character; one headed by the husband, involving his children, and that family's life history and unique developmental structures; and the current family, or blending of families, that the couple is trying to create.

Accordingly, the family's progression through life stages can take many varied forms, represent many useful and different paths, and reflect the shifting exits and entrances of different family members. Couples do not always meet when they are young and grow old together; children do not always live in a family with two parents. Children often have stepparents with whom they must also negotiate important and crucial relationships.

If a family is to grow and change, as it must to develop and thrive, then it will need to attend to important cultural tasks, including the care and protection of children. The family must do certain things, negotiate and master specific stages that unfold to deepen and enrich a family's developmental present, or, in other circumstances, jeopardize it. Figure 3.4 represents the

Figure 3.4
Current and Longitudinal Development: An Integral View

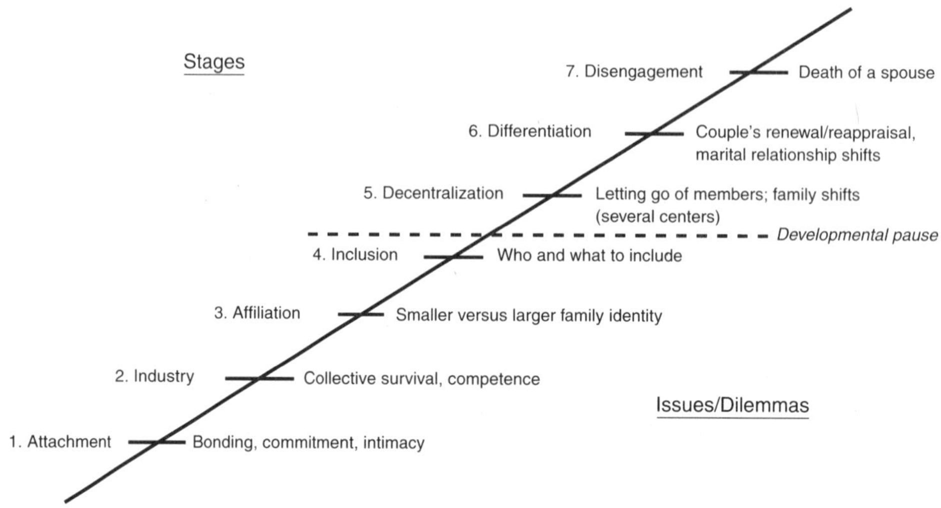

- The line or continuum depicts progression of family development over time (the family life cycle).
- Current family development, shown in Figure 3.3, is also occurring and is available for assessment.

integration of the concept of "family passages," blueprints for success and survival (Andreozzi, 1980, 1988), research on child and family development (Andreozzi, 1978, 1979d), and Kantor's concept of family development and organization. As Figure 3.4 shows, families face a series of challenges, or cultural prescriptions. These challenges, broadly speaking, reflect important and strategically timed changes in boundaries—an expansion and contraction of the system from within—that provoke and engender new structural arrangements.

The family begins with the couple. In our changing society, couples sometimes bring "ready-made families," children from previous marriages, to the process of creating the new family system. Regardless of whether each partner brings children, renegotiating these stages anew in the creation of the present family system, or whether the couple starts out without children, incorporating them later into the family system, all families traverse developmental milestones. Families must do certain things to ensure that the family system continues. With the shifting trends in current society, family development or the family life cycle, in addition to expressing chronologically unfolding stages, reflects the four levels of family organization. In this light, family development is less time-driven and more task- and dilemma-oriented.

A couple's meanings and preferred models are largely undeveloped and unshared when they start out. A couple's meanings, the concepts and images of self and family, are implicit guides that they carry around inside them. A couple's preferred models for child and family development are tentative and relatively rudimentary at first, except in transactional blueprints they call on for future reference. A couple's meanings and preferred models serve as the filters and guidelines, a map, so to speak, for what takes place in the family, as a changing and evolving system when the couple takes on life's tasks together. As Figure 3.4 illustrates, these successive tasks include bonding/attachment, industry, affiliation, inclusion, decentralization, differentiation, and disengagement. Figure 3.4 represents an expansion and elaboration of Figure 3.3 in which family developmental life tasks or dilemmas are superimposed, indeed integrated, into the picture of multilayer, co-occurring family development.

A decisively absent link, highlighting a crucial gap in family therapy practice, theory-building, and testing (which was described in Chapter 1), involves the need for a comprehensive, research-derived Child-Centered Model. The invisibility of children and the need for reappraisal of their minimal role and participation in family practice, as well as the development of practical methods for incorporating children in the family therapy process, reflect a serious collective concern of child-oriented practitioners. Consider the following examples of the status of children in family therapy: A preliminary review and content analysis of a sample of workshops and panel discussions devoted to children at national family therapy conferences (e.g., the 1991, 1993, 1994, and 1995 National Conferences of the American Association for Marriage and Family Therapy) highlights the marginal attention that children's issues have received. The percentage of presentations focusing on children are far less frequent and disproportionately underrepresented compared with adult-oriented issues. This is not to say that adult issues, in relation to family therapy practice and development, are not important, but rather asks the question, "Where are the children in family therapy process and theory-building?" An illustration of the reawakening recognition of the crucial role and need for family practitioners involved in child development is seen in the current call for involvement of family therapists as collaborators with National Head Start that appeared in the October 1994 issue of the American Association for Marriage and Family Therapy's *Family Therapy News* (Staton, 1994).

As an evolving practice, science, and professional community, the field of family therapy stands at a critical social and historical juncture. Family therapists, by nature and definition, have always found themselves embroiled in the currents of social change. As a community, we continue to respond sensitively and responsibly to shifting societal trends and priorities. We now need to turn a serious eye to the rights and needs of children, reclaiming the role of child development in family therapy.

From its pioneering days, the family therapy profession has taken on social problems and stood at the forefront of advocacy and change. The work of bringing about positive change, the act of intervening in the lives and transactions of troubled families, puts family therapists in the thick of things, making therapists "social agents" and "activists" on the cutting edge of broader social trends and changing values. Our society, in the form of cultural tasks, norms, and customs, flows through and is filtered by the family. The family, in turn, influences the course of society through the quality of its socialization, including how well the family teaches, nurtures, and guides its children. Family therapists, as architects of change and facilitators of human development, often mirror society back to distressed families with feedback that suggests positive, corrective measures are urgently in order.

Family therapists, as wise and well-informed observers and arbiters of family process, embody society and, almost of necessity, by the sheer will and act of what therapy is and does, forecast the family's progress and relay the changing experiences of families back to society. Children and child development are vital predictors of a family's as well as society's future. Where are the children in family therapy? What technical and conceptual bridges between child and family development, in the form of cohesive models, are available to the practitioner? The Child-Centered Structural Dynamic Model provides a comprehensive developmentally focused framework and method for incorporating children in family therapy.

The Child-Centered Model synthesizes multilevel perspectives of child and family development, and provides the practitioner with flexible and adaptive methods and techniques of access, assessment, and change facilitation that fit and simultaneously address the needs of families who seek help for problems (crisis and early intervention) as well as the enhancement of effective, healthy family process (prevention and enrichment). The Child-Centered Structural Dynamic Model fills this need, offering the practitioner an array of conceptual and practical tools that can be shaped and molded to fit individual families, different system types, and the professional orientation and context (treatment setting) of the practitioner. The model is designed to give the therapist a broad range of choices and a fluid, dynamic method of application.

Children in Family Therapy

Integrating child and family development is an exciting and involved task. The task is challenging and stimulating. There is much to absorb and also to distract the practitioner. In a family of five, for example, consisting of two parents and three children, there can be a range of developmental stages—from infancy to adolescence—clamoring for attention. A therapy hour of families with children is often noisy and unpredictable in energetic ways. The practitioner is faced with differing worlds and the challenge of communicating in a blend of child-oriented and adult-compatible ways. The therapist needs to find a common "language" that meets each member's developmental capabilities and readiness. Often the language the therapist uses to speak to the family must, by the nature of childhood cognition and socioemotional development, extend to include far more than words. Therapists' "talk" with children combines words, actions, and the symbolic activities of play.

A child's play sequence expresses the child's nonverbal story. *Behavior is the child's message, and actions are the child's preferred medium.* What a child *cannot, will not,* or *does not* yet *know how to say,* the child will *say* through his or her *behavior.* Symptomatic behaviors, as well as the more benign features of a child's play, are a child's "metaphorical speech," or their telegraphic, condensed, and compelling "messages" to therapist, family, and others in the world around them. What a child's play reveals—what the child's stories, symbolic play, emotional vocabulary, and family behavior can accurately tell us—is contingent on their age- and stage-specific developmental maturity.

A practitioner working with 2-, 5-, 9-, and 16-year-old children in the same family can and should expect vastly different things from each child. The therapist, therefore, not only has to be well versed in child development theory, but must also track and simultaneously design "communication methods" that meet, bridge, involve, and positively change all participants. This is certainly a formidable but enriching challenge posed to the therapist's creative powers and clinical skill, involving the integration of diverse family member paths of knowing, learning, emotional expression, and understanding.

In addition to thinking about the therapist's cognitive, conceptual, clinical, and interpersonal focus in the practice of therapy with families of children, there is the "therapist as self" to consider also. What does working with families of children require and elicit from the practitioner? First, a comprehensive, detailed knowledge of child development is essential. As the practitioner is being asked in any given hour to be a master juggler of interactional detail, much is demanded of the therapist's powers of observation and cognitive synthesis. Also, there is the entire question and issue of the practitioner's personal comfort level and experience with the child's world and play. Going a step further, even if the therapist is relatively at home with being playful, and with the riskiness and vulnerability that play can bring out, there is the added consideration that play is not a unidimensional, monolithic activity. Each family type—open, closed, and random—responds to "play-guided" interventions quite differently.

My emphasis on the role of therapy involving families, when children are engaged as full participants and vital sources of information and emotional understanding, is intended to open the door to practice with children and invite the practitioner in. As Figures 3.4 and 3.5 illustrate, the Child-Centered Structural Dynamic Model offers the practitioner quick access to

Figure 3.5
Integrating Child and Family Development

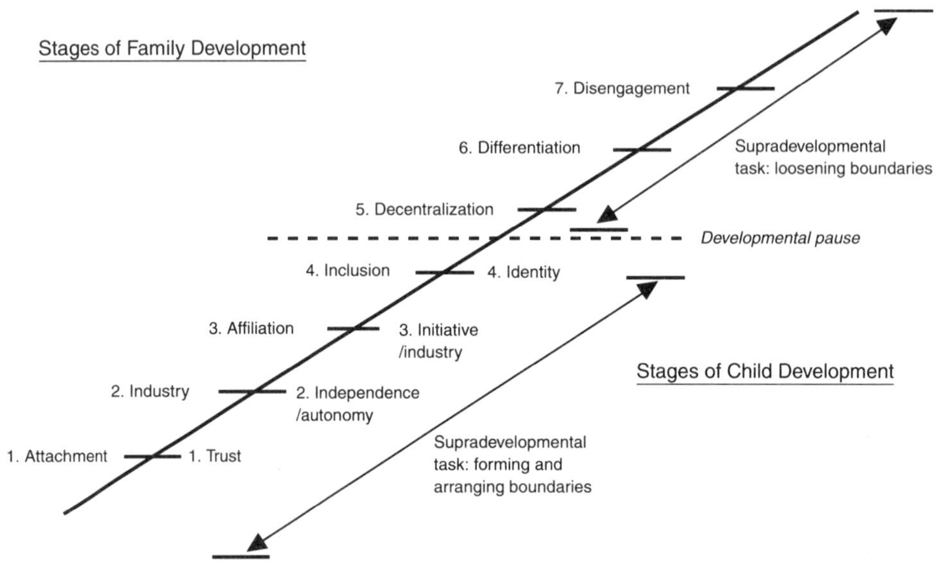

- The line or continuum depicts progression of child and family development over time.

integrated child and family development. Figures 3.4 and 3.5, when combined with the developmental descriptions in Table 1.1, provide the practitioner with ready and immediate access and a means to assess and arrive at a multilevel view of development.

Pinpointing where a family is now—the current dilemmas, tasks, problems, and developmental challenges it faces, including its enabling and problematic structures—is the first, essential step toward staging family change. We need to know what a family is and where it now stands before considering therapy options or strategies for moving a family forward and back on its chosen course.

Returning to Figure 3.4, we can envision this diagram as representing the first of a sequence of steps in our child-centered family observation and assessment. Figure 3.4 depicts an integral view of family development which considers current family organization in relation to family development over time. In Figure 3.4, we can also superimpose the "cutaway," layered view and perspective on contemporaneous system development shown in Figure 3.3 which integrates the Child-Centered Model's concepts of child development structures and parent-child structures with Kantor's theory of family organization, unique to the Structural Dynamic Model. The sectional view of family development depicted in Figure 3.3 forecasts to the practitioner a developmentally focused process perspective on family change. This figure communicates that child and family development are equivalent to the quality and structural complexity or richness of family organization. Family organization is conceptualized and studied as a layering effect. Figure 3.3 also indicates that, while the model and meaning levels or structures are mediated through the observable world of family interaction, the action and pattern levels or structures are visible in family transactions. At each of the four levels of family organization, we find corresponding child development and parent-child structures that influence family process and provide a rich source of assessment information for family change.

When a family comes to therapy, we see its problems and competencies in its actions and patterns of actions. This is our first view inside the family. Keeping this knowledge of the family's preferred transactional sequences and favored psychopolitical configurations in mind, the practitioner will later add knowledge of the family's model structures (preferred system type) and meaning structures (the sources of elements in critical identity conflicts) as this knowledge unfolds in conversation and interaction with the family. For the therapist, Step 1 is gaining knowledge of all four levels of family organization, action, pattern, meaning, and model. This will provide the practitioner with a complete picture of the organizational quality of the family's current developmental stage.

A full grasp and appraisal of developmental continuity involves a few important additional steps. There is the layered view that represents current development. However, there is also development over time, and fixing the family's place on the life-cycle. This step involves assessing the family's experiential history, including how it dealt with earlier stages. At each progressive stage, which contains its specific system task, cultural prescriptions for the young, and dilemmas to resolve, we find this cross-sectional view of organization. For example, as the child grows and develops, each ascending child development stage and task intersects the family life cycle, longitudinal development, and current family organization. Each level of family organization—meaning, model, action, and pattern—evokes and has embedded within it corresponding child development structures and parent-child relationship structures. The child's growth and development at any point on the life-cycle continuum represents a crossroads between child and family development reflected in multilevel, cross-sectional family organization. The task for the therapist is to identify:

- The current family development stage.
- The child development stage and task or competency primarily in conflict or at risk.
- The family's prior experience and degree of success with the developmental stage in question.
- The viability of parent-child relationship structures and child development structures expressed and observed in all four levels of current family organization.

In fact, we can think of this current view of family development as undergoing transformations at each successive stage. We can also envision this layered view of current family organization as progressing along and intersecting the continuum of family development. Think of the multilayered cross-section of family organizational development as a conceptual and practical tool a therapist can use for rapid calculation and cross-reference: plotting of child and family development to pinpoint the convergence of stages, problems, and competencies.

Family Development: A Timetable of Changes

Identifying the family's developmental stage and qualifying its prior experiences is Step 2. As Figure 3.5 shows, a family negotiates a series of progressive tasks essential for system development and continuity. Each successive dilemma that a family handles and resolves enriches and deepens the family system, its structures and process. These transformations set its developmental course and destination in motion. Family stages encompass child development, integrating children into the family's broader patterns, roles, preferred strategies, and style. Similarly, a child's developmental stage and experience with a particular developmental task exert reciprocal influence on the family. Child and family development interact to create and move the family system forward through time.

In this second step, the therapist identifies the current dilemma that the family is trying to negotiate and resolve, and gathers information, or a general impression of the quality of earlier developmental tasks, specifically how successfully prior tasks and dilemmas were handled. Just as individuals can move forward chronologically, carrying with them earlier partially unresolved personal developmental tasks, family systems can and often do progress in time, carrying within them a residue of partially unmet prior tasks. For example, a family that faces the challenges of industry may bring to the tasks of this stage strands of unfinished dynamics, or crisis, around the first system stage of attachment. Earlier system stages are relevant in terms of the light they shed on current system development and family organization.

Figure 3.5 depicts a series of continuous stages along the family life cycle timeline shown as an ascending arc, symbolizing the idea of progression or growth. Figure 3.5 charts and interweaves unfolding child and family development and represents the integration of child development theory, the concept of family passages (Andreozzi, 1980, 1988) and Kantor's concept of family development. Each system stage contains an essential task and primary dilemma for family and child. The choices of the family system and its individual members—the unwitting and tacit decisions often expressed in predictable behaviors and transactions, although rarely overtly discussed in the conversational life of the family (except in the context of therapy and enrichment)—affect the system in profound and practical ways.

Bonding and Attachment

Similar to the human infant's striving to bond with parents and work out the details of intimacy, the first stage a couple or blended family faces is Attachment. The tasks of Attachment evoke issues surrounding bonding and commitment, trust, loyalty and, for the couple, sexual intimacy. The central dilemma revolves around the successful organization of interpersonal dynamics and family structural arrangements concerning intimate contact. The couple and family experimentally work out the interplay of patterns that balance union with individuation and autonomy. For example, a spouse who repeatedly has affairs can reflect the couple's difficulties with the unresolved, anxiety-provoking side of attachment. Attachment, as the initial step in system development, expresses the central metaphor or guiding principle of Structural Dynamic Therapy, namely, distance regulation. In working out patterns of intimate contact—compatible rhythms of joining and separating—a couple and the family are working out the interpersonal and personal blueprints that form the foundation of human interaction, and the quest for emotional and physical closeness, touch, and community.

On the one hand, the couple and family seek union and collective identity: an intimate, emotionally nurturant environment. On the other hand, the couple and family seek to preserve and protect personal autonomy. The desire and expectation, or the positive pole of this dilemma, is connection and belonging, a sense of being known and knowing others intimately. The negative pole, or fear underlying this dilemma, involves the perceived risk and threat of engulfment, loss of selfhood, and loss of personal freedom and autonomy. The dilemma, as Kantor aptly describes, is one of "invasion versus loneliness," expressing the most fundamental risk and venture we all face in our life journeys. This first dilemma, embodying the precipitating initial step in family formation, sets the stage and lays the crucial psychological and interpersonal groundwork for future system development. Again, we see here one of many variations on the family theme of regulating "sameness and difference," a supra- or metalevel task resonating, to some extent, throughout all developmental stages.

As a couple bonds, attaches, and commits, there is the simultaneous task of detaching from past lovers, or loosening in intensity and transforming the emotional ties of prior relationships, including friends, or exspouses, and extended or family-of-origin relationships. This can be a fluid, overtly rocky, or quietly tumultuous time for the couple or blended families where the gaze, focus, and concentration temporarily turn toward the "new family" and away from or at an angle to outside relationships. This is a time when centers shift and the couple, at least for some stabilizing period, needs to focus mainly on each other and the new uncharted family map and territory ahead of them. This involves the important and plain work of boundary negotiation where the couple or blended family draw and test their margins.

Consider Rachel Clarke and Don Harris, and Rachel's two teenage sons, Ryan and Alan. The following is an excerpt from therapy:

Rachel Clarke is 40 years old and has never been married. She loves books, pantomime, and Native American dancing. She has a master's degree in child development and works with handicapped children. She is quiet, warm, sympathetic, and appealing. There is a childlike quality about her.

Her fiance, Don Harris, is 64 years old. He is divorced and the father of eight grown children. A blend of Native American and African-American culture, he sees time and life differently. He has rediscovered his heritage, draws great pride from it, and works managing security for the Indian reservation. He has deeply disciplined emotions, believes strongly in inner strength, and passionately demands the truth from those closest to him. Yet he seemed more a bystander, sometimes a wary observer, a rather reluctant participator in life. Each calls the other a paradox too difficult and enigmatic to figure out. Underneath it all, however, Rachel and Don are more alike than they are different. Problems with Rachel's two teenage sons, Ryan and Alan, are the reasons that brought the family to therapy.

Rachel and Don have an on-again, off-again relationship. For them, although they have not actually said this aloud, "One relationship is too many and a thousand relationships are not enough." They have been living together for three years, struggling with what they call their "own private demons" around intimacy and commitment. Each yearns for yet fears it at the same time, going through cycles of passionate fusion followed by cycles of bickering, criticism, and bitter despair. They realize that they are "stuck" in trouble spots coming from their own personal relationship histories, not all a part of what is going on with them in the here and now. It seems once every 6 months, like clockwork, either Don abandons Rachel in an hour of need or Rachel, in a ritual to declare her emotional independence, sends Don, bag and baggage, packing. This is part, but not all, of this couple's developmental crisis.

On the face of it, there is also the developmental crisis for which they initially came for help. At their wit's end, they did not know what to do with Rachel's sons. Neither knew how to handle Ryan, on the brink of adolescence, and Alan, in full hormonal bloom. Don sees Rachel as too permissive; Rachel views Don as too stern and authoritarian. She is unclear about either the limits or entitlements of boundaries, and unsure about how to assert herself with each "man-child" living in her house—boys growing in leaps and bounds who now tower over her in height and strength. Rachel finds herself alternating between angry criticisms of herself and the boys. Not knowing quite where he fits in, or what role he should play, Don is trying to figure out his place in this family. The incendiary rocket that set this family off in search of frantic answers is Alan's sexual behavior and sexual confusion that came together in a troubling incident the boy had experienced at work after school. For Rachel, her son's troubles have a much deeper, reverberating meaning that has unnerved her—a meaning that goes far beyond the borders of his experience and enters her own.

This late Friday afternoon the family can be seen through the waiting room window as they make their way up the path, drawing a wide arc around the low sprawling branches of the Chinese red maple tree that stands as a landmark outside the clinic. As the family negotiates the first turn, Don gives Rachel what looks like a hurried and embarrassed kiss; then they drift apart. Ryan and Alan lead the way. Rachel follows with Don, now lagging several feet behind them. Rachel seems childlike tonight, girlish and vulnerable, somewhere between the ages of 10 and 12.

Her walk, a characteristic one, is even more slow and exaggerated tonight. Shoulders hunched, eyes cast downward, she gives the impression she will not allow herself to see anything of life above ground level. She looks as if she does not want to make eye contact with the world or with anyone in it. Looking into someone's eyes, she has explained, makes her feel "naked" and "transparent," as if she could almost be "seen clear through," and there are no protective borders—lines of differentiation—between herself and others.

Once inside the session, as has become her habit, she immediately abandons her earlier body language. She appears now alive and strong and talks openly about the sexual abuse, the incest and violence she experienced in her childhood family. This is a subject that both Don and her sons know only too well, a story that has been hashed and rehashed repeatedly inside the family. Tonight however, it is being talked about differently. Rachel and Don sit opposite each other, their chairs strategically positioned at angles, half facing each other. Almost simultaneously they both move their chairs so that they now are looking directly at each other. The boys have chosen to sit on the couch in the middle, about half way between Rachel and Don. The look on Rachel's face, the stance she takes (if it was given words) is "Don't trifle with me. Don't mess with me now." For a moment, Don looks as though he wants to reach out to her, to touch her hand or hug her, showing her some kind of affection, but he stops. Instead, digging his heels in, he says "I never lied to you. I never made any promises. You know how I am. You know that my people, the tribe, come first and mean everything to me."

Alan and Ryan, sitting in the center of this, look on. Amid their cool MTV impressions and macho man stances, there are expressions of bewilderment on each of their faces that seem to say, to varying degrees, "Please, find me . . ."

Although this family may have appeared on the surface to be farther along on the family life-cycle progression, handling the practical daily tasks of industry, the couple, in fact, was still grappling with attachment dilemmas. The couple had evolved a stormy, yet predictable style of union, bordering on fusion, punctuated by sharp and abrupt separations when the risk, fear, and intensity of commitment and attachment came too close to home. They evolved patterns of avoidance or disharmony, strategically mismatched or ill-timed approaches or moves toward each other that thwarted, instead of facilitated, emotional access.

The couple had tacitly agreed to block each other, not to be "ready" or "available" when their partner initiated access and intimacy. This tacit but painful agreement kept the couple on familiar but unhappy and despairing ground, and kept the direct confrontation of intimacy and attachment safely at bay. While this primary distance regulation model—the psychological equivalent of "star-crossed" lovers—worked to forestall the couple's attachment dilemma, keeping them on ironic, unsatisfying, interpersonally familiar ground, it created a strong sense of insecurity and bewilderment for the children, Ryan, aged 14, and especially Alan, aged 17. Alan eventually began to act-out sexually the unfinished or, more exactly, the "missing and unarticulated pieces" in the family's troubling and "unclaimed" developmental script.

Don and Rachel brought to the relationship their separate reasons for ambivalence over commitment and trust of another human being. On one level, the family, voiced through the words and expectations of Rachel, was in search of a "home." On deeper levels, because of the more potent force of potential disappointment, they tacitly chose not to venture into attachment. For them, not to have what they fervently sought, to worry and distract themselves over the "terrible problems" they were having that "kept them apart" was more palatable than to risk finding authentic commitment and intimacy. They could not allow themselves to luxuriate in the experience of comfort and intimacy, as they were so certain that the bond would be broken and lost. All four family members contributed to the developmental impasse. Each offered a crucial piece—playing a dynamic structural part—in the overall puzzle of unmet needs and expectations. Their crisis, I will illustrate in later chapters, reflects the coalescing of individual critical identity images into a collective struggle that structurally expresses the family's developmental conflict.

THE SUPRADEVELOPMENTAL TASK OF ORGANIZING AND ARRANGING BOUNDARIES

The next three successive developmental tasks the family faces, Industry, Affiliation, and Inclusion, express the family's overriding supratask of structuring and arranging boundaries. Boundaries signal structure and structure is the hallmark of system development and change. In the first four stages of development, the family faces tasks specific to each new stage but also continues throughout all four stages to refine, adjust, mold, and reshape its boundaries. The primary emphasis in this suprastage is on inclusion and expansion in terms of the depth and breadth of the family's structural, emotional, and pattern life. In this vigorous time of growth and exploration, the family is evolving the substance of its rule-governed behaviors and expressing the quality of its own brand of family process, reflecting its own variations on and interpretations of the fundamental tasks common to the continuity and development of all family systems.

What the family does, essentially, is to imbue these stages with the family's unique identity and character, bringing to common tasks the stamp of individuality. Over time, as the family reaches the fourth stage, Inclusion, the family has had enough practice being itself. The family has persisted long enough over time now to know itself and to be generally known to others. This knowledge is often more tacitly felt than verbalized or consciously discussed. As research has shown, through an intensive study (Andreozzi, 1978, 1979d, 1979e, 1985a) of families negotiating and relating their experiences at each stage, families do have access to this knowledge. Families know who they are and how they work, and can effectively organize and use this knowledge when they are provided with technique-guided activities designed to build and support unfolding system awareness.

Child development, nested within the wider family system, is influenced by and influences family development. The timing, content, and process surrounding the appearance of successive child developmental stages is crucial to consider. Each child development stage and task from trust to autonomy and independence to initiative and industry, along with the parent-child process it generates, can evoke one of two responses: Either child development content and process mesh or they conflict and are at cross-purposes with family development, raising the ghosts of the unclaimed and unfinished puzzle pieces of family development and identity. For example, a family grappling with broken bonds and shifting emotional and structural arrangements of divorce (uncoupling) or a marriage on the rocks will be at cross-purposes, and thus a poor match at this developmental moment to optimally respond to the developmental imperatives of a child's sense of trust. Or, a child's burgeoning expressions of autonomy may fare poorly in a family that is united by its losses and hides its separation doubts under the blanket of denial. In this way, each child development stage offers its own content or theme and child-centered process to add to the mix of family development. Families can learn to "read" and consciously direct both content and process and their reverberating effects on current and future child and family development, as will be shown in Chapters 5 through 8.

Developmental Stages, Problems, and Early Intervention

The stages of Attachment, Industry, Affiliation, and Inclusion compose the early or formative years of system development. Together, they create an important transitional period and distinct change-facilitation opportunity for the practitioner. The family is forming itself and, therefore, is pliant and amenable to influence and redirection. Consensus among clinicians supports the benefits of intervention in the early stages of a problem or crisis, while it is still forming and structural arrangements have not fully crystallized. Ideally, we also should intervene early in a child's life, during the infant-toddler-preschool period, when behavior is less likely to have become fixed or habituated, when human potential is more plastic and "open" to influence, and when the problems are inchoate and newly emerging.

Family systems also have "early" lives when structures and process have not fully solidified. During the Attachment-Inclusion transition, which spans four developmental stages and usually coincides with the family's early child-rearing years, the family is testing, evolving, blending and renegotiating its model, meaning, action, and pattern levels of organization and development. This makes this sequence in the family's life cycle fertile ground for change, and ideally suited to early intervention.

The term *early* has been used so far in a variety of ways, requiring clarification. *Early intervention* with children usually means intervening in the lives of at-risk children in the infant-toddler or preschool developmental stages to promote optimal development by ameliorating developmental delays and environmental or societal disadvantages. This term also applies to intervening and supporting families in developmentally formative system stages. The other way the term *early* is being used here focuses exclusively on the notion and onset of "problems." A problem is often most efficiently resolved when the problem itself (not necessarily the child or family system) is in its early stages. Therefore, regardless of what stage along the life cycle a family is experiencing, it makes practical sense to begin with a family at the problem's earliest sign or symptoms.

The Child-Centered Structural Dynamic Model, through its commitment to three levels of systematic family access, intervention and support, and methods of change (prevention, early intervention, and crisis) makes use of both meanings of the term *early.* The model adheres to several important principles that will be discussed throughout this book. One of these principles deals with the early stages of development, falling under the broadband grouping of Attachment, Industry, Affiliation, and Inclusion. These stages are optimal times for facilitating system growth and enhancing positive system change. Children usually accompany the early stages of family Inclusion. As children, and the tasks of raising them, are embedded in wider system process and interaction, a family's child-rearing practices and child development outcomes become critically dependent on and reflect the overall quality of family process. Child development and family development, as such, overlap, again making a compelling case for the Child-Centered Model.

In addition to and apart from the family timetable of development, "problems," which can arise at any system stage, have their own sequence: a beginning, middle, and end. Problems have their own developmental life, moving from initial stages to entrenched, stultifying stages. The Child-Centered Structural Dynamic Model advocates intervening sooner rather than later in a problem's stages and provides the practitioner with specific methods to do so. Prevention is a vital part of each level of the model. In work with families in crisis, for example, the model devotes part of the therapy (usually in anticipation of closure) to rehearsal, asking the family to anticipate and devise ways of handling similar problems in the future as well as planning for future developmental tasks.

Industry

Returning to Figure 3.4, Industry forms the next system dilemma after Attachment. This stage, once again, is a collaborative stage as the couple or blended family works out patterns, rules, and processes of accountability, entitlement, responsibility, and autonomy. The family needs to set its course and develop its plan for collective survival in the everyday practical and social world. This task includes economic survival and the concept of work, or family competency, as well as the family's means, methods, and themes around sharing resources. The family needs to decide who gets what and what "provisions" and "prices" are exacted from members.

To use a common example, does the family give the children weekly allowances without strings attached? Or does the family pay children for chores, communicating that money is not automatically given but instead is earned? A more complicated example of this dilemma involves the decisions a remarried couple may make around allocating the respective financial resources each partner brings to their current family. These decisions revolve around what the couple is willing to share with each other, as well as what they choose to invest in the new family system, which may consist of "his," "her," and "our" children. The crucial dilemma in this stage, as Kantor expressed, involves "freedom versus constraints."

As clinical practice and research have shown (Andreozzi, 1978, 1980, 1988), "accountability" is a focal task. Accountability has far reaching implications for child rearing and the psychological and moral development of children: the kind and quality of their character and the person they will become. Accountability issues, while associated with a family's economic life, extend well beyond it. Certainly today, as always, money, or its lack, is a great source of underlying tension in many marriages and families. Money problems can quickly destabilize a family, wreaking havoc and ill will among family members. Like food, however, money has multiple and deeply felt meanings. A family's money patterns often indicate more global and generalized emotional and interpersonal patterns raising basic issues of availability versus unavailability; this dilemma centers around issues of abundance and feelings of "having" or "there being enough" versus scarcity, the feeling of amplitude versus the feeling of "precious resources withheld," or an anxiety of "perceived deprivation." These patterns, which begin around money, tell us a great deal about the family's spirit and generosity. In addition, when financial difficulties are beyond the control of the family's work resourcefulness and competency, as when there are job layoffs, how a family rallies and responds to the crisis expresses the family's strategic patterns around problem solving in the face of adversity. However, there is also the concept and question of psychological and interpersonal accountability—the rules parents establish and the lessons the family imparts to children in the areas of behavior and impulse control.

Affiliation and Inclusion

Affiliation and Inclusion, the next two developmental stages, continue the family's process of expanding and deepening its capacities and structural variations. Not only are the family's distinct patterns and boundaries undergoing adaptation and transformation, changing fluidly in the dynamic ebb and flow of accommodating to developmental challenges, but also the family is increasing in its structural complexity. The richness of a family's themes, the varied and multifaceted nature of its pattern repertoire, are strong indications of a family system's viability. At this point in system development, the family is acquiring its fullness, filling in, shading, and layering the rudimentary structures of earlier stages. This period is one of energetic physical, conceptual, and practical expansion. Children are born, careers are begun, a future is envisioned, and the family builds from the inside out.

The dilemma that surfaces in Affiliation centers on the decision over what Kantor aptly describes as "smaller versus larger system identity." This dilemma can evoke conflicts around the competing demands of home and work as well as the tension between commitments to social and work relationships and responsibilities, and the obligations of marriage, parenting, and the intimate world of the family. The stage of Affiliation raises, in a new guise, issues of attachment combined with availability. This stage focuses primarily on the extent to which the family invests and extends its association to social systems (school, work, community) outside the family. This kind of family system expansion concentrates on the family's boundaries and wider community. Like the latency-age child, the family is venturing out and incorporating new friendships and competencies as identity (self-concept) stabilizes and takes shape.

In the fourth stage, Inclusion, which represents a cumulative or supratransitional stage, highlighting the overall quality of family development, the family turns its attention inward toward the system. Whereas in Affiliation the family's gaze was directed outward, in the direction of expansion beyond its system borders, in this developmental stage the family faces tasks around "inclusion." Having extended its boundaries outward into the wider social community, organizing and identifying distance regulation patterns and pathways, the family system now decides to open its boundaries inward. The family makes decisions about who or what to include.

A couple may choose to increase the family size by having a baby. Or, the family may engage in system building and enhancement in more symbolic ways by adding to the family's conceptual life or its meaning dimension through the development and elaboration of family myths, stories, lore, legends, and history. The family increases its thematic complexity while it simultaneously enriches a world of private, intimate knowledge available mainly to family members and individuals, like therapist and friends, whom the family, granting entrance and access, chooses to include in the system. A family's conceptual life, the meanings it ascribes and attaches to events and experiences, is a potent source as well as explanation of human behavior and a child's competencies as well as problems.

The Family as Collective Interpreter

A family system's meaning dimension, where inner and outer worlds of experience blend, and events are transformed and embellished over time in the family's evolving oral history, strongly influence how family members think, perceive, emote, and behave. Salvador Minuchin (1974) refers to this as the family's "collective mind." I like to think of it as the family's invisible legacy and history, the subjective imprint a family impresses on events, everything the family is and does. This collective interpreter and family style of coding, classifying, and labeling events, is a powerful shaper of human behavior, for good or ill.

One research family member, Barbara Wells, described this omniscient family interpreter as analogous to a family having a double life, or living on two simultaneous levels. She said, "It is *as if* there is the family you see, moving about, talking, interacting, doing daily chores and activities . . ." "On the surface," she further explained, "everything can look calm. But, underneath it all, there is a whole other teaming life of meanings going on, chattering to people just below the surface about *who* they *are*, *who* they *are like*, *who* they *can* and *cannot* be, and *what* the family tells us we *can* and *cannot* become or do." Barbara continued, "To find out a family's collective mind and know the contents of what a family thinks, we almost need to turn the family's actions and words upside down and read family experience from the inside out." Barbara is a 28-year-old wife and mother with two preschool children, who participated in our early intervention program and is one of the families followed intensively over almost a 5-year period. Barbara's analogy is insightful and revealing because often what a family brings to therapy are these two worlds or ongoing lives: the family it formally enacts and presents itself to be and, on a deeper, less visible level, the family that it believes itself—and actually shows itself—to be.

Family myths fall within the interior life of family beliefs. Myths are compelling, hypnotic motivators that can direct and influence the outcome of family transactions. For example, myths surrounding a child's birth, or the legend built around a parent's or relative's persona, accomplishments, character, or deeds can significantly affect how a child perceives self, the world, and his or her future place in that world

In the Brimmers' chaotic and troubled multiproblem family (see Chapter 2), John, aged 12, is the presenting child whose health is so seriously at risk that the courts may not allow him to return home to the family after his surgery. He was born several months after his father's death and had never been told the actual circumstances of this traumatic event. Instead the family, mainly under the mother's direction and bidding, spun a glowing and ideal myth about the father's virtues. Instead of uplifting John's spirit, this myth had enshrouded and depressed him. His anger, masking apathy and indifference, was not about the family lie, that his father was "wonderful and perfect," for John knew otherwise through familial conversations and collusive alliances. His anger and apathy were due to the persistence of the lie. Until family members communicated straightforwardly with each other, the myth and its underlying family secret continued to have a life or zeitgeist of its own, with its tenacious influence.

I have seen families come to therapy symbolically carrying and accompanied by their myths. During family conversations, these myths can become reified, taking on the proportion, significance, status, and sense of real presence associated with another person, *as if* an additional family member had joined the family in the room, *as if* the myth itself had suddenly increased the family's size by one. Myths can become that powerful and real to the family, acting as a "chattering subjective interpreter," talking nonstop in the background. Sometimes a family myth has gained such momentum and centrality in a family's conflict and struggles that I have encouraged family members to address the myth directly, acting *as if* the myth were sitting there invisibly in an empty chair. I have urged family members to talk directly to the "myth," asking questions and requesting answers of this nonstop interpreter, which has obscured the truth of actual family events and experiences for so long. Using this technique, when appropriately and sensitively timed to fit a family's readiness, may open the way for family members to talk directly to each other.

A DEVELOPMENTAL PAUSE OR A LOOSENING OF BOUNDARIES

All four stages—Attachment, Industry, Affiliation, and the supratask and stage of Inclusion—mark a decisive turning point in system development. By this point, boundaries, having endured the pressure and pull of growing pains, begin to settle into shape; family structures are fairly well drawn out and clearly sketched; family themes and patterns are evolved and recognizable; family transactions and psychopolitical configurations are fairly predictable and set. In a sense, a "developmental pause" occurs now, to some extent. While system development continues, there is a certain quiescence. Some of the helter-skelter, jarring, awkward movements of a young system trying on many different forms gives way to slower, steadfast growth. The family system, much like the young adult who comes of age knowing approximately who he or she is and where he or she wants to go, can now move more slowly, filling in with greater patience and security the broad outlines of an emerging identity.

The family, too, knows who and what it is becoming. The general features of the system's blueprints now having been drawn, the family can take its time filling in the fine lines of detail. Unless there is a major upheaval, either an emergency from outside or an identity crisis from within, the imprints of family structures, both formal and content structures, are fairly well cast. Their outlines are clear and set. The task that stands now before the family is to gradually fill in these outlines, smoothing and refining rough spots and jagged edges of the system's stabilizing structures and boundaries. Simultaneously, children are testing the system, pushing and prodding its limits, while absorbing what the family has to teach.

Paradoxically, just as the stages of Attachment, Industry, Affiliation, and Inclusion are settling, the family turns another corner. While Attachment, Industry, Affiliations and Inclusion involve expansion, extension, and elaboration of boundaries and family structures, the next three stages evoke system transformations in an opposite direction. As Figures 3.4 and 3.5 show, the remaining developmental stages are Decentralization, Differentiation, and Disengagement. Simultaneously, as the family arrives at a stable structural maturity and identity, a process that has all along incorporated the dynamic, artful interplay of joining and separating, the opening and closing of its physical and metaphoric boundaries, the family system now shifts its emphasis. Instead of movement in the direction of expansion, the family prepares for a loosening of its boundaries. In this life-cycle period, the family will grow smaller, decreasing in physical size. The family will "let go" of some family members as adult children create their own families, embark on their own lives, and, as one spouse inevitably faces the loss of another.

Initially, we might wonder, are these stages ones of diminishment and depletion for the couple and family system? "Having less" or "being less" does not always signal loss; instead, it can engender growth and development of a different kind and quality. These stages represent important qualitative shifts occurring in the family that have decisive effects. Potential growth opportunities are available to all family members. The family system is growing in a crucial, qualitatively different way. While the physical size of the family may appear to be shrinking as its collective and interpersonal boundaries loosen in favor of personal autonomy and the independent lives of its members, the family is actually undergoing vital and exciting change. The family has become "smaller" only in the literal sense that all members are now no longer living under the same roof. The family's composition is essentially the same. Family members are still integral to the system but in new, interpersonal ways.

Relationships transform to accommodate the increasing autonomy of adult children; distance regulation patterns enlarge and increase in complexity. Parent-child relationships have the potential to deepen in new unexpected ways as the demands of parental supervision relax in light of the adult child's quest for autonomy. The opportunity arises for mothers and daughters to know each other as women; for fathers and sons to know each other as men; and for parents and children to discover and experience one another much as they might encounter and explore the relationship offered to them by a new and intriguing person entering their lives. This can be an important time for reclaiming lost moments, asking still unanswered questions, exploring and fulfilling missing parts of the self—emergent in the unfolding puzzle pieces now available in the changing parent-child relationship.

Similarly, the family center has not diminished; the family system has diversified, dispersing into several, even many centers. In the crucial work of boundary renegotiation, boundaries loosen in the sense that they become, ideally, more flexible and pliant in a durable way. The developmental continuity of interaction and communication goes on; however, these conversations now span greater geographic distances and are expressed in metaphors of acknowledged personal autonomy and independence. As adult children leave home, return for temporary visits, and leave again (as has become a shifting and increasingly frequent trend in our society), the couple takes stock of their relationship. Unresolved problems camouflaged by the distractions and absorptions of parenting will resurface, clamoring for the couple's renewed attention, as will the possibility and excitement of new intimacy and reawakened personal autonomy.

A Fluid Picture of Family Development: Focal Issues and Stages

In Figures 3.4 and 3.5, family system development is shown as the interplay of current and historical patterns. The arc of family life stages is intended to convey continuity of development, and the overlapping cutaway slice (shown in Figure 3.3) symbolizes multilevel family organization to create a fluid picture of family development. Development flows and unfolds from stage to stage. Stages are meant more to convey the opportunity for qualitatively new system shifts in boundaries and family structural arrangements. Stages are not fixed but movable points along the life cycle that signal the advent of focal issues, core dilemmas, and developmental tasks. With each stage comes crisis, a normal occurrence and catalyst of growth. Children are immersed in the process of these stages, influenced by, as well as influencing the family's developmental progress. As a visual rendering, the diagrams are simplifications. While Figures 3.4 and 3.5 show family development as a linear process, this notion falls short, as two-dimensional visual schemas often do, in fully communicating the dynamic nature of system development. Family system development, while tracing a linear course and expressing a linear direction, is cyclical, coiling its self-elaborating advances forward and self-reflective gazes backward.

In essence, while each stage highlights a focal dilemma, the tasks and issues of other stages also are present, to a lesser extent. At each developmental crossroads, the family system faces a primary issue, as bits and pieces of prior or future stages also cycle through, giving the family repeated and reframed opportunities to "get it right this time," to mold and shape family process, and change. Attachment, affiliation, inclusion, and differentiation issues appear in new and varied forms in all stages. The couple or family who is working out the bonds of attachment simultaneously, by seeking connection and intimacy, may grapple with the rhythms of satisfactory and essential individuation, tasks of "being separate" and autonomous. The evolutionary pathways of system development and change are, in this way, never quite complete, but open and relatively unfinished, as they should be.

CHAPTER 4

The Child in Family Development

Welcoming Children and Families to Child-Centered Structural Dynamic Therapy

To this point, the focus has been on a view and assessment of current and historical family system development. There is still the question of incorporating child development into the special circumstances of family therapy and enrichment. A practitioner who sees a family with a presenting child or is involving children in family sessions must attend to and incorporate child development considerations. This is the third developmental view or context that is integrated into the practice of the Child-Centered Structural Dynamic Model. Table 1.1, combined with Figures 3.4 and 3.5, provides a useful guide, overview, and decision aid to the practitioner, a framework for melding and shaping treatment plans, therapy process, and change facilitative techniques that maximize positive outcomes by matching the goals of therapy to the goals, capabilities, and developmental readiness of children and families.

Engaging Children and Families in Therapy

Several considerations face the therapist who, for example, is seeing a family with children 3, 6, and 10 years of age. The therapist's preparation, in terms of the cognitive and developmental process of therapy, centers around the "model" for "seeing" the family. The model is a lens for viewing problems and strengths and enables the practitioner to evaluate, understand, and assess child-centered problems as part of the therapy process. A practitioner engaging a family with children is being asked, in the context of family therapy (with the active involvement of parents), also to do child therapy. Children, regardless of how young or developmentally immature, cannot be left out; their full participation, according to their readiness level, is actively sought.

Family therapy is all about inclusion. The risk and fear of venturing into the unknown, of discovering something "bad" or "unspeakable" about the self or others diminishes, and the prospect of learning something important and new about self and family grows. The commitment and hard work that go along with changing behavior strengthen in an atmosphere where all participants are invited in, and feel valued and known. Inclusion is the first sign of such an invitation the therapist can extend to the family, a "welcome" that the therapist symbolically offers to the family who stands on the threshold of change, at the door opening onto the understanding that therapy can bring.

When we strip away the fancy labels and window dressing terminology of our major nosologies, the symptomatic classifications of childhood disorders (e.g., *DSM-IV*), when we distill childhood problems to their essence in the realm of human affairs, the problems children show reflect a plain and simple, yet profound transactional statement: that children are, in some way, not being *seen* or *truly known*. I cannot stress this enough, especially in light of what families willingly have confided, and what I learn from them in the change process during the special circumstances of therapy and intimate family conversations over time. This view was further reinforced by the revealing "window of insight" and opportunity into family process and development provided by the research families who participated in an intensive 5-year outreach program (Andreozzi, 1978, 1979d, 1979e, 1985a).

Presenting Child Problems and Diagnostic Categories

Before going on to explain Child-Centered Structural Dynamic Therapy, an important point needs clarification to avert a potential misreading of what I have said. I do not mean that practitioners should ignore assessment classification schemas or diagnostic taxonomies of childhood disorders. To do so would be patently unwise, unethical, and professionally irresponsible. There is the child, after all, to consider, and important clinical signs and symptoms to watch. Also, descriptive classification systems such as the *Diagnostic and Statistical Manual of Mental Disorders* (*DSM-IV*; American Psychiatric Association (1994)), or the taxonomy developed by Achenbach and colleagues (Achenbach, 1985, 1993, 1995; Achenbach & Edelbrock, 1983, 1986, 1987; Achenbach & Howell, 1993; Achenbach & McConaughy, 1987; Stanger, Achenbach, & McConaughy, 1993) although not without problems, signify major advances and contributions to the field of child development and our understanding of psychopathology. Consider the "comorbidity" factor: that symptoms and subtypes of childhood disorders can overlap, making classification categories not always clearly discernible and mutually exclusive as they ideally should be. For example, diagnoses of Oppositional Defiant Disorder (ODD) and Conduct Disorder (CD) have not been well validated as separate clinical entities. The high rate of overlap between diagnoses of ODD and CD may arise artifactually from the lack of a valid distinction between them, rather than from potentially informative clinical distinctions between two different disorders. The clinical literature and research suggest that ODD represents an earlier, less inclusive cluster of features that predict or are associated with the broader symptom-constellation known as CD.

As the history of the classification of childhood disorders reveals, the description and categorization of childhood symptomatology received minimal and cursory attention simply because childhood behaviors were thought of as precursors to adult psychopathology. The few systems that resulted mainly reflected downward extrapolations of adult symptomatology and terminology. Childhood disorders, in this way, were viewed primarily as replicas and predecessors of analogously named adult symptomatology and terminology. In this way, children's developmental needs and disorders have been obviated and confused by adult perspectives on the course of psychopathology and mental health. Currently, we know differently; there are considerably different presentations in children and adults. For instance, we know that depression in children can present differently than in adults. Depressed children do not always sit forlorn in a corner and cry. Nor do they always withdraw socially or retreat into apathy, showing the same kinds of psychomotor retardation or vegetative symptoms we see in adults with depression. Instead, children can become aggressive, angry, distracted, and agitated, often acting out in frenetic and disruptive ways.

The point made, here, is not to abandon diagnostic labels but to incorporate and then move beyond them. After giving the child's behavior and presenting symptoms a "name," using these labels to fulfill the purposes and needs, for example, of interdisciplinary teams, case conference consultations, and the requirements of health care providers and managed care programs, the practitioner can translate these labels into transactional statements. Diagnostic and assessment categories are a tool, as well as a form of professional distancing in terms of the way information is organized and bracketed. There is also the intimate and less clinical side to a child's problems and the labels we designate to express the disturbance or disorder.

Labels aside, children who present in families communicate their distress: Their needs have gone unmet. Either they have been overprotected or constrained or given unwarranted license. Either they have been lectured and scolded too much, or they have been not listened to in serious ways. In both instances they have not been genuinely heard nor have they been authentically seen. The sense of *not being seen* is often at the root of parent-child struggles. Children act out and develop symptoms *to be seen.* A harsh light at least draws some attention to the child and, from the child's point of view, is better than obscurity. The therapist can communicate to the family and child a potent message declaring the importance of that child by preparing the physical environment and the emotional climate to welcome the child and child-centered family process.

Preparing the Room for the Family

How the therapist creates and communicates this message is one of the first and most important inroads the therapist is making with the family in terms of engaging them. The therapist prepares in two related ways. There is the arrangement of the room, the design of physical space, and the materials and objects that are offered and contained within the room. The room, obviously, needs to be big enough to accommodate a large family and allow for the propensity of children to use and explore physical space. Ideally, the seating arrangement encircles the play area so that children can play while therapist and family talk. Placing the children's play area in the middle of the interaction communicates that children are central in the participation of family process. The metaphor communicated through the physical, spatial organization of the room is one of belonging and inclusion. The seating, obviously, should accommodate adults and children. Child-size chairs are important to have. Also, an ample number of chairs, eight to nine, should be available.

Child-Centered Materials

Regarding materials and play-objects that work best, I suggest a carefully chosen finite group of toys. Ideally, toys and play materials are age-appropriate and stage-dependent and also contingent on the type and nature of the child's problem, if prior to initiating therapy, a presenting child has been identified. For example, when a child displays Attention Deficit Disorder with or without Hyperactivity, distractibility and difficulty focusing and staying on task are part of the child's frustrations. Because these children tend to flit from activity to activity and are more prone to holistic, but fragmented, rather than sequential cognitive and emotional processing of stimuli and information, the best environment is a structured one that offers enough but not too much stimulation. An orderly environment, displaying a few inviting toys and materials, can have a calming and soothing effect on the child, creating an ambience that promises guidance and nurturant supervision.

It makes good sense, generally, if some but not too many play options or enticing toys are available, in order not to overwhelm children or tax already worried, anxious, and frustrated parents. A therapist's standard fare or staples can include paper (easel-size as well as standard drawing size), crayons, markers, and pencils. Play-Doh is also useful. Blocks, the most universal and abstract toys, combined with figures of people, animals, and vehicles, are essential for encouraging fantasy play and symbolic transactional enactments. Blocks of different sizes and composition (wood or plastic; rigid or flexible; smooth or interlocking) are useful to accommodate children's gross motor skills and the dexterity of small fingers and hands. Blocks are familiar childhood territory, and even reserved parents often become absorbed and intrigued by this activity, joining in their child's fascination with the building process. Play is the important and revealing work of child-centered family change. Other essentials include dolls (representing adults and children, both genders, and varied racial and ethnic characteristics), puppets, and most notably, the centerpiece symbol of family work—some form or representation of a "family house."

COGNITIVE AND EMOTIONAL FRAMES OF REFERENCE

The therapist also prepares her- or himself cognitively and emotionally for child-centered family practice. One crucial, informational aspect of this preparation involves an accurate assessment of each child's range of developmental capabilities. When there are several children in a family, the therapist's preparation is twofold from the perspective of the children. The practitioner identifies capabilities (limits and potential) of each developmental stage and then synthesizes this knowledge into an understanding that encompasses all the children in the family. This understanding is the precursor to developing therapeutic strategies and designing child-centered family activities that have the maximum effect on and elicit the fullest participation possible from all family members. The integrated developmental knowledge of the children in the family is next combined with the therapist's grasp of the family's organization and interaction, for processing the developmental tasks, focal issues, and dilemmas it is facing.

Table 1.1 was developed as a teaching, supervision, and consultation tool to community centers, child development programs, and mental health clinics who used the Child-Centered Structural Dynamic Model. An adaptation of this developmental table was also devised for parents and incorporated in family enrichment and early intervention levels of the Child-Centered Model. The application and integration of child development theory (contained in Table 1.1) will be explained and illustrated in Chapters 5 and 6. Table 1.1 will be referred to again in Chapters 7 and 8 on families in crisis, delving into it in greater depth, combining and illustrating its use and application with the model's detailed method of assessing family development.* Part of the comprehensive assessment method referred to earlier in Chapter 3, a genogram, treats and consciously tracks developmental stages as crucial structures in the network of relationships and developmental patterns that reveal a family history. Family assessment in the Child-Centered Structural Dynamic Model is unique, unlike the assessment perspectives of other therapy models. Later chapters explain the assessment process as it relates to all three tiers of the model, prevention or enrichment, early intervention, and crisis.

Table 1.1 offers the practitioner epitomized, highly condensed profiles of children at different developmental stages. The descriptions provide simplified normative "still photographs" or "developmental snapshots" of what a child is capable of and what can be expected of the child according to the developmental stage. This table addresses the child's cognitive, social, emotional, moral, and language development, communication, and self-help skills.

For example, a 2- to 3-year-old child asks and can respond to "what" and "where" questions, shows frustration at not being understood, enjoys simple storybooks and stories, and responds to simple directions such as "Give me the block." At this developmental stage, the child will play near older siblings; watches other children, joining briefly in their play; symbolically uses "objects" and "self" in play; defends his or her own possessions; participates in simple group activity; knows his or her gender identification; and begins to play house.

A child 5 or 6 years of age shows a greater facility. At this stage, the child likes to play with words, often creating rhyming songs, word games, or phrases; plays with and makes up words with similar sounds; can draw a person with two to six distinctly recognizable parts, such as head, arms, and legs. The child's attention span is longer now, and he or she learns through observing and listening to adults, as well as through exploration. Exploration as a mode of learning and emotional access is the bridge between the 2- to 3-year-old child and the 5- to 6-year-old child. However, the 5- to 6-year-old child shows a broader understanding of the concept of function, part-whole relationships, and time. The child can talk about yesterday or last week, which often seems like a long time ago, as well as today, and what will happen tomorrow.

Dramatic play is also more pronounced and closer to reality, with attention paid to detail, time, and space. In the brief developmental sketches

*For further information and a comprehensive training manual and set of child-centered family process materials, including *Parents' Family Guide* and *Therapist's Family Guide*, please contact the author at P.O. Box 174, Kingston, RI 02881.

drawn and illustrated, we can begin to see the connections between child development and family access and goal dimensions. Children are active shapers, interveners, and intuitive explorers of family process in these key areas. We also can see how developmental knowledge, particularly of a child's communication skills and levels of symbolic representation, aids the therapist in framing questions appropriately, and developing action-oriented techniques to facilitate a combined child-oriented and adult-compatible family understanding.

Critical Identity Images, Family Crisis, and Child-Centered Family Change

We have seen that there are positive, growth-oriented aspects to crisis, and that in the Child-Centered Structural Dynamic Model, crisis is viewed as a normal developmental occurrence. Crisis can precipitate system elaboration and self-initiated change in some families. These families may hardly notice a change. They flow smoothly, or with moderate difficulty, from one developmental task and transition to the next. It is not that these families are immune to difficulties; they sometimes experience problems and trouble spots in moving the system forward developmentally, but they manage those problems more effectively. For whatever reason, the family at this point in its developmental history can handle the disquieting tumult and shifting disequilibrations of structural change. But for other families, or for the same family at different developmental turning points, the crisis continues unresolved, threatening the system balance.

In those situations, either an emergency from without or a developmental conflict arising within will send unresolved crisis reverberating throughout the family system. There are signs that tell us when a family, through its collective consciousness and interpersonal efforts to settle a tumultuous developmental episode, has touched on a deeply felt identity crisis that is generating and maintaining the family conflict. The source of the conflict pattern can be traced and linked to the developmental crisis inherent in the mismatched and jarring puzzle pieces of individual family member identity, child and adult alike.

When we distill the crisis pattern to its developmental essence, we find critical identity images in conflict. Children's critical identity images differ from those of adults. Children's images differ in the form they take, the method by which they are shown, and the ways the therapist accesses children's imagery, as will be illustrated in two family scenarios, "Justin and the Blue Bird" and "Sarah and the Make-Believe Heart" described in Chapter 7. As therapists, we can recognize, trace, and engender family understanding around the content, meaning, and behavioral expression of these images. The child occupies a special place of inclusion in the Kantor critical identity image concept of family crisis, instability, and change.

When we see a family with children in crisis, we do not see its model and meaning structures. The identification of these structures, giving these levels of current family organization embroiled in the crisis a name, mainly aids the clinician as agent and facilitator of change. Meaning and model structures are conceptual entities or reifications. Their importance lies in the understanding they provide the practitioner and family, illuminating problem dynamics. Meaning and model structures "hold" the family's symbolic, "image-life" as well as the guidelines it has tacitly agreed on or grudgingly settled on for regulating interactions and structuring interpersonal relationships. At the model level, the therapist finds, for example, the family's preferred system type: open, closed, or random, which offers invaluable insight around system change. Here, the clinician explores the family's transactions, how it modulates interpersonal access, contact, and the style the family develops for reaching family and personal goals in the areas of nurturance and intimacy, power and competency, and identity.

Model structures also highlight the family's style, or its homeostatic ideal, self-correction, and change. We note this in the family's orientation toward the expression and response to sameness and difference in family members, and in the rules it has laid down and calls on for acting on disturbance, or the onset of system instability either in the form of an obstacle from without or a developmental crisis stirring within.

Family System Problem-Solving Styles in Response to Crisis

When we situate and apply the Kantor system typology of open, closed, and random system types in the context of child-centered family therapy and the domain of child development and parent-child problems, clinical practice and research (Andreozzi, 1985a, 1988, 1993a, 1993b) have shown that each family type presents a different profile and orientation to problem solving and signs of crisis. A closed family system type, experiencing stress and instability it perceives it cannot or does not know how to handle, will close down, rigidify, and bring the process of problem resolution to premature and unsatisfactory closure. The open family system type, which generally blends individual and family perspectives and works on the premise of consensus, will vacillate and stall in indecision and ambivalence around the integration of the claims of family members and the rights of the family as a whole. The random family system type, prizing individuation, carries it too far in a developmental crisis, devolving into competing idiosyncratic patterns, veiled and confusing personal quests, and conflicting pathways of personal autonomy and self-expression.

The closed family system tends to shut down the developmental dilemma prematurely, requiring a pseudounanimity of members. The open family system loses its consensual balance, falls prey to indecisiveness, and wavers between the worlds of individual and family. The random family system ends up a disjointed disconnection of individuals in search of contradictory goals and personally defined identities. The personal and private worlds of family life overshadow the collective sense of the family to such an extent that often it is difficult to perceive overt systemic interaction, although the system does indeed still exist. Here, at the model level of family organization, we also find a family's models of parenting, those deeply felt ideologies and tenaciously held worldviews and beliefs about what a child is, what a child's place in the family is and should be, and the role of parents in guiding children's development and behavior.

At the meaning level of organization, we come to know the family's store of images and thematic content: its favored symbols, icons, myths and lores, and the family's legacy, as well as emergent imagery. Here, we find the family's personal legends about childhood and the value the family and the individual members attach to the concept of being the child and childhood experience. The therapist can discern and identify crucial parent-child and child development structures in the form of primary process, emotionally laden personal and interpersonal imagery. On this level, we will eventually trace and connect child-centered critical identity images (drawn from the Kantor critical identity image concept) among family members. At this level, additionally, we discover the foundation of the family crisis as both historically significant and currently emerging hierarchies of personal, interpersonal, and family imagery collide and compete to be known, heard, and seen. I will show how the clinician can detect and identify the "crisis dynamic" on these levels, illustrating, through an excerpt of a family case, how knowledge of model and meaning structures can shed light on the family's problem, and how knowledge of each contributes to problem resolution, family change, and positive, redirected child development.

What we do see in a family crisis are the family's actions and patterns of action. Although the crisis is simultaneously present and, therefore, implicated on all four family levels—meaning, model, action, and pattern—and there are corresponding parent-child and child development structures for the therapist to consider at each level—what the family reveals through its transactions is a breakdown in its problem-solving strategies. The family shows crisis in two striking and overt ways. The family's usual decision-making, problem-solving strategies do not work as effectively. Previously familiar and reliant patterns that have effectively steered and kept the family on course, fall short. Families are perplexed and do not know what to do. They are unable to generate new effective strategies, or to call into play novel or inventive solutions. What happens next? Not knowing what to do and unable or unwilling to discover viable alternatives, the family falls into a vicious cycle of repeating patterns and strategies that do not work, and paradoxically, this effort makes things worse when what the family wanted was for things to get better. The family system, in this way, perseverates and developmentally comes to a halt in its absorption in the crisis.

The most overt signs of crisis are seen in the stereotypic roles family members resort to and adopt. In crisis contexts, family members assume highly predictable, self-defeating and system-counterproductive positions at critical transactional moments in the crisis cycle. People essentially constrict their behavior, freezing and limiting their options, reverting to old and less effective patterns. They do this for a variety of reasons, including fear, force of habit, confusion, disappointment, and anger. It is as if the family system has lost a degree of its personal and interpersonal generosity; the system dynamics, tensing under the crisis, appear to have lost their pliancy. Roles, actions, and patterns of actions become inflexible.

Child-Centered Family Therapy, Critical Identity Images, and the Crisis Cycle

Critical identity images take on additional, special meaning when applied to children in the context of family therapy. As shown in Chapter 1, the Kantor critical identity image concept is distinguished from other types of images in several important ways. In the family's ritualized impasse, we see the symbolic "image" representation of crisis. The ritualized impasse involves recurrent, episodic enactment of the identity crisis. In these transactions, family members are polarized as they assert their separate realities, personal claims, and unmet expectations. They feel misunderstood and often betrayed. When they are not standing in direct opposition to one another, expressing their anger and disappointment openly or through tacit withdrawal, their transactions can take on a different, more ironic, ill-timed quality.

One spouse may move toward the other, making a brave overture of access while the other spouse pulls away. In this way, the cycle continues and the crisis escalates. Next, the withdrawing spouse may offer tentative access, usually at an inappropriate moment. Upset at this ill-timed gesture, the spouse who had ventured out earlier and was rebuffed, rejects the partner's efforts to bridge and join. This happens much in the same way with parents and children. We see a highly ritualized pattern of moves and countermoves that thwarts people's emotional and physical access to each other. Nothing meshes interpersonally or blends transactionally; the artfully timed rhythms of mutual access and approach are lost. The family feels alienated and polarized. The crisis that is created is particularly poignant and compelling for vulnerable children who stand at the center or on the periphery of the conflict and who are often emotionally torn and confused.

Family members, including children, as they make known the source of frustration they are experiencing, discover deeply held beliefs of self and others, relationship plans and blueprints gone awry, at the center of the problem pattern. When honed to essentials, the developmental crisis revolves around critical identity images in conflict. However, before describing the special nature and application of the Kantor critical identity image concept as shown in Child-Centered Family Therapy (Andreozzi, 1985a, 1988, 1993a, 1993b), we may wonder: "What are critical identity images?" Step back for a moment to consider the term "image" on its broadest level. The link between the formal structures (e.g., its transactional patterns) that a family develops over the life cycle and the content that is the foundation of communicational life, both behavioral and symbolic, is the image. Images form the basic creative elements of an individual's knowledge structures: what a person will and often does come to believe to be true. Images are internalized mental representations. In the context of family practice, images can be thought of as highly condensed, emotionally laden, interpersonal and transactional scenarios. The separate imagery, both personal and interactional, in the form of preferred transactional "moves" around certain themes, creates and builds into family images as family members interact and the family system develops over time.

Images equal the subjective, affective, and cognitive knowledge structures (observational and vicarious learning) that the family and children show through their behavioral enactments. How people act toward one another reveals their guiding and idiosyncratic interpersonal imagery and relationship metaphors. For example, is the world a "dog eat dog" jungle in which a person feels compelled to attack before being attacked? Physical or emotional combat, or sparring for self-protection and defense is the guiding metaphor here. Or, are the world and the intimate relationships within it seen as gifts that are stingily given, with strings attached? This reflects a transactional metaphor in guiding relationships with others that combines a notion of "self-sacrifice will win out" with a sense of preciously limited options. What I have just described are emergent critical identity images, what children are creating in the dynamic process of self vis-à-vis others in the parent-child relationship and the intimate family environment.

We can think of these images as pictorialized representations of emotionally crucial and interpersonally salient events or internalized memory pictures. As David Kantor has expressed (1980), "It seems to me best to view the image as an integration of sensibility and intellect, as sensate and cognitive experiences merging into pictorial thought schemas" (p. 148). Critical identity images can be approached as thoughts in visualized form, or as pictorial thought schemas. This accounts for how and why the Family Photograph

Technique, an activity specifically developed within the Child-Centered Structural Dynamic Model (Andreozzi, 1979c), works well at appropriately and sensitively timed moments to elicit and allow family members to discover their separate, guiding critical identity crisis images and to give them a name. I will explain this process as it applies and can be used in all three tiers of the model (enrichment or prevention, early intervention, and crisis) in later chapters.

The point here is that these images are highly condensed action-structures, views of the self as experienced by, and experiencing, others. These images provide the "automatic pilot" instructions, if you will, that guide, predict, and explain the often cryptic or quixotic behaviors of family members toward each other. These images are accessible and are revealed through mental visual descriptions of interpersonal scenes or moments of import in a person's life. The active development of mental representation is the work of childhood, and because children are action-oriented and think concretely, with a sense of immediacy and literal richness, their images provide an important inroad to child-centered family change. What I have found in practice and research with families in the process of change and crisis resolution, is that the family member with the most interpersonal sensitivity, the richest and most multifaceted worldview and relationship imagery is often most disqualified or unheard in the family. I refer to this euphemistically as the "Cassandra Family Complex."

In Greek mythology, Apollo gave Cassandra the gift of prophecy to win her love. When Apollo was thwarted and spurned in his efforts to win her affection, he, who had given her prophetic powers, betrayed the intent of that gift by decreeing that although Cassandra would clearly see events and the future with deep insight, she would be doomed to endure the repeated experience of no one taking her seriously or believing her. Children often occupy precarious and untenable positions, as their direct and simplified insights and unconcealed awareness into family systems go unnoticed and are given little credence or, in the worst scenario, are completely disqualified. In this way, a child's place in a troubled family can be likened, in certain contexts, to Cassandra's cursed and invisible prophecies, messages that are lost to overwrought or oblivious parents.

Two Central Principles of the Child-Centered Model

Two central principles integral to the Child-Centered Model draw attention to the bidirectional and reciprocal link between individual biopsychosocial development and the structural interplay of system development. The emphasis in both principles is on positive mental health and the developmental genesis of human vulnerability. To explain more fully, the first principle states:

- *Regardless of the level of health or crisis characteristic of a family system at any given time, the level to which the family system may potentially aspire may be contained within and reflected by the highest level of perception (sensibility, cognitive and interpersonal sensitivity) manifested* by *current system membership.*

The second principle continues:

- *The strength, sensitivity, adaptability, behavioral and interpersonal insight expressed by one family member, once validated and made important and credible by an influential, trusted, objective source (in this case, the therapist) and integrated by the family as useful system information, may carry the family forward into increased states of health, deepened and more authentic communication, and toward a process of interpersonal repair.*

I have found that children, seen at first as the most unlikely initiators, when given guidance, structure, and support, can and do lead the family system forward in uncanny and unabashedly inventive ways, as I will illustrate in Chapters 5 through 8.

FEATURES OF THE IMAGE

The Kantor critical identity image concept is recognizable through a number of salient features that make its application to children evocative and multidimensional—a precise, efficient, developmentally focused method and technique ideally suited for children. These images are primarily visual and spatial and action sequenced, involving the self and at least one other significant intimate other who, together, with the image bearer, creates a scenario of interaction that is either implicit or explicit. Critical identity images display unusual vividness and intensity, what David Kantor (1980) refers to as their "arousal value." While images derive from past experience, their power and influence continue to shape current relationships. As such, critical identity images extend well beyond memories alone and are not to be confused or viewed as synonymous with childhood recollections. These images are fully developed or broadly sketched outlines of behavior. They are intuitively practiced interpersonal scripts that can lead to good or ill, as is the situation in unresolved crisis.

While critical identity images may explain the source of alienation, divisiveness, and despair that a family in crisis is experiencing, they also represent positive personal assertions and interpersonal claims. Just as I have spoken about the underlying original good intention gone awry in the development of individual symptoms, or a child's problem behavior in the family, critical identity images have their positive side, what David Kantor (1980) has termed, "critical identity claims." As these images are shown in families and to family members, and the child's inchoate imagery is explored and named, the original search to be authentically known, seen, and heard by someone highly valued in the person's life becomes clear.

This illumination occurs as we, practitioner and family, turn the image around, so to speak, moving and inverting it to transform negative, interpersonally distancing features of these images into positive personal and interpersonal affirmations. In this way, to refer back to the words of Barbara Wells, the 28-year-old mother who described the experience of exploring her family system in Chapter 3: It is *as if* the ideal work of therapy is to turn these images inside out, to reveal their affirmation, standing them right side up on their positive and inviting side rather than focusing on the negative and troubling side visible in the original "ritualized crisis" that the family brings to therapy.

Through the content of critical identity scenes (e.g., one spouse's ridicule or derision of the other spouse while a child looks helplessly on) and through the mood climate associated with these scenes (e.g., shame, fear, or even a strange, captivating excitement), critical identity image scenes embody the thematic and qualitative character of the family system's developmental crisis. The behaviors of an individual vis-à-vis others, embedded in the originating action-scene, that is, a person's learned transactional style, are as important as the details (content) of the critical identity scene each family member brings to the family crisis. As David Kantor (1980) emphasizes, what people store in memory experience "is not only the special memory content of the image and the psychopolitical configuration, but an energy component associated with the original experience, reinforced by new experiences along the way" (p. 149).

The Power and Tenacity of Images in Child-Centered Family Crisis

Critical identity images touch and strike deep emotional cords in children as well as adults. These images, or what the image conveys about self and others, are cherished, deeply fought-for and fought-over views of self, family, and relationships. We know when we are in the midst of an emerging critical identity struggle by the tenacity with which individuals, including children, cling to, defend, and refuse to relinquish these images. Unresolved critical identity image conflicts have claimed more than one couple's marriage in divorce. Some are the route of physical or emotional violence and spousal and parent-child abuse. Still others account for a child's troubling symptomatic behavior. When pushed, it is the line that people draw, the last ground they will not surrender, the one they refuse to have violated, the one some will fight for to the death.

The Stones

I return, by way of example, to the unfolding crisis of the Stones—Lila, Ted, and Keith, their 6-year-old son—to show how the child's and adults' separate critical identity image scenes meld to create a three-way family developmental crisis:

In the initial therapy hour, Lila is tearful and distraught, full of worry. Ted looks on in sullen and silent resentment. The spouses refuse to look at each other. Tensely sitting at cross angles, they signal the polarization and alienation they feel. Barely concealed anger and disappointment is palpable between them. They communicate disillusionment. Keith sensing the familiar tension between his parents, seizes the moment. Stealing the attention from their angry and bitter silence, he does something. He draws the attention onto himself and becomes the negative focal point. In a burst of energy, he jumps into the center of the space before his parents. Brandishing an invisible whip in one hand and making a small, menacing fist with the other, this boy, dressed in a medley of brightly mismatched clothing, recognizes intuitively that something must be done to move things one way or another. Knowing his part well, he declares in a family that now refuses to freely declare anything, "I am the Ring Master. I am the Ruler of the universe. I will save her . . ." Keith's frenetic behavior, his odd and compelling costume (e.g., black top hat made out of paper; insulated winter vest on a warm day), and precocious demeanor hide a child's sad and angry bewilderment.

In Chapter 2, in the discussion on psychopolitical configurations, or the family's development of a unique transactional style composed of combinations and variations on four strategic social interaction positions (mover, follower, challenger, and bystander), the Kantor Four Player Model was extended to include the enactment of transactional roles according to the child's age- and stage-appropriate development. Child development tasks and the child's unfolding cognitive and affective readiness were linked to parent-child dynamics and situated within the broader ebb and flow of family development. The "bystander" role was conceptualized as a vitally active system function and characterized in the Child-Centered Model as the family's capacity to observe, communicate, and reflect a system view of family dynamics. In Chapter 3, a vignette about the Stones involved an episode around food:

In a vivid scene that the family relates, Keith comes home from school and runs straight to the refrigerator, a behavior typical of most children his age; when Ted the father is home, he blocks and opposes Keith's access, preventing him from getting a snack. Ted does this for a number of reasons, some clearly known to him (e.g., he hollers at Keith, who flings the refrigerator door open, "Get out of there! You're letting all the cold air out!"); other reasons, unclear to him, are contained, as with Lila and Keith, in personal emergent critical identity images. Each image contributes to the evolving three-way image-crisis. In this scenario, Keith becomes more rebellious at every move Ted makes to control him. Soon the mutual opposition escalates into shouting and screaming. A scuffle ensues in which father and son are hitting each other. The noise of the violence and commotion draws Lila into the fray, and, fearful that Ted will injure Keith and angry at what she interpret's as Ted's childish and controlling behavior, she steps between them and literally pulls them apart. Feeling vanquished and humiliated, Ted skulks away like an angry, reprimanded child to his workshop in the garage. Lila and Keith are now together. Lila hands Keith a cookie from her stash of "goodies" that Keith calls his "mommy's treasure trove," something Lila believes is hidden from Ted.

In this brief scene, several salient features of the crisis and the Stone's style of family process begin to appear. First, if we did not look beyond the surface dynamics, we might miss the obscured positive assertions each family member is trying, underneath it all, to make known to each other. Ted's behavior might be seen as childish, petty, and controlling. Lila's contribution might be seen as that of an overprotective and engulfing mother who is choosing son over husband. The son may appear as an unruly and undisciplined child who mischievously stirs up trouble, intensifying the dissension between parents. These initial observations hardly approximate the whole picture. The intensity of the Stones' developmental struggle will persist until the crisis around identity images is clearly known, and new behaviors are introduced transactionally.

In both of the brief scenarios given, a repetition of family patterns, strategic transactional parts, learned and chosen or compelled, falls routinely and problematically into place around certain family themes, one of which is the giving and taking of food. The Stones are in a rageful and desperate fury over food, something that obviously has deep, multifaceted, reverberating meanings for them. In our earliest encounter with the Stones, introduced in Chapter 2 and more fully described here, we can begin to appreciate the family's repetitive, problem pattern. Lila begins the conversation, acting as the mover, while Ted has the option to participate, by following Lila's overture. Instead, Ted chooses silent opposition to express his position. Keith, wishing to break the mounting tension between the parents whose care and nurturance he needs, takes action to redirect, or somehow "save" the interaction. He acts out and, as such, safeguards the family's status quo for the time being. Now everyone can worry and wonder and complain about him, his odd-looking clothing, and behavior. By making this behavioral statement, Keith is also opposing his father, challenging him, as he announces he will save his mother (the child's transactional part and purpose is twofold: He is an opposer to his father and simultaneously a follower to his mother).

In the second scenario around the refrigerator, food, and surreptitious snacks, the pattern further distills and clarifies. Ted and Keith physically oppose each other, an image that has become a working metaphor of their relationship. Neither can soften their highly predictable position and give in or follow the other with the necessary follower-moves that would ameliorate the conflict and improve their relationship. Both have become thwarted and ineffective opposers. Obviously, Ted, as the adult, has more refined cognitive powers and should be capable of perceiving this "choice-point" better than his son, who is developmentally inexperienced. I mention Keith's involvement here because he has learned his part and contributes to the course and direction of the interaction. Lila is also caught in highly ritualized opposer-follower moves. She stereotypically opposes what she sees as her husband's "bad parenting" and "childish behavior" with her follower position in relation to Keith. Their son shows his opposition to both, although when he heeds directions or requests, it is mostly his mother whom he obeys. He sees her as available and more sympathetic, one who knows and understands him better. The Stones are a family of disempowered movers and disqualified opposers with few, well-timed and effective follower moves. This is the emergent problem pattern or distressed psychopolitical configuration—the behavioral piece important in identifying the critical identity image conflict.

Before Keith was born, the couple managed to keep their model differences or clashing system types under control. Lila prefers an open system characterized by generous access, fair play, and equal representation. Ted, on the other hand, favors a closed family system style. He likes order, control, and structure, sometimes to excess. He prefers measured access, earned and hard-won rewards, often withholding the "precious gift of himself" because he feels Lila or Keith does not "deserve it." When he does venture out emotionally, offering either intimacy to Lila or nurturance to Keith, as Lila later described, he "offers it out in teaspoons."

After Keith was born, and the couple was faced with working out the details of joint responsibilities in raising their first child, their differences emerged sharply. Conflicts that had been smoldering underground and were contained within the boundaries of adult marital intimacy began to surface decisively after the birth of the baby. The litmus test of system type difference polarizing the couple emerged around parenting ideologies. Not only did the couple vehemently disagree about parenting, they were in a war about it, especially around what it is and means to be a child. The problems arose gradually, becoming overt when Keith was about 3 years old, a developmentally appropriate stage for testing limits. Keith was clearly experimenting and expressing his personhood. He had language now and was no longer a quiet infant or easily distracted toddler. Ted had to face his child as an emerging person with a unique self and will to contend with and accommodate. The child development stage that Keith presented, characterized by his growing independence and accompanying episodes of opposition, stirred up, ironically and prophetically, unresolved family developmental issues around opposition and inclusion, autonomy, deprivation, and shame.

A third excerpt from a therapy hour later in the therapy process sheds light on the critical identity conflict imbuing the crisis. Again, the problem conflict occurs around *food.* The family relates the following scenario:

It is dinnertime, Keith is dawdling with his food in a way that is beginning to irritate Ted. Lila and Keith sit beside each other at the table. Ted sits opposite them. Keith sometimes plays with his food, as children do, not eating in a clockwise pattern from every category of food on his plate, something that infuriates Ted's need for order. Ted, whose anger is beginning to rise, instructs Lila "Take charge of Keith before I lose control." Lila begins to tense and tries to coax Keith to cooperate, which only exacerbates the problem further in this family of underdeveloped followers locked into rigid patterns of opposition and confrontation.

The predictable cycle of violence erupts. Keith, who is hungry and now eating consistently, asks for more chicken. In this family, the father controls the food and the portions that he serves are small and meagerly given. Ted refuses his son's request, railing at his son's poor table habits, as Lila looks on in dread and anticipation of what she knows will happen next. Keith, feeling challenged by his father's merciless criticism, picks up a plastic container of children's vitamins and slams the bottle down hard in protest. The bottle cap flies off and vitamins spill and scatter.

Now Ted is furious. He jumps up, ready to attack Keith. Ted is screaming at Keith who, instead of shrinking away, screams back, further enraging his father. As Ted moves threatingly toward Keith, Lila quickly rises and stands between the two shouting, "Don't you touch him!" Ted shoves Lila out of the way. She pushes him back. Their son withdraws against his chair, his eyes moving from one parent to the other. Suddenly, feigning an injury, a small cut that had opened around a cuticle, the father shouts "Look what your mother has done!" (The father's whiny, angry shouting sounds more like a child's than an adult's, as if erupting from a memory of another time.) "Look, your mother drew blood!" Ted displays the superficial cut. Keith is frightened by the blood and begins to cry, not knowing what to believe.

At this point, the intensity deescalates and the interaction comes to a halt, having reached its emotional crescendo and transactional threshold. The ritualized violence and real aggression have served their purpose according to this family's current homeostatic ideal, and proceed no further.

After the foundation is laid for the image exploration, Lila and Ted and Keith communicate the following: When asked to recall an interactional scene similar to the present family transactional scenario, in which a similar role occurred, Lila eventually describes the following:

Lila, who is the middle of three children, has just returned home from a hospitalization surrounding asthmatic complications. She is about 7 or 8 years old. She is lying in bed resting, a small mug of soup beside her on her night table. Outside her bedroom door, there is the chatter of her brother and sister and the family having dinner. She hears her mother praise her older brother for his good work in school. No one, it seems, is going to look in on her. After dinner her father walks past her door without a word. Lila feels alone and very small. As the hours pass, feeling excluded and abandoned, hungry and ill, she softly cries herself to sleep. Later that night, when her father goes into her room to kiss her good night, she turns her face away, pretending to be asleep. She opposes what she believes her father and family will not give freely, belonging and warmth.

During therapy, Lila speaks about this recurrent image when she describes herself as always feeling as if she were in search of recognition from her parents. She explains, *"While my older brother and younger sister were always on the 'gravy train,' I felt I always had to be on the 'grateful train.'"* Seeing herself as a bereft and lonely child, due to what felt like a peripheral and tentative status in her childhood family, she vows when she is a parent *"to do the opposite and to champion her children, giving to them generously and freely."*

Ted relates what may seem like a different circumstance but, on closer examination, conveys a remarkably similar experience:

Ted is about 8 or 9 years old. He has been sent to the store to buy a loaf of bread. The scene begins in a playground near his house. Ted is small for his age and a number of older neighborhood boys bully him. They intimidate and rough him up a great deal, as does his father, who is short tempered and stern, and who believes in corporal punishment. Frequently, when angered, he pulls Ted's hair. Ted responds reflexively to violence with rage. On the way home from the store, several boys encircle him, taking the money and tossing the bread on the ground. Enraged and feeling inadequate, Ted runs home and tries to explain to his father what has happened to him, wishing for concern and sympathy. He receives neither. His mother, more afraid of her husband than in touch with Ted's shame and embarrassment, chastises him further. For his punishment, he is sent to bed without dinner. Hurt, humiliated further, and feeling betrayed by a weak mother, he cries himself to sleep. The lesson he has learned in relation to his nonsupportive mother and oppositional father is, as he describes, "This is a dog-eat-dog world."

Through this and the coalescence of several other particular visualized scenes, Ted's critical identity image begins to emerge and crystallize.

Ted and Lila's son Keith's emergent imagery is expressed symbolically through action-oriented play:

Keith says, referring to the playhouse before him, "This house (meaning Keith's house) is an empty, haunted house." When asked about what is going on in his family, he says, "I have to fight my father. That's my job because," he hesitates, "he's a bad man." He looks quizzically at his mother for her agreement. Confused and ambivalent about how to answer this question, she turns her face away. Keith becomes tearful but he does not cry. He begins to pound two people-figures together. When asked what is making him sad and angry, he answers, seemingly out of nowhere, "My Uncle Paul died." (His Uncle Paul, Lila's uncle and Keith's great uncle died years before Keith was born, an ally and protector of Lila, his mother. Lila has spoken of her Uncle Paul to her son often. Uncle Paul has emerged over the years as a kindly, strong, and protective presence. Keith clings to the mythology as a protector of his mother, internalizing the hero figure, and by association seeks protection for himself.) Before referring out of the blue to Lila's deceased uncle, Keith, in his vigorous play, was pummeling and talking about "stabbing" a "bad guy." When asked if besides thinking about his Uncle Paul, had he maybe been thinking also about his father, Keith bursts out, "I don't want my Dad to leave . . . Mom, can we move back to the old house?"

The family had moved 3 years ago when Keith was about 3 years old. By changing houses, he wishes to return to less troubled times. Keith has been denied access to other important transactional roles. In his desire to return to "the old house," he is expressing his frustration at being locked into a disqualified and disenfranchised opposer role. His comments bring the family on the verge of positively reawakened system awareness and a vitally important system-level perspective. This is the work of Child-Centered Therapy shown in greater detail in the following chapters.

The Role of the Therapist in Child-Centered Structural Dynamics

Up to this point, the major building blocks that form the fluid system concepts of the Child-Centered Structural Dynamic Model have been described and illustrated. These building blocks comprise the practitioner's basic conceptual lens as well as practical tools for structuring family change, facilitating family growth, and organizing "therapeutic strategies" around family crisis and development. As the word "dynamic" in the Child-Centered Structural Dynamic Model is meant to convey, the building blocks of the model can be flexibly and creatively applied by the therapist. The therapist may, for example, use all or some of the building blocks, emphasize some of the conceptual and practical tools more than others, or mold the concepts and methods to fit the special circumstances of a particular family and the context in which family change may be occurring, including enrichment, early intervention, or therapy.

The Staging of Family Change

The therapist considers a number of sequential steps in planning family interventions or the staging of system change. The method of Child-Centered Structural Dynamic assessment, essential to the formulation of developmentally focused treatment plans, involves consideration of the model's central building blocks and concepts of change. Each building block highlights a step in the overall assessment plan and change process. For example, the therapist considers:

- System types in relation to engagement in therapy and the family's response to crisis.
- Access and goal dimensions, family patterns, combined with an understanding and assessment of children's perspectives and developmental readiness.
- The sequence of transactional roles, child and adult parts, in the problem pattern.
- Levels of current family organization, including the assessment of the viability of parent-child and child development structures.
- Critical identity images and developmental impasse in the form of family identity crisis.

Content and formal structures have also been highlighted. To translate these concepts of family process into everyday life, we can think of a family's system type as its rule book and compass for guiding the family's course and telling it what to do when it encounters difficulty. The disturbance can be anything—physical, psychosocial, or symbolic—that challenges the family's model for living. The most obvious challenge to a family system's sense of itself comes in the form of difference, for example, an acting-out child or deviant behavior. All three types of families, in Kantor's system typology, open, closed, and random, handle disturbance in clearly different ways as child-centered family therapy research and practice on the effects and features of family system type difference show (Andreozzi, 1985a, 1988, 1993a, 1993b).

To draw on "families" in our pop culture, television icons who have become familiar models in our cultural consciousness, *The Waltons* illustrate an ideal closed family type; the Cunninghams of *Happy Days* the ideal open family system; and the families in the films, *Places in the Heart* and *Steel Magnolias,* the ideal random family systems. Access and goal dimensions express cross-cultural human quests and goals. Regardless of the preferred distance a family establishes in its patterns of intimacy and individuation, visual and symbolic relationship expressions a family develops as its preferred style, the family, if it is to be a family, carves out its space, organizes time, and modulates its energies, both physically and metaphorically. By doing so, the family guides how family members choose to work out their interpersonal plans for reaching the primary human needs of contact, connection, affection, and belonging (intimacy and nurturance), competence (effectance and a sense of power and influence), and identity, or a sense of meaning and purpose. The family in crisis over intimacy and nurturance, and depleted in this area, is often on the verge of emotional bankruptcy. A family that loses its sense of influence and collective competence will flounder aimlessly. Without a sense of collective purpose, the family is often in the throes of an identity crisis that can lead, with its unresolved, deeply felt conflicts over personal and interpersonal identity, to emotional or legal divorce, and the family's dissolution as we know it.

Identifying the Problem Pattern as a Sequence of Predictable Parts

Family parts or the roles of mover, follower, challenger, and system-conscious observer (described in the Kantor Four Player Model and adapted to child-centered family practice) simply refer to the "moves" individuals make in an interaction. Imagine the following scene: A wife is coming up from the family's rumpus room in the basement. She hears footsteps bounding down the stairs from the upstairs floor. It could be any of a number of family members: her husband, her 13-year-old daughter, or her 11-year-old son. She calls out, "Good morning. Who's there?" In a gruff and annoyed voice, her husband answers, "Who the hell do you think it is anyway?"

Here, the first word or "greeting" of the day that the husband extends to his wife is one of opposition. He opposes her. Had he said "Good morning, it's me, honey," then he would have been "meeting her halfway," moving in to join her as a follower to her initial greeting rather than blocking her with his challenging and provocative remark. Had their 13-year-old daughter just at that moment, come down the stairs, she would have overheard her parents' strained interchange, and said, "Why is it that everything in this family lately is such a struggle? What's the big deal? Why don't we just get along?"

The daughter then would be acting as a witness to family process. She would have, in that comment made specifically to neither parent but to the "family," activated or stimulated the family's capacity for self-evaluation and self-reflection. She could elicit the family's powers of self-observation, or the system consciousness function crucial to system viability and change.

As illustrated and emphasized, the four transactional parts from Kantor's Four Player Model live a double life in the Child-Centered Structural Dynamic Model. The family parts offer a "transactional flowchart," a framework of interpersonal options for understanding a family interaction. In effect, the clinician identifies the mover and then the combinations of co-movers, follower, opposer, and witness or impartial system arbiter (referred to in Kantor's Model as the "bystander"), and then asks four interrelated questions:

1. What is the aim of this family interaction?
2. What is its theme?
3. Is it successful and effective, or is it ineffective and a problematic sequence?

4. What are the roles children typically take and what are the implications for the family's current conflict and broader patterns of child development?

TESTING FOR THE INFLUENCE AND PRESENCE OF UNRESOLVED PERSONAL AND INTERPERSONAL IMAGERY: THE PUZZLE PIECES OF FAMILY CONFLICT AND IDENTITY

Children think in images. They attach feelings to thoughts and express their hopes and doubts, worries and fears about important relationships in their lives through feeling images and imagery. Behavior is also a potent medium and a crucial form of symbolic action language that children call on to express what they are experiencing in family relationships. The depth, detail, and specificity of a child's images, and the technical methods that the therapist adopts in child-centered family image exploration, are a function of the child's developmental readiness and the family context (nature of the problem and level of family distress). Children's images are concrete, condensed, often one-word descriptions of the family's problem and the child's place in it, as illustrations in Chapters 5 through 8 will show.

Critical identity images are what individuals argue over, fight for, and stand up for in heated and impassioned ways. These deeply felt, tenaciously held interpersonal and personal images contribute to and create the transactional scripts we enact that bridge psychic life and family interaction. The critical identity image merges the personal world of the individual's past history, as shown in internalized scenes of crucial transactions, with systemic or current family interaction. To test for the influence and operation of these images at work in an interaction, watch for emotional intensity and what we can think of as a "raw-nerve" level of arousal. Also, with children, watch for silences. Take two examples from everyday life. One involves an apple pie and the other, a telephone.

What could be more innocuous or innocent than "apple pie?" Imagine the following two versions of the same family scene:

Two children are in the kitchen; a 6-year-old boy and his 8-year-old brother. There is one piece of Mom's apple pie left, and although the older brother has had his share at dinner and this piece is being "saved" for the 6-year-old, who had dinner at a friend's house, the older brother, knowing he is bigger and at an advantage, claims ownership. Eating the pie with delight and relishing his superiority in this sibling rivalry, he says, "Finders keepers, losers weepers. Too late! Get out of here squirt." Angry, the younger brother reaches out to grab his brother's arm and get the pie. But even before he can yell "That's mine. No fair," the last morsel of pie is gone. The younger brother looks on as the pie vanishes, resentful of his older brother who always "pushes his weight around and takes advantage." He calls "Mom!," and runs out of the kitchen, feeling vanquished and helpless and cheated, and maybe plotting to "get even" and "turn the tables" on his big brother.

Just then, moments too late, his mother enters the kitchen and says, "What's going on here?" looking first at her older son who is standing there with a "cat that swallowed the canary" grin on his face and then at her younger son, whose face is as red and angry as "a traffic light."

For both boys, if the scene and this type of sequence repeats itself enough times and across enough contexts, we have critical identity images in the making, or "emergent images." For the mother as well, who walks into the kitchen, the scene may elicit the faint recollection of earlier scenarios, similarly meaningful transactional sequences in her own life.

The sight of her two sons and the empty plate may stir her to act in a familiar way reminiscent of important earlier family transactions. She may choose to adopt a role that flows from or satisfies her own unfinished or unresolved personal-interpersonal puzzle piece and identity image, roused around the theme of siblings, family, and fair play. This image may prompt her to assume a familiar transactional role. She may decide to move in and side, follow, or support, her younger son while simultaneously she admonishes the misdeed of her older son. In effect, she may take her younger son's part, viewing him as the "underdog" and her older son as the "bully." Or she may adopt another viewpoint. The position she takes flows from the details (content structures or themes and formal structures, past family of origin transactions) she has absorbed and experienced and she feels are expressed in the current sequence. The moves she chooses to make in the here and now family interaction with her children—the transactional part she elects—is the potent, visible, overt sign of the critical relationship guide and system blueprint informing her behavior.

Drawing on the same "apple pie" caper, we can expand the scenario. Imagine, instead, that both parents hear the boys' commotion in the kitchen:

The father enters moments after the mother. The mother is asking the children, "What's the matter?" The father interrupts, saying, "It doesn't matter who ate what or when. Why don't you boys just split the piece of pie and call it quits. You're brothers, aren't you? And brothers share." The older son capitulates saying, "Yeah!" supporting and liking his father's suggestion. The younger son shouts "No fair!" At that point, the mother pipes up, "It belongs to him," pointing to her younger son, and says to her older son, "Don't be so greedy." The boys start to squabble over the pie, grabbing at the pastry, each swiping little pieces with their hands. They start to laugh, caught up in the game. Their father, frustrated with the whole fiasco, intervenes. Yanking the plate of half-eaten pie away from both boys, he throws the pie out. "Now no one gets it! That will teach you boys to share." Upset at her husband's actions, the mother says "This is not about sharing. It is about what's right and fair!"

If we traced each critical identity image back to the individual family members and then forward in terms of each image's contribution to the family behavioral sequence, then we would find four separate images or transactional puzzle pieces all coalescing around the common theme of "justice and fair play," and the dilemma of balancing individual and collective rights and responsibilities.

A second example of how critical identity images can show up in everyday life revolves around the telephone—that multidimensional symbol and instrument of communication. How many disputes between parents and children, especially adolescents, or arguments between spouses have erupted around the telephone? The telephone triggers and often carries deep emotional significance. It may mean connection, contact, access, availability, even, in some instances, mobility, transporting one person "interpersonally" and instantaneously to the location of a significant other. A busy signal, no answer, or "phone off the hook," "a phone line out of order," a message not returned, or a "promised" call forgotten, or the blocked access and emotional distancing at times created by continually getting an answering machine can raise all kinds of interpersonal imagery. Individuals can feel abandoned, betrayed, slighted, ignored, helpless, isolated, and even denied access at crucial moments of need, and out of control and humiliated. This accounts for the abuse telephones take; the reason they are slammed down, thrown, unplugged, or even ripped from their connections in the wall. Referring to the telephone as an instance of "broken or unmet communication" is often a frequent and revealing theme running through family practice.

I have found that interactions around the telephone evoke particularly intense imagery. Consider the following examples from marital and family practice: A spouse who cannot reach her husband (who is away on business) at a hotel may wonder about the possibility of her mate "having an affair." A husband whose wife is frequently on the telephone with relatives and friends may come to resent the telephone, seeing it as blocking his intimacy and access to his wife, feeling he comes in a "poor second" to more important people in her life. The roles in this example can be interchanged or reversed; they are not gender specific. Husbands can be suspicious of unreachable wives off on business. Wives can resent husbands whose work or work-related phone calls take or keep them away.

If we traced the couple's or family's transactions to the meanings family members ascribe to the behaviors of others, then we would eventually find powerful critical identity scenarios around themes of "broken promises of access" and "broken intimacy" evoked by the symbol of the telephone.

Child-Centered Structural Dynamic Therapy: A Model of Professional Development and Self-Supervision

The discussion has focused on the practitioner's use of the building blocks of the Child-Centered Model in relation to the family. Our gaze has concentrated on the building blocks as practical and conceptual tools for understanding family process, the dynamics around crisis, and child-centered family therapy. But what about the practitioner? These building blocks can also serve a second, important metalevel purpose: to aid the therapist's professional development. Each "building block" has its companion-counterpart for the practitioner, acting as an aid to professional development and self-supervision. In this sense, the gaze is directed toward the practitioner, and the beam is turned on the practitioner to illuminate the therapy process. This self-understanding involves:

- The therapist's wise and well-informed use of self and self-knowledge.
- The therapist's model versus methods.
- The impact and interplay of the therapist's technical mastery and evolving relationship skills.

These concepts and self-supervision tools act as decision aids to the therapist, creating a system of evaluating and tracking family process to maximize outcome. This is an example of how the model incorporates, through the practitioner, a method of ongoing self-development and supervision. This self-evaluation of interactions with families and overall progress is accomplished through the use of the Rainbow Forms (Kantor & Andreozzi, 1985). The multidimensional application of these forms will be fully explained and illustrated in Chapter 7.

Included in the central proposition of the Child-Centered Structural Dynamic Model are aspects of self-reference that arise during attempts to influence others. In traditional treatment approaches, most signs of self-reference, including countertransference in psychoanalytic therapy or non-neutrality in systemic family therapy, are viewed as problematic, if not breaches of good clinical form when they are out of awareness and remain unmanaged. In the understanding of clinical realities achieved with the Child-Centered Model, however, self-referential phenomena are viewed as inevitable occurrences in the therapy process. It is not that self-reference occurs, but rather, how the clinician makes use of the phenomenon. Self-reference, as an emotional and cognitive response, demands from the clinician a finely honed sensibility and alert attention to subtle nuances with an informed use of self.

There is a point worthy of clarifying regarding the therapists's influence and the term "self-reference." When I am speaking about the therapist's involvement or personal self-reference, I am not suggesting a solipsistic self-absorption or preoccupation, or that therapists should make a study of themselves that overshadows the rights and needs of the family in treatment. To do so would be patently absurd. I am intentionally exaggerating this point to prevent a misreading of my meaning of self-reference in family therapy.

To look at the role and impact of the personal background and professional influence of the therapist in the therapy process is not to suggest that therapy is a total social construction devoid of objective truth. The concept of self-reference, here, intentionally stays clear of the murky waters surrounding the current re-emergence of the 1980s "epistemology" fray in the new guise of "constructivism" as a school of therapy. The therapist does have the larger responsibility as the trained professional in the therapy partnership. The plain research and clinical truth is that the therapist's self-reference has been seriously overlooked. The point is a practical one. Therapy is not a total or completely relative social construction where participants are indistinguishable and problems are viewed as subjective creations. Otherwise, problems could not be identified and their solutions could not be objectively evaluated or found.

There is, and should be, an objective basis to the practice of psychotherapy. We see this, for example, in the accepted and recognized catalog of family patterns and problem types that have come to be known as "family practice"; that is, patterns that are recognizable and common across families. Also, in contrast to the constructivist family therapy view, responsibility stops at the therapist's door. The therapist is the prime mover and the objective guide. Our expertise (i.e., a family has sought us out for our specialized knowledge), regardless of the level or degree of assumed participation offered to the family, means that it is the therapist who bears ultimate responsibility as a supervisor or monitor of the therapy process, safeguarding the family's rights, confidentiality, and well-being.

When referring to the focus on the role of the therapist, we are considering thoughts such as these: A therapist may like or dislike some families or some family members more than others; a therapist may feel more comfortable and function more effectively with some family system types more than others; a therapist may find some family members more attractive than others. These personal preferences, or self-referential phenomena, influence practice. To the extent that such influences are out of the therapist's awareness, they can affect practice in numerous unidentified ways. To the extent that self-reference phenomena are known to the therapist, they can be used positively and consciously. The self-supervision offered in the Child-Centered Model blends two types of awareness:

1. The therapist's understanding of self, including their critical identity images.
2. Attention to practice issues, including developing and checking the outcome of a session plan or chosen intervention strategy.

Together, the facets of this professional understanding can help the practitioner systematically track therapy as a building process; that is, a series of small outcomes that can create positive change.

Self-Knowledge and Clinical Practice

Translating this concept of self-knowledge into the world of practice, we can think of self-reference as shown in the clinician's tendency to perceive individual and family patterns (competencies and problems) according to social categories derived from personal experience in key former and current relationships. Similarly, the practitioner tends to behave in familiar patterns when encountering client characteristics that resemble and reawaken key relationship structures and foundation experiences from the therapist's own past. Critical identity images, internalized thematic and interactional scripts, account for the tendencies of the therapist to perceive and act in predictable ways in specific contexts. In the interactional field of therapy, these tendencies inevitably lead to evolving relationship structures (Andreozzi, 1985e; Kantor & Andreozzi, 1985), on which I will elaborate.

The reason for paying attention to the emergence of self-reference in therapy is the potential impact these phenomena have on the course and outcome of therapy. The most striking way the therapist's uninformed self-involvement makes itself known and palpably felt occurs when there are differences between the family's and the practitioner's styles, models for living, and modes of approach.

"Resistance," "no shows," or "early terminations" in therapy can often be traced to undetected differences in client and therapist personal orientations. The problem is not that these differences exist. We can and should expect therapist and family, at times, to hold different models for living and relating as well as sometimes quite differing views of how the world works and what needs to change. These are welcome issues that make interaction and the therapy process varied and interesting. The problem arises not because these differences exist or self-referential factors occur, but because they go unnoticed and can interfere with the therapy process. Once the practitioner knows the particulars of "self," the practitioner is free to make more informed clinical decisions.

The therapist's personal background and life experience can influence the course of therapy in a number of crucial ways. The first influence pertains to the therapist's experience and comfort level with different family forms or types. Consider Kantor's system typology. For example, does the practitioner work better with and feel more at home with open family systems, closed family systems, or random family types? What style of family process does the practitioner lean toward based on early experience? What style of organization is the therapist most drawn to? Sometimes, this is a matter of which family style the practitioner had most experience with in his or her own life while other styles represent "undeveloped pieces" in the therapist's life, accounting for why the therapist may work better with some families than others. This awareness which can be systematically known, often remains at the level of "impression" for the therapist. Asking ourselves a few pointed self-supervisory questions, as shown in Chapter 7, can turn these impressions or déjà vu insights into knowledge of the therapist's patterns of interaction across family cases.

The therapist's professional orientation and school of therapy will also reveal the practitioner's tendency toward a preferred style of relating and mode of engagement and intervention vis-à-vis the family. Recall Kantor's Four Player Model and the roles of mover, follower, opposer, and bystander. For example, although all roles are required to keep the therapy process ongoing, is the practitioner more of a mover? A supportive follower? A challenger? Or a self-reflector to the family? While exercising all four roles to some extent, which role, if the therapy relationship is to thrive and continue, best fits the practitioner's personal style and professional image of self? Given the premise that practitioners will, at times, like some families more than others, consider the following.

The practitioner who regards him- or herself centrally as a self-avowed mover, when encountering a family with a strong "take charge" style, may find the members "assertive." A therapist less inclined toward the mover style, may see the same family as "intrusive." The practitioner who sees his or her style as supportive may view a family who follows as "cooperative." Another practitioner, less inclined toward the follower role, may see the same family as "timid." A practitioner who defines his or her professional style primarily as confrontive may view a family of challengers as "gutsy" and "feisty" and "strong." Still another practitioner may view the same family as "abrasive," "blunt," or "tactless."

These attributes are important considerations because treatment plans usually flow from them. This is not to say that practitioners do not notice these things, nor that practitioners, by training, are not able to identify and handle them. The point is not that the practitioner should attempt to neutralize preferences, or remove them (sometimes this is not possible because some self-reference can be out of awareness), but by consciously tracking or paying attention to when such feelings (or factors) arise, transform this information into self-knowledge and then use this knowledge to improve practice.

Professional development is a continuous process that includes not only increased skill and expanded, refined technique, but a wise and well-informed use of self. We know that communication is the sine qua non of effective therapy. We also know, for example, that curative factors (leading to positive therapy outcomes) are linked to the treatment milieu and a "generic picture" of the effective therapist (Bergin & Garfield, 1994). Positive family therapy outcomes are positively associated not only with technical competence and skill but also with the interpersonal climate that the therapeutic process engenders: the family's perception of the therapist as warm and empathic and the environment as safe and initially nonconfrontational. When a practitioner knows the strengths and limitations or "growth areas" of their professional identity and personal development, the therapy process, and family, invariably benefit in several ways: Clients' rights are safeguarded. The therapy process becomes less encumbered and slowed down due to "out-of-awareness" issues or "rival" agendas. Therapy problems can be anticipated, and success can be framed in terms of practitioner-family matches or acknowledged and effectively used differences.

Another feature of the therapist's selective perception and preferred behavioral orientation relates to one or another thematic domain. Consider the three communicational domains identified by Kantor, affect, power, and meaning. Is the therapist finely attuned to feelings, dealing with themes of intimacy, nurturance, and affection readily? Or, does the therapist "tune in" on issues of rights and responsibilities, first recognizing and responding to themes of power, equity, and fair play? Or does the therapist first note conflicts around the family's meaning dimension, including themes of identity and purpose?

Therapists recognize and respond to favored themes: What the therapist notices first when encountering a new family and what the therapist chooses to focus on or deemphasize affect the course of therapy. Again, favoring and feeling attuned to some domains more than others will flow from a practitioner's own personal experience and history and, as issues of self-reference, can become part of the therapy. Self-reference phenomena, by necessity and circumstance, are part of the therapist's professional practice. The influence of these phenomena grows only when they remain unknown and unexplored. Their potential to assist and improve therapy outcomes increases, in contrast, when knowledge of the therapist's preferred professional and personal patterns is available to the family practitioner.

A set of interrelated concepts developed by Kantor in 1983 and introduced in subsequent publications (Kantor & Andreozzi, 1985; Kantor & Neal, 1985) provide a means of managing self-referential phenomena in therapy. These concepts include formed versus forming structures (what Kantor calls the "boundary profile wheel") and two other clinical concepts, the therapist's model and method. All four concepts or manifestations of these self-referential operations, as they appear and are noted in the therapy process, are studied both for their pattern of influence and for their overall effect (Andreozzi, 1985a, 1985d, 1985e). In this way, the supra- or metalevel, self-supervisory tier of the Child-Centered Structural Dynamic Model provides a means of attending to professional self-development and also a method for accessing and positively influencing family therapy process, outcome, and change.

Models, Methods, and Use of Self

Psychotherapy is all about the skillful use of self and self-influence. Therapy is also all about communication and learning by example. Successful therapy is like an ongoing intimate conversation aimed at bringing about positive change in the participants. Returning to ideas introduced in Chapter 1, family therapists are a particular kind of social scientist, a social "meteorologist," as Lynn Hoffman (1981) has aptly called those of us who chart the course of large, moving "weather systems" and track the "variable weather" of the human "soul." Philosophical issues aside, family therapy, on very practical grounds, is all about social intervention and change. "Change" or "helping families change" is a responsibility with strong real-life implications, especially when the lives of children are involved. Therefore, the therapist's influence, among other things, is a crucial factor with its own set of real-life ramifications for families. How a family should change, or the best way for a family to change, is not always clear-cut. The preceding examples, showing the ways self-reference issues can arise in therapy, are simplified and a bit stereotypical. Still, there are other ways in which the unresolved puzzle pieces of the therapist's personal development and identity can show up in therapy. A therapist's model for living, for example, can be remarkably different from that of the family's worldview.

These models can differ radically and can flow from cultural, socioeconomic, or sociological differences, or even from a difference in personal backgrounds, belief systems, and life histories. This is often the case when a clinician works with a family with different ethnic or racial experience; or when a male therapist works with a single woman and her children; or when a therapist who is not disabled or who has had no experience with disability issues works with a family with a disabled member. Surely, an experienced and sensitive practitioner would have moved in close temporarily to consider and understand the family's world before staging change and working to restructure the family. Is it true that the practitioner's view, simply because it represents the "expert" view and carries more weight, is the "right" view or correct way for the family to change? Family work is mediated by a large gray area of social factors. For example, is divorce a positive outcome of therapy? When is it best for a child to be removed from the family? Value judgments are invariably a part of the family practitioner's terrain. The point is that it is imperative to know where the borders between the therapist's experience begin and the family's end; to know when aspects of self-identification and self-involvement are muddying up the therapy waters; to identify when the therapy process is steering into the personal domain of practitioner.

Formed versus Forming Structures

In 1983, Kantor introduced the concepts of "formed" and "forming" structures. The intersection or juncture between both concepts, the bridge between technical aspects of therapy and the developmental aspects of the therapist's personal identity, provides a convenient vehicle for organizing and responding to self-reference. Formal structures relate to the technical domain of therapy and the therapist's evolving professional skill. Forming structures, on the other hand, pertain to the relationship patterns that actually evolve in therapy or the client-therapist relationship. Formed structures are drawn from the therapist's theoretical perspective, from what the practitioner is prepared to see, on theoretical grounds, in a troubled family. Formed structures are what therapists usually treat. These are the structures and existing characteristics that the family brings into therapy and that the therapist is trained to understand. Therapists view these formed structures as external to themselves. Formal structures are what therapists are trained to "see." Different schools of therapy are attuned to different formal structures of the family. Some examples of school-based formal structures include attention to diffuse boundaries (structural family therapy), a couple's complementary projective identification (psychodynamic or family object relations), a role reversal between parent and child, a family "triangle," and so forth. Regardless of the type of family structure that the therapist sees, all theoretical orientations view formal structures obviously as separate and apart from the therapist. Formal structures equal professional understanding of families.

When a therapist treats a client, individual, child, or family, a second kind of structure begins to form. This forming structure develops out of the client-therapist interaction and evolving relations. Forming structures can evoke personal issues for the therapist. Forming structures exist whether or not the therapist pays attention to them. Just as therapy schools divide around the degree of professional distance that the therapist should keep in the therapy process (Kantor & Andreozzi, 1985; Kantor & Neal, 1985), schools also divide around the extent to which the practitioner should pay attention to forming structures. When we consider forming structures as relationship structures, family therapy school differences become clear. For example, structural and strategic therapy, favoring a more restrained involvement, keeping a moderate distance, forces the therapist to concentrate on formed structures. Constructivist, symbolic-experiential, and existential approaches, relying more on the therapist's use of self and closer engagement with the family, consider forming structures as well as formed structures.

Because both formed and forming structures actively mediate between the therapist and the therapist's use of technique, they often have more bearing on therapy outcome, both positive and negative, than do the therapist's more readily observable formal interventions. Any attempt to understand more fully the mutual, reciprocal relationship of process and outcome (i.e., of therapeutic process to differential outcomes) must inevitably and systematically address these phenomena of self-reference and influence. To ignore their emergence and unfolding in treatment is to proceed blindly through the therapy process at great expense to both client and therapist.

Chapter 5 will focus on the first two tiers of the model, prevention and early intervention. The building blocks and role of the therapist will be examined in these contexts. Techniques and interventions directed toward facilitating family-initiated and therapeutically guided change will be described and illustrated. Chapter 6 provides a step-by-step plan and series of concrete activities for promoting child-centered system awareness in families. The goal of the Child-Centered Structural Dynamic Model, through the special role of the therapist and cumulative effect and intent of its systematic program of activities, is to provide families with cognitive, affective, and experiential knowledge about child development and family process. The Model's ultimate aim—as will be shown throughout case illustrations and activities described in this book—is to awaken, nurture, and strengthen in families, the crucial capacity to observe, comment on, guide, and direct family process, and to make informed decisions about family development. In effect, the aim of Child-Centered Structural Dynamic Therapy is for families to become their own "system experts."

CHAPTER 5

Primary Prevention and Early Intervention

The First Two Tiers of the Child-Centered Model

When individuals and families seek help, entrusting themselves to a professional, what they invariably seek is to be *known, seen, heard,* and *found* for *who* they *are,* and *who* they *want* to be. Technical elegance, skill, and training aside, when therapy is honed to its essence, these messages of human contact, connection, and continuity emerge and constitute what the therapy relationship and the intimate conversations of therapy and family enrichment are all about.

The Psychological Voices and Vocabularies of Children

The desire to be known and seen, heard and found is particularly compelling when children are involved, because children's "voices" are subtle and unpracticed—often being either too quiet, lost, and overshadowed, or too loud, and thus dismissed or ignored. In contrast to the vocabularies of adults, children's psychological "vocabularies" are largely unformed, with their words and word choices being sparse and unrefined.

"Voices" and "vocabularies" mean more than the physical voice and range of words a person has available. It refers to the emotional vocabulary—the language, images, and mental representations we bring to the expression of human needs—combined with the desire to communicate to self and others who we are, as well as how parents and children in families seek to be known, seen, and heard. Children often express their personal needs, relationship confusions, and desires about self and family through their behavior. They act out their inner stories. The psychological voice of children is often reflected in what they do as well as in what they refrain from doing. The message in children's behavior is their language.

Continuity and Connection through the Child-Centered Model

Just as the essence of the therapeutic relationship as well as other meaningful intimacies revolves around the simple yet profound experience of being seen, known, and heard in genuine ways, when the concept of "mental health" is distilled to its key elements, two fundamental ingredients emerge: a sense of continuity and of connection. Emotional and physical cutoffs, such as the symbolic closing of a door on the past, parts of the self, and crucial long-term relationships, can signal interpersonal difficulties and emotional distress around attachment, commitment, and patterns of conflict resolution. Abrupt ruptures in important family relationships, the use of geographic distance to deal with unresolved interpersonal conflicts, unexplained emotional withdrawal, years of silence that can stand between family members and characterize a family's genogram history provide important assessment information about continuity and connection. For Child-Centered Structural Dynamics, such emotional rifts and signs of interpersonal alienation illustrate the negative and unproductive results of the emotionally expensive strategy involved in attempting to solve relationship problems through premature closure on these conflicts without comprehensive understanding and resolution.

The Child-Centered Therapy Model utilizes a family history in an unusual way, paying careful attention to former as well as current patterns of emotional connection and alienation, specifically, patterns of joining and separating, and their implications for parent-child relationships. As shown in Chapter 7 and 8 on clinical practice, the model consciously considers, as central to the assessment process, the family's transgenerational patterns in relation not only to people (important relationships), but also family patterns focused around child and family development. In this light, developmental stages (as described in Chapter 3), as well as family relationship patterns, are viewed as important structures of family assessment and change. The problems of discontinuity, including broken emotional bonds and interpersonal connections, can be remedied through early intervention. When individuals and families come to therapy, or participate in enrichment and prevention, the group experience offers a sense of community, and extends an invitation to open the doors onto self and family understanding. A sense of community is important to the emotional health of all family therapy participants. Isolation can slowly erode self-esteem. Emotional isolation—the absence of social and emotional support—combined with an intrafamilial problem can be a family's undoing, diminishing and overtaxing its group capacity to cope.

As will be shown, the Child-Centered Structural Dynamic Prevention and Early Intervention Model (in the way the building blocks and techniques are applied) offers families a sense of continuity and connection through a variety of techniques. In the Child-Centered Model, participants are gathered into groups. The groups can consist of 8 to 10 parents and children, 4 to 5 couples, or 3 to 4 families. Continuity and connection develop along three perspectives and in three concrete and symbolic ways:

1. There is the family group itself. As the group forms and grows, it acts as a living model of community and provides a real sense of network to participants. The group process can also be used to illustrate how systems develop. The group facilitator can draw on examples that show system processes of organization and change to illustrate the Child-Centered building blocks. The clinician or child development specialist can ask, "What kind of group are we becoming? An open, closed, or random one?" "What parts do each of us find ourselves playing?" "Around what issues and themes?" "What do space, time, and energy feel like in this group?" "What is the group's sense of being effective?" "What is the group's emotional climate like?" "What is the group's identity, purpose, and meaning?"
2. The group setting also provides a learning laboratory for personal and family exploration. Through the model's structured activities, couples, parents, and children can make important discoveries about self and family. When participants express what they have learned, interchanges among group members can highlight both how families are unique and what families have in common, communicating the concepts of normative development and individual differences.
3. The group context teaches and models observational skills. Through the group, individuals and families can become informed guides, sensitive observers, and initiators of family change, as they are encouraged to act as positive movers in the direction of child and family development. A central goal of the prevention and early intervention phases of the model serves to strengthen, within families, the crucial capacity to emotionally mediate: to stand back and gain a broad, objective perspective on family events. This important observational and evaluative capacity is reflected in the impartial, thoughtful observations that a therapist usually offers to a family, a view that considers the group as a whole and is intentionally nurtured in families participating in the model's activities.

This chapter illustrates how a branching continuity and connection are created within and between families in the Prevention and Early Intervention phases of the Child-Centered Model.

Throughout the book, I have referred to the common theme and desire expressed by individuals and families: to be seen, heard, known, and found, as the essence of the therapy experience. What does this actually mean? Is it unconditional approval and acceptance? Not exactly. More to the point, the kind of acceptance that individuals and families seek is an acceptance that they rarely believe will include total approval. Families do not intuitively want, nor expect, that the therapist will approve of everything they do, which is why they come to therapy in the first place: for the honest feedback they both yearn for and fear. What individuals and families seek is an acceptance of self—"warts and all." They seek an acceptance of who they are magnified by the possibilities of what they can become. Like therapy, the enrichment and early intervention environment creates a safe and nurturing "holding environment," an emotionally accepting relationship that is expressed through the climate of the group and role of the facilitator (family group leader). This environment allows participants to take risks, to show both their vulnerabilities and strengths. This kind of acceptance enables growth, combines the uplifting and the sobering, the humorous and the disquieting into a well-rounded understanding of family and self. In conversations with families, I find that once a family and individual feel this kind of authentic acceptance, once they are seen, known, and respected enough to be entrusted with honest feedback, they will begin the necessary work of change.

An experience with a stormy and irascible client, with whom I formed a strong and positive bond, epitomizes this point. During one of our sessions, we moved into particularly sensitive issues around sexual abuse and parenting. All at once, at the end of the hour, she became irate, jumping to her feet, grabbing her coat, and walking to the door. As she turned, she said, "I've had enough of this crap. None of it is true!" Then she walked out and slammed the door behind her. A second later, she opened the door. Peering in, she said, in a quiet voice, "Same time next week?" I nodded, "Yes."

The Process of Primary Prevention

Before delving into fuller descriptions of case examples, including the steps and techniques of this model, several comments need to be discussed regarding the process and objective of the Prevention and Early Intervention phases of the Child-Centered Model. The first objective pertains to the painful experiences that individuals and families may inevitably discover and relate about their lives in parent and family groups or during a therapy hour. The second objective involves primary prevention and assessment-related issues raised earlier in the book. It is not wise or beneficial to dwell too long on an individual's and family's pain. To do so can delay and obscure the real work of change and self-growth that lies ahead.

The therapist should convey a sensitive understanding regarding the emotional toll that the painful experience has taken on both individual and family, communicating a genuine acceptance, understanding, and palpable sense of being with and beside the family. The therapist should also join with them in recalling and remembering. Then the therapist, by way of leading the family beyond the painful experience, should ask, "What can we make of this? How can we take this misfortune and turn it into a strength? You have survived it. By doing so, this says something important about you. These experiences, painful and unfair as they may be, are part of you, making you who you are now, showing your ingenuity and courage." This is an approximation of what a therapist might say; the words and message will vary with the situation. Surviving childhood incest, rape, an acrimonious divorce, living with the unpredictable behavior of an alcoholic parent, or the chronic experience of social prejudice—each of these experiences is quite unique, as is the intensity of an individual's and family's response to it.

The therapist's primary objective is to create acceptance—knowledge that the painful memory and event can be contained, held, seen, known, and heard in a safe and accepting environment and then incorporated or left behind. Like therapy, prevention and early intervention are about practical family matters. After relating a traumatic event, individuals and families are looking for practical solutions: What can be done to improve a family problem or make a personal situation better? I raise this issue now, because often in enrichment and early intervention groups, there can be "surprises." Participants can reveal highly personal and intense experiences as they explore child and family development process and experience change. It often becomes the responsibility of the facilitator, as the guide, to create protective borders and safe boundaries around participants' self-disclosure.

This objective leads naturally to the second point—the scope of primary prevention. In 1981, L'Abate proposed an intervention classification framework that still holds today. The categorization schema of family interventions incorporates three levels: primary, secondary, and tertiary prevention. This framework has been chosen as a springboard for a broad discussion of family assessment, because the term "prevention" unites all three levels, supporting the central twofold principle of the Child-Centered Structural Dynamic Model, which is that healthy and counterproductive processes can coexist within the same family and that troubled, multiproblem families express aspects of healthy family process. The term prevention, as L'Abate suggests, calls attention to the present and, at times, submerged growth and change-oriented processes ready to be awakened and strengthened in all families.

"Primary prevention"—the first level of intervention—includes short-term skill training and enrichment, and is associated with "normal" or asymptomatic families who seek to enhance healthy family process. A deepened family understanding and strengthening of family relationships, including parent-child bonds, are often the goals. "Secondary prevention" is usually associated with children and families at emotional risk. At this point, presenting child problems are typically in the early stages and fall within the mild to moderate range of intensity. The treatment of choice may involve preliminary, precrisis, and early intervention family therapy. "Tertiary prevention" involves families experiencing crisis or emergency (e.g., suicide), families with chaotic and entrenched multiproblem histories (e.g., transgenerational parent-child insufficiencies), and families with a seriously disturbed (e.g., psychotic) member. These families do not appear to respond well to brief therapy or skill training alone. Instead, they often require and respond more positively to long-term, intensive psychotherapies.

Frameworks of levels and interventions are never clear-cut. In the world of family therapy practice, levels of intervention overlap. Borderline gray areas exist between modes of intervention (Levels 1, 2, and 3) or primary, secondary, and tertiary prevention. Similarly, types of families who participate in different levels of treatment, as well as types of families who participate in the same level of intervention, may overlap. Just as intervention levels cut across family types, family types cut across intervention levels. System states (from fully functioning, to symptomatic, to crisis and instability) also may vary within a given family's experience, and across developmental stages.

Because families hold different images, and face different dilemmas around the prospect of therapy and the experience of asking for help, families travel a variety of paths to find the professional guidance and assistance they need. Some families follow the enrichment and educational route; other families seek help through therapy. Occasionally, there can be a surprise or two in prevention and early intervention when, for example, a troubled family finds its way through this route; when a stable family encounters a crisis during the program; or when an individual, during family exploration, discovers and reveals a family "secret." This is illustrated with case examples later in the chapter.

Prevention and Early Intervention in the Child-Centered Model: The Whole Picture

The model that is about to be described and illustrated has evolved through systematic empirical research and practical interaction with a broad range of families of different educational and socioeconomic backgrounds, and ethnic and racial experiences. The model has also been applied in a variety of practice settings, including Head Start Programs, community schools, child development centers, and community social service programs. The model and activities have been specifically developed to reflect sensitivity to racial and cultural differences, as well as the needs of families and therapists in different treatment contexts.

The idea of "family" embraces diverse forms: one-parent families, blended families, large, extended family networks, and so on. The initial message given to participant families is one of acceptance. This acceptance of diverse family forms sets the stage and encourages participants to become active "researchers" and "explorers" of family process and the family environment. The model's ultimate goal is to promote positive and optimal child development through an understanding of wider family patterns and full family involvement.

Throughout the preceding chapters, I have emphasized and illustrated the transactional role of the therapist as a warm, empathic observer and impartial arbiter for the family. As a sensitively attuned observer, witness, and interpreter of events, the therapist has a vital transactional role. Just as we seek to instill in children, as learners, the importance of careful eyes, careful ears, careful hearts and minds, adults in the family can similarly come to trust their observational skills, which support their capacity to reflect on family process and to remind family members, through an insightful and impartial grasp of the whole family picture, when the family is veering off course, when family members are inconsiderate of one another, and when the family is losing sight of its goals and sense of identity. Awakening a thoughtful observing ego within the family is the equivalent of developing a family-system perspective. When a family has perspective, the family has influence and direction, as well as the crucial capacity to self-evaluate. I have found (through research and therapy) that the key to sustained positive gains in prevention and early intervention lies in deepening the "group consciousness" and observational capacity in families.

The prevention and early intervention phases of the model and activities integrate this developmental principle with a special kind of systems consciousness that has family members as "system guides." The model's objective is to stimulate family awareness in participants by engendering, within individuals and families, the sense of a benign observing ego, a sense of self-reflection that can guide family development by understanding family process, "naming" what is taking place, and then constructing change. Self-initiated change, derived from the goal of encouraging parents to become sensitive and informed family guides, is the primary objective of the Child-Centered Model. Because parents are not taught but rather are shown, they organically and consciously build and center their knowledge of child and family development within personal and family experience. Parents are encouraged to fit the systematic knowledge they obtain through the Child-Centered building blocks (activities and techniques) to their own evolving model of family and child development. Participants, accordingly, stand at the center of family change as informed observers.

Four Modes of Integrating Child and Family Development: Families as Informed System Guides

The Child-Centered Model consists of four interactive modules (Andreozzi, 1976, 1977, 1979d, 1979e). These modules provide contexts for facilitating family growth and are the equivalent of different perspectives on child and family development. The modules are:

1. Parent and family group.
2. Children's playgroup.
3. Home teaching and home-based intervention.
4. Family resource lending library.

The components can be thought of as movable parts that fit the therapist's, family's, and community's specific needs.

PARENT AND FAMILY GROUP

The centerpiece of the Child-Centered Model is the family group. It can be organized in several ways: parents, couples, or families. I suggest 8 to 10 participants when working in a parent group; in a couple's group, no more than 4 to 5; in those groups involving whole families, 3 to 4 work well. The group is the primary vehicle for exploring family process and parent-child relations.

CHILDREN'S PLAYGROUP

The second component involves the infant-toddler or children's playgroup. Classroom observation can be combined or substituted for the children's playgroup when the children of participating families are older and/or when the therapist has access to school involvement. This component can be variously applied in combination with the family group. For example, group meetings, which usually last 2 to 2½ hours, can incorporate parent-child interaction through the playgroup experience. A portion of the parent-group time can and should involve interaction with and observation of children. Just as the family group can act as a living model of group process and, symbolically, offer a vivid illustration of how a family develops, the family time provided by the playgroup can create a spontaneously dynamic and invaluable parent-child human relations laboratory.

When parents and children interact in the playgroup context, opportunities arise for observational learning. Opportunities emerge to intervene naturally and unobtrusively through example and interaction. Through subtle ways that preserve the parents' dignity and strengthen the family's self-esteem, the therapist (group facilitator) can show the parent, through modeling, more effective ways of relating to children. I cannot stress enough that to usurp a parent's dignity or misread a family's strong sense of identity is a risk that could ultimately cause the child, who is the center of our positive goals and intentions, to lose. Small gains are better than large or dramatic ones, especially when a parent's core sense of self may be at stake.

Additional benefits of parent-child interaction in the playgroup context include the family's opportunity to experience their child in a new environment and to see how the child interacts with other children in a social setting other than home and family. The playgroup experience exposes parents to different family viewpoints on child rearing and parenting styles. Similarly, children's socioemotional and cognitive development are enriched and enhanced by interaction with other children and families.

Home-Based Intervention

The third component focuses on the family's home environment. The same activities used in the family group can be adapted within the home and individual family. The model, its building blocks and activities, can be applied to families. This, to some extent, can turn the tables on the professional, who becomes the one attempting to gain access to the family, instead of the family seeking access to the professional. Ground rules change. The therapist is inside a family's borders and on the family's own turf. Home-based education and family intervention assume various forms. A visit with a family can center around imparting child development information in conversational ways as the therapist illustrates more effective parenting skills and strategies. The Child-Centered Model makes distinctions among three factors:

1. The child's behavior.
2. The parents' expectations.
3. The meanings and intentions ascribed to behavior.

Highlighting the positive aspects of the parents' style, the therapist can also explore, clarify, and separate the parents' experiences and perceptions (interpretations) of the child's behavior from the child's actual behavior. When the issue of self-reference arises (when a parent recognizes and distinguishes self-experience from the experience of the child), the parent will become more receptive to age-appropriate child development expectations.

In the Child-Centered Model, the role of the home-based professional who meets with the family is intentionally broad, both in its goals and in the range of professions that can be involved. The home-based visitor can be a therapist, early childhood educator, or parent involvement coordinator or family educator, as was the case in the 5-year Family Outreach Project (Andreozzi, 1976, 1977, 1979d, 1979e). The professional or paraprofessional acts as a:

- Supportive listener to the parent.
- Link between community resources and the needs voiced by the family.
- Demonstrator of child development activities, and creative learning activities for parent and child.
- Consultant to the family on basic child development information and questions.
- Facilitator of the parents' awareness and understanding of family patterns and process, including how children and child development fit into the picture.

One unusual and outstanding feature of home-based early intervention is the central emphasis and theme of involving and stimulating family system understanding and nurturing in parents the capacity to act as an observing ego, a self-reflecting teacher, guide, and interpreter of family process. Once a family knows itself, what it is, how it transacts, what it values, its strengths and vulnerabilities, the family, with professional guidance and encouragement, can bring about self-initiated change. When families participate and are consciously aware of how change takes place, the change is theirs to "own," offering the best method to ensure sustained gains, and assuring that positive change will last. Change that happens out of family awareness or happens in ways unclear to some family members, can be short-lived or "blind change." This kind of change can work for a while, but it ultimately leaves families unprepared for new problems. The principle emphasized here, central to the success of the Child-Centered Model, requires the absolute involvement of parents as explorers of family process on cognitive-affective or experiential levels, as will be shown in the next chapter on the Child-Centered Activities, and also in Chapters 7 and 8 on the clinical model.

Although the main focus of the home-based component of the Child-Centered Model involves the nurturing of the developing child and family, thus enabling the child to develop fully within the special circumstances of each family, a crucially important companion purpose is violence prevention. To intervene early in a family's life, when parent-child conflicts and the child's behavior problems are nascent, can save a family from greater future distress. To become a warm, accepted, empathic observer in the family's own physical and social space, before the onset of more difficult problems that continue over long periods and take root further down the road, can spare great emotional expense to parent, family, and child. In the intimate conversations with families of early intervention therapy, and even prevention, common themes frequently expressed are scenes of psychological and actual aggression: subtle nuances as well as overt scenes that show some form of symbolic or actual violence against body, mind, relationships, and the human spirit.

Violence does not always take the form of physical aggression and physical injury to others, although this is often the case when family abuse escalates and becomes overt. There are other equally damaging, subtle forms of violence that take their toll: A parent's inability to see a child for who the child is; a parent's indifference to a child's strivings; a parent's discouragement or, worse, a parent's steady, deprecating criticism and emotional rejection of a child can have profound effects on a child's mind, spirit, imagination, empathy, and expectations for the future. It makes sense to prevent the occurrence of these emerging, psychologically damaging parent-child scenes rather than to try to erase them later on; since, in fact, they cannot be erased. While the process of therapy strives to transform these foundational scenes of self-in-relation to others, imprints remain that will, to some extent, always be there for the individual, parent-child, and family to deal with. Therapy can illuminate for the individual (parent and child) his or her strength and capacity to forgive, as well as provide him or her with an understanding of the ways in which patterns can continue. The best preventive measure is to help families early, to nurture strong, emotionally responsive bonds of attachment, to support the capacity of responsive, parent-child relationships, including a parent's awareness of self inside the relationship—separating out child's and parent's needs and emotional issues—combined with solid, accurate knowledge of what to expect from children at different developmental ages. Infants and toddlers are incredibly malleable and adaptive; the bonds of attachment, patterns of autonomy, and the rhythms of emotionally gratifying or conflicting and frustrating parent-child relationships begin here.

Creating Therapeutic Relationships: Family System Types

The key to home-based intervention is the family change that takes place in the family's own living space, its natural environment. As shown in earlier chapters, emotional warm-up periods, timetables of access and approach, and different models of physical and social distancing (visual relationship styles and statements of engagement and intimacy) can be anticipated and expected with each of the three family types: open, closed, and random. This provides another example of how knowledge of the family's preferred system type (the Kantor system typology and communicational domains) can benefit therapist and family. This knowledge can facilitate and guide the therapist's actions, and significantly enhance rapport.

For example, the closed family system values sameness, tends to favor less effusive shows of emotion and enthusiasm, and relies on clear traditional rules, roles, and family hierarchies. This family type can be more authoritative and, when counterproductive, authoritarian. An open family system tends toward order, but less so than the closed family system. Sameness is important, but difference is also encouraged. The open family system works from a premise of consensus, viewing itself as egalitarian. This family favors clear rules for how children and parents should relate, but allows greater latitude in interpreting and applying rules. Rules can and do change more readily in the open system. There is a conscious sense that rules are context dependent and situation specific. A strong believer in difference, the random family system is the most idiosyncratic family type. Rules favor the individual's (parent's and child's) personal expression. This family can often be effusive, intense, and emotionally extravagant. Emotion and enthusiasm can be openly and outwardly expressed.

There is a strong relationship benefit for the therapist in communicating differently with each family type, consciously choosing words and styles of physical and interpersonal access and emotional expression that meld with the family's capacity to "listen." Helping families to shape and direct, from within, their self-initiated change, the therapist begins to join the family's view of itself and the world, offering information and emotional access in ways familiar to the family's "mind."

Harper Lee's (1960) *To Kill a Mockingbird* relates a story about a school-age brother and sister, Scout and Jim, their widowed father, Atticus, their town, and their town's strange outcast, Boo Radley. The novel describes the world through the children's eyes. In the story, it is Scout and Jim who, with uncomplicated understanding and clarity of perception, look beyond the myth surrounding the town recluse, Boo Radley. As the children's relationship with him grows, they gradually discover a warm ally and protector, a silent and caring observer who saves them from harm. The children are the first to sense and respect Boo Radley's quiet dignity, and to see him not as odd, menacing, and "crazy," but as humane and astutely aware.

At the end of the novel, Atticus, Scout and Jim's father, has learned profoundly from his children. He realizes the town's mistake: that no one took the time to look beyond the outward, odd appearance of their curious neighbor. As Boo Radley stands with Atticus and Scout, Scout asks: "Daddy, can we touch Boo Radley?" Atticus responds: "You can shake Mr. Radley's hand, if that's alright, with you Mr. Radley?" Atticus then adds, "Scout, we can never really know a person until we walk around in their shoes for a while and see the world from their front porch." He explains that to disrupt Mr. Radley's private world by bringing him too quickly into the town's light would be a little like killing a mockingbird who disturbs no one and just perches in a tree and sings.

A similar parent-child problem will be explored within the following three family perspectives, showing how the therapist and early childhood educator can shape their language and mode of access to match the sensibilities of the three family types. Joining the family raises the therapist's awareness and illustrates the importance of making the family conscious of its use of self and self-knowledge. The process of engagement, building the therapeutic alliance, highlights the ways in which the therapist's and family's style of relating are compatible or mismatched, an issue that will be explained in greater detail in Chapter 7.

Newcomers to the Neighborhood: Rita, Antonio, and Toddler, Alicia

Rita and Antonio, both in their mid-20s, and their 19-month-old daughter, Alicia, are a closed family system facing a potential early intervention problem. Immigrants from South America, they are ambitious and energetic "go-getters" committed to a strong work ethic. Antonio works two jobs while Rita stays home, caring for Alicia and organizing the family. She talks about feeling isolated, cut off from family support 3,000 miles away. Rita has been losing her temper more quickly with Alicia recently. Antonio is often too tired to provide her with reassurance and the intimacy she needs. In the face of increasing isolation, a world that seems to be growing smaller, Rita must find constructive ways to deal with Alicia, a vigorous and curious toddler as determined and intense as her parents. The parents describe Alicia as a blend of their fiery tempers ("quick to flair up; quick to cool down"). Alicia is meeting her mother's requests for compliance with blatant daily resistance. Rita complains to the home-based teacher, "All I get from pretty little Alicia is 'No'!"

The house is immaculately clean. In the corner of the small living room, Rita has set up Alicia's play-yard. Toys are lined up neatly around the play-yard edge. On the walls are pictures of saints; a small votive candle burns. Although it is a sunny afternoon, the window shades are drawn. Rita knows none of her neighbors and only on rare and special occasions can she afford the long distance telephone call to her mother and sisters whose guidance she misses and needs.

Thumping her hand on the Bible, she says "Spare the rod and spoil the child. Even the Bible tells you that." It is very close to dinnertime, and Antonio is home between jobs. He supports and continues his wife's theme, "We believe that children should respect their parents. Alicia cannot defy us as she does." Next, he subtly shifts the focus of the conversation from their (the couple's) joint decision and beliefs onto his wife alone. He adds, "My wife can't take Alicia's disobedience."

This family is a closed family partly because of the models of family life, order, and stability each spouse brought to and has agreed on in the marriage, and partly because the family is new to the neighborhood and is living in a community of strangers. Respect and tradition are important to the couple—more vital now since the family perceives itself as being alone.

Before the family can be open to the idea that "no" does not mean "insolence," but rather is Alicia's testing of the normal limits of her independent learning and exploration of self, the family centrality must be emphasized and upheld. In contrast to an open or random family, in a closed family system type the route to parental receptivity begins with emphasis and support of family values and beliefs. Closed family systems strive for traditional order. This family type prefers clear parental hierarchies with explicit distinctions between roles. Parental authority is highly valued and not a matter easily open to dispute. To challenge the "spare the rod, spoil the child" cultural-religious belief would have alienated the couple. After some discussion with the early childhood educator (noting that the child was indeed not being physically hurt), and several weeks of early intervention, Rita and Antonio softened and later abandoned this notion of discipline.

The Fowlers

The Fowlers, Mary and George, in their mid-40s, and their five children, ranging from adolescence to toddler age, live in a close-knit, urban, ethnic neighborhood—a network of interconnected and attached apartments and tenement houses. The houses are so close together that, in the summer when windows are open, the sounds of families overlap and blend. The Fowlers live in the same neighborhood where they were born. They are an open family, in many ways, an extended family.

The Fowlers were having difficulty with Jason, their toddler, when they began the early intervention program. Although the family's values and traditions were deep-rooted, as a result of having raised four children, combined with the couple's belief in open disagreement, they favored and enjoyed exploration of ideas, including child rearing.

Several weeks of parent group, home visits, and playgroup experience changed the Fowlers' concept of discipline. In this open family, who agreed to disagree, child development was given priority. The couple realized that Jason did not always intend, nor understand, the full extent of his mischief.

Open family systems can be approached more directly. Suggestions about new parent-child strategies are absorbed and seen by the family as variety and as possibility. Closed family types, on the other hand, respond to more sensitively timed and slower approaches. Whereas the gatekeepers in the closed family are usually the parents, this is not always true in the open family.

The Gardners

Karen and David, in their 20s, along with their two young children, live in a three-room, rural farmhouse. Karen bakes bread, believes in telepathy, and feels that plants have souls. The Gardner family has four cats, a dog, a gerbil, and a hamster for their

3-year old. Karen is still breast-feeding her younger, 18-month-old child. The family sleeps together in a "family bed." The house is strewn, helter-skelter, with clothes, toys, books, and projects in progress. Everything is open; there are few private spaces. Karen is having trouble setting limits. The concern she and David describe centers on boundaries around the children. They have few rules. The children, who are chasing the family into decisions over safe bounds and limits of autonomy, are quickly growing into wild spirits. The Gardners are a random family system.

Random family systems, of all the family types, can be the easiest to join on the surface, simply because they are so individualistic. The random family type thrives on spontaneity. The dilemma here is not necessarily one of access, but one of structure. Random family systems can often typically show early intervention problems stemming from too fluid and arbitrary parent-child rules. There is also an absence of clear limits that reassure a child that the power and influence is not too great to overwhelm them.

Family Resource Lending Library

The fourth module and companion-part of the Child-Centered Model is the development of child and family resources that a participating family or parent can borrow from the program. This is a practical component. A therapist may or may not choose to develop this "family resource center," based on such considerations as the nature of the therapist's practice, the needs of the families seen, and the financial resources available to child development or mental health centers.

The family resource lending library does not need to be elaborate. It can be quite simple, filled with practical, inexpensive items. Some suggestions include hand puppets, a container of blocks, several family board games appropriate for various children's age ranges, a "recipe book" of parent-child activities, a handful of well-chosen children's storybooks, books on child growth and development and parenting, an inexpensive Polaroid, or simple box camera. For example, as the early intervention and prevention program develops over time, either the therapist can collect or ask families to contribute (write down and add to the recipe book) parent-child and family learning activities and suggestions—offering future family participants the benefit of their experience. Families are quite eager and enthusiastic about passing on their knowledge. This symbolic connection to other families can create a "living sense" of social network, a message of the common experiences families all share. For example, several of the parent groups developed what they called their *Family Newsletter,* which they circulated among themselves and then, at the end of the program, gave to me to use in my work with other families.

In addition, a Book of Child Development Activities, written in plain, everyday language, with examples, can be easily compiled by consulting a local preschool. Many of the activities parents can do with their children to promote learning and increase interpersonal connection do not require any special extra materials and can be organized around everyday items that the family already has at home. For example, the game of peek-a-boo teaches object constancy, that the parent is there and does not disappear; Cheerios (cereal) can be used for counting, different-size buttons for sorting and categorizing, and so forth. Suggestions about the use of household objects and materials as readily available resources to promote child development should always be tempered with discussions around child safety and recommendations for childproofing the home for young, inquisitive explorers. The inclusion of a camera in the lending library is to provide families of limited means with the opportunity to take new family photographs and create new relationship images, as will be explained and illustrated in Chapters 6, 7, and 8. The act of taking new family photographs, in itself, provides a graphic means for transforming parent-child and family imagery; the message conveyed is the prospect that relationships can and do change in positive ways. Photographs are crucial ingredients in one of the five Child-Centered Activities used in all three tiers of the model.

I have found the act of lending these materials and resources to families, entrusting them with something they take from the therapist's office or community center into their homes, communicates an important message of belonging or being part of the process, and a sense of responsibility: that the family is competent, valued, and capable. This can be a profound and potent message of welcome to families at risk.

Identifying and Treating Emergent Critical Identity Images through Prevention and Early Intervention

The following illustration from everyday life shows what a critical identity image is and how an identity struggle can evolve. The example selected is drawn from early intervention and enrichment with an extended family. The emerging family crisis and identity struggle center around Peter, a 7-year-old boy, his Aunt Phoebe, and her 21-month-old, Raoul.

Peter's parents refer to him as a "late arrival" in the family's life, a "change-of-life baby." His brother and sister are teenagers and Peter, as one of the few boys who lives in a neighborhood mainly of little girls, often feels he has too few playmates. That is why when his cousin, Raoul, was born to his Aunt Phoebe and Uncle Bob, Peter seemed delighted. He now had a chance to "be a big brother." Peter was always, his parents explained, very gentle with the baby, amusing the baby while showing a strong sense of protection. Peter talked about how "taking care of baby Raoul" made him feel "big and important." He was beginning to derive meaning and a strong sense of self-worth from his role and image as hero and protector.

However, as Peter became more ensconced in his position, other changes were happening in the family, pulling his Aunt Phoebe, the gatekeeper to baby Raoul, in a different and opposite direction. Phoebe, who confided that she was unsure of herself as a parent and often felt like "all thumbs" as a mother, was becoming increasingly frustrated by baby Raoul's behavior. Her anxiety and frustration grew in direct proportion to every increasing step baby Raoul took away from her, separating and declaring his toddler independence. The precarious, unpredictable mobility of Raoul frightened her and heightened her sense of feeling out of control. As Phoebe explained later, she had no image of herself as a mother, nothing to draw on from her past, which filled her with self-doubt that she tried to hide.

The more she pushed to instill control, the more little Raoul resisted her. He would not let her dress him, change his diaper, or feed him without a "royal battle." When Phoebe tried to put him in his car seat, she explained, "He stiffened out like a board."

Feeling helpless and defeated, Phoebe, afraid to admit her frustration to herself, began to silently resent Raoul's behavior toward her. To invite sympathy from extended family and support from her husband, she began to tell vivid accounts of her difficult child: what a "terror," what a "wild and uncontrollable," "physically strong and deliberately disobedient child" he was becoming. Her ambivalence showed as she swung back and forth between overprotectiveness and subtle but abrupt disengagement and emotional withdrawal from her son. Either she hovered too closely to Raoul or, distracted, rushed in almost at the last minute. She had become preoccupied with Raoul somehow getting injured or being hurt. Peter's parents, and even Phoebe's husband Bob, wondered to themselves, reluctant to tell Phoebe that they could not decide whether she wanted to hug or scold the child.

What happened next was a change in a family pattern, shifting from a positive to a problematic one in which Aunt Phoebe and Peter's relationship began to get into trouble. Because of her own insecurities about parenthood, a vulnerable area of self-concept that she experienced from childhood, she began to scold Peter and block his access to baby Raoul. She would harp on everything Peter did, good, bad, and indifferent. Peter no longer seemed to like his aunt and her sense of his "doing everything wrong"; experience of being criticized and opposed by her was spreading to his feelings about his cousin, Raoul. Peter began complaining that he did not want to visit his grandparents anymore. When asked "why," he answered, "Because Aunt Phoebe will be there with the baby" (he said "the baby" in a singsong, childlike way that conveyed his feelings of jealousy and rejection). In a family meeting, when his parents said, "But we thought you loved baby Raoul. We thought you couldn't wait to play with him. You're such a big help," Peter adamantly shook his head "no" and said (to his parents) "Not any more!"

When I asked him if he could tell us what had happened, what had changed his good feelings, he sprang from his chair to show us. Peter was eager to role-play his emerging relationship image and experience with Aunt Phoebe and the baby.

Peter stood before us, leaning forward, arms bent at the elbows, neck and head bent forward, and began to run frantically in place. His arms and legs gave the impression that his body was going in all directions. He pulled out his shirttail and said, as he ran continuously in place, "This is my Aunt Phoebe." Then he threw his arms up and out. In the role of Aunt Phoebe, he whines, "My baby! My baby!" Then, moving even faster in place, resembling a cartoon caricature showing us his child's image of Aunt Phoebe, he explains for us, his bemused audience, "Aunt Phoebe's cheeks get all puffy. Her eyes bug out and her jacket puffs out all around her, flying behind her in the wind. All she keeps yelling like a 'big butt-brain' is 'Peter don't do this, Peter don't do that' even when I'm being good with the baby." Then he says, "She's nosey and never leaves us alone," adding. "Why can't I do anything right? . . . I don't like Aunt Phoebe. Maybe she's turned into a witch or something."

Peter is communicating an emergent critical identity image that, if left unresolved, may not only turn what was a positive relationship with his aunt and cousin into a troubled and conflicted one, but may also crystallize into a guiding relationship image with authority figures that will affect future patterns of relating to others in the world. The content of the image revolves around themes of Peter's desires to nurture and be nurtured and to show his competence, as well as have it positively affirmed. The transactional message Peter is learning in his role play and obviously internalized interaction scene is of self as a thwarted mover or "doer" in relation to an aunt who once supported or encouraged (followed) his affectionate relationship with the baby and now blocks (opposes) his good gestures and emotional access. Aunt Phoebe is pushing Peter away, increasing the emotional and physical distance between herself and Peter, as well as between Peter and baby Raoul. Her behavior becomes comprehensible when we know her critical identity image and how it fits like a matched puzzle piece to Peter's developmental strivings.

Phoebe, who participated in the early intervention, reveals crucial interpersonal scenes in her own life where she becomes blocked and, like Peter, a thwarted mover who seeks to show parents her skill and competence as a "caregiver." Phoebe and Peter were the youngest among much older siblings, having in common the psychological experience of being an "only child" with limited social access and expression. As shown throughout the book, these foundational image scenes (transactional scenarios) lay out the blueprints for taking on familiar roles and create the unfinished relationship areas children carry into adulthood as they seek positive resolution and better outcomes. The next chapter will present, in depth, the five Child-Centered Activities. The activities of the Child-Centered Structural Dynamic Model are consciously designed and developed to stimulate system-level awareness of parent-child relations and family process and to promote family change.

CHAPTER 6

Five Child-Centered Family Activities

Routes to System Understanding

FIVE PRIMARY FAMILY activities interact to build understanding of family process, parent-child relations, and child development. These activities, designed and developed to work on all three levels (prevention, early intervention, and therapy), form the heart of the Child-Centered Structural Dynamic Model:

1. The Family Notebook.
2. Photographs in Family Process.
3. The Family Network Drawing.
4. Living Sculpture.
5. Family Role Play.

Family awareness of all five building blocks of family process flows through and emerges out of parents' and children's involvement in and self-guided learning through the five Family Activities. Each activity can be used by the therapist and family to illustrate, explore, and consciously make apparent the influence of some or all of the child-centered building blocks (derived from the integration of child development, with the Kantor system typology and communicational domains and the Kantor Four Player Model described and illustrated in Chapters 2 and 3). The building blocks include the understanding and identification of:

- The family's network of relationships.
- Space, time, and energy dimensions.

- Affect (nurturance between parent and child and intimacy between spouses); power (competence, mastery, and learning); meaning and identity.
- Player parts.
- Family types.

Any of the five activities can be effectively used to illuminate the network of family relationships; the family's use of space; how the family spends time; the family's style of energy; its sense of power, competence, and mastery; its nurturant images and style of intimacy; the family's and individual's identity; the player parts that family members seem to play routinely; and the type of family (open, closed, or random) that the family sees itself as being. The activities are specifically designed to provide the most flexibility to therapist and family.

The point emphasized here, as research and practice have shown (Andreozzi, 1977, 1978, 1979a, 1979b, 1979c, 1979e, 1988), is that all five activities do not always need to be used. Any one or two activities, carefully chosen and strategically timed, can stimulate parent-child awareness and facilitate family change. Each activity offers technique-guided methods of accessing families' knowledge of all the family process, child, and family development building blocks. While guidelines accompany all five activities, including how to use them, the order of introduction of activities, and clinical suggestions based on research for maximizing the impact and efficacy of the activity, the decision of which activities to use and when is left to the therapist's judgment, firsthand knowledge of the family's needs, and special circumstances. The five activities have been purposely designed and adapted to work both together and alone, and in all three settings (parent group, the therapist's office in one-to-one relationship with the family, and the family's home as part of the home-based context). Together, all five activities create a comprehensive program of family-system understanding.

There are two other important aspects of overall application and decided strengths of the activities. The first feature is that each activity has been consciously adapted in two ways: to be used with adults and also to be used with children. The second feature involves the multiple ways that families learn. The activities offer multilevel learning. Families are involved cognitively and affectively. The activities elicit "thinking" and "feeling" awarenesses around family process. Learning is personal and interior (surrounding the self), group and family-oriented and systemic, and experiential. Parents and families in early intervention and prevention have described the process as "learning with both our hearts and minds." Finally, the activities work on a child and family development level. The child's needs for nurturance, self-expression, and growth are central.

The Family Notebook Activity

Space is location. Time is sequence. Energy is vitality and intensity. Power is competence, constructive efficacy, autonomy, the capacity to make one's own decisions. Affect is perceived nurturance, the giving and acceptance of support, a sense of intimacy and felt connection and attachment. Meaning is equated with intentionality, a sense of purpose and destination. Identity connotes integrity, a sense of integration, a blending of the unique and special with common features that are shared. Each of the family dimensions of the Child-Centered Model branches out into multiple levels, connecting in some way with every other dimension in the family's social space with simultaneous implications for the family, the family's interpersonal and interactional life, and the personal worlds of self. This model is about selfhood and system integrity, communication, and change.

The Family Notebook Activity (Andreozzi, 1979b) is the first learning experience in the model, the organizing activity that sets the stage for family awareness and the activity around which family change is built. The premise, confirmed through clinical practice and prevention/early intervention research (Andreozzi, 1978, 1979d, 1979e, 1985a, 1988), is that increased system awareness, knowledge of one's own family, combined with general knowledge of how the family interacts and develops as a group is the first step toward family understanding. Families who understand family relationships as a whole and what can be thought of as the puzzle pieces of a family gestalt, in turn, create opportunities for self-initiated family change. This premise about family change may seem clear, obvious and practical, but the principle may require some clarification.

What is described here is not family change based on an academic understanding of systems theory and concepts of family process. The learning and knowledge available through the Family Notebook Activity (as with the other activities in the model) extend far beyond cognitive awareness. What families gain is experiential knowledge: their own self-formulated view of family process explored through observation and understanding of everyday concrete family events and interactions. This unfolding family view and developing awareness is communicated and shaped by the family's personal experience, emotional vocabulary, images, symbols, and metaphors using nontechnical language. We know an individual, child and adult, as well as the family through their personal images and images of self and others that shape and guide their behavior, interactions, and ultimately reveal the way they see the world. When families grasp a view of the family as a whole—an overview of the interplay of relationships—they can begin to see parent-child relationships, child development, and the meanings, goals, and expectations of children and childhood behavior in a new and fresh light. The path is open to move beyond guilt and blame and the parent's overpersonalization of the child's behavior—often the first signs that a parent-child relationship problem may be forming. The Family Notebook Activity is purposely designed to shift parents' attention away from an individual focus toward an expanded view of the individual self, adult and child, in the family group and wider community. The activity has a twofold objective:

1. To stimulate an awareness of circumstances and the impact the physical, psychological, and social environment (both within and outside the family) can have on the parent-child relationship.
2. To create in families a sensitivity to context, a view that considers and values the individual, but also sees the broader picture—the role and influence of the surrounding environment.

Well-intentioned parents may encounter difficulties with their children because of an unsupportive environment.

SHIFTING THE FOCUS FROM SHAME AND GUILT TO SHARED RESPONSIBILITY

Parents who are on the verge of developing abusive patterns of behavior, who show the early parent-child relationship signs of subtle withdrawal or emotional unpredictability with their children, can also benefit from the psychological "pause" that an expanded family view offers. This view can provide the crucial interruption and vital transition time a family needs to regroup, self-reflect, and regain its composure and sense of purpose: in essence, to "think about" what the family is doing in a broader perspective. The importance of introducing an expanded family view in the early stages of parent-child problems is similar to and serves much the same purpose as "eye blinks." We cannot stare at a single, stationary object or scene too long before we begin to feel uncomfortable and need to break away, turning our gaze to something else to provide our eyes with visual relief. The same is true of the mind. We cannot concentrate attention for hours on a single task without losing accuracy and perspective. The mind, like our eyes, thrives on variety, a shifting gaze. Similarly, turning parents' attention to a family view provides psychological relief. Parent and child can temporarily recede out of what often can become a harsh, negative, unforgiving spotlight into a softer and broader family view, as parent and child are reintegrated into the total picture with a more positive light.

In Chapters 2, 3, and 4, problem transactions, painful, mutually disqualifying patterns, in the vicious cycle of unmet needs and lost expectations were likened to a cat chasing its tail and going nowhere. Early intervention and prevention can break these cycles before they take hold in families. For example, the sigh of relief families breathe is palpable and audible when the therapist can say to a worried and frazzled parent: "Okay, let's look at some practical things in your environment such as how your family organizes its living space, spends time, and uses its energy. Let's see how these things may also be contributing to the problem. Some solutions may be right there in the environment waiting for us to find."

The Family Notebook Activity forms the family's first introduction to and exploration of space, time, and energy, power, nurturance and intimacy, identity and the meaning of selfhood in the family. The focus is on the environment; the aim is increased interpersonal perspective. The purpose of the Family Notebook Activity is to orient families to their contexts, to create an understanding of the power and influence of the environment—the family's capacity to stand back and see events, behavior, and the self in perspective. The central goal of the Family Notebook Activity is to encourage relative versus absolute thinking, and to nurture the capacity to evaluate and reconsider a child's and parent's actions in a broader and fuller light.

To understand context, essentially to put life events and relationships, positive, negative, and traumatic, into perspective is a unifying theme and common goal of all good and effective therapy. The particular modality of therapy (e.g., dyadic, group, or family) or the particular theoretical orientation within a family of therapies (e.g., structural, strategic, or object relations) does not matter. The goal of effective therapy is to help individuals see the forest from the trees; to encourage them to stand back and gain perspective; to expand their cognitive and emotional awareness beyond the "hurt"; and to encourage alternative explanations.

This expanded view grows out of a sense of emotional maturity around the events, and is reflected in the depth and diversity of possible explanations a person brings to a description, as well as understanding of what has happened to them in their lives. Clinical practice and research (Andreozzi, 1978, 1979d, 1985a, 1988) have shown, for example, that individuals and families who can consciously recognize additional relevant factors affecting the problem, who consider and identify a larger number of plausible theories about the problem (how it got started, who and what is involved, and what contributes to its development and maintains the difficulty) tend to make more rapid progress. This expanded perspective and maturity of thought, a combination of affect and cognition, begins with a palpable awareness of a wider world around us—the environment. Self-knowledge and change through self- and therapy-guided exploration grows out of the experience and heightened sense of emotional connection, an empathy for self and others that can arise out of an expanded view and appreciation of circumstances. Nothing in the world, plants, animals, societies, can live without some connection, or thrive for very long in isolation. Autonomy is grown first from the experience of interdependence.

How the Family Notebook Activity Works

The Family Notebook Activity consists of a series of questions that families are asked to answer. A few practical suggestions should be offered here. While The Family Notebook is composed of a set of family questions designed to encourage families to think as a system, the Activity can involve keeping an actual physical notebook (though this is not essential). Some families who have difficulty reading and writing, or who do not feel comfortable expressing their thoughts on paper, can be encouraged to approach the questions as "things to think about." Because the questions are practical and concrete but also extend into social aspects of the family's group life, I have found in practice that the questions raise their curiosity and capture their imaginations as they think about family life and their children in new ways. Parents do not necessarily need to write their thoughts down in a journal. They can be encouraged to talk about their opinions and answers to the questions in the parent group or one-on-one with the therapist. A group facilitator can choose two or three questions as the focus of each weekly group discussion, or the therapist can ask the family together to discuss their thoughts, impressions, and observations around one or two salient questions.

Questions can be introduced in two ways within the group. The group facilitator can choose two or three questions in advance and organize the group discussion around these questions. Or, at the end of each group meeting, the group facilitator can give parents two or three questions written on a sheet of paper that they can take home and think about during the week. I have worked with a broad spectrum of families (who have been described earlier) that provided detailed and thoughtful feedback. Based on their evaluation, from parents with 8th- to 10th-grade educations through parents at university laboratory schools, the common theme they expressed was excitement and enthusiasm around the questions; the activity stimulated new ways of looking at the intimate family world around them and helped them to change and improve their family's living space.

Parents are urged to develop a running account of their observations, reactions, and growing awareness about family interaction and child development. The Notebook Activity can be introduced variously as a "notebook," "diary," "journal," "log," or "family story." Parents are encouraged to choose the name that best fits their personality, personal image, and preferred style of communicating. They can be as objective or subjective and personal in their "books" as they wish. The goal of the Family Notebook Activity is not written composition per se, although a large number of parents discover intellectual strengths, gain confidence in their cognitive/academic skills, and have gone on to complete high school educations or have returned to college. The goal of the Notebook Activity is self-expression and the nurturing of crucial life skills and important parental abilities: a capacity to observe, to self-reflect, to trust their awarenesses, to sense the extents and ranges of influences in their lives, and to identify available alternatives.

Another integral aspect of the Family Notebook Activity involves parents observing a child (one of their own children or preschool children in a playgroup) and then relating child-rearing beliefs and styles of parenting to their childhood experiences. A central goal of the activity is to make the family's style of parenting conscious through the parent's self-initiated identification. This preserves the family's dignity and strengthens existing competencies while forming the trust and rapport between family, facilitator, and parent group that will enable parents to face parent-child vulnerabilities and provide them with the psychological incentive and courage to change. I will illustrate this process in the two family vignettes that complete this chapter. Anticipating the possibility of change and also guiding this positive outcome, the group facilitator (therapist) can suggest to families that over time they may be surprised to see how their opinions about children and child rearing have changed.

For example, the therapist or family group facilitator can offer encouragement in the form of the following practical suggestions to parents:

- Relax. Think of your written voice and speaking voice as one and the same. Write down your thoughts as you would speak them.
- Imagine you are talking to someone who is very interested in you and what you have to say. Pretend you are talking to someone who knows you and really wants to know you better. Hold an imaginary conversation. The Notebook can become your "best friend" and act as a trusted confidante.
- Imagine you are writing an important letter to a loved one or to a friend you have not seen and want to tell the person something important about yourself, your children, and family.
- You can also choose a favorite photograph of a family member, or someone you trust and feel emotionally close to, and keep that photograph in front of you as you begin to write. Write down your thoughts as if you are talking directly to the person(s) in the photograph. Keep the photograph in your Notebook.
- Think of yourself as a teacher. Imagine that a group has asked you to explain family life and children to them. They do not have the knowledge; you do. They need you to explain how families work. The group or person is intently listening and needs your help and the benefit of your experience.
- Be natural. Dictionaries are for spelling and grammar for school compositions. The meaning of what you have to say is most important. You are telling your child's and family's story.

Some families who have participated in the prevention and early intervention model have developed detailed and thoughtful journals that the families have proudly referred to as "family books." Some parents have suggested keeping their journals and giving them to their children when they are grown. One participator, for example, characterized the Family Notebook as a companion, an important part of the family history, something to treasure and reflect on as one would a family photograph album or a child's baby book.

The Family Notebook is the first activity used with participating families for several reasons. As mentioned briefly, the activity shifts the focus to the family's consideration of the environment, specifically basic elements of the environment. What can be more fundamental and intuitive a part of family life and human interaction than space, time, and energy? Like clay, these are the mediums through which we shape our lives. Everyone is familiar with these concepts. Space, time, and energy are concrete realities of everyday life. Families are immersed in these dimensions. Another vital reason speaks directly to child development and brings the child's needs and unique child's view of the world onto center stage and into clear family focus. Part of the work of childhood is the development and exploration of spatial concepts and the concepts of time. Through space and time, children learn the important concept of function, how things work, and also sequence, what to expect next. For example, a child learns that flipping the light switch makes the light go on. Or, after naptime, big brother comes home from school.

A child's view of space and time is remarkably different from the views of adults. Parents will discover and appreciate these differences as they observe children's orientations to time and space, and will connect this awareness with observable characteristics of their family's social living space and family's patterns and rhythms of time. As I will show in the case of the Appells (a family in prevention), and the Rexfords (a family who participated in early intervention), changes in the family's physical environment that can be made quickly and easily are often all that are needed to circumvent problems. Parents are often encouraged by the almost instantaneous positive changes they experience. These intermediary measures, which shift the interaction between parent and child, constitute enough of a positive direction to satisfy and motivate the parent to explore further and to attempt additional changes. Blaming the arrangement of the family's living space is preferable to blaming a child or overpersonalizing a child's behavior.

THE CHILD'S EXPANDING WORLD IN SPACE AND TIME

Children are vigorous explorers. Their world is one of practical intelligence as they learn through trial and error and active experimentation. Their repetitive play (performing the same action over and over) is the way they learn intentionality and discover concepts of cause and effect. The toddler accidentally pulls on a rug while trying to get a toy out of reach and discovers that, by pulling the rug closer, he or she can obtain the toy. Active investigators of space, toddlers deliberately seek novelty and act to produce new, unexpected, and interesting results. The child empties cabinet drawers, pots and pans from cupboards, opens and closes doors. From the early stages of infancy, the child's sense of object permanence begins to form determining how the child perceives self in relation to objects in the world, as well as how the child perceives relationships among objects in relation to self. While the child invests objects (including people and relationships) with some permanence in time and space, the child's conception of cause largely remains egocentric. Nothing happens in the world except as a result of the child's own wishes. The child sees the moon through a glass patio door. The child walks and the moon walks with her. Because she moves, the moon moves, following her.

Gradually, the child internalizes spatial and temporal relationship patterns. Space exists on two levels, physical and imagistic. The child no longer always needs to physically experiment with objects to solve problems, for example, carefully nesting four teacups. Instead, the child represents the objects mentally and cognitively combines and manipulates them. In effect, the child is cognitively inventive. At as early as 18 to 24 months, the child shows active and innovative problem-solving awareness. The child uses a stick to poke and prod a toy outside the play-yard and beyond reach, pulling the toy closer, until it is within grasp. Similarly, the child begins to represent and act mentally on absent objects and events. Imagination and a rudimentary memory take hold. The child's symbolic life and the seeds of spatial relationship patterns, in short, self-concept in relation to family transactions, begin to form.

As language grows, the child's symbolic world expands, and family relationships take on psychosocial and representational meaning. The child becomes concretely aware of the implications of the family's social living space. As shown in Table 1.1, a child's principal achievement between the ages of 2 and 7 is the development of the capacity to represent the external world internally through the use of symbols. Symbols and symbolic play free the child from here and now boundaries because they can now represent past and future concepts and events. In this preoperational and intuitive thinking stage, the child's problem-solving is strongly guided by visual perception and the child's problem-solving approach flows from what the child senses to be true. (Table 1.1 outlines the gradual deepening and expansion of the child's cognitive and social world, highlighting the literal, concrete immediacy of the child's environment.) What makes young children vulnerable is the child's concrete perception or sensory-dependent interpretation of events. What children see happen is what they believe. Because the capacity to adopt and shift points of view is developing but fairly limited, when there is family conflict, they cannot see both sides.

Consider the Stone family vignettes described in Chapters 3 and 4. During dinner, the son, 6-year-old Keith, in a fight with his father over food, angrily slams the vitamin bottle down on the table, spilling vitamins all over the floor. This act provokes his father and draws Keith's mother into the conflict. As the conflict escalates into violence, the father turns toward his bewildered son. Holding up a small cuticle cut on one of his fingers, the father says to the boy, "Your mother drew blood!" This remains a vivid image in Keith's mind and emotional life. He is too young to stand back and analyze the situation. He is unable, cognitively, to shift between both parents' points of view, and he is unwilling, emotionally, to split his loyalties and favor one parent over another. No child should have to make such a choice. Such violent and divisive relationship imagery can be forestalled through early intervention.

Some of the Stones' problems, as with other families, arise out of the family's misuse and poorly constructed organization of the environment. While there is more at stake, early signals of an erupting episode of anger and aggression can be traced to cues in the family's ironic use of space, colliding energy styles, and patterns and perceptions of time. The Child-Centered Model averts the full escalation of crisis by preparing families to be careful observers of these family dimensions and to undertake practical solutions. Changing or rearranging the physical environment can positively alter parent-child interactions. The goal of the model is to prevent debilitating family crisis.

FAMILY NOTEBOOK ACTIVITY: THE FAMILY AND CHILD'S SOCIAL SPACE

The following are some practical and concrete activities and questions used across all three tiers of the Child-Centered Model to increase the family's awareness of itself as a system, and the parent's increased understanding of the child's world. The answers to these questions (parents' self-reflections and observations) can lead parents to make important positive changes (reorganization) in the family environment. The therapist can introduce the following activities and questions by stating:

Describe (draw) the physical layout of your home. Indicate rooms, doors, windows, stairs. Put in the furniture. Now take a look at the way the house is arranged and how this influences your family: How people move around, the natural flow of interaction created by the locations of doors, walls, furniture, stairs, room positionings in your home. Can you see some advantages? Some disadvantages? For children? For adults?

There are two kinds of space. There is physical space and social space. Physical space is the visible living space (house, yard, etc.) in which the family lives. There is also social space. A family's social space may be more than the actual architecture or physical walls of the family household. Social space may be the way we feel about our family relationships and interactions in the physical living space. Social space may be, in fact, the way individual family members regulate emotional distance (being together and being separate or apart) in the family's physical living space. The therapist can continue:

A person's physical living space may be small yet the person may feel that he or she has enough space in which to be separate and together with other family members. Or, a person may feel that his or her physical living space is too cramped, too close for being comfortably together and separate in the family. Which feeling have you experienced most often in your family?

Next the therapist can raise the following system consciousness questions:

- As a parent, do you feel that your family has enough physical living space? If yes, why? If no, why?
- Are there objects, furniture, or rooms in your home that are "off limits" to your children? If so, what? If not, why?
- Are the doors to rooms in your house more frequently open or closed? Which doors are open? Which doors are closed?
- Every family has a "safe area." How far beyond your front door do you feel safe? Sometimes this safe area extends beyond the physical walls of the house. Sometimes this safe area does not exist inside the home. Where does your child usually play when he or she plays inside the house? Where does your child play when he or she plays outside the house?
- Do you allow many people into your home? A few? Very few? Why?
- Give an example involving the person(s) outside your immediate family (relatives, friends, neighbor children) who, when they enter your home, seem(s) to exert a powerful and important influence on your family and children. What kind of influence?
- A new family has just moved in next door. What do you do? Do you greet them or do you let them introduce themselves first? Do you watch and wait awhile, until you think they look friendly enough, and then strike up a conversation?
- Describe some advantages of living in your neighborhood. Describe some disadvantages of living in your neighborhood.

The preceding activities and questions reflect a salient but small number of the range of activities and practical suggestions for exploring family space, parenting, and child development in the Child-Centered Model. Full descriptions and research-practice based recommendations for effective application and maximum positive child and family outcomes are contained in the *Parents' Family Guide* and the *Therapist's Family Guide:* two full-length manuals available through the author (see p. 163). The activities and questions presented here were selected because they highlight four major aspects of the family's awareness and the child-centered knowledge that builds systemically. The activities and questions communicate the influence of physical space on family interaction, physical and emotional safety, physical access, and emotional boundaries.

The Influence of Physical Space on Family Interaction

The layout and physical structure of home and community, the actual locations of doors, walls, fences, room partitions, and relationships, have a strong often unnamed impact on how family members relate to one another and the social relations that develop. Like the walls and paths of a maze, the way the environment is arranged guides family interaction and can be instrumental in creating and maintaining family patterns. For example, children's play areas may be placed too close to a parent's work area, causing competing priorities and a conflict of parent-child needs. This undue tension, the overlapping noise and interference as children and parents pursue parallel activities, can be minimized and eliminated by moving the children's supervised play area to another location in the house.

Physical and Emotional Safety

The emphasis on "safe spaces" in the house draws attention to the important issue of safety, both physical and emotional. Children need to feel they are living in a safe environment in order to develop the positive, emotionally nurturant bonds of attachment. A child's feelings of being secure arise from two interactive features of the environment. One aspect of the environment involves the physical safety, order, consistency and predictability of the home arrangement. For example, can a child count on his or her toy-creation (block tower, painting in progress) remaining where the child left it, undisturbed? Can the child expect his or her room to remain relatively the same as the child has come to know that space? Do relationships have predictable places in the family's emotional climate: How predictable, consistent, and safe are emotional expression and affective exploration of relationships in the family? Often conversations initiated by therapist or group facilitator around child-proofing the home environment—ways to ensure the physical safety of the developing child—form the "icebreaker" that opens discussion around issues of emotional security, attachment, and parenting.

Physical Access and Emotional Boundaries

The family's organization of its physical living space conveys and influences social-psychological patterns of joining, community, and separation, personal autonomy, privacy, and the individual. Through visual-spatial statements, such as drawing the layout of their home—the concrete, observable structural arrangements of the house—the family discovers what kind of access is offered to members, parents and children, and participation in the family. For example, are there too many or too few boundaries? Are children afforded privacy, spaces that they can call their own? (This does not necessarily involve the child having his or her own room. It can be as small and simple and clear a statement as the child having a "goodie box" to hold his or her special toys and treasures, or a particular part of the bedroom the child shares with a sibling designated just for him or her alone.) As parents physically walk through the rooms, corridors, nooks, and crannies of the physical layout of their house, taking note of family interaction, they gain a graphic understanding of the ways the family naturally as well as intentionally organizes space to create patterns of access and also boundaries to important interpersonal experiences and relationships in the family.

Family Notebook Activity: Family Time Patterns and Boundaries

The Family Notebook questions and activities focus on time patterns as both accesses and barriers to interpersonal relationships. The activity highlights linear and nonlinear time, introducing families to the child's view of time, including the importance of fantasy, symbolic representation, and play. Time is explored and expressed as sequence. Sensitizing family awareness to sequence—including the order of events—draws participants' attention and observational focus to patterns, preparing families to think systemically. Without using terms such as "pattern" or "sequence," parents begin to notice how events and interactions unfold, what happens next as they explore physical and symbolic time in the family, with the children, and as part of the developing parent-child relationship. This objective is accomplished through concrete examples and experiential exercises.

For example, parents are asked to compare and consider the different timetables, time styles, and schedules of family members. They are encouraged to contrast a child's time sense with the adult's time experience, as well as to note individual differences among their children. The therapist or group facilitator can introduce the topic of time and family process in the following ways. The therapist can state:

Time may be measured in terms of seconds, minutes, hours (clock time), days, weeks, months, years (calendar time). Clock and calendar time, together, combine to make up our past, present, future (our own personal history) and the history of our family as a group.

The therapist can continue:

Time also takes the form of dreams, fantasies, folklore, myth, meditation (our subjective history). Consider (think about) these time aspects:

- Seconds, minutes, hours, days.
- Weeks, months, years.
- Dreams, fantasies, folklore (old wives tales), family legends, and stories.
- Family history.

Look at all these different forms of time and come up with a brief statement that expresses how you feel about these time forms and what your relationship is to these time forms. Think about the seconds, minutes, past, present, future, dreams, aspirations, fantasies and decide which ones of all these seem to be most important to you in your life.

Now answer this question as you think the other adult(s) in your household would answer this question, what you think they would say if they were answering this same question.

Think of each one of your children (infants, school-age, adolescents, young adults). Beside the name and age of each child, indicate in one or two sentences what form(s) of time seem(s) to play a more important role in the child's life and how you arrived at your conclusions. Does the child seem to be more:

- Moment-to-moment time bound?
- Hour-to-hour time bound?
- Day-to-day time bound?
- Fantasy time bound?

Consider these questions:

- Describe a typical daydream or fantasy that you have about yourself.
- Describe a typical daydream or fantasy that you have about your family.
- Describe an important fantasy or daydream that you have about each child.
- Describe a typical weekday schedule for you. Choose a day of the week that you feel is most representative (sums up) what a typical day in your week is like.
- Describe a typical weekday schedule for each child.
- Describe a typical weekday schedule for each other adult.

- Describe a typical Saturday or Sunday schedule for you and your family; choose the day (Saturday or Sunday) because the day sums up best what weekends are like for you and your family.

The therapist can elaborate further:

Time is a means of access to what we want or need: people, objects, resources, events, ideas, opportunities. We say things such as:

- "We're right in time with one another."
- "Sure, I'll give you my time."
- "My time is yours."
- "For you, I'll make the time."

Time is also a means of keeping people, objects, information, and relationships at a distance. We can keep people away from us and each other by not having enough time. Time boundaries can keep events from happening with us (as a part of that other person's time). We say things like:

- "If time permits."
- "I haven't got the time right now."
- "Sorry, I didn't make it in time."
- "This is no time now."
- "Hurry up, make it quick."

Time is a boundary that can separate people. Time often can stand between people.

The therapist can pursue these relationship issues through the following questions:

- Think of a recent situation in which you have had a time problem (felt out of phase) with one of your children. Describe the situation. Describe how you handled the time problem.
- Describe a situation in which you had a time problem with your spouse or partner (an adult) in your household. How did you resolve the time problem?

The Family Notebook: Temperament, Parent-Child Relations, and Family Energy Styles

The majority of parent-child problems, especially involving young children, can evolve around the parent's misreading of the meaning and intention of a child's energy expression or misinformation about children's energy levels.

In addition, parents often hold unrealistic expectations about the child's capacity to self-contain: to hold and bridle their enthusiasm and outpouring of pent-up energy. A parent's image of an obedient child may be one in which a child either sits quietly or complies immediately with a parent's request that the child "settle down." Further dilemmas arise when parent and child are temperamentally mismatched; when, for example, an exuberant, high-energy child interacts with a laid-back, low-keyed parent. The following questions and activities are designed to facilitate the parents' and family's understanding of energy styles and energy images and to stimulate in parents a reconceptualization in energy endowment and expression. The therapist can introduce the Family Notebook Activity by saying:

Energy is motion, movement in, with, and through the world. Energy is a way of acting and approaching: a way of moving through space and time toward people, activities, events, objects, tasks, and goals.

We all develop our own style of "energy approach," our "energy image," and our "energy pattern." It often helps us to identify how we use our energies and what our particular energy pattern is in our daily living.

Once we understand what our particular energy style is and identify our "energy image," we gain one more piece in the puzzle of self-knowledge. When we identify our energy image, we, in fact, identify an energy pattern or approach that characterizes not only our way of being-in-the-world but also our way of being-with-the-world: a way of being with people, objects, events, and ideas. Energy is vitality and intensity.

- In meeting the demands of daily family activities, do you feel that you have:

  A high energy level?

  A medium energy level?

  A low energy level?
- Describe what you mean by a high energy level, a medium energy level or a low energy level.
- Are you satisfied with this energy level?
- What image do you have of yourself as you carry out day-to-day family responsibilities? How do you think others see your energy level?
- What factors or circumstances (*outside* yourself but *inside* your family) help contribute to your particular energy level?
- What energy level characterizes each of your children (child's approach to people, objects, and events)? Give the name and age of each child. Explain why you think your child has developed this style of energy expression.
- As a parent, are you satisfied with each child's energy style? Does your style of energy mesh better with one child than with another child? Give an example.

The therapist continues:

There are many different energy feelings. Read through (think about) the following two energy feelings and decide which one best describes you:

- *Energy Feeling 1:* I seem to release more of my energies, investing more in people, activities and events, than I seem to have given back to me by the people, activity, or event that I invest in. I feel depleted and emptied just as though all my energy were drained out of me. I feel that I put into life more than I get out of it.
- *Energy Feeling 2:* I feel frustrated with no real outlets for my energies. Although there are a great deal of activities to keep me busy, these activities somehow just don't seem to be the right outlets and activities for me. I feel like I have much more energy than I can use.

What we like to invest our energies in, often tells us what we value:

- Looking at what you invest your time in, what would you say you value?
- When you look at what each child seems to spend his or her time on, what would you say the child values?
- When you look at what your spouse (partner) or other adult(s) in the household seems to do with his or her time, what would you say he or she values?

Think of how you typically approach and carry out an activity:

- Do you have difficulty getting started (impetus), keeping the activity going (momentum), or finishing the activity (impact)?

Think of your family as a group carrying out a family activity or task:

- As a group, what would you say your family has difficulty with: beginning, sustaining (maintaining), or completing an activity?

Think of each child and adult in your household in terms of approaching and carrying out an activity:

- Next to the name and age of the person, indicate whether you think the person has difficulty with the beginning, middle, or the completion of activities?

Think of what you described as your own particular approach to activities (your energy image):

- Is there anyone in your family (child or adult) who bothers you because that person's expression of energy (energy image) seems to oppose yours?

Energy is a means of approach. Think about your children:

- How does each child approach you? What differences do you notice between your children? To what extent does the age of the child make a difference?

The Family Photograph Activity

The second, integral Child-Centered Activity, Family Photographs, provides another illustration of the conscious ways structured activities have been strategically designed and developed within this model (Andreozzi, 1977, 1978, 1979c, 1988) to capitalize on familiar materials (photographs) and everyday experiences that make concrete (by visual means) ongoing family processes and patterns. The Photograph Activity has proven effective in eliciting and organizing powerful, immediate, and graphic participant awareness of child and family development in a variety of ways. Photographs involve families emotionally. While the Family Notebook Activity is introduced to participants as the first means of exploration into family process because the Activity is primarily cognitive—nurturing families' analytic and observational abilities—the Photograph Activity is palpable, affectively charged, and can create immediate access to emotional content and expression. In essence, the Family Photograph Activity, as shown in prevention, early intervention, and family therapy process analysis research, has proven to have positive and important effects on promoting family change. The Photograph Activity, when appropriately and sensitively timed, provides the bridge to critical self-awareness and, accordingly, the bridge for positive family change.

The Immediacy and Graphic Awareness of Family Photographs

Photographs provide an extraordinary source of awareness and exploration. Photographs are graphic and visual, engaging families on multiple levels, cognitively and emotionally, and depicting an array of system concepts of awareness in concrete, observable ways. In effect, photographs are "still life" pictures of ongoing family process. They provide participant families, therapist, or group facilitator with concrete observable scenes and events in a family's life to point to, talk about, and explore. The Photograph Activity can be used to highlight all the building blocks of the Child-Centered Model, including family subsystems, networks of family relationships, preferred family structures, personal and interpersonal imagery, family dimensions and favored transactional parts. A few examples of application will illustrate this point.

A Chronicle of Evolving Family Identity

Photographs record and reflect the family's stream of consciousness, the history of its evolving system identity in graphic imagery. They show recurrent themes. Photographs depict what a family selectively notices, values, remembers, and likes to talk about. As such, photographs provide observable access to the family's foundation and meaning level of family organization.

Relationship Statements

Photographs capture important relationship statements and show maps of connection (alliance) and cutoff (rifts) in family organization. The group snapshots of a family often reveal spatial arrangements, physical and metaphoric statements about the degree of emotional closeness and alliance, and the degree of emotional distance or separation between family members, spouses, parents, and children. These photographs clearly depict family structure. This intuitive knowledge captured by the camera's eye, reflects the family's organization (usually someone in the family directs the members, deciding who stands or sits where in the family photo). Once this knowledge is named, it can be put to conscious, positive, and constructive use by the family.

Transactional Roles and Family Parts

Photographs highlight preferred transactional roles. Over a series of photographs, a family and therapist will notice who typically is in the center of the interaction, the mover; and who is the challenger, either seen, for instance, in a member's conscious absence, facial expression (frown, grimace, or "forced smile") or in the family member's body posture (turned away from or at an angle to the group). Followers are also apparent, as is the important, emotional mediation role of the wise, observing witness of family process. This moderator and impartial interpreter of family events is not necessarily found on the edges or peripheries of scenes. Rather, this impartial arbitrator, crucial to family balance and perspective, can be observed visually as the advisor or comforter the family most often turns to as a group. It may be one of the parents, grandparents, a favorite aunt or uncle, an intimate family friend who has become an adopted family member, or an especially interpersonally aware and sensitive child.

Family Development

Photographs communicate an immediate and unified understanding of current family structure. Photographs also show recurrent themes in terms of the activities families engage in and the events they remember and value. The typical transactions among family members in a particular photograph, or the transactional patterns that recur across photographs, can highlight the impact and interplay of current family dynamics and unresolved developmental issues. Family photographs provide powerfully condensed pictorial stories of a family's life. They offer vivid accounts of a family's history, development, and current transactions. This illustrates another instance of how historical content (linear time as personal history) and family patterns (the family's current developmental stage and degree of organizational complexity) converge. A guided exploration of a series of carefully chosen photographs, spanning childhood (family of origin), and current family development can illuminate transgenerational themes around the expression of intimacy and nurturance, the family's sense of competence, accomplishment, and its common threads of group identity from one generation to the next.

For example, one member of the couple, after organizing and presenting her photograph selection, may discover that in her childhood family, the expression of the power dimension (the constructive use of personal influence) was an unresolved issue. After exploring his family of origin photograph choices, her partner may notice that his photographs reveal a family revolving around unmet affective needs and unfinished issues around emotional expression, nurturance, and intimacy. Together, with the guidance of the therapist and candid, insightful, and supportive comments of the parent group, the couple may begin to recognize that some of their marital difficulties surrounding commitment and parent-child dilemmas around discipline flow from the missing and unexplored puzzle pieces of affect-power carried forward into current family development.

Personal and Interpersonal Images

Family photographs can express deep personal and interpersonal meanings. Photographs literally convey visual images. Sometimes families are unaware of the types of images evolving around each child, as well as ones that are associated with different family members. A conscious and careful visual journey through a chronology of photographs, for example, depicting the unfolding stages of a child's development, can generate an incisive awareness that extends well beyond a simple behavioral observation, or a comment offered by a trained observer such as the therapist. Literally, to parents, it is like looking at a series of slides in very slow motion where the integrated cognitive-emotional understanding can be profound, reinforcing the therapist's facilitative comments. Parents can begin to see how children grow into roles inside the family, how images of a "good child" and a "bad child" subtly form over time. Parents can be encouraged, for example, to find a "least likely" photograph of the child emerging as "the difficult" or "problem" child. Families, in this way, are being urged to expand their perspective, and their usual characterization of the child, to cast him or her in a new light that will open the pathway for a positive view of self and self vis-à-vis others; as perceptions change (expand), behavioral change naturally follows.

Similarities between Self and Child

Another palpable source of awareness can also arise when parents note remarkable visual similarities between self and child. This includes psychological as well as physical resemblances. A parent and child may not only look strikingly alike; they may share personality traits and play similar parts in their respective family experiences. For example, a parent who was typically labeled the challenger in their childhood family may be drawn into conflict with the child in the family who challenges parental authority the most. Similarly, a parent whose emotional experience in her family of origin was one of having been a sensitive and disqualified observer may be drawn intuitively to the child she perceives as most misunderstood, who stands outside the mainstream of current family experience. Here, parent and child are implicitly and symbolically united as allies by virtue of their unvalidated and nonshared family experience, namely, that both feel they are on the periphery of family influence, nurturance, and group identity. Such thematic and transactional role repetitions include physical and psychological similarities, as well as friction and conflict. The Family Photograph Activity can quickly bring these bonds and tensions to the surface.

The Family Photograph Activity and Its Clinical Uses

The basic feature of the Family Photograph Activity, an instruction that guides its effective use, is to limit participants' selection around a specific theme or family concept to no more than three to four photographs. Limiting the number of photographs the participant uses to express his or her understanding helps to structure the activity, guiding parents' in the process of making meaningful and informed choices. The decision process itself, including who keeps the photographs and what the family member had to do to obtain them, are also important information and "grist" for increased family understanding. For example, when parents decide to explore family of origin photographs, they often discover who is the family gatekeeper as well as the "official holder" of the family photograph collection—the member who has been entrusted with the responsibility for the safekeeping, care, and protection of the family's symbolic, pictorial "visual history."

The other important aspect of the activity involves participants making decisions regarding the order in which they present their photographs to the parent group, therapist, and other family members. Participants are encouraged to "tell a story" with their photographs. An important part of that story is the sequence of the photographs, which are analogous to pages or chapters in a book or scenes in a moving picture. When the order and the meaning of events change, the parts-to-whole relationships change as well.

The Family Photograph Activity has proven to be effective around five objectives. The activity can be organized around the following family explorations:

1. Participants can generally explore past childhood (family of origin) experiences and whole family process.
2. Participants can focus on current family system dynamics (the family as a whole).
3. The parent(s) can examine parent-child relationships over time. In terms of each child, they can concentrate on transforming an early problematic or troublesome parent-child relationship into a positive one.
4. Parents can trace, relate, and connect knowledge of current parent-child relationships to the parent's childhood experience, changing roles and vantage points as the parent recalls the experience of having been a child and the relationship style the parent developed with his or her own parent.
5. Partners can explore and communicate to each other the relationship patterns, affirmations, unmet needs, and repetitive behaviors they bring to the marriage and the developing family system.

Participants can discover the critical puzzle pieces of their psychological and interpersonal identity, voicing to others and themselves the sources of their hopes and frustrations. Photographs, because of memory content, emotional immediacy, and intensity create an activity that involves and captures the imagination, interest, and enthusiasm of even very young children. Just as children like looking into mirrors, they enjoy gazing at themselves in photographs, with children under the age of 3 often referring to themselves in the third person as "he" or "she" or "baby." Children can also tell simple stories around the photographs, contributing to the family group activity. The Family Photograph Activity draws its appeal and effectiveness from the plain and simple, almost universal phenomenon, that as human beings we are continuously fascinated with the prospect of explaining ourselves to ourselves and, as the circle of community and connection grows, communicating this knowledge to others.

The Family Notebook Activity can serve as a visible and observable introduction to family exploration, through the access dimensions of space, time, and energy. The Family Photograph Activity effectively elicits awareness of the qualitative dimensions of family life, power, affect, and meaning. Family space, time, and energy can also be explored through the photograph activity. Because family photographs reflect significant events (developmental milestones) and are often taken to record and recall important memories, the Family Photograph Activity lends itself naturally to a full exploration of power, affect, and meaning on personal, interpersonal, and family levels. Clinical practice and research on the Child-Centered Model (Andreozzi, 1979d, 1979e, 1988) have indicated that the first introduction of the Kantor Four Player Model pairs well with exploration of transactions centered around the themes of personal autonomy, family efficacy, influence, and power. The Family Photograph Activity equally accommodates exploration of themes of nurturance and intimacy, affect, and meaning or identity.

Family Photographs, Power, Efficacy, and Self-Influence

The therapist or group facilitator can introduce exploration of the family's power dimension in the following way. The questions and activities can be tied into the Family Photograph Activity by encouraging participants to select photographs that highlight the central theme of each question. The therapist may state, for example:

There are many ways to be powerful and effective in daily interactions in order to influence others. In our group, we will explore and identify ways of getting things done, being and feeling powerful, being effective, feeling and expressing our influence. We will also identify our own strategic patterns (typical ways) of coping with and handling daily power encounters with adults and children.

Before we explore our particular transactional roles (player parts) in the everyday "power dramas" that fill our lives, let's take a broad look at ways of dealing with power, ways of being-in-the-world-with-our own personal sense of self, who we are and how we wish to be seen (recognized) by others. For our purposes, we can divide power into two types: there is the use of power that controls and limits people; there is also constructive power that influences and guides.

Next, the therapist frames the following questions and activities:

- What kind of power do you think happens most often in your family? Explain. Choose a family photograph that shows how power feels in your family.

Consider these roles or parts:

- **Leader (mover).** Moving others to action (e.g., rallying others to move, get going, speak up, take part). The mover motivates people and begins activities.
- **Follower.** Following someone else's lead, being in agreement with the leader and following his or her actions, opinions, ideas. The follower gives support and makes it possible for others to reach their goals.
- **Opposer.** Taking a stand that directly challenges that of the leader, the opposer is not necessarily a villain. The opposer simply challenges or questions the position (actions, opinions, ideas) held by the leader.
- **Impartial observer or witness.** The person who stands on the outside of the act/action, activity, event, or transaction. He or she does not take a position but remains neutral and watches. This person may act or voice opinions, but essentially is noncommittal, not making his or her point of view known, in terms of a personal stake in the interaction, but trying to mediate by taking into account everyone's interests.

Consider the following:

- Which part do you find yourself most often playing in your family? Under what circumstances? With whom?
- Think about the four parts. Next to the name and age of each child, put down the part or role the child seems to express most often in the family. When? Under what circumstances? With whom? Explain why you think your child seems to continually play this part in the family. Choose a family photograph that best expresses your part and the part (images) of each child. Do the same for adults in the home.
- When you are a leader, whom do you feel most comfortable leading?

  (a) Adult men?

  (b) Adult women?

  (c) Young children?

  (d) Older children?

  Why do you think this is so?

- When you are a follower in your family, who most often is leading the way for you? Who are you being led by?

  (a) A man?

  (b) A woman?

  (c) A certain child?

  Why?

- When you are an opposer in your family, whom most often do you find yourself challenging?

  (a) A man?

  (b) A woman?

  (c) A certain child?

  Why?

- When you are a witness (remain neutral, refuse to enter into the act and take sides), whom or what do you find yourself most often watching without trying to interfere or exert influence over?

  (a) The activities of children?

  (b) A certain child?

  (c) The activities of adults in the home? Men or women?

  (d) A certain adult?

  Why?

- Describe a situation in your family that you feel powerless to change, that is, you feel it is best to leave the person or situation alone because you believe your influence probably would not have any impact or effect. Next, describe a situation in your family when you did have a direct impact on the outcome. What made you feel influential in one situation and not in the other?

- Complete the following sentence: I feel strong and in control inside my family when . . .

- List the name and age of each child. What role (leader, follower, opposer/challenger, or witness/observer) does the child play most often when interacting:

  (a) With children, older brothers and sisters (if any) in the family?

  (b) With younger brothers and sisters (if any) in the family?

  (c) With adult female figures in your home?

  (d) With adult male figures in your home?

  (e) With a teacher in school?

  (f) In school with other children?

Why do you think that your child acts differently with different people in different circumstances?

- Complete the following statements:
  When I want my children to listen to me, I . . .
  When I want adults in my family to listen to me, I . . .
  When I want the outside world to take notice of me, I . . .
- Think of your family as a group. Which of the following images first comes to mind when you think of your family:
  (a) Rising up.
  (b) Falling down.
  (c) Holding back.
  (d) Holding in.
  (e) Holding the line.
  (f) Down for the count.
  (g) Hands in the air.
  (h) Reaching for the stars.
  (i) Hands tied behind its back.

  Explain your answer. Add a different image if none of the preceding fit.

FAMILY PHOTOGRAPHS, NURTURANCE, AND INTIMACY IN THE FAMILY'S SOCIAL LIVING SPACE

The therapist can organize child and family development around the idea of nurturance and intimacy. Observing from a different vantage point, the therapist can explore patterns of connection and emotional cutoff, as well as styles of access to intimacy. The family dimension of intimacy and nurturance can be introduced as follows:

Each of us, like the family we belong to, seeks our own balance between being together and being apart. The way we approach people for support and comfort, nurturance, and intimacy, is as important as what we ask for. Our approach to others, our partner, and our children, affects how they respond to us much in the same way as their style of approaching us for nurturance, comfort, and emotional support affects how we react.

The therapist can then select from the range of the following consciousness-raising child development-family system questions:

- How do you let your spouse know that you want to get close? How do you show your affection? How do you convey intimate feelings? Come up with an actual example, a visual scene or image of how you physically and psychologically approach your partner.

- On the other hand, how do you let your partner know that you want to be apart, that you want and need some distance and separation? Or as someone described, "Get some breathing room, . . . space"?
- Similarly, how do you let your children know you want to get close to them? Give the names and ages of all your children and the ways you convey this message to each child differently.
- How do you let your children know that you need some private time and space, want to be apart, that you want some distance and separation from them for a while? (Again, breathing room.) Give the name and age of each child and the ways you convey this to each child differently.
- How does your partner let you know that he or she wants to get close to you? How does your partner also indicate the need for personal space? Give an example, a visual image.
- How does your spouse communicate to the children that he or she wants to get close to them? Give the names and ages of all your children and how your partner shows nurturance to each one. How does your partner, on the other hand, let the children know that he or she needs personal space and wants some distance and separation?
- Describe what immediately comes to mind when you think of "affection." Choose a family photograph (one from your childhood family and one from your current family) that shows affection.
- How can a person in the family show his or her affection for others? Openly? Excitedly? With reserve? Quietly? Whenever the person feels like it? Only at certain times? Add to this list.
- What can a good mother do to show her children that she cares? What is a bad mother? Give an example.
- What makes a good father? What can a good father do to show his children that he cares? What is a bad father? Give an example.
- Describe an affectionate experience that you recall happening in your family of origin (the family you were born into and grew up in). Describe an affectionate experience that happened between you and your parents, describe what this affection felt like.
- List the names and ages of all the children in the family and describe how each child lets you know that he or she wants to be close to you, needs you. Can you relate this to what you know about child development?
- List the name and age of each child and describe how each child lets you know that he or she wants to do things for him- or herself. Can you relate this to any child development theory? Also describe how each child lets you know the child needs his or her personal space and time

to be alone, that the child wants to do things all on his or her own. Can you relate this to what you know about child development?

FAMILY PHOTOGRAPHS, MEANING, AND IDENTITY

In illustrating the family's group identity, and personal as well as interpersonal levels of identity, images, and meaning, the therapist or facilitator may state the following:

The idea of meaning happens at the very center of our lives. Ironically, it seems only when people, activities, events, ideas, and human relationships lose meaning for us do we suddenly become aware of being without something important. We recognize that some personal center of meaning has vanished or dissolved. Or, we are aware that meanings are clashing. The most striking example that comes to mind is the adolescent boy or girl battling with parents over meaning: what it means to be a 16-year-old in the world.

Let's look at some other concrete situations that have been emptied of meaning. Most of us have had the experience of performing a monotonous job; meeting an old friend and finding that there is nothing left to share or to say; going through a traditional family event only to discover that the event did not have the old meaning and excitement it used to have (i.e., family holiday get-together); ending a relationship, falling out of love, or we might say, falling out of "meaning" with our loved one; and reviewing our past only to discover that some event or self-image (image of ourself in the event) no longer carries such monumental significance for us (i.e. childhood nickname).

When we review these experiences, we discover that having meaning, being meaningful happens as the result of relationships: us in relation to the world. Meaning can involve a relationship with ourselves (purpose and self-worth), a connection with other people, or events in the world.

When we talk about meaning, we are talking about identity, purpose, worth, and industry. We are talking about having something in common with others or desiring to share something important about ourselves with them. Meaning involves self-images, shared images, and emotional connections.

The therapist can explore the following:

- What does it mean to be a parent in your family?
- What does it mean to be a child in your family or a specific child in your family? What do you think it means for each one of your children to be a child in the family?
- What does it mean to be a man in your family? A boy in the family? Do you like this image? If yes, why? If no, why? What does it mean to be a woman in your family? A girl in the family? Do you like this image? If yes, why? If no, why?
- What kind of image of yourself do you think others in your family have of you? How do you think each family member sees you? Give the

name, age, and image/impression of you through other's eyes. Do you like this image? If yes, why? If no, why?

- What kind of image do you think others in your family have of themselves? Give the name, age, and image, and the way you think the family member thinks others see him or her. Do you think the family member likes this image? Has the person been locked into this image? Do you think the person wants to change this image? (If you get stuck on this question for very young children, think of the child's actions as part of the expression of self-image. A child's actions/behaviors reflect their image, what they feel about themselves and are too young to express in words.)
- List the names and nicknames of family members. How did the child or adult name or nickname come about? Tell the story behind a name or nickname if you think the story is important.
- All families experience disagreements. Families experience meaningful differences between and among members. Family members always have some differences. List some issues around which family members hold strong differing opinions and beliefs.

The Family Network Drawing

The third activity consists of the Family Network Drawing (Andreozzi, 1979a, 1988). The activity can be modified and adapted to the various developmental capabilities of children. For very young children, the Family Network Drawing is similar to play therapy techniques associated with children's art. Children can simply be asked to draw a picture of their family. (If the child is involved in a difficult parent-child relationship or the early intervention family is experiencing crisis, the therapist may want to initially modify the technique slightly by asking the child "to draw a picture of a family.") Older latency-age children and adolescents can follow the same steps outlined for parents regarding the completion of the Family Network Drawing. In an hour with the family, this activity, like all of the model's activities, can be effectively applied in a variety of contexts: parent/family group, as part of a home-based family intervention, and in the therapist's office.

The Family Network Activity: The Family's Visual Relationship Map

The Family Network Drawing visualizes the family map. The activity organizes a family's thoughts and awarenesses of the family as a whole, along with the network and interconnection (quality) of relationships that comprise current family development. In Chapter 3, two concepts were explored and illustrated: a view of current child and family development, and the concept of family types (the Kantor system typology and communicational domains)—open, closed, and random. In a concrete, practical, and graphic way, the Family Network Drawing depicts this system awareness. The activity draws a family's awareness to:

- The quality of relationships that make up a family's current network, including a visual statement of family structures.
- The family boundaries, particularly the system's boundary and, as such, an initial knowledge of its preferred system type.
- The family's degree of connection or isolation.

The Family Network Drawing provides a family's view of itself, a map of what is included inside the family and what is distinguished as outside the family's borders of identity. This activity vividly illustrates and catalogs the family's developmental stages, particularly Bonding and Attachment, Affiliation and Alliance, and Inclusion. As a research tool and intervention technique, the Family Network Drawing (Andreozzi, 1978, 1979a, 1979d, 1979e, 1988, 1993a, 1993b) offers a rich and concise qualitative as well as quantitative assessment of family change. The activity also highlights a family's meaning, model, and pattern structures (described in Chapters 2 and 3)—three crucial elements that reflect the quality and viability of family organization and development. To introduce the activity, the therapist can state:

We may think of a family network as a living tree of the people, places, and relationships influencing the "here and now" of our lives and the lives of our children. A network drawing is a tree of current relationships. We are all familiar with the idea of a family tree. Family trees tell our history, where we came from, who came before us, and who our ancestors were. In creating a "family network" such as the one we will be drawing today, you will begin to recognize the people, places, and relationships that are presently helping to shape, change, and direct, in short, to influence your family and children.

The therapist continues:

Think of the network as a living tree, its branches being the connections—the influences. For example, mother and toddler may form one connecting branch. Mother and toddler, as one connected branch in the tree may, in turn, be connected to the toddler's playgroup. The branching lines, along with each connection you identify in your drawing, signify a relationship. The connection between mother, toddler, and playgroup expresses an important relationship, much in the same way that branches in a tree intersect. The branches can extend and continue. For example, mother may be connected to her mother, and she may also be a wife connected to a husband, and so forth. Each branching relationship extends, intersects, and influences directly or indirectly aspects of the family tree.

While a network includes family members, it can also extend beyond the family to include people, places, and relationships outside the family. The network may show the impact of the outside world on family life. For example, the positive support provided by a good friend, the influence of a school or a peer group on a particular child, or the influence of a particular institution, such as the Social Welfare Department, all affect a family's image of itself, its competence, and its capacity to cope. People and places influencing each other constitute a relationship. All the preceding examples may be considered relationships—child-school, home-school, and family-social institution.

Questions Participants May Ask

Some of the questions participants may ask follow.

Participants may wonder:

- What is a network?
- Why should we do a network activity?
- What is so important about a network anyway?
- How does this activity help parents and families?
- How and when should parents use this activity?
- What can parents learn from family networks?

The therapist can state:

The network activity helps people to recognize that they are not as isolated as they may have thought. Parents may no longer feel that they are parenting alone, carrying the entire weight of the family world.

For parents who discover that their network is in fact limited (e.g., a single parent who has recently moved into the area and has no close friends or family around), the parent group itself may become an integral part of the network.

The Family Network Activity helps parents to identify support that is either already available to them in their existing network or that could be available to them. Parents begin to identify positive support and personal strengths in either unexpected places (e.g., parent group) or "taken-for-granted-places" (e.g., long-standing relationship with a good friend). The awareness of a limited, sparse, or almost completely absent sense of network can motivate and encourage families to develop new relationships through actively pursuing social support and community resources.

The Family Network Activity helps parents to visualize the possibilities for change. With the realization that a network is a living tree of changing relationships, that is, of growing children and a developing family, participants discover an alternative view regarding both their present and future.

Parents may ask, "Do networks change?" The therapist can state: Yes, they certainly can and often do change. If, for example, you completed a network of the people, places, and relationships influencing you and your family 2 months to a year ago, and then compared it with a network you drew today, you, like other families, might see differences between the two networks. You would see change, movement, and growth.

Networks are not only living trees of the here and now; they also point the way to the future. Networks show us where we are at a given moment, as well as indicating how our social networks are organized at a certain time in our lives. Family networks also record our direction. Anyone who has drawn and kept their family networks from 6 months to 2 years can tell you that these networks act as a barometer of the social factors and influences in the family's life. Networks change and shape direction. An unexpected pregnancy, the birth of a child, a child's transition from grade school to the middle school, the growing incorporation of the parent group (supportive network of parents), these or other changes, when occurring in a family's life, are examples of significant network changes. Family Network Drawings record and give credence to these changes.

CONSTRUCTING A FAMILY NETWORK DRAWING

A few basic materials are needed: paper and pencils, as well as crayons, colored markers, or colored pencils for children. After explaining the general nature and purpose of the Family Network Activity, the therapist can pass out sheets of paper (larger sheets of paper for children) and offer the following guidelines:

Network Membership: Step 1

Begin by thinking about the people who exert an influence on your family life and family relationships. These people can include people both inside your family (family members) as well as people or groups outside your family, for example, persons in the Head Start center, your boss at work, a neighbor, a friend. Make a list of these important people or groups of people.

Choose those people who exert a powerful and significant influence on you and on your family's life. These should be the people or groups who immediately come to mind when you think about your family, or your day-to-day routine and activities, ones who are part of your life and play an important role. Their influence can be positive or negative, strong or weak, direct or indirect. The important issue is that, from your point of view, you consider these people as centrally involved in your life and in the network of family relationships.

The therapist can give young children a simple instruction:

Draw a picture of your family.

Or

Draw a picture of the really important people and things in your life.

Two Methods of Application: Individual and Family Collaborations

The process involved in creating the Family Network Drawing provides a family with access to important system awareness. The Family Network Drawing offers a highly condensed diagrammatic illustration and "picture-story" of the family's current structure. The activity can be applied in two ways. For example, each family member can draw his or her individual version of the family network. Then separate perceptions of each family member can be integrated into a "family view." In this instance, family members complete their Network Drawing, after which each member, in turn, presents and explains his or her drawing to the family group. In this application, the family process surrounding the family's presentation and explanation of individual Family Network Drawings is equally illuminating and revealing for both therapist and family, as is the process involved in each member's construction of his or her individual drawing.

Another method of application involves the family, as a group, actively collaborating to create a collective Family Network Drawing. In this instance, the family creates one Family Network Drawing. The family's observable interaction, including how individual viewpoints are expressed and treated (incorporated or discarded), sheds considerable light on family process as the family negotiates a collective view around the Family Network Activity. The family group application of the Network Drawing Activity can offer direct access to parenting styles and parent-child relations as parents guide, respond, and react to children's contributions to the drawing. The family is then able to see to what extent children's thoughts, perceptions, feelings, observations, and suggestions are acknowledged and validated (affirmed) or minimized and ignored (disqualified).

Creating System Awareness and Change

The Family Network Activity graphically communicates to families a number of central system concepts that, in turn, generate increased system awareness. Family Network Drawings are literal and visual maps that depict a family's perception of current family structure. As a map of family structure, the drawing serves as the family's counterpart to a therapist's map of system structures (family diagnosis). This is not to suggest that the family's view is a substitute for the therapist's assessment, or that a family's and therapist's views are always similar and, in this sense, equivalent.

As family therapy process-outcome research has shown, confirmed by a salient set of empirical findings obtained in family therapy outcome research on Child-Centered Structural Dynamic Therapy (Andreozzi, 1985a, 1993a, 1993b), a family's and therapist's perceptions of the problem can be considerably different. However, in contrast to regarding divergent viewpoints as discrepant outcomes, such indications suggest different relevant perspectives. When the therapist's and family's view (a perspective often overlooked in process-outcome analysis) are treated as complementary sources of data, a comprehensive picture of family progress and outcome emerges. The Family Network Drawing serves as a technique for assessing change, as well as an activity for stimulating system awareness.

The Family Network Drawing depicts other important system concepts. For example, it displays diagrammatic family relationships. As participants connect individuals in their drawing, they are literally formulating personal and collective statements about their perceptions of family relationships and distance patterns of "relating." The quality of relationships as well as the awareness of physical and metaphoric space, a concept explored throughout the book, is expressed in the Family Network Drawing in several ways. As part of the process of constructing a drawing, participants indicate relationships by connecting people. The physical distances shown in the drawing (how close or how far apart individuals stand in relation to one another) often indicate the metaphoric and symbolic distance a family member perceives.

Participants also depict family awareness and a systems view of family development and current process in the relationship structures that they represent. For example, are the relationships primarily dyadic (two-person), triadic (three-person), or family triangles (three persons with one person acting as a "go-between")? In addition, participants, using a devised, standard set of symbols, indicate the quality of relationships (positive, negative, or conflictual). The kind and quality of relationships portrayed in Family Network Drawings can communicate a vivid, visually compelling story about an individual's and family's perceived sense of community or felt isolation. The connection and continuity versus disconnection and isolation apparent in the drawings provide another illustration of an individual's and family's intuitive understanding of the system concept and organizing principle of the Child-Centered Model: the capacity of families to become "informed system guides" and "system experts."

The preceding examples describe how the Family Network Drawing is purposely designed to promote system awareness by engaging families as active explorers and conscious influencers of family development. The activities of the Child-Centered Model have been carefully developed to achieve a twofold objective:

1. To provide families with concrete, practical, thought-provoking activities that motivate and engage their curiosity about system awareness.
2. To translate complex system concepts and theory into everyday, observable family system understanding.

This twofold objective supports a central guiding goal of the Child-Centered Prevention and Early Intervention applications of the model: To make participants into "family therapists" and "family researchers," in effect "family explorers."

The premise underlying family change is a straightforward one: The more a family knows about itself, the more prepared it is to solve problems, cope with normal developmental crises, and direct a course of positive change. The following corollary also holds true: When a family lacks or temporarily loses the important sense of perspective provided by self-knowledge, including sensitive observation and awareness of family process (events, relationships, and interactions), the family may become vulnerable to crisis. A family that loses its group perspective (capacity to self-reflect, self-evaluate, and self-monitor) is analogous to a ship traveling through uncharted waters with a faulty compass, blindly navigating a course without benefit of orientation or radar. The work of prevention and early intervention in the Child-Centered Model is designed to equip families with system awareness, combined with practical suggestions (plans) to improve a family's problem-solving capabilities. A family's "system compass" comprises its problem-solving strategies.

Identifying Important Relationships: Step 2

To return to the therapist's role in facilitating the Family Network Activity, after asking participants to list important people, relationships, and organizations (groups of people) in their lives, the therapist can move to the next step. The first step required participants to peruse their social living space and reflect on who and what is an important influence in their current lives. The next step in constructing a Family Network Drawing encourages participants to focus on and express their perceptions of family structure. The therapist can introduce the next series of Family Network guidelines by stating:

Take another blank sheet of paper. Imagine that this sheet of paper is the world. Imagine that all this empty space is yours. You are the architect, artist, and designer. On this paper, you will construct a drawing that shows how you see relationships between/among important people in your life.

Kind and Quality of Relationship Connection: Step 3

The therapist can continue with the process by stating:

Draw a circle on the paper. This circle represents space inside your family. The circle should be large enough for you to draw in and arrange people inside the family circle (see Figure 6.1).

What is inside this circle is your family. What is outside this circle is the outside world.

The therapist explains:

The circle acts as a boundary to indicate where the inside family world ends and the community and outside world begin. Now, referring to your checklist of important people, begin to arrange people. Show family relationships as you experience them. Place people anyway you like. Do not be concerned about being factual or how good your drawing is.

At this point, the therapist can introduce the three to four basic symbols for representing individuals. For example, circles, squares, triangles, and ovals can be used to designate men, women, children, and groups (organizations or social institutions). The therapist can also distinguish between the "facts" versus "feelings" phenomenon often associated with relationships. For example:

- *Fact:* A parent may say: "My brother is part of my family; he is living with us."
- *Feeling:* "My brother is often quite emotionally distant. He feels like a stranger to me. This makes me want to place him outside the circle. What do I do?"

Figure 6.1
The Family Network Map

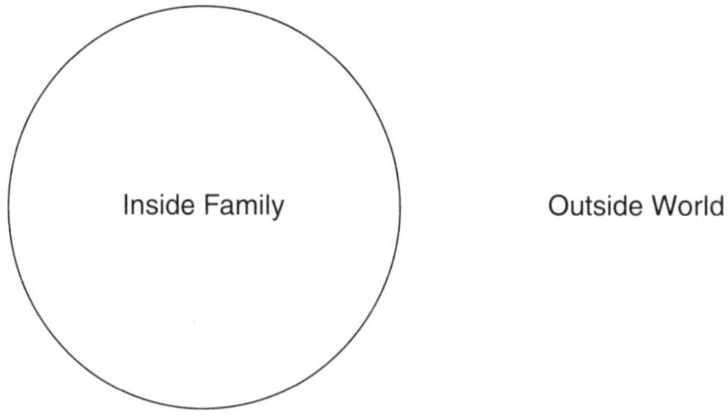

The therapist can state:

If you feel your brother is an outsider to your family life, place him outside the circle in your Family Network Drawing.

Naming the Types of Network Influence: Step 4

Moving to the next step, the therapist explains:

Review the list of the names of people and/or important organizations (groups) influential in your life and begin arranging them on the paper. You may want to begin at the center of the paper (circle), starting with the most important persons (relationships) and gradually move outward. Your list may contain people who are both inside and outside your family. Place them where you feel they belong. Fill in, add, and connect people. Continue until you have connected all the people and groups on your list and you are satisfied with what you have drawn. The important issue is not how neat or artistically drawn your network is. The important issue is your opinion and perception of the way people are connected to form relationships in your network.

As part of the process of completing the Family Network Activity, individuals and families must make decisions about the kind and quality of the relationships they draw between (attribute to) people. Participants connect people in their Family Network Drawing using a variety of symbols and different types of lines.

Interpreting and Applying the Family Network Drawing: Relevance and Meaning

The relevance of the Family Network Activity extends beyond the actual lines and circles that compose the drawing. Because the Family Network Drawing symbolizes relationships, it is interpretive: it tells a symbolic story of an individual's and family's relationship experience. A number of salient relationship dimensions emerge from the thickness of the family circle, the relative size of the symbols representing individuals, the length of the line drawn to join and connect people, and the designations assigned to depict the kind and quality of relationships. I will briefly illustrate the family system relevance and type of system awareness associated with each dimension in clinical practice.

The line drawn to form the family circle as well as the size of the circle can be significant. The line (thick, thin, perforated; drawn in a heavy or faint stroke) can symbolize a family's sense of integrity and communicate its perceived relationship to the world and outside community. For example, does the family's group boundary appear thick and impervious, permeable, or fragile and tenuous? This can open discussion around a family's image as an impenetrable fortress or a precarious, vulnerable unit. Each image conveys a palpable sense of either having too many or too few protective borders. The size of the family circle, demarcating inside and outside family experience, is also revealing in a number of ways. In some instances, the family circle can be large, enveloping almost the entire sheet of paper and leaving little room for "outside experience." In other cases, the family circle can appear relatively small, positioned in the middle of a large "expansive" outside world. In the first example, the family claims, asserts, and literally "takes over" large amounts of social space. The second example suggests that a family may feel "small" and, by inference, overwhelmed by the outside world.

A second important dimension available for family conversation involves the portrayed sizes of individuals vis-à-vis one another. Relative size can connote a variety of meanings: indications of actual differences in physical size (a parent drawn larger than a child), or psychological differences and a sense of social inequality (when one person feels small and overpowered in the presence of another). For example, an individual may communicate the symbolic and psychological experience of a particular relationship by stating, "I feel smaller than my boss. When I'm around her I feel like I'm unimportant."

A third related dimension of the Family Network Drawing pertains to the positioning of individuals relative to one another. For example, power and control issues characteristic of a relationship can be represented vertically by placing one person higher than another in the drawing. A parent may express the following: "I have no control over my teenage daughter. She does not listen to me or my husband. She does just what she wants. I feel she controls us." On the other hand, a relationship that reflects equality depicts people on the same level. Spatially, the individuals may be drawn side by side or facing each other on the same line. A parent may say, for example, "I finally feel that I can talk openly with my daughter's teacher." Another parent might say, "Since I became a mother, I believe my mother is seeing me as an adult. We are getting to know each other as women."

A fourth dimension involves the quality that an individual and family attributes to particular relationships. This is visually expressed in the kind of connecting line chosen, as well as in the length of the line drawn. A longer line may suggest distance; a shorter line may convey perceived emotional closeness. The line can also be straight (indicating a direct relationship), curved (indicating an indirect relationship), or broken (suggesting an uncertain or strained relationship). The Family Network Drawing can qualify important relationships further. Parents have used double lines (two parallel lines) to express and differentiate extremely strong relationships. For example, a mother explained, "Carrying this second baby, I feel really connected. I feel a strong bond between myself and the baby. My life seems to be all wrapped up in waiting for this birth."

Relationships can also be portrayed as negative or ambivalent. Parents have discovered inventive ways of communicating these relationships, including using a minus sign to indicate a negative relationship and a lightning bolt (zigzag line) to suggest emotional friction and ambivalence. An example of a negative relationship directly stated would be, "My sister and I can never agree on anything. We have never gotten along."

Examples of conflicted, ambivalent, and "go between" or indirect relationships include the following: A 40-year-old woman describes, "My mother and I have always had a very strong and deep relationship. However, we have a number of issues to work out. We are close and I want to remain close. She is a real support. But lately we really clash on our ideas about how to raise children. She is always giving in to my children; on the other hand, I want them to have some limits." A 16-year-old girl states, "The way things work in our family, when I really want something badly enough, like a new dress or permission to stay out late, I always ask my mother first. I ask her to see if it is alright—I try my plan out on my mother before I ask my father. Sometimes I even ask my mother to ask my father for me." A 51-year-old man confides, "My father is very inaccessible. I don't know how to approach him. I seem always to have to beat around the bush before I tell him what is on my mind. It does not seem to matter that I am a husband and father with grown children of my own."

The Family Network Drawing provides a map of family structure, a visual depiction of the branching relationships in the family's here and now. The activity translates the family's relationship experience into a "parts-to-whole" diagram, or picture of family structure. The Family Photograph Activity explores family structure imagistically. The Family Photograph Activity puts faces and memories into the structure of family relationships and can be a means for exploring both past (childhood) and current family organization. The Family Network Activity, on the other hand, focuses exclusively on present family development. Comparing Network Drawings over time provides access to the family's awareness and perception of change, showing that family relationships evolve, transform, and are far from fixed and static.

Living Sculpture and Family Role Play

The fourth and fifth activities, Living Sculpture and Family Role Play, are experiential techniques well known in the family therapy community. Living Sculpture is a technique that allows either a therapist or family member to physically move and "position" family members to portray the sensibilities and experiences of family relationships: how the individual perceives self in relation to others and others in relation to self. An individual (family member) actually creates a living sculpture. An individual "places" (positions) family members, instructing family members to strike poses, assume facial expressions, and enact gestures. An adolescent may, for example, position him- or herself with back turned to parents as he or she simultaneously positions parents, arms joined, in a stance that indicates a united front in opposition to the "fleeing" and "rebellious" adolescent.

In another instance, a mother who has become the family's harried and distraught emotional "switchboard," may place herself in the center of the room and arrange other members in various relationship positions around her that show "clinging," "pulling," and "clutching" behavior. She (the mother) or the family (when another member creates the sculpture) may literally have children tugging her on one side, and a husband tugging her in the opposite direction. Living sculptures offer an immediate, mind-body understanding of the impact of family relationships and interactions. Living Sculptures express family transactional patterns and are comparable to the effect of having the images in the Family Photograph Activity and the structure of the Family Network Drawing come to life.

The benefits of the Living Sculpture Activity involve its interactional immediacy. During a sculpture, the individual who has created the interactional family portrait (positioned family members in the room) can ask questions of the family. Similarly, a therapist can explore how and what family members feel regarding their relative spatial-emotional positions vis-à-vis others. For example, the mother whose sculpture depicted her as interactionally torn between family members may express feelings of exasperation and a defeated sense of helplessness as she "tries to be all things to all people in the family." A therapist can also take the opportunity to ask other family members to literally "step into the mother's shoes" by suggesting that family members, in turn, switch places with her and experience her family role from her literal spatial vantage point.

Family Role Play functions similarly as a technique and is extremely effective in heightening awareness. For example, role plays are powerful experiences in dramatically creating child development awareness. In family groups, parents and children can be encouraged to reverse (play) each other's role. In addition, parents can be encouraged to imagine (via role play) what it feels like to be a very young child and to experience the world directly from a child's eye-level view.

Creating Family Change: Families as "System Experts"

As clinical practice and research on the Child-Centered Model confirm, parents, children, and families can become system experts who, strengthened by that awareness, bring about positive family change. This is the enabling system quality and central developmental objective of prevention and early intervention. Most individuals carry within them an intuitive understanding of how their family works and how relationship patterns are organized. This knowledge is often expressed in the stories individuals and families tell about themselves, and in the images that color their memories and connect important events and relationships in their lives. A child's palpable and immediate account of the connections in the family emerges in the stories he or she tells through play, and in the intuitive system awareness about self-and-others-in-the-world that the child expresses through the language of behavior.

The five Child-Centered Activities described in this chapter have proven effective in heightening, organizing, and focusing family awareness. The activities draw together strands of awareness and integrate individual viewpoints—validating, clarifying, and revising this knowledge into a total picture of family development, interaction, and change. The research-based activities that form an integral part of the Child-Centered Model consciously encourage and strengthen a family's capacity to observe, reflect, evaluate and, accordingly, generate new solutions: the foundation of systems theory and the essence of change. When families learn about systems by first learning about themselves, when they can name the dynamics they see in family interactions and relationships, and when this knowledge strikes a balance between thought and feeling awareness, they are far better equipped to handle crisis. Families can become conscious creators, as opposed to helpless victims of an unowned family future. The activities are purposely designed to stir in families the self-reflective capacity to state, "We see what is going on. Do we want to continue this way?" Simultaneously, the activities provide families with new action-strategies (parent-child and system problem-solving skills), helping them to recognize and approach problems more effectively, and guiding them along a positive developmental path. As numerous cases in the research depict (Andreozzi, 1979d, 1979e, 1985a, 1988, 1993a), one compelling benefit reflects a certain psychological wisdom in terms of the emotional expense spared vulnerable children: Early intervention can be synonymous with violence prevention. In this light, the contribution to positive developmental outcomes in children (more well-adjusted, emotionally healthy adolescents) is immense.

How the Five Activities Integrate System Awareness and Family Change

All activities included in the Child-Centered Model integrate cognitive and affective awareness. The activities (Andreozzi, 1977, 1978, 1979d, 1979e, 1988) were consciously designed to provide families with a concrete, practical translation and understanding of system concepts in order that families, equipped with this knowledge, may initiate self-guided positive change and development. The central principle is system consciousness: to put system concepts into the "minds, hands, and imaginations" of families. The premise is that as parents shift from an individualistic to a group perspective, the tendency to blame self and others (child, spouse) decreases in favor of adopting a collaborative view that parts relate to wholes and that individuals contribute to situations and overall outcomes. This level of awareness, alone, can create a profound and positive intervention. For example, self-critical, emotionally unsure, and unprepared parents who doubt their parenting capabilities can begin to recognize the influence of other factors on the quality of parent-child interaction. Parents who can think more kindly of themselves and feel less guilty about relationship vulnerabilities and shortcomings, become more emotionally generous with the child.

As all the five Child-Centered Activities illustrate, the educational process guiding the Child-Centered Prevention and Early Intervention Model emphasizes a system orientation in several ways. The subject matter, the content families focus on, is the family as a whole and the interrelationship of unfolding stages of child and family development. Another system aspect emerges in the way the concept of "system" is taught: how the five activities of the model (Family Notebook, Photographs in Family Process, Network Drawing, Living Sculpture, and Child and Family Role Play) are consciously utilized by family participants and therapist-facilitator. The activities are purposely constructed to build and layer awareness.

Curiously, when a system view emerges, the individual is not lost in the group. To the contrary, a system perspective which recognizes the self as both independent and interdependent with the environment ultimately increases personal autonomy. As described in Chapters 2, 3, and 4, the Child-Centered Structural Dynamic Model focuses on the individual-family system interplay. Both the self and the system—the family group—are equally emphasized. Similarly, the activities facilitate self and family growth, building and integrating all three levels of awareness:

1. Personal (self).
2. Interpersonal (parent-child, marital).
3. System (family group).

The activities cycle and reintroduce child and family development through three perspectives: self, interpersonal, and system. The common theme and goal of the activities is to enlarge a family's perspective: to guide parents and families to think "system" and explore the environment, particularly how the environment influences the child and parent-child interaction and contributes to child development.

The Family Notebook Activity introduces family exploration of the environment. The activity stimulates an understanding of the family environments, specifically concentrating on space, time, and energy expressions as access or boundaries to personal (self), relationship (interpersonal), and family goals. The Family Notebook Activity is purposely introduced first because it is cognitively oriented, relatively neutral (nonthreatening) and is concrete and practical. Although the activity centers around physical aspects of the environment (e.g., the physical arrangement of the house, including children's play areas), the activity begins to create in the family a growing relationship awareness of metaphorical space, time, and energy. Ultimately, the activity's system purpose is to sensitize families to context: parents begin to enlarge their theories and views of parenting, child development, and the parent-child relationship. The power in the system perspective is its capacity to dispel attitudes of "overpersonalization" and negative self-reference, which, research has shown, are central factors and salient predictors of negative parent-child relationships and potential abuse.

The Family Photograph Activity primarily elicits affective awareness through exploration of a family's symbolic life. The Family Photograph Activity provides the next step, logically and naturally building on a family's awareness of its physical, metaphoric, and relationship environment. The access dimensions of space, time, and energy are connected with and integrated into the affectively oriented system awareness generated by the Family Photograph Activity. The Family Photograph Activity is employed to guide exploration of current as well as transgenerational themes and images around critical family and child development tasks (goals), including affect (nurturance, bonding, and intimacy), power (competence, achievement, and autonomy) and meaning (identity and purpose). Awareness of family member parts is also drawn in and consciously elicited through both the Family Notebook and Family Photograph Activities. These activities, which intentionally designate the participant as the mover (initiator and explorer) inside the special circumstances of his or her family world, are combined with the practical observation of children in classroom and playgroup settings. Collectively, the activities and experience are designed to draw together two simultaneous, increasing types of knowledge: one of self and family; the other of child growth and development. The learning laboratory is a family's home environment and interpersonal world; the lessons are practical and, at the same time, systemic.

Throughout the book, the terms *content* and *formal structures,* drawn from the Kantor critical identity image concept, have been repeatedly emphasized and related to the emergence and resolution of parent-child conflicts. Content and formal structures have been shown to represent, in their interplay, the intersecting bridge that joins both a conceptual (family systems theory) and experiential (concrete, transactional) understanding of family development. Content and formal structures are central ingredients in critical identity conflicts and, as such, are integral to the work of Child-Centered Therapy. Content and formal structures are accessible (available to a family's understanding and a therapist's grasp) through the Family Photograph and Family Network Activities. These activities translate and elicit these crucial system concepts, making them apparent and observable to family and therapist.

The Family Photograph Activity provides vivid illustrations of content structures in several salient ways. Photographs elicit memories, and memories are content structures. The details and nuances (atmosphere, emotional climate, mood) of a photograph can organize an individual's awareness of the impact and imprint of important "relationship lessons" or "relationship turning points" (critical identity scenes) and, hence, crucial identity images. Photographs are all about images and the awarenesses they evoke and create. The Family Network Drawing, on the other hand, approaches structure less from a content (memory and image) route than from a form or formal sense. The Family Network Drawing communicates the form (or formal arrangements) of a family's current relationships according to the perceptions of family members. The activities work synergistically, building layer on layer. The participant begins with a broad view much like the preliminary sketch and outline that an artist draws in the early stages of rendering a painting. The basic pattern and outline are sketched. Next, the participating family, like the artist, begins to fill in, smooth rough edges, revise and refine detail, add nuances and shading. Gradually, the family sketch takes shape and reflects depth, contrast, dimensionality. Families return to the activities throughout the prevention and early intervention experience, using them as benchmarks that show the steady and consistent increase in family understanding. Each activity repeats central concepts, reintroducing them in new ways and from different angles. For example, to develop the unifying theme of family patterns of separation and connection, visual and metaphoric relationship statements are explored throughout all five activities. Like system theory and the sensory-perception-dependent worlds of the child, Child-Centered Structural Dynamic Therapy is a visually oriented model. Together, these activities elicit, condense, and visually illuminate family patterns, making system awareness readily and quite practically available to family and therapist.

The Appells

The Appell family, Frederica and Jason, in their late teens, their two twin boys, Danny and Jimmy, and Frederica's mother, Francoise, sought help through the prevention route. Frederica and Jason, both barely 19, were the parents of two vigorous and independent 3-year-old boys. When I met the family, the couple was estranged. Frederica was symbolically (and for all intents and practical purposes) a single mother struggling on her own. Although the couple (who married when they were just 16) were not officially divorced, they were emotionally headed in that direction. Jason was literally in and out of the home, sometimes staying away for a week at a time. Jason vacillated between wanting to be a rowdy adolescent boy—"joyriding with his friends"—and a responsible father to his children. Frederica, as mother and stabilizer of the family, did not have this existential and emotional luxury.

The Appells live in an urban public housing complex—rows of small, attached two-story buildings. Physical and psychological space are at a premium. Frederica, Jason, and their sons share one apartment; Francoise, Frederica's mother, lives alone in the apartment next door. Jason works as a busboy at a local restaurant; Frederica works part-time at a convenience store in town; and Francoise is surviving on disability insurance due to progressive arthritis. (For years, Francoise worked in a food processing and packaging plant. The cold temperature, combined with the continuous assembly-line activities, caused permanent injury to her wrists, crippling her fingers and hands.) That fall, Frederica had enrolled Danny and Jimmy in Head Start. Frederica and Francoise, acting as family emmisaries, sought help through the prevention route. Several weeks later, more curious and skeptical than convinced, Jason also joined the Family Support Program. This proved to be a breakthrough for the Appells with the Child-Centered Activities promoting family growth and change.

The first level of system awareness that stimulated family change involved what the Appells learned about how their family is organized: the concrete and visual recognition of family structure. Frederica, Jason, their two sons, Danny and Jimmy, and Francoise live in apartments that literally touch, sharing a common, adjoining wall. In this community of crowded social space, lives are often tightly interwoven, and the physical and metaphoric walls between families (the Appells and Francoise) cease to exist. Family structure and interaction revolve around the "experience" of Francoise who is fast becoming the "backbone" of the family and sole support of her daughter, Frederica. Boundaries and interactions are fluid in the Appell family, often crossing generational and functional family role lines. This development has taken place for a number of vital system reasons; some protective, others practical. Francoise is clearly acting as a "mother" to everyone, including Jason.

The family arrives at this collective recognition through the visualized relationship maps depicted in their individual Family Network Drawings. Frederica, Francoise, and Jason each place Francoise in the middle of the "family circle," although each qualifies her relationship and involvement in the family differently. Frederica and Francoise view Francoise's influence as strong and positive. Jason expresses mixed feelings. He values and, at the same time, resents her involvement. The children echo and confirm the substance of this family experience, adding their own awareness, as they often call Francoise "Mommy" and their mother, Frederica, "Grandma."

The Family Photograph Activity reveals striking relationship themes. Francoise, who is in her late 30s, was divorced at 24. She never remarried. Mother and daughter seem joined around a common, unfolding history: Francoise, involved in a brief and stormy marriage, was deserted by Frederica's father when Frederica was 4. Frederica appears to be traveling down a similar path of broken bonds and emotional abandonment. Both women choose photographs that reflect similar themes around affect and meaning.

At the center of her Family Photograph story, Francoise proudly displays a photograph of a festive holiday table. There are six place settings. The table is a small chrome dinette in the middle of what appears to be a dimly lit, tiny kitchen. The table is beautifully set. It is clear to see that Francoise has gone to great lengths, and taken great pains, "scrimped and saved," as she explains, "to create just the right picture-perfect home and holiday." But no one is in the photograph. The photograph, like the plates, glasses, and chairs, is empty.

Frederica produces a similar kind of photograph in their family group meeting:

She holds up a photograph of her children's nursery (actually a small corner of the bedroom she shares with her husband). There are bright clown figures on the wall and a teddy bear in the crib. Beside the crib is a small, old desk painted green; on it, there is an opened book. "The twins weren't born yet," she explains, "This picture was taken a month after Jason and I got married when I was about 9 months pregnant. We had both dropped out of high school by then."

In addition, Francoise and Frederica's photograph selection and their raised awareness around family patterns showed individuals trying to create order and beauty (meaning) out of a frugal environment (poverty), and the arbitrary and difficult circumstances of their lives (divorce, teen pregnancy). The common thread across the Family Photograph and Family Network Activity was a striking absence of people. Both Francoise and Frederica's Family Network maps were sparse, and the borders (boundaries) separating family and community were thick, suggesting a closed system orientation in relation to the outside world. Family Network Drawings over time indicate graphic changes in a family's view of itself. The Appell family's views shifted: Networks enlarged and the family gradually began to "let more of the world in" (Head Start Program, center staff, friends) as it simultaneously ventured outward.

Jason's photographs revealed a different set of self-images and family themes. His images revolved around meaning or identity through power. His photographs expressed another important puzzle piece and crossroads in the family's and couple's development:

In the family hour, Jason, electing to be the last individual in the family to present photographs, proudly arranges a series of photographs that depicts a boyish-looking Jason in various macho poses: on his motorcycle, playing pool with friends, holding up a high school wrestling trophy. (In this photograph, his father, a burley and somber-looking man, stands beside an animated Jason.) None of Jason's photographs include his wife, Frederica, or his children, an awareness that within moments, becomes apparent to the whole family. On this issue, Frederica confronts him.

There is another reason for Francoise's increasing family involvement. Jason has begun to drink. He is staying away from home more frequently; when he does return, whether he is or is not under the influence, he is short-tempered. He flares up angrily and then becomes quiet and sullen. His anger has not risen to the level of abuse but it is on the verge. Frederica and Francoise are worried about the vivid impressions Jason's "short fuses" and "fiery temper," combined with his erratic presence, are having on the children, Danny and Jimmy. In a family group meeting, Frederica and Francoise describe an incident with the three-year-old boys:

Frederica explains, "When I walked into the room, I found Danny and Jimmy marching around in circles. They were yelling out orders saying 'Do this. Do that. You idiot. You fool. Can't you do anything right.' At least that is what it seemed like they were saying. Their voices were loud and they sounded just like 'little Jasons.'"

Frederica is worried about the children—the scenes of bravado, psychological violence, and emotional intimidation that they are witnessing and absorbing:

"Will what the children see—Jason's outbursts—hurt the children later on?" Frederica wonders. Francoise, who is drawn to more practical, action-oriented solutions, simply wants to protect the children now.

Francoise intuitively recognizes the family's (especially Jason's) need for guidance. Although Frederica showed greater maturity and responsibility, often steadying the family's course, both she and Jason, as Francoise saw it, were "still children raising children." This experience mirrors Francoise's adolescence, as she explains, "Both Frederica and Jason have had all their freedom taken away before they could explore things—find out who they really are. Frederica didn't even get to go to her senior prom."

Francoise recognizes Jason's particularly urgent need for a "mother" given his current emotional cutoffs with his family. She also recognizes the importance and structure that her presence provides: keeping the system in check, reminding and guiding, and telling Jason that there are limits. What Francoise and the whole family learned later, through an evolving series of Family Photograph Activities and Family Network Drawings (as well as the conversations that the activities opened up) is that Francoise's role is only temporary.

Jason's involvement and full participation in the Family Support Program (his willing use of the activities, including the self-awareness, as well as the system awareness they provided) proved to be a positive sign that bodes well for the family. Something inside him stirred him to join Frederica, Francoise, and his 3-year-old sons in the process of family change. This awareness communicated to all that below the surface of his boyish, reckless behavior, there were elements of and a desire for genuine commitment to Frederica, as well as the pull of strong bonds toward fatherhood and the nurturance of his children. At a 5-year follow-up, the couple was still together, the children were doing well in elementary school, and Jason was not drinking.

The Rexfords

Marilyn and Arthur Rexford, in their mid-30s, and their daughter, Ella, aged 22 months, and son, Kenny, aged 5 years, own their own home in a modest, suburban neighborhood. Marilyn has quit her job as a bookkeeper in a law firm to take care of Ella. Arthur often works double shifts and holidays at the post office to cover Ella's rising medical expenses. Marilyn talks rapidly. Her speech is pressured and urgent. Her husband looks on empathically. He is sitting beside her; almost imperceptively, he grasps her hand. He lets Marilyn do the talking. Before them, their 22-month-old daughter, Ella, sits propped up in her stroller, smiling. Ella seems half thrust out in front of the family for all the world to see and half drawn back under its "protective wing."

In unison, each parent grips a stroller handle, keeping Ella near them, closely in place. Kenny stands to the right, seemingly alone and apart from the family. Marilyn races on, "Ella's got such big blue eyes. Look at those thick, dark lashes. All she has to do is bat those eyes. That charm of hers will get her through life." The Rexfords found their way to family growth and change through an early intervention route. Kenny's preschool teacher urged the family to seek counseling for his "helpful" behavior which had begun to border on "intrusive."

The couple's commitment to each other is strong, although the daily quality of their interaction is strained due to the difficult circumstances they face. Marilyn's guilt, sense of shame, and despair is palpable. It is seen in her face, and her averted, downcast gaze, and is felt in the pressure of her speech. For months, she has not stopped blaming herself. Although Kenny's behavior is the primary reason for therapy, Marilyn repeatedly draws the conversation and attention back to her concerns about Ella.

"If I could only do things over, if I just had that moment back, if only . . ." she cries openly. When Ella was 13 months, she developed flulike symptoms. Marilyn telephoned their pediatrician as Ella's fever rose. Alarmed, Arthur wanted to take Ella to see the doctor. Marilyn thought this was unnecessary (she had phoned the doctor); she thought it best to wait a bit longer, overriding Arthur. Several hours later, when Ella's fever would not break but, rather, continued to rise, the family rushed Ella to the emergency room, where, after examination, she was immediately admitted to the hospital. During Ella's hospitalization, her persistently high and uncontrollable fevers led to brain injury. Ella was now developmentally delayed. Due to Ella's developmental stage, the full extent of her acquired disability could not be assessed. The uncertainty of Ella's

developmental future, like the certain guilt that Marilyn felt, hung over the family and stood as an unnamed worry for Kenny, who was searching for a way to help his family out even though he was too young to understand. Feeling outside the orbit of his family's attention and unable to understand and control the emotional roller coaster his mother was experiencing, Kenny decided to be the "bestest" boy he could. Gradually, however, in search of his own attention in the family, his "helpfulness"—laced with the tacit, telltale signs of his anger—led to behavior problems at school: He both wanted "to help" and also "needed help" so badly that he "pushed" himself intrusively on children, disrupting school activities (other children's work and play).

All the features of Kenny's (the presenting child's) problem emerged over time. An illuminating breakthrough for the family occurred during the Family Photograph Activity, which provided an opportunity for Marilyn to openly express her "guilt" and need for understanding:

Marilyn chose a set of photographs that revolved around a recent family vacation at a summer resort and amusement park. The photographs were all about Ella in various poses and relationships with family members. Ella's position was central; Kenny's presence was peripheral. One of Marilyn's photographs was remarkably revealing. In the photograph, Marilyn is smiling. She is wearing sunglasses and her head and hands and arms are in an old, New England town replica of a public pillory. The symbolic and visual contradiction between Marilyn's smile and the atmosphere of the park with the "pillory" as "punishment" and a vehicle for "public scorn" is compelling.

At the end of the early intervention experience, Marilyn wrote the following on her Family Assessment Questionnaire:

Since participating in the early intervention program and receiving counseling, I have gotten back my own identity. I realize that Kenny's problems at school were not because of a lack of discipline, but rather the problems at home. He is a bright child who was overlooked in the difficulties our family was facing. He is easily bored when not challenged or when left to fend for himself as he was during times when I was too busy or preoccupied with my own worries. Since counseling, his behavior has improved due to better socialization (social skills) with peers and a little more of the right kind of freedom.

My marriage, though it has never been a problem, also improved after counseling, once stresses were relieved. I look forward to returning to college soon with the total support of my husband.

My daughter's "handicap" no longer worries me. I know she is getting the best possible education and will do her best. Basically, I am calmer and more in control of situations than I was before counseling.

The next chapter focuses on the Child-Centered Family Therapy phase of the model.

CHAPTER 7

Children and Families in Therapy

Critical Identity Images, Growth, and Change

THROUGHOUT THIS BOOK, I have explored the overlap and interplay of development from various perspectives, including the self in relation to the system, and the child in relation to the family. The focus has been on family growth and change. Family crisis has been viewed as a normal developmental occurrence, an opportunity for creating positive change. A family's current development and the place where a therapist joins a family are reflected in the current state of family organization, the here and now of family transactions, as well as in the impact and imprint of prior developmental stages. How well has the family handled each developmental challenge? Within a developmental view that considers the family's current system integrity in relation to family life-cycle stages, the needs and concerns of children have been interwoven, including ways to nurture positive parent-child relationships. Developmental crises, much like the opening phases of therapy, have been portrayed as turning points: crossroads that branch into several paths.

In Chapter 1, five developmental paths were broadly sketched and illustrated. For example, a family can rise to the occasion and successfully resolve the developmental crisis. In this case, a family, much like the individual (child and adult) in human development, moves on to the next developmental challenge, transformed and deepened in structure and strategy by these successful experiences. A family may also decide to temporarily delay the developmental crisis, momentarily "putting the problem off" in favor of more pressing family priorities or emergencies. A family may intuitively or consciously recognize the limits of its resources. A family may wisely sense that circumstances (e.g., coping with an unexpected job loss or the recent diagnosis of a family member's illness) may have stretched a family's interpersonal and problem-solving resources to the limit. To try to do too many things at once—to try to solve a developmental crisis in the midst of adjusting to a financial emergency or a health crisis—may just be too much and may overtax the most viable family. Like the self-reflective individual who inventories and assesses his or her current capabilities and resources in light of extreme environmental demands, the family recognizes its vulnerabilities and waits for a more opportune developmental moment. In this instance, a family briefly sets aside the problem to resolve it later when the family is better equipped and more fully prepared. This is an assertive and positive, system-protective move.

Taking another positive developmental route, a family may choose to externalize the problem or adopt a position of collaborative responsibility with the outside world. The family accurately assesses the source of the emerging crisis and, drawing on its deep sense of positive, group identity, in a system affirming move, locates the problem completely outside the family (e.g., prejudice or discrimination) or develops joint problem solving strategies (e.g., with the child's school). Like the individual whose behavior is guided by a firm belief in self and a realistic appraisal of the problem, the family evaluates the source of the feedback, judging the problem to be unjustified (outside the family's real concern) or the family looks to discover collaborative solutions.

On the other hand, a family's delay and partial resolution of a developmental challenge may take destructive forms, sending a family down different paths. The family may either externalize the problem, completely denying responsibility, and blame outside sources (neighborhood, community, society) or the family may ritualize and internalize the crisis, turning the conflict, so to speak, "on" or "against" itself.

A tacit decision to delay dealing with a developmental challenge may amount to denial. A family may avoid the problem or attempt a partial, unsatisfactory resolution of the problem, glossing over the dilemma superficially. In this example, a family may literally move on (progress) to the next developmental stage, carrying along to the current developmental task the puzzle pieces of unfinished development. Like "ghosts of unresolved relationships past," denied and unresolved developmental tasks can and will emerge at some point in a family's development, clamoring for the family's recognition and full resolution. It is at various points down this road that we encounter families in therapy, when crisis and family instability have reached the level of overt struggle.

This chapter will focus on children and families in therapy. The progress of Child-Centered Structural Dynamic Therapy will be explored and illustrated in several ways. A broad overview of the therapy process (stages and steps in facilitating family change) will be presented. Child-Centered

Structural Dynamics offers the therapist an effective, proven model for guiding, assessing, and staging family change. In Chapters 2 and 3, the main building blocks of the model were explored in depth. The five building blocks, which are drawn from Kantor's theory of structural dynamics, integrate child development and child-centered family therapy; they are:

1. Network of family subsystems.
2. Family access dimensions of space, time, and energy, combined with the child's conceptions of space, time, function, causal relationships, and temperament.
3. Family goals of affect, power, and meaning, combined with the child development tasks of trust/nurturance, competence/autonomy, and identity.
4. Child and family transactional roles or parts.
5. Family system types.

In Chapter 6, I described and provided examples for five Child-Centered Family Activities specifically developed and designed to heighten system awareness and nurture the family's capacity to self-evaluate and initiate purposeful, self-guided, positive change (Andreozzi, 1979a, 1979b, 1979c, 1979d). The aim of the five activities is to increase family awareness: to awaken in families a palpable, integrated (thought-feeling) awareness of parent-child and family patterns. The ultimate goal of the program of activities (the model's overall orientation and technique) is to nurture and support a family's capacity to observe, reflect, revise, and change, in essence, to create a "therapist's" capacity and perspective in families. (Andreozzi, 1979e, 1988, 1993a). The activities are:

1. The Family Notebook.
2. Family Photographs.
3. Family Network Drawing.
4. Living Sculpture.
5. Child and Family Role Play.

The activities are equally effective in the context of therapy.

In Chapter 4, the role of the therapist, including concepts and issues relating to professional development and self-supervision, was explored. In this chapter, the concepts, activities, techniques, and orientation for family change and growth, explored and described throughout the book, will be drawn together and illustrated. To round out and complete the picture, this chapter will also focus on the therapist. A model for professional development, supervision, and training (Kantor & Andreozzi, 1985) will be fully explained. This chapter will first focus on the goals, phases, and subphases of Child-Centered Structural Dynamic Therapy. Next, the role of the therapist, supervision, and model of family therapy training will be examined in depth.

Child-Centered Structural Dynamic Family Therapy

The process of the Child-Centered Model revolves around the inclusion and active participation of children in family therapy, allowing parent-child critical identity images to become visible, and providing for the culmination of individual awarenesses into positive transactional change. The Child-Centered Family Therapy phase (tier) of the model represents the integration of child development theory (age/stage-specific child development competencies and tasks) with Kantor's Structural Dynamic Therapy and the adaptation of the Kantor critical identity image concept to the developmental requirements and special circumstances of therapy with children. The model represents the adaptation and application (Andreozzi, 1985a, 1988, 1993a, 1993b) of Kantor's (1980) structural dynamics to therapy with children and the treatment and resolution of child-centered presenting problems. Central to the therapy process is the positive reframing of interpersonal imagery, the view of relationships (self vis-à-vis others) that motivates and guides individual and family behavior.

When we are working with children, the Kantor critical identity image concept, a potent clinical tool in therapy with adults, requires modification in the way the method is applied. Children see the world differently. They often "act out" rather than "talk about" what they are experiencing. Their behavior often spells out the problem, telling us what they think and feel. Therefore, action-oriented, play-guided activities and techniques work best. On the broadest level, the model and therapy involve turning images around, taking a critical identity image and transforming the image into a positive one. The image explorations turn a critical identity image inside out and upside down, symbolically "standing the image on its head." The metaphors of turning images inside out and standing images on their heads in the search for positive affirmations may seem to be an unusual way to illustrate the process of family change. This is not true when we think of the goal of Child-Centered Therapy and the *Alice in Wonderland* world of children's thoughts and feelings. The model is about children. To view therapy in this light is to approach therapy with families and children through playful imagery.

DIFFERENCES BETWEEN CHILDREN'S AND ADULTS' CRITICAL IDENTITY IMAGES

There is another reason the metaphors of turning images inside out and standing images on their heads work well. This reason relates directly to the differences observed between a child's and adult's critical identity images. Critical identity images are emotionally charged transactional scenes that an individual internalizes over time. They are powerful, visual and mental representations—vivid memory pictures. These image scenes are deeply felt perceptions about self-in-the-world and self-in-relation to intimate others. Critical identity scenes often involve an individual's sense of unmet needs and emotional misfortunes. The scenes for adults and children alike, although expressed in different psychological voices and vocabularies, reflect moments of real and imagined abandonment, rejection, shame, and betrayal.

While the content of children and adults' image scenes reflect similar themes, there are a number of salient differences. The first pertains to the extraordinarily different ways in which children and adults think, feel, and see the world. Children interpret events with concrete and literal immediacy. Children lack the sophistication of standing back and gaining perspective—the kind of cognitive, reflective frame of reference that adults have. For example, a father and mother are arguing as a child looks on. The father, angry at his wife's criticisms of him, walks out of the house, saying "I'm getting out of here. Don't expect me back." The child believes: My father is *never* coming back. In contrast, an adult may recognize this as the "same old pattern" and knows, from experience, that the father will, after he "cools down," come back home as he always does.

The second difference relates to the nature of children's and adult's critical identity images. Critical identity images peak between the ages of 8 and 11, and their acquisition tapers off in adolescence and adulthood. Young children, age 5 and under, are gathering and internalizing the elements of these images. The grade school (latency-age) child is busily and actively acquiring (internalizing) whole image scenes. When we view the normal, patterned developmental path of the child's unfolding object relations, depicted in Table 1.1, we can think of the critical identity images of children (their acquisition, internalization, and developmental receptivity) as occurring along a bell curve. Most of these images occur between the ages of 7 and 13, with the highest concentration falling in the center of the curve between ages 8 and 11. At the right end of the curve, critical identity images gradually taper off from the age of 17 and beyond. On the left side, or opposite end of the curve, children, ages 6 and below, are just beginning to have developmental awareness on a rudimentary, concrete level of image elements.

This bell curve has strong implications for therapy with parents, children, and families. This curve shows the relationship between critical identity images and the psychoanalytic view of development in terms of a set of internalized interpersonal experiences and images. Psychoanalytic theory holds that between birth and age 5 the unconscious is created. As system therapists, rooted in overt behavior and the family's here and now transactional patterns, we do not subscribe exactly to the concept of the "unconscious." What we need to know, to bridge individual and system development, is that underneath the surface, transactional views that we may or may not call the unconscious are being absorbed by children. These are the image lessons that families are teaching children.

These image lessons (critical relationship images) are recorded by children in "acts of creation" (mental representation) as they begin to understand how the system works, although these imagistic stories may be imperfect ones. Children are growing into intuitive system experts. Starting at about age 5, children intuitively grasp family patterns. It is as if they say, "Ah ha, this is a message about me and the world that I tease out of my experience." For example, they can begin to recognize the impact of parents' influence. Children may see the demonstration of parents' power as a "power to enhance me" but also as a "power to hurt me by betrayals." These interactions spin off of parents' imperfections. The process comes full circle as parents' critical identity images interact with the child's emerging ones.

Adolescents and adults whose critical identity images are formed, are acting on these images and using these salient identity scenarios to guide and structure intimate relationships. For example, the tenacity, emotional quality, and power of these images can cause an individual to be attracted to one person and not attracted to another. The type of person(s) an individual is attracted to can, in many instances, be traced to important image scenes. A person fits a crucial puzzle piece of an individual's critical identity image in one of two ways: either the individual validates (provides and fulfills) an unmet need or continues to withhold that need. Or, sometimes, the image bearer does both.

For example, a woman is initially attracted to a man who champions her, offering her the emotional protection she sought in her family but did not receive. Or a woman is attracted to an emotionally distant man because his "aloof style" reminds her of the experience of the protection she strives for and is unable (afraid) to get. Both experiences are familiar. Adults act on their critical identity images. Children in grade school are actively acquiring and organizing core sets of these images. Young children are slowly constructing them. Children's critical identity images are emergent ones. Because these images are, in fact, evolving, they can change, which makes the work of Child-Centered Therapy poignant, crucial, and, in many respects, preventive.

Knowledge that an adult's critical identity images are formed and a child's images are emerging leads to a third important distinction that pertains directly to the process of therapy. The core of an adult's critical identity image does not change. Critical identity images, like self-concept, are deeply interwoven in an individual's personality and sense of integrity. Like self-concept, these images can reflect the substance of an individual's identity. These foundation images often express deeply held assertions about self vis-à-vis others: the important ways an individual chooses to be known, wishes to be seen and, often in the case of therapy, wishes to be found by those an individual cares about and assumes care for him or her.

The differences between a child's and an adult's critical identity image affect and, therefore must be considered in, the therapy process. Only certain aspects of the image change in therapy. As a result image exploration is different with children than with adults. The similarities and differences between children's and adults' critical identity images relate directly to the goals, phases, and clinical steps of the therapeutic process.

Overview of the Therapy Process

Images are centrally important in Child-Centered Family Therapy. In life, as in therapy, images provide a powerful medium for expressing identity. Images are the currency of communication and are key to the conversations of therapy. Adults think imagistically. When individuals are pressed or urged to speak (self-disclose) either because the individual wishes to communicate something important about self or others, or because the individual is confronted to disclose, individuals will turn to the vivid immediacy of imagery to express how they feel. In the therapy hour, a wife says to her husband, "I feel like a worn-out dishrag." Her husband then retorts, "If you're an old dishrag, then I'm the world's biggest doormat." Another woman (mother of eight children) says to her bewildered family in a therapy hour, "Who am I? God knows! All I feel like is this incredibly shrinking woman. Poof! I'm gone. All that is left is one huge breast tottering around on two tiny feet, running here and there to take care of everyone's needs."

Children are also spontaneous and adept at communicating their thoughts, feelings, and experiences through imagery. Magical thinking, discovery and fascination with language, and amusement with the cadence and literal meanings of words can make children "image innovators." For example, during a therapy hour, in response to his mother's question about why he got into mischief, a 6-year-old boy states, "I don't know why, Mom. First I thought 'no.' Then I don't know what happened. All of a sudden, the fun just jumped into my head and I couldn't stop." In another family therapy conversation, a similar situation arises. When asked by her father for an explanation for her "rascally" behavior, a 5-year-old girl, answers, "It was my silly bone, daddy," pointing to her elbow, "The silly bone made me do it."

The most efficient way of learning something significant about both the interior life and patterned social life of parents, children, and families is to know something about the nature and scope of their images. An individual's and family's imagery serves as a basic frame of reference for their ideas about the world. For example, is the world a "jungle," a "dog-eat-dog world?" Images can convey important messages about behavior. Images can suggest transactional scenarios. For example, if individuals see the world as dog-eat-dog, then the expectation (anticipation) of confrontation may cause them to meet interactions aggressively. An individual may decide, based on this preconceived image, to "attack" before being "attacked." This image can carry with it guidelines for structuring intimate relationships. From the image, expectations follow. Expectations, in turn, shape behavior. What happens when a parent who perceives life as a dog-eat-dog world is challenged by a child or spouse who is declaring autonomy and independence of mind?

The work of Child-Centered Structural Dynamic Therapy is all about this special kind of critical image, what may be best described as relationship thoughts in visual form. They are the highly charged, unmet needs and unvalidated personal assertions that parents and children bring to therapy. These images reflect the family's struggle. These images are the ways parents and children, husbands and wives compete to be heard, seen, and known. This developmental impasse that a family takes to therapy expresses its struggle, and once an individual's critical identity images are understood, what emerges is the disappointment of not being found. This is the essence of image exploration with parents and children. The hidden emotional energy in the developmental crises that families generate as they attempt to nurture and perfect a family that "works" for the different family members, constitutes critical identity struggle.

The process of Child-Centered Therapy revolves around the articulation (expression) and acknowledged affirmation of these potent images. The focus of image exploration and the therapist's staging of change is directed to crisis resolution in the context of the family's repetitive, unresolved, developmentally focused transactional patterns. The nature of critical identity images and image exploration communicates an exciting aspect of Child-Centered Structural Dynamic Therapy. The excitement, and indeed the preventive aspect of Child-Centered Therapy, lies in the developmental differences between children's and adults' image exploration. As Kantor (1980) rightly emphasizes, when we are working with adults, we do not change images. We change the behaviors associated with an image, and we change the meaning associated with an image. For adults in therapy, this process involves bringing about a change in the meaning of an image without disturbing the image itself.

To try to do so is to challenge and disrupt a person's basic identity, in essence, to violate an individual's psychological integrity. Adults are formed. The changes that occur in therapy are mostly behavioral. An individual "owns" these images, and they form the fabric of personal identity. To tamper with the essence of these images is to tamper with the continuity of an individual's identity, who a person is. This is the single most important lesson of therapy for therapist, child, and family. The message of the lesson is one of maintained continuity and connection. Trauma, if it has occurred, is part of an individual's identity and personal history. To try to discard the image is a clinical as well as interpersonal mistake. Even if a therapist thought it "good" or "wise" to change an individual's or family's image, a therapist could not, for these memory imprints are indelible—they do not erase. A therapy that tries to alter the substance of these images will fail, or at least meet with a great deal of resistance. The goal, when engaging adults in family therapy, therefore, is not to change the essence of the image, but rather the meaning and, in turn, the behavior. In fact, changing a person's behavior (proposing alternative transactional strategies) will, paradoxically, also bring about a change in the meaning (interpretation) of the critical identity image. Gradually, through the process of therapy, the positive underside (affirmation) of negative or unproductive behavior will emerge.

Children, on the other hand, are emergent developmental systems. They are in process. Their self-concept, sense of identity, and efficacy are being actively formed. The therapist, in partnership with children and family, can, as an image guide, help create new image opportunities for children. Children's family experience can be imbued with new, alternative meanings and family relationships, particularly parent-child, can be transformed. The excitement of image exploration and family change in the context of children is twofold: not only can family patterns change and family development resume a positive course, but a therapist can structure opportunities for optimal child development and avert crisis and further vulnerability for children at risk. The interior life, cognitive and affective mental landscapes, of the developing child are rife and ready for the suggestion of a "positive future" and the promise of better relationships. Unlike adults, children are often the first to forgive.

Image Explorations

The Child-Centered Model focuses on three aspects of critical identity images:

1. The behaviors that flow from the image.
2. The intentions (meanings and motivations) that guide the behavior.
3. The expectations associated with the behavior.

In essence, when working with children, the critical identity image is viewed as both the source and explanation (cause and effect) of what each family member does and does not express through his or her behavior. This returns us to the idea of image exploration that relates to turning an image upside down—symbolically standing an image on its head. The therapist's aim is to discover and identify the positive claims of each family member's negative and conflicting critical image. For example, a child who perceives he or she is not valued or wanted may literally develop intrusive behavior. The child may "push" him- or herself onto parents and siblings in an attempt to gain access to nurturance, a sense of belonging, and intimacy. The child's behavior, because of its intensity, may be misperceived. Instead of providing the interpersonal access and emotional validation that the child seeks (the positive inside-out version of the image), the family rejects the child.

When the positive meanings and positive expectations associated with an individual's (parent's and child's) behavior or symptom are revealed and validated by the therapist and family, the behavior(s) associated with critical identity images are transformed. What is both exciting and compelling about Child-Centered Structural Dynamic Therapy is that children's images are malleable and inchoate, not yet formed or fixed. Children under 8 or 9 are still actively constructing, creating, organizing, and testing these salient identity images; these images have not taken root. A wonderful opportunity is open to the therapist. Consider, for example, the 5-year-old boy who constantly pokes his younger sister, pinching her cheeks and pulling on her hair. When his behavior is viewed in context, it appears more playful than intentionally aggressive. However, this vigorous child is quickly earning a negative image and label in the family. When the therapist names this behavior as "playful," while offering the child and family alternate child management strategies, the child's behavior and self-image now become "free" to change. Therapy with young children immersed in a family struggle can transform and even curtail the development of negative, interpersonally counterproductive images. The emotional expense spared children can be profound.

The Staging of Child-Centered Family Change

In Chapter 3, an integrated framework of child and family development was presented and illustrated. The framework expresses a multilevel view of family development that considers and combines two perspectives on family change. One view involves the family's here and now, including their current quality and style of organization. This current picture of family organization focuses on four ongoing levels, drawn from Kantor's theory of structural dynamics: a family's meaning, action, pattern, and model structures. Each level of family organization incorporates evolving child development and parent-child structures with implications for optimal or problematic development. The other interrelated view involves development over time: how well a family has negotiated prior stages and developmental tasks. Seven system stages were described: Attachment, Industry, Affiliation, Inclusion, Decentralization, Differentiation, and Disengagement.

When families with children are involved in therapy, it is usually the first four to five stages and focal issues that create a family's history, influence its current style and organization, and are important to assess. Because "usually the case" is far from "always the case," sometimes families with young children can present quite different developmental paths and scenarios. For example, a blended family or a one-parent family (either through divorce or death of a spouse) may have experienced, to some degree, the later stages and dilemmas of family development. The first four stages of family growth reflect the meta- or supradevelopmental task of forming and arranging boundaries. This is the time in a family's life and natural history when the system is being shaped, molded, and consolidated as individuals "work out" a collective "model" of family: what they want the family to be and how they see themselves in it. Children are active ingredients and participators in this act of creating family identity.

The second supradevelopmental task covers the last three stages of Decentralization, Differentiation, and Disengagement. In this phase of growth and change, a family faces a loosening of boundaries and qualitative shifts in the system. The family center diversifies into multiple centers as the family opens wider pathways of growth and exploration, as adult members (parents and grown children) increase in their sense of personal autonomy and set out to create new models of family or discover and fulfill parts of themselves. A family who has experienced divorce has dealt with the developmental tasks associated with later life-cycle stages. Boundaries are loosened as the "idea" of "family" changes. When a blended family with young children comes to therapy, each spouse (along with the respective families of children each spouse takes into the marriage) brings an individual family history to consider.

These separate histories and separate families make their imprint on current family development. In this sense, the current family system that the couple and children are creating reflects and contains some degree of experience and knowledge of all seven life cycle stages. Blended families and families of divorce know and often have cycled through the full range of experience of the family life cycle. To some extent, they have had practice and first-hand experience with the core dilemmas of every phase of family growth and change, from creating bonds of attachment and commitment to the emotional process of "letting members go."

Assessment

Integrated within this view of current and historical family development, we find the child. In Chapters 2, 3, and 4, this framework of family development and assessment was enlarged to include the child. Child development tasks and dilemmas were interwoven. Child and family development are occurring in a family simultaneously. Stages overlap and influence each other, at times causing crises. In the Child-Centered Model, when a therapist takes a family's history to help form a system diagnosis and facilitate the process of change, a therapist considers three aspects:

1. The family's current development (organization).
2. Its collective family history.
3. Child development stages of the children (including the developmental history of the identified child when a particular child is presenting).

Figures 3.1, 3.2, 3.3, 3.4, and 3.5 in Chapter 3, combined with Table 1.1 in Chapter 1, provide an outline of assessment issues and can act as an efficient and useful decision aid to a therapist. The Child-Centered Model charts a family's history in a special way. In addition to mapping the structure of current family relationships, as well as the family tree of significant people (genogram), development is traced along life cycle and child development lines. When mapped, child and family development stages are also treated as structures that provide important assessment information on the staging of change.

Because the physical and emotional well-being of the child is tantamount in Child-Centered Family Therapy, the first level of assessment focuses directly on the child and child development. This is absolutely essential for several reasons. First, it is unethical to do otherwise. Symptomatic children are often in considerable distress. Symptoms mean real or symbolic pain, the result of psychological and interpersonal disturbance. Therefore, the therapist's first priority is to assess the extent (acute or chronic nature) and level of intensity (severity) of the child's distress. The ultimate goal of therapy is the resolution of crisis and redirected positive development.

Another reason for attending first to the child is the nature and common predicament associated with troubled families. Symptomatic children are symptomatic (often develop symptoms) precisely because they are isolated, lost, or overlooked in overwrought or emotionally bereft families. To gloss over the child's plight (symptom/behavior) and move prematurely to consideration of broader family patterns may amount to repeating the family pattern of dismissing or minimizing the authenticity of the child's claims. Whether a child is overcontrolled or undercontrolled, overprotected or underprotected, sad and fearful or aggressive and angry, whether the child is depressed and withdrawn or oppositionally defiant, these children share a common experience: that the family, on some level, is unable to truly "see" (recognize) and respond appropriately to their developmental needs. Their needs as children, due to one circumstance or another, have gone unmet.

For this reason, the therapist's first line of inquiry and exploration in a structured family assessment is the child. The therapist can either literally ask some or all of the following questions or can incorporate them in a "mental checklist." Some highlighted areas, major points around which a view of the "problem" is organized in the Child-Centered Family Assessment (Andreozzi, 1985a, 1988) include:

- Developmental history of the presenting child, including pregnancy (mother's health, experience during pregnancy, quality of social/emotional support), birth (difficult delivery), use of medication, birth weight, special neonatal care; medical history (long illnesses, hospitalizations, allergies, current medications); physical, social, emotional, and intellectual development (acquisition of developmental milestones); parents' perception/awareness of anything unusual, different or special about the child's development.
- Onset of the problem, including initial identification (by whom), family's reaction, family's "theory of the problem" (etiology), "solutions" applied, and types of help (intervention) sought.
- Description of the problem in behavioral terms, a transactional picture or scenario of the problem as it is experienced by each family member and the family, including when it occurs, how it occurs (sequence of interactions), where it occurs (home, school), who is primarily involved, what major issues (recurrent themes) arise and seem to be at stake.

The therapist then organizes this information to shed diagnostic and developmental light on the problem. The therapist begins to formulate a developmentally focused view of the problem on two levels: the problem as it occurs in observable behaviors that build into repetitive problem transactions, and the emotional process that appears to surround the problem.

This developmental assessment can be done quickly and can be incorporated easily into conversations with the family. Even when there is no presenting child, in the Child-Centered Family Therapy Model, the therapist charts child development, taking note of recurrent family patterns in relation to child development stages. For example, is this a family who has difficulty "holding on to" (creating nurturant bonds of intimacy and attachment) or "letting go of" (nurturing autonomy and independence) its children? In this light, child development stages are treated as evolving family structures and are charted across time.

The next level of assessment involves the family, specifically how child development is nested within the family and its relationship to the family's current developmental crisis and problem. When a family comes to therapy, we see its actions and patterns. These are the two levels of family organization that we can observe through a family's behavior. Its model and meaning structures we learn about later through image exploration. All four levels of family organization contain corresponding or counterpart parent-child and child development structures for the therapist to assess or consider. For example, the therapist gathers preliminary information about the family's guiding ideals in relation to child development and a sense of the "group" or family purpose that children fulfill. The therapist also formulates a working understanding of what it means to "be a child" in the family, including the family's image and concept (social construction) of childhood, explored from the children's and parents' experience and perspective. During identity struggles, individuals (spouses, parents, children) confront each other, not with the competing critical identity images themselves, but rather with competing assertions about reality: about how things are and how things ought to be. Individuals do not confront each other with these images because they are beneath the surface of awareness, and usually remain there unless they spontaneously surface or are clinically elicited, as shown in Chapter 4 and as I shall illustrate in Chapter 8.

Therefore, the next step in assessment involves the identification of the positive assertions underlying family member behaviors. These assertions about self-in-relation to others are always specific and contextual and reflect positive values. The therapist seeks to discover the positive meanings and the expectations motivating an individual's behavior. This is what the therapist seeks to name (affirm) and make visible. When the positive strivings—meanings and expectations guiding an individual's behavior—are explicitly known (stated), behavior changes can and do take place. The converse is also true: As individuals in therapy change their behavior (transactions and styles of approaching others), paradoxically and simultaneously, meanings and expectation will also change. This takes on special meaning in Child-Centered Family Therapy. When working with children, the therapist identifies these positive assertions (hopes and wishes about relationships) by "reading" the message and action-statement contained in the child's behavior.

Changes in behavior can often transform the message of the behavior. The message that a behavior conveys (an individual's experience of self-in-relation to others and others-in-relation to self) will also change as new, positive behaviors are learned and replace negative ones. Similarly, as family members understand the meanings (motivations) and expectations of each other's behaviors and also claim (take responsibility for) the expectations and meanings (motivations) guiding their own behavior, family change will take place. In either case, both routes lead to the same kind of family change. But the place the therapist starts is with the concrete behaviors of family members (spouses, parents, children). The therapy begins here at the level of behavior, action, and pattern.

For example, take the following situation and common parent-child problem. Some children will literally throw themselves at inattentive or preoccupied parents. The frenetic activity of a child who is trying to be noticed can be perceived by a parent as intrusive, annoying, or hostile. This is the negative behavior message. (Children will often develop teasing behavior as a last resort to be noticed in some way. Negative attention from a parent is better than no attention at all.) Once a parent understands the positive message (intention and expectation) that a child is communicating through the language of behavior and the parent increases or initiates emotional access, a child's frantic search "to be noticed"—negative behavior—will settle down, taper off, and, through therapy, eventually change in a positive direction.

Phases in the Therapy Process

The developmental framework described throughout this book is incorporated into the treatment steps that form the process of Child-Centered Family Therapy. The model draws on the Kantor critical identity image concept and Structural Dynamic Therapy (1980), adapting the therapy process to the situational demands and developmental context of child-centered therapy. Kantor's overall treatment process reflects a number of interrelated steps, ranging from locating the key ritual struggle, isolating the psychopolitical configuration (player parts) and making preliminary behavioral changes; identifying the competing critical identity images and image elements; rendering the images more visible and changing the behaviors associated with these images; and sharing the theory with the family. Kantor's process of facilitating (structuring) change involves drawing out through visualization (mental imagery) the critical identity images of each family member. In making the image visual and known or, as Kantor aptly calls it, in "fixing the image and image-elements," the treatment process integrates the inner experiences and systemic life of the family.

Child-Centered Family Therapy carves out distinct pathways of inclusion, understanding, and intervention for children in the conceptual and clinical landscape of structural dynamics. This therapy molds this treatment process and integrates techniques and activities to fit the child-centered, developmentally focused nature of the therapy (Andreozzi, 1985a, 1988, 1993a). These changes include modifying some phases, while emphasizing others considerably more. For example, the Child-Centered Activities described in Chapter 6 (Andreozzi, 1979a, 1979b, 1979c, 1979d, 1988) were developed to structure the treatment process for meeting the developmental needs of children. Similarly, therapeutic techniques (a process of assessment and intervention) have been devised to weigh, equally consider, and balance (engage) the full participation of children and adults.

In the Child-Centered Model, system crisis is viewed from a developmental perspective. Child development and parent-child structures are charted and assessed in relation to family process, organization, and development. In viewing the child's and family's problem as an unresolved developmental struggle, a therapist organizes diagnostic and treatment activities around the main task of locating the recurrent "problem" transactional pattern, what Kantor (1980) terms, the key "ritual impasse." On a practical level, however, before considering the dynamics of the developmental crisis, the therapist must often work to set priorities. This step involves careful consideration and sensitivity to the cluster of complaints that the family brings to therapy counterbalanced by the therapist's judgment regarding the most serious problem. If the therapy process is to succeed and the family is to remain committed and feel valued, then treatment plans should weigh and balance the family's agenda of change. Some symptom relief should be offered. The therapist seeks to free the system and nurture its development forward through an understanding (analysis) of the current identity struggle that is creating conflict in family transactions. The conflict is examined from two simultaneous perspectives, child and family.

Confirming the Developmental Crisis and Identifying Family Parts in the Problem Pattern

When parents and children come to therapy, the first task of the therapist is to confirm that the problem(s) the family presents reveal(s) the key developmental conflict. The therapist accomplishes this in several ways: First, the therapist considers the developmental dilemma and task that the child and family are having trouble with. Is it attachment and trust? Commitment and bonding? Independence and autonomy? Second, in locating the key developmental crisis, the therapist looks to see what features define the context of the identity conflict. For example, what is the theme around which the struggle occurs and recurs? Is it affect, nurturance, and intimacy? Is the theme one of power and personal autonomy? The therapist also observes the overall pattern or sequence of family member behaviors and the outcome of this sequence. The therapist explores the unproductive transactions among parents, children, and spouses. The theme, combined with an understanding of the way the conflict unfolds, as well as which part each family member plays (including children) defines and reveals the family's developmentally focused conflict.

Next, the therapist identifies the transactional parts that each individual (child and adult) contributes to the crisis pattern. For example, does a parent repeatedly oppose a child's initiating behaviors? Does a child come between (oppose) both parents when they begin to argue? The therapist does some preliminary work to alter these frozen, repetitive, and unproductive behaviors. (Family change begins at the level of observable behavior.) Then, at an appropriate, sensitively timed moment, the therapist elicits the crucial images associated with each child and adult in the crisis pattern.

The critical identity images of children and the puzzle pieces of behavior that they contribute to the conflict pattern are explored differently. The therapist begins image exploration with children primarily through the medium of play, or if the therapist does not employ play exactly, then the route to children's store of these images is accessed and communicated through playful ways. Several techniques for opening the door to image exploration with children will be illustrated in a later section. The route to straight answers and candid insights from children is often best accomplished through the multifaceted indirect world of play. The power of play to open families, especially vulnerable children, is directly related to the capacity of play and playfulness to assuage anxiety and dissipate shame, a point I will illustrate in two family cases.

When we ask children to show us the relationship image guiding their behavior, we are asking them to tell us something important and private about themselves. Some children, either because they are developmentally unpracticed or because they have not been given acknowledgment for verbal expression or an opportunity to develop this skill, may shy away from language in revealing these potent images. For these children, the therapist can, once again, turn to the rich store of information offered in the child's behavior and mode of play.

There are two guiding principles of image exploration with children: Keep it simple, and use repetition. The therapist explores imagery on three interrelated levels: behavior, expectation, and intention. For example, the therapist can frame image exploration by asking: "What do you do (behavior) when the problem starts? What is your part in it? Then what does (parent) do? What do you think (expect) will happen (reaction from parent, family) when you act (behave) that way (consequence)? Tell me what is the 'good thing' (positive intention) you want to happen when you act (behave) that way?" The same type of questions can be posed to parents and to each individual, child and adult, vis-à-vis the family. The consistency and repetition of this form of "behavior-expectation-intention" circular questioning provides structure to image exploration and the process of change.

Planning for Predictable Lapses in Progress

When family members have expressed their personal images, the therapist can expect and usually gets some immediate progress. Then, as the family (parents and children) experiences getting into and out of conflict, some retrenchment is also likely. These are the halting steps forward, hesitations, and steps backward that can accompany change. Family change never proceeds in a straight line. Family change patterns are varied, circuitous, and uneven. Growth happens in spurts. There are also plateaus, and we can expect temporary lapses back to old patterns. Change can be a daunting process; sometimes it takes a number of valiant efforts to get it right.

Structural Dynamic Therapy (Kantor, 1980) and Child-Centered Structural Dynamic Therapy (Andreozzi, 1985a) identify and plan for these temporary lapses and view them as signs that authentic change is occurring. This phase of therapy provides the therapist with a rich source of additional insight and observation into the family system: its strengths as well as its conflict patterns. The therapist uses this "lull" period or plateau to identify each individual's image more precisely by eliciting from each member a "picture" of the family member and other key people in interaction. This image scene relates to the way each family member feels now in the family crisis.

"This picture," a therapist explains, *"is one you have put together from important experiences and events and relationship moments in your life. This memory picture is vivid and powerful. It is the scene that immediately comes to mind, that you see (visualize) when you think about yourself in relation to important people in your life. This memory picture or scene is telling you how to be and how to behave. This picture is also telling you something important about yourself, who you are, and what you expect of yourself and expect from others."*

Eliciting Critical Identity Imagery

For adults, the images are drawn from the past and continue with considerable emotional intensity to affect current intimate relationships: husband-wife, parent-child. Adults' images begin as "thoughts" that are gradually organized into detailed visual scenes. With the therapist as guide, individual family members visualize these images, filling in the concrete details of the image scene much in the same way that an artist brings a painting from mind to canvas. The concrete details of image scenes are crucial: Who is, as well as who is not present, the mood, theme, emotional intensity, and interpersonal behaviors; all these factors add up. Each family member's critical image provides an important puzzle piece of the family conflict. What the therapist focuses on in image exploration is the relationship of the critical identity image scene to the current developmental crisis. The therapist is looking at behaviors, expectations, and intentions in preparation for the important process of changing the meanings of images and, in turn, facilitating family growth and behavior change.

Children's images are elicited differently because they arise in more concrete ways. Children will enact their images, symbolically representing their images through their behavior. Children's behavior is their language and the therapist is there as the translator. We see a child's emerging imagery of self, self-in-relation to the world and self-in-the-family, through a child's actions. They express their "image-worries" (what will happen to me and my family?) and their "image-wonders" (Am I good? Am I smart? Am I important?) through play and in the way they relate to others, including the therapist. Because a young child's imagery (including critical identity ones) are either not yet formed (the very young child) or still taking form (the 4- to 7-year-old), their images or "image-elements" are more concrete, immediate, and plainly seen.

Children's images are remarkably accessible. When rapport is built, a child often will candidly and spontaneously offer his or her images in a combination of words and actions. The child's imagery and image scenes are more impressionistic and considerably less detailed than adults' image recollections. A child's sense of self in the family and view of his or her relationship with a parent can be succinctly conveyed in a one- or two-word metaphor. The therapist needs to listen carefully for this imagery. Also, as is the case with children, this imagery may never be spoken, but rather acted out and shown in subtle ways (facial expressions, body posture, physical and emotional distances from family members). In a therapy hour, a 7-year-old girl, as she shrugs her shoulders, staring down at her hands, not raising her gaze once, communicates the image of her relationship with her biological father when she states, "You're not my real daddy. You're not the man who married us."

THE POSITIVE PROCESS OF CHANGE

While eliciting images differs with adults and children, once the images are apparent the therapist has two immediate tasks. The therapist needs to recognize, respond to, validate and, in some instances, draw out the feelings aroused by the image. The therapist also needs to identify enough of the key elements to solidify the image scene in the individual's awareness. This is a balance of empathy (feeling with the family and child) and planning (directing the therapy process). A therapist who guides family members in the full exploration of an image (image details), is going about the important work of stabilizing the system.

When each family member's image is made visual, concrete and known, the borders as well as boundaries between past and present are set, and the hidden, distracting energy in images (that have remained unmet and unnamed) diminishes. This takes some of the "heat" and "fire" out of the conflict, calming the family struggle. I have found that once critical identity images are known and become part of an individual's (child's and adult's) awareness, family members can be more available to one another.

Several important things take place at this juncture in the therapy process. Family members are beginning to see each other in a new light. As each member grows in knowledge of his or her own images, members gain an understanding of the wants and needs of others. The ultimate goal of Child-Centered Structural Dynamic Therapy is reciprocal validation: family members' mutual appreciation and respect for each other's images and positive identity claims. To facilitate mutual understanding, image exploration should, to some extent, focus on all individuals in a session. This conveys an important message of continuity and connection. It tells the family, through the therapist's attention to all participants, *"You contribute to each other's behavior. You are a group."* Image exploration can signal to the family the excitement that something new is about to happen.

Behavior change takes place when an adult's and child's image is known. This is a therapy firmly rooted in behaviorally anchored change: restructuring of system interaction. The therapist and family do not stop at a perceptual level of awareness alone. Images are explored, assessed, and communicated on three practical levels: concrete behaviors, expectations, and the intentions (motivators) underlying family members' relationship patterns or styles. The goal of the Child-Centered Structural Dynamic Therapy Model is to change the meanings of critical identity images. When we change the behaviors associated with an image, we change the meaning of that behavior. The goal of changing the meaning of an image is intimately tied to changing family transactions, specifically the parts parents and children and husbands and wives typically enact. The therapist directs the treatment so that each family member, including children, will shift that aspect (transactional part) of the behavior that contributes to the struggle (and flows from the critical identity image). As children and adults shift and expand their transactional behaviors (interpersonal strategies available to them in the family), system structure and interaction also change. In this model, change is viewed developmentally and therapy occurs at the place where personal and system, and a child's and adult's worlds meet. Considerable time and attention is devoted to the integration of child development (positive parenting strategies) in conflict resolution. The Child-Centered Family Activities (presented in Chapter 6) are integral to the model's practice, forming both the foundation and bridge to improved parent-child relations, and positive, redirected child development outcomes.

In bringing the therapy to closure, the therapist can communicate (summarize), explaining the puzzle piece quality of critical identity images and their power to influence the outcomes of relationships. This system awareness can be communicated in simple, graphic ways and in a language that children can understand, as will be illustrated in several family cases in Chapter 8. The notion of explaining the change process is rooted in the model's commitment to giving the family a strong sense of ownership of the process of change: to communicate to the family the full measure and importance of their participation and active involvement in creating and maintaining positive change. Next, in the preventive and developmental spirit of the model, family and therapist can prepare for the future. This may involve helping the family work through concrete changes and decisions in the present (e.g., should a particular child change schools?) and anticipate developmental issues that may arise (e.g., "How will you handle your oldest child leaving home?"). The following two examples illustrate techniques of fantasy-guided play with children in image exploration.

Justin and the Bluebird

Justin, who is 9, "acts tough." He is frequently truant from school and has threatened and, on several occasions, has actually run away from home. He picks fights with children at school. When he is reprimanded or punished either by teachers (detention) or his mother (loss of privileges), his response is simply, "Go ahead. Do what you got to do." In a blend of surface indignation and sullen defiance, he adds, "Who cares." In the first therapy hour, he refers to himself as "Stone Crusher," a brief but incisive view into his critical personal and interpersonal imagery. Then, as if to reinforce his assertion about his position in the world, he jumps to his feet and begins shadowboxing (kicking and punching) an invisible assailant or enemy. Looking first toward me and next toward his astonished family, he announces, "I have big muscles." Flexing his arm, he continues, "No one better mess with me or I'll kick their raggedy butts to the ground!"

Justin lives with his mother, Betina, his six brothers and sisters, and Thelma, his grandmother. The family lives in an urban housing development. Justin's father, who is in prison, has not seen Justin since the boy was three. The family is facing hard times on multiple fronts. They are in difficult economic straits and also confront the growing challenges to their parental authority and influence posed by the "mean streets" and "rough neighborhood" that surround them and now lure Justin. Thelma and Betina, mother and daughter, describe that lately they have been fighting like "cats and dogs." In a later session, Justin adds, (via image exploration) that he is "the hate between them."

Thelma is a strong initiator and prime mover of family organization and events. She is an equally formidable challenger, often assuming the negative or oppositional side of this family role. Betina is similarly strong willed and deft at mover-challenger roles. In the presence of her mother, however, Betina is no match. Both women are in deadlocked opposition. Ironically,

Justin, who has two "maternal voices" fighting over "what is best," has no "real mother" to guide him.

When vulnerable children have grown up too quickly and have developed "protective covers," when life lessons have inured them, hiding their "image-worries" and "image-wonders" under tough and hardened exteriors, the therapist must literally coax these children out. This involves reconnection, reuniting them with the world of childhood and earlier, important developmental periods and tasks that were overshadowed, minimized, or lost in the circumstances of their life and family experience. As a rule of thumb, we can say that the tougher the demeanor (behavior and attitude), the more fragile is the child's sense of connection and self-esteem. What works best is to reawaken in children the psychological wonder and challenge of earlier developmental stages and tasks: to return and reconnect children with the world of childhood through fantasy, playful imagery, and symbolic play. These techniques can have a twofold benefit and message, and exert a powerful, liberating effect on the adults in the family.

A well-timed guided fantasy can break the spell of a family's deadlocked, vicious cycle of distress, add "surprise" to intervention, and introduce wonder once again to child and family. Consider Justin and his defiant, disordered behavior. Below the surface of his tough guy exterior and rude behavior that bordered on insolence, there was a bewildered innocence and confusion. Justin was a 9-year-old boy who had not learned to be 7.

In a therapy hour that focused on the preliminary stages of our image exploration, a week when Justin had been particularly aggressive and distraught, I said, "Let's pretend that there is a bluebird right there perched on your shoulder. The bluebird can talk to you and you, in turn, can talk to the bluebird. The bluebird is your friend and can keep you company. The bluebird is something that your mother and grandmother and all of us want to give you. The bluebird is hope." First Justin appeared skeptical, then puzzled and surprised, then, caught up in the wonder and magic of it, he smiled.

Gradually Justin opened up emotionally; clearer generational lines were drawn; and the family began the work of restructuring. The bluebird became a source and symbol of nurturance, humor, and hope in a family facing harsh circumstances (poverty and single parenthood) where relaxation had become a "luxury," and "worry" (anxiety and tension) had become the rule. The family needed to find a way to "feel safe"—to give permission to its members—to "let down their guard" of intense work (survival) long enough to allow nurturance a chance to surface. They needed to allow playfulness to again have a "place" (role) inside the family. The bluebird created a metaphor and justification (reason) for Justin and his family to feel all right about emotions and emotional exploration.

As a technique, the bluebird plays a similar role to the invisible, six foot tall rabbit Harvey in Mary Chase's play of the same name (1944). Elwood, the protagonist, says of his large, invisible companion, "Einstein has overcome time and space. Harvey has overcome not only time and space—but any objections." Elwood's sister, Veta, notes that Harvey's special qualities mirror the differences between the concrete nature of a photograph and the depth and impressions of a painting. "A photograph," she says, "shows only the reality; a painting shows not only the reality but the dream behind it." Like Harvey's powers to bemuse and transform the people he meets in the play, technique guided fantasy (exemplified by the bluebird example) can create new structures, structural opportunities, and interpersonal possibilities for overworked family systems. For this family, children and adults alike, the bluebird notion evolved to symbolize a "safe place" and served as an emotional mediator, confidante, and time-out from life worries, the equivalent of Mary Chase's six-foot, invisible rabbit, Harvey. At the end of therapy, when I asked Justin what the bluebird "stood for" (meant to him), he said "truth."

Sara and the Make-Believe Heart

Children show their evolving images and image stories through the fabric and substance of their everyday life. Unlike adults, they do not put a frame around their experience and label this creation a "story." They live their images and communicate through the language of symbolic interaction (their behavior) what they are internalizing about important relationships. We see the models of relating that children have incorporated and transformed through the active "language" of their behavior. Consider Sara and her family.

Sara, who is 7, is an only child. She lives with her parents, who both are on the fast track of two independent, professional careers. Sara is a frail child who has been prone to physical illnesses from birth. She was recently hospitalized and has undergone a number of surgeries to correct a congenital problem. Sara is increasingly sad and withdrawn. Her mother describes finding Sara sitting in the den one afternoon crying. When her mother asked what was wrong, Sara explained that her "doll" had been left in the "spare room," and she was worried that her doll was "cold" and "alone." In school, where Sara usually excels, she will complete her addition problems but refuses, for some reason, to subtract (although she knows how). Changes in Sara's behavior at school prompted her teachers to recommend that the family seek help.

Sara's parents have a stormy relationship. They bicker constantly. However, when the couple is confronted with a direct challenge to their union (status as a unit), they join together in strong defense of each other. This couple threatens to divorce, but will never do so. Sara stands in the lonely center of this enmeshed and alienated family. Sara's parents, who are facile with language and cognitively sophisticated, provide "intellectual imagery" or intellectualized explanations of the problem and the critical puzzle piece each spouse contributes to the marriage and child rearing. When individual image scenes are distilled to their essence to form a collective family image underlying the crisis, a common theme emerges. Both parents camouflage their feelings of loss in busy achievement. They keep "doing" activities (an interpersonal distancing strategy) to buffer and avoid emotions. Similarly, both parents are, under the surface, frightened by Sara's physical frailty. It raises uncomfortable feelings of loss, human weakness, shame, and vulnerability. Through ritualized approach-withdrawal patterns that deny authentic emotional access (intimacy), they provide materially for Sara, but fail to see her emotional and developmental needs. Unlike her verbal and intellectually confident parents, Sara is emotionally reticent and tentative, and needs coaxing.

When asked to find "something special" to her that will show us what she is feeling, Sara returns the next week with a shoebox full of stones. She carefully removes three rocks of graduated size and arranges them in a straight line on the floor. She explains, "These are my make-believe hearts." She points, "This big one is my Dad's. The next one is my Mom's. And this teeny-tiny one is mine." (The rocks have the rough outline and shape of hearts.) "I keep my make-believe heart in this box under my bed. That's where I put all my feelings at night." Sara then carefully collects the rocks, placing the smallest one aside, separate and apart. Sara's parents are stunned.

Her simple, uncomplicated symbolic statement (in words and actions) opened a door in the family on authentic exploration and expressions (discussions) around loneliness and loss. Through therapy, Sara's parents learned to face (no longer deny or cover up) feelings and to balance competence (work) and nurturance (intimacy and emotional closeness). They recognized and now responded appropriately and directly to her poignant isolation inside this busy, well-intentioned family.

Three Clinical Propositions of Child-Centered Family Change

Three clinical propositions focus on the treatment of children in family therapy, the role and function of presenting child symptoms, and intervention in child-centered family systems. These propositions or principles about change are derived from research and practice (Andreozzi, 1985a, 1988, 1993a, 1993b) on the Child-Centered Family Therapy Model:

1. The presenting-child problem reflects a conflict between subsystem functions as well as a problem between individuals. Focusing on the

individual-family system juncture serves to balance and equally value the psychological reality of each family member and the psychological reality of the family as a whole. Alternating treatment-emphasis between the individual and the social context will result in system change.

2. The child's symptoms (problem) often serve to protect a healthy part of the family. Naming that aspect of health is central to family change.
3. Regardless of the current state of system distress, the level to which the family system may aspire is contained within and reflected by the highest level (behavior and perception) of current system membership. The sensitivity, sensibility, and behavioral flexibility (adaptability) expressed by one family member (the intuitive "system expert"), once validated and made credible by an objective source (e.g., the therapist), will lead the family forward to increased states of health throughout the process of healing.

The third principle requires further explanation. This principle is intriguing because, given what we know about systems, it may seem, on the surface, counter intuitive or contradictory to system-level intervention. First, there is the intersection or juncture where the worlds of individual and family meet. Next, there is the emphasis and attention drawn to the quality of system membership—that the identification of the individual with the highest degree of interpersonal (emotional sensitivity) and behavioral flexibility (adaptability) can most effectively bring about family change. Ironically, as clinical research and practice on the Child-Centered Model has shown (Andreozzi, 1985a, 1988, 1993a) the family member who expresses the highest degree of sensitivity and flexibility is often, paradoxically, the member most disqualified in the family. "Disqualification" is a common process in the disordered patterns of troubled families, partly explaining how the family became troubled in the first place.

Troubled families have a tendency to invalidate (nullify) the experience of their most astute member, or intuitive systems expert, and as I have found in clinical practice, these intuitive system experts are often children. Once the experience of these disqualified but abundantly insightful guides is validated by the therapist (consciously considered and "given a voice"), then the family is free to move on developmentally. Thus, a primary goal of the Child-Centered Model is to identify and create "moments of validation" for the intuitive system expert, the most available and also most vulnerable family member, who can help lead the family forward. Children who are ignored and discounted in a distressed family often function on a deeper level as the family's invisible Greek chorus; a benign, observing ego; a family's "ears" and "eyes" and "mind," the entity that the family no longer heeds. Validating this member liberates the system, and the work of change begins. Frequently, the leaders of lasting family change are children, as will be shown in full case illustrations in Chapter 8.

On the global level, the therapy process, embracing a set of task and change-oriented strategies, unfolds as follows:

- Identifying and listing the presenting-child problems for which the family seeks help.
- Identifying and focusing on the problem to which the family assigns greatest priority (response to most immediate distress).
- Exploring the problem through the family's own language, perceptions, emotional (feeling) vocabulary, and expectations (the problem from the family's worldview).
- Identifying the most influential subsystem(s) involved in the creation and maintenance of the problem-pattern and the key elements (membership, function, etc).
- Reframing the problem as a conflict in personal (self) imagery and interpersonal transactions, as well as subjective experiences and the associated behaviors and expectations among family members.
- Expanding the view of the problem and restating it in transactional, developmental terms, shifting from shame, guilt, self-recrimination, and blame to shared responsibility.
- Exploring and introducing alternative behaviors and family problem-solving plans, including positive parent-child and child development strategies. This includes the shift toward emphasis and identification of family strengths, skills, and resources.

The following discussion of the role of the therapist and a model of self-development and supervision will complete the overview of the Child-Centered Model.

The Role of the Therapist in Child-Centered Structural Dynamics: A Model of Training, Supervision, and Development

When aspects of self-reference (personal history, preferred style of relating or the unfinished puzzle pieces of evolving personal and professional identity) remain out of awareness and unnoticed by the therapist, these elements can interfere with the process of therapy. Efforts to maximize and positively influence family outcomes and the process of therapy must focus on two aspects of training and supervision: technical skill (professional development) and the therapist as self (personal development). Therapist, supervisor, and trainee ultimately need to turn the spotlight onto the therapy process to illuminate it in two important ways: How well is therapy progressing technically (in terms of mastery of systems concepts, therapy planning, efficient and effective use of techniques) and how well is therapy progressing interpersonally (in terms of the therapist's informed, positive use of self). From these principles, a model of professional development, training, and self-supervision flows.

In response to both aspects of effective and positive therapy outcomes—increased clinical skill and an informed use and awareness of self—this model of supervision and training has been developed. The model for family therapy training and supervision (including ongoing self-supervision) consists of a series of forms, a set of instruments we (Kantor & Andreozzi, 1985) term the *Rainbow Forms.* The model of training and supervision includes the use of the actual forms but also extends beyond them to the message that the forms convey. The Rainbow Forms track the progress of therapy as well as the therapist's growing awareness of self, including the conscious as well as unwitting and tacit ways the phenomenon of self-reference (described and illustrated in Chapter 4) can affect therapy.

Using the Rainbow Forms has a twofold objective: to promote positive therapy outcomes for families by consciously and systematically charting the phases of therapy process, including the therapist's role and involvement in it. The Rainbow Forms simultaneously guide and nurture professional and personal awareness by systematically posing questions to the therapist about the progress of therapy with a family. As a method, model, and program of family therapy training, supervision, and personal as well as professional development (self- or peer-supervision), the Rainbow Forms can be flexibly applied. For example, a therapist can actually use the forms, filling them out to systematically chart the process of therapy or, over time, the forms can become an internalized structure: a framework of self-evaluation and self-reflection that a therapist integrates in his or her practice. In this light, the forms, whether actually used or incorporated as thought process, can improve therapy outcomes.

Therapy process revolves around a plan, a series of intervention strategies (moves) designed to help the family progress and change. This plan, which flows from a therapist's system hypothesis about change (a description and explanation of the family's predicament or source of trouble), is akin to a problem-solving strategy. Similar to most problem-solving tasks, therapy and, by inference, the therapist's behavior and thought process (the equivalent of "therapy process"), consist of a structured sequence of actions. The therapist plans to get from Point A to Point B by specific means (techniques or strategies) through the linear process of problem-solving we call therapy.

All therapies, on the most generic level, must have a plan. A "plan," by definition, unfolds by stages (first "A," then "B," then "C"). Although family systems therapies are built on circular models of interaction, influence, and feedback, they must also incorporate practical, linear problem-solving plans. Without the linear, predictable steps and stages associated with a therapeutic plan, therapy process will disintegrate into chaos.

In some therapy approaches, the staging of change or stage theory is central; in others, implicit; in still others, not to be found at all. The model's position on this issue, which trainees can challenge but not replace, is quite specific: The staging of change is one of the most important keys to efficient therapy. It is the compass that guides clinical practice; the checks and balances we use to assess and gauge the progress and the quality of the developing interpersonal relationship that we call "therapy." Items on the Rainbow Forms address this issue, eliciting therapists' views about how they deal with this therapy process dimension in their practice.

A therapy plan also contains a concept of "duration," or a time frame. The therapist's estimation of the amount of time it will probably take to reach designated therapy goals is a prediction or forecast. Some therapies are explicit about the prescribed length of time. For example, brief strategic therapy calls for 8 to 10 sessions (e.g., the Mental Research Institute group); other therapies suggest that therapy should be brief but do not specify a specific time period; and still others, whether they address this specific issue or not, imply that therapy may take time. To ensure that therapists consider the length of time that the treatment of specific cases may require, the Rainbow Forms contain items like these: "How long will it take to reach your therapy goals?" "Who in the family is likely to agree or disagree?" Raising such issues through the instrument items not only calls the therapist's attention to the theoretical function of time factors inherent in different family therapy approaches and theories of change, but also sets the stage for an even more fundamental issue. It draws the therapist's attention to the way in which the interfacing of the family's model, the therapy model, and the therapist's personal theory often alters the "official reported method" to produce, in contrast perhaps to what is described in final case summaries, the actual model that unfolds in the therapy process.

The Rainbow Forms and Their Clinical Application

The Rainbow Forms consist of eight color-coded forms (color-coded for quick identification in the practices of busy therapists). Each form corresponds to an important phase (aspect) and represents a different vantage point on the therapy process: Engagement (Pink—two forms), Assessment and Working System Diagnosis (Blue), Case Summary and Presentation (White), Therapy

Process (Beige and Yellow), Reviewing Therapy Progress (Green), and Termination/Transfer (Gold). Integral to the Rainbow Forms (as a set of instruments and framework of supervision) is a specific concept of effective therapy. This concept of what constitutes effective therapy flows directly from the Child-Centered Structural Dynamic Model's organizing objective: The emphasis is on the therapist's capacity for self-understanding (self-disclosure) and on the validation and encouragement of affective expression (therapist as an empathic witness who supports the family as it understands the strengths and struggles in its images) combined with the importance of structure and planning. The forms, thus, highlight and stress the therapist's informed use of self (interpersonal skills) and the technical competence of therapy (professional skill).

The Rainbow Forms contain three types of items (Kantor & Andreozzi, 1985):

1. Sensor.
2. Assessment.
3. Flag.

Each type of item is a signal to the therapist and has an important self-correcting function. Sensor items sensitize the therapist to factors in the therapy process, especially those introduced and/or generated by the therapist that originally remain unnoticed or, if detected, unattended (e.g., aspects of the therapist's personal history, background, and subjective experience that may interfere with or alter therapeutic process). Sensor items call attention to self-reference issues, including the extent to which the therapist's feelings toward the supposed resister are similar to (reminiscent of) the therapist's past relationship experiences; the extent to which the treatment plan reflects the therapist's personal views about how to solve life problems; and what about this family contributes to the therapist's certainty or uncertainty about whether the therapeutic plan will work.

Assessment items focus on the therapist's facilities for comparison and critical self-evaluation. These items address clinical issues: whether the therapist has a definite plan; to what extent does the therapist's plan borrow from the type of plan associated with the therapist's method of choice; how certain is the therapist that his or her plan will work; and who in the family is likely to show the most resistance to the therapy plan. Flag items encourage the therapist to "yell for help," acknowledging the therapist's professional and personal vulnerability and, therefore, increasing his or her awareness of reciprocal involvements in the therapy process. Typical flag items alert the therapist to the ramifications of not having a plan and ask the therapist to consider the consequences of this position. For example, the therapist is asked to consider whether he or she prefers routinely to work without a plan, needs more time to discover a plan, or is confused and needs help. All three reciprocal functions, and the items that represent these functions, help the therapist develop the power to make informed discriminations and decisions about events in the therapy process.

ENGAGEMENT: THE PINK FORMS

The first two Rainbow Forms focus on and track issues involved in the engagement process, the initial rapport-building and information-gathering phase of therapy. Engagement consists of two companion forms, each highlighting a different and progressive step. The first Form (Pink-1), "Setting Up the First Family Meeting," addresses the therapist's earliest reactions to the family and clinical formulations about change (see Figure 7.1). For example, the therapist is asked to describe the experience of the initial telephone contact, including the family member to whom the therapist spoke and the quality of the interaction. The therapist is also asked to state working hypotheses generated, including salient history obtained. Additionally, items on this form begin to elicit the emergence of the therapist's informed use of self. The therapist is encouraged to note his or her reactions to the family, conceptions about the problem, and perception of the family's response to the therapist and notion of treatment.

The next Form (Pink-2), "First Face-to-Face Contact," consolidates the events of the first therapy hour (see Figure 7.2). Items draw the therapist's attention to the importance of this bridging session that can often signal a turning point, either in the direction of early termination or strengthened commitment to change, a fact well known in the psychotherapy literature. Items invite the therapist to reflect on forming relationships and the level of

Figure 7.1
Pink Form 1

SETTING UP THE FIRST FAMILY MEETING

Therapist ______________________ Case #/Client Last Name ____________
Supervisor ______________________ Date of Service ____________________
Date of Form Completion ____________

NOTE: Staff are not required to complete items marked with SO (Staff Optional), but are urged to do so.

(SO) 1. What was your most honest reaction to reading the intake form?
1) ____ eager and interested 2) ____ neutral 3) ____ overwhelmed
4) ____ other (briefly describe):

2. Before the first therapy session, with whom did you speak? (in rank order)

(Continued)

Figure 7.1 (*Continued*)

Rank	Who	Length of Contact in Minutes
____ family member	____________	____________
____ intake worker	____________	____________
____ team leader	____________	____________
____ supervisor	____________	____________
____ other agencies	____________	____________
____ other (specify)	____________	____________

3. a. If you spoke to a variety of sources, was there consensus among them regarding reasons for referral? 1) yes ____ 2) no ____
   b. If no, what different reasons were given?

(SO) 4. What were the goals of your first phone call to family? (Check all applicable):
____ I just wanted to set up a meeting and hang up
____ I tried to figure out who to ask in for the first session
____ I got a lot of family history
____ I tried to clarify the presenting problem
____ other (describe):

5. How did the family member respond to you? (Check all applicable):
____ interested and cooperative in scheduling appointment
____ didn't know who I was or why I was calling
____ angry
____ indifferent
____ gave me more information than I wanted
____ tried to establish a "special" relationship with me by talking about other family members in certain ways
____ said not everyone would come to first meeting
____ struggled with me over convenience of meeting time
____ other (describe):

(SO) 6. How did you respond to this (or these) move(s)?

(SO) 7. Whom did you ask to the first meeting and why?

8. Do you have beginning hypotheses about the family system from your phone call(s)? 1) yes ____ 2) no ____ If yes, what are they?

(SO) 9. What areas of inquiry will you follow up from phone call in first meeting?

10. What are your feelings about the anticipated first face-to-face meeting with the client(s)?

11. Rate your degree of satisfaction with your first phone contact (Choose one):
1) very dissatisfied ____________ 4) satisfied ____________
2) dissatisfied ____________ 5) very satisfied ____________
3) neutral ____________

(SO) 12. In retrospect, what, if anything, would you do differently in your early phone contact(s) with family member(s)?

Figure 7.2
Pink Form 2

FIRST FACE-TO-FACE CONTACT

Therapist ____________________ Case #/Client Last Name ____________
Supervisor ____________________ Date of Service ____________________
Date of Form Completion __________ Planned Contact Unit ____________
Contact Unit Seen ______________

NOTE: Staff are not required to complete items marked with SO (Staff Optional), but are urged to do so.

1. Did you need to have more than one phone contact with family before you actually saw them in treatment? 1) yes ____ 2) no ____ If yes, describe the kind of outreach you needed to do:

2. Did family member(s) appear on time? 1) yes ____ 2) no ____

3. a. Did the family constellation you requested appear? 1) yes ____ 2) no ____ If no, what was different?
(SO) b. How do you feel about this? (Check all applicable):
1) challenged ____ 2) upset ____ 3) happy ____ 4) angry ____
5) confused ____ 6) curious ____ 7) indifferent ____
8) other ____ (describe briefly):

(SO) 4. What was the "feel" of the meeting in the first 10 minutes? (Check all applicable):
1) happy ____ 2) sad ____ 3) chaotic ____ 4) relaxed ____
5) anxious ____ 6) cool ____ 7) guarded ____ 8) angry ____
9) neutral ____ 10) other ____ (describe briefly):

(SO) 5. a. Did everyone, especially the children, have an idea of why they were meeting with you? 1) yes ____ 2) no ____ 3) not applicable ____
b. If no, how did you handle this?
1) ignored it ____
2) I explained why I thought they were there ____
3) I asked parent(s) to talk to children about why they were meeting with me ____
4) other ____ (describe briefly):

c. What special techniques or methods of inclusion did you use with the children? Were the techniques/methods an appropriate match for each child's developmental stage/level?

(SO) 6. As best you can remember, list order of family members you addressed; briefly describe what you talked to them about, and whether you felt connected enough with them very early in the meeting:

Who and Their Age	What Talked About	Quality of Connection (Good, Neutral, Poor)
____________	____________	____________
____________	____________	____________
____________	____________	____________
____________	____________	____________
____________	____________	____________

(Continued)

Figure 7.2 (*Continued*)

(SO) 7. Why did you choose this order?

8. a. How do you feel now about the amount of time you spent trying to connect with each family member? 1) about right for everyone ____ 2) I should have spent more time with ____________, ____________, ____________ 3) I could have shortened the time with ____________, ____________, ____________

   b. List the developmental age/stage of each child. Do you feel more comfortable/less comfortable with each stage?

9. Did you spend more time with (Check one):
   ____ 1) adults
   ____ 2) children
   ____ 3) particular adult, if so whom
   ____ 4) particular child, if so whom

   Explain briefly:

(SO) 10. What is your typical way of joining a new group? (Check all applicable):
   1) guarded ____ 2) quiet ____ 3) joking ____ 4) friendly ____
   5) boisterous ____ 6) distant ____ 7) shy ____
   8) cautious ____ 9) follower ____ 10) professional ____
   11) other ____ (describe briefly):

11. Was there an easy fit between your style and that of each family member?
   1) yes ____ 2) no ____

   If no, what was the problem and possible consequences of the mismatch?

12. a. Did you modify your typical style with the client(s)? 1) yes ____ 2) no ____ If yes, how? If no, do you think you should have and why?
   b. Did you develop or use specific play-oriented or non-verbal techniques with younger children?
   c. Do you have a sense of the family problem from each child's perspective (cognitive and perceptual view)?

13. Who gave the most information about the presenting problem?
   1) mother ____ 2) father ____ 3) child (who?) ____________
   4) other family member ____

14. Who initiated information about the presenting problem? 1) mother ____ 2) father ____ 3) child (who?) ____________ 4) other family member ____

15. Who wanted to talk about it? 1) mother ____ 2) father ____
   3) child (who?) ____________ 4) other family member ____

16. Who was free to talk about the problem? 1) mother ____ 2) father ____
   3) child (who?) ____________ 4) other family member ____

17. Who was not free to talk about it? 1) mother ____ 2) father ____
   3) child (who?) ____________ 4) other family member ____

(SO) 18. What information did you learn about the family boundary in your first few moments of contact with them?

(SO) 19. a. What clues did you get about the family structure as you observed how each family member interacted with you and with each other in the very early part of the meeting?
   b. What is the role or "place" of children in this family's structure?

Figure 7.2 (*Continued*)

CONDITIONS OF THERAPY

20. Was team/supervisor behind the mirror? 1) yes ____ 2) no ____
If yes: was family comfortable with being observed? 1) yes, all were ____ 2) yes, some were ____ 3) no ____

    Were you comfortable being observed? 1) yes ____ 2) somewhat ____ 3) no ____

21. Did you raise possibility of videotaping sessions? 1) yes ____ 2) no ___
If no, why not?

    If yes, did family agree to videotaping? 1) yes, without many questions ____ 2) yes, after discussion between themselves and me ____ 3) no ____

    If family *refused* videotaping, what was your reaction? (Check all applicable): 1) relief ____ 2) I let it drop ____ 3) frustration ____ 4) I tried to talk them into allowing videotaping ____ 5) I'll talk to them about it again in the next meeting ____ 6) other ____ (describe briefly) 7) not applicable ____

22. Are you clear about what family wants from you? 1) yes ____ 2) no, they gave me conflicting reports ____ 3) no, family was vague and elusive ____ 4) no, their version of why they are there differs from that of referral source ____ 5) no, my style is to find out what family wants over several meetings ____

23. a. Did you establish a clear, explicit treatment contract?
1) yes ____ It is:
2) no ____, because:
b. If the family identified a range of concerns, did you qualify (prioritize) these problems?

(SO) 24. a. With this family, did you set out other "rules" of therapy (for example, the pass rule, using "I" statements)? Note: Not all therapists do this because it depends on therapist preference and the treatment model you are using. 1) yes ____ 2) no ____
b. *If yes,* what?

ASSESSMENT OF ENGAGEMENT

25. How "hooked" do you think the client/family is into treatment? 1) all committed to therapy ____ 2) some are engaged ____ 3) I think it will take more meetings before I can say ____ 4) not engaged ____ 5) I don't know ____

(SO) 26. Whom do you feel most engaged with and why?

(SO) 27. Whom do you feel least engaged with and why?

(SO) 28. Given these different beginning connections, what will you do differently at the start of the next meeting?

29. How sure are you that the family will return? 1) sure ____ 2) I don't know ____ 3) not sure ____

(SO) 30. a. What is the most important thing you learned about your engagement style and how it interacts with this particular group of people?
b. Is your engagement style different with children? Explain briefly.

31. Are you more comfortable with children or adults?

family member involvement including signs that some members may not be fully engaged.

For example, the therapist is asked to evaluate the amount of time spent "trying to connect with each member," the order in which members were addressed, and reasons for this decision. Building on the therapist's evolving profile from personal and professional characteristics elicited in Figure 7.1, items specifically ask about the therapist's typical style of joining a group and whether there was an "easy match" between therapist and each family member. Assessment items introduce structural evaluation in, for example, questions surrounding who in the family "initiated conversation," who "talked the most," and who in the family appeared "free" or "not free" to talk. This leads directly to clinical process around children. The question is asked, for example, "Did everyone, especially the children, have an idea why they were meeting with you? If no, how did you handle this?" This form also stimulates self-reflection around technical aspects of effective therapy, ethical issues, and client rights, including the importance of developing a clear, explicit contract, establishing the ground rules of therapy, and planning for the next session.

ASSESSMENT AND WORKING SYSTEM DIAGNOSIS: THE BLUE FORM

The Blue form—the first of the Rainbow Forms to be completed following the forms on engagement—charts the therapist's assessment of a client system. On this form, the therapist answers questions about the problem from multiple, concurrent vantage points (e.g., the perspectives of the family, the referral source, and the therapist). These questions tend to validate the notion that there are often different perspectives among various people and contexts on many system levels (e.g., between family members as well as between the treatment agency and the referral source).

One major cluster of items on the Blue Form is designed to help the therapist select an appropriate method of treatment for the particular family. This form organizes and makes explicitly known the implicit thought process (sequence of decisions and observations) that contribute to and influence the therapist's formulations around a working system diagnosis. The Blue Form highlights the selective observations (relevant details) the therapist chooses to notice (attend to) and weigh within the assessment process (see Figure 7.3). For example, the therapist evaluates the primary problem on a family member level (perceptual and behavioral). This knowledge then builds to an interaction or pattern level analysis and developmental assessment of the problem. The construction of the form is thus a statement in itself. It encourages therapists to make informed decisions as to the proper

Figure 7.3
Blue Form

ASSESSMENT AND WORKING SYSTEM DIAGNOSIS

Therapist ____________________ Case #/Client Last Name ____________
Supervisor ____________________ Date of Service ____________________
Date of Form Completion __________

NOTE: Items marked with * are Personal Model Clarification questions. Beginning therapists are usually not aware of their models, but are encouraged to try answering these questions and to talk them over with supervisors. Intermediate trainees should try to complete these items, and if you cannot, to think about what you need to learn to answer them. Advanced trainees should fill out all questions. Staff are not required to complete items marked (SO) (Staff Optional), but are urged to do so.

THE FAMILY SYSTEM

1. List all people in family system (Continue on back of page,if necessary):

Name	Role	Age	Occupation	Education	Live Home?
__________	__________	___	__________	__________	______
__________	__________	___	__________	__________	______
__________	__________	___	__________	__________	______
__________	__________	___	__________	__________	______
__________	__________	___	__________	__________	______
__________	__________	___	__________	__________	______
__________	__________	___	__________	__________	______

2. Draw genogram (include ages, ethnicity, religion):

3. List referral source, relationship to family, agency name (if applicable) and phone number:

4. List all other people involved in primary way with family's problem (including extended family, school personnel, clergy, other therapists):

Name	Relationship	Agency	Phone #
____________	____________	____________	____________
____________	____________	____________	____________
____________	____________	____________	____________
____________	____________	____________	____________
____________	____________	____________	____________

5. What is the family's developmental stage? 1) Attachment ___ 2) Industry ___ 3) Affiliation ___ 4) Inclusion ___ 5) Decentralization ___ 6) Differentiation ___ 7) Disengagement ___ 8) other ___ (what?) __________ 9) not familiar with developmental stage theories ___

6. What are the current developmental tasks, stages, and dilemmas of each child? List the name, age, and stage of each child.

(Continued)

Figure 7.3 (*Continued*)

7. What is the relationship (connection) between the family's current system-level crisis and the child development tasks it is negotiating? Where are individuals (parents/adults and children) potentially at risk?
8. What are the transitions, changes, and stresses the family has experienced or will experience in the next year? (Check all relevant events):

NOTE: You may not have all the information to fill out item 8. This may be because you don't yet know how to gather it efficiently, because the family therapy school you are using doesn't require this information, or because of something else. Simply be prepared to account for your clinical decision.

	Happened in Past	Expect to Happen in Next Year	Who Involved
LOSSES AND TRAUMAS			
death of spouse/partner	______	______	______
divorce	______	______	______
separation	______	______	______
death of close family member	______	______	______
death of close friend	______	______	______
miscarriage, abortion, SIDS	______	______	______
serious injury/illness	______	______	______
give up child for adoption	______	______	______
child placed out of home	______	______	______
child leaves home (for school, work, own apartment)	______	______	______
homicide of family member	______	______	______
rape/sexual assault	______	______	______
ADDITIONS TO FAMILY			
marriage	______	______	______
remarriage	______	______	______
start of serious relationship	______	______	______
pregnancy	______	______	______
birth	______	______	______
gain new household member	______	______	______
WORK AND SCHOOL			
family member begins, drops out, ends school	______	______	______
severe change in finances	______	______	______
retirement	______	______	______
fired/demoted at work	______	______	______
promoted at work	______	______	______
change jobs	______	______	______
problems at work	______	______	______
nonworking partner starts job	______	______	______
change in work conditions or hours	______	______	______
OTHER			
change residences	______	______	______
minor infractions of law	______	______	______
major infractions of law	______	______	______

Figure 7.3 (*Continued*)

DEFINING THE PRESENTING PROBLEM

(SO) 9. a. Describe each family member's perception of the primary problem, including their behavioral description of the problem, when it began, their assessment of its severity and its impact on other family members.
b. Describe the presenting child behavior (when applicable).
c. Describe the behavioral contribution of each child to the problem—scenario. If possible, identify the developmental "motivators" influencing the behavior of each child.

10. Have you talked to the referral source? 1) yes ____ 2) no ____ 3) not applicable ____

If yes, what is their perception of the family's primary problem?

11. PROBLEM CHECKLIST: Check difficulties experienced in family, which they may or may not list as the presenting or primary problem.

NOTE: You may not have all the information to fill out item 11. This may be because you don't yet know how to gather it efficiently, because the family therapy school you are using doesn't require this information, or because of something else. Simply be prepared to account for your clinical decision.

Problem	Yes	Who Involved	Problem	Yes	Who Involved
wife abuse	____	____________	child abuse/neglect	____	____________
incest/sexual abuse	____	____________	substance abuse	____	____________
eating disorder	____	____________	blended family	____	____________
peer problems	____	____________	marital problems	____	____________
adoption issues	____	____________	infertility	____	____________
mental retardation	____	____________	psychosis	____	____________
juvenile delinquency	____	____________	runaway	____	____________
discipline problems	____	____________	communication	____	____________
school problems	____	____________	sexual problems	____	____________
court involvement	____	____________	DSS involvement	____	____________
divorce/separation	____	____________	parent/child fights	____	____________
other problems	____	____________	(describe briefly):		

STEPS TOWARD A SYSTEMIC HYPOTHESIS

(SO) 12. Use the Minuchin system of mapping or any other system suggested by your method to map the structure of the family, paying attention to triangles, alliances and coalitions, boundaries, closeness/distance between family members, and the overt and covert power structure.

13. a. Describe the family type: 1) random ____ 2) open ____ 3) closed ____ 4) other ____ (describe briefly):
b. What evidence do you have for your decision about the family type? Explain.

INTERACTIONAL SEQUENCES

(SO) 14. When you review your first impressions of the client and/or family, what is most striking to you about the family process (for example, you may be struck by the presence of secrets or violence, by the degree of emotionality or distance, or by disturbed hierarchy or communication problems, or something else)?

(Continued)

Figure 7.3 (*Continued*)

(SO) 15. a. Describe the major pattern of family process using any system you prefer. If you wish, use psychopolitical roles of mover, opposer, bystander, follower in the dimensions of power, affect, or meaning:

b. Focusing on the most problematic features of parent-child relations, what role(s) is each child free to play? or restricted from playing? What is the impact on child development?

(SO) c. I did not fill out 15a or b because: 1) I am using another family systems framework to describe family process, but I am not familiar with how to detail it ____ 2) I'm not sure yet how to describe family process at all ____

16. a. How do the children's transactional roles contribute to the problem interaction?

b. Can you relate child development stage theories to the behaviors of children in families, in terms of mover, follower, challenger, and bystander roles?

17. With a focus on the primary problem, and keeping in mind your observations of family structure and process, describe YOUR systemic hypothesis about the presenting problem. Include how often, when and with whom the problem occurs, what each family member does, how the problem ends, and then how it begins again. When forming a systemic hypothesis, consider your hypothesis on three developmental levels: behavior, perception, and expectation (or motivation). Description of interactional sequence should be fully circular.

NOTE: Be sure to describe how the symptom may serve an adaptive function for EACH family member. One helpful way to think about this is to ponder what would be lost or changed in a negative way if the symptomatic behavior were to disappear.

(SO) 18. Did you do anything in session(s) to test this hypothesis? 1) yes ____ 2) no ____

If yes, what were the results?

If no, why not?

(SO) 19. If you did not complete any part of this section on developing your systemic hypothesis, why not?

____ 1) I don't know how to get this information and need some help
____ 2) the information I didn't give isn't necessary given the family therapy method or school that I am using with this client
____ 3) I need more time
____ 4) other (describe briefly):

SETTING GOALS

(SO) 20. In concrete behaviorally or emotionally specific terms, briefly describe what each family member hopes to have changed and what each family member hopes to keep the same. You can often read this type of information through the child's behavior. Translate the child's behavior into an emotional statement on the current family conflict.

(SO) 21. Briefly describe what family member(s) have tried in past to solve problem. What has and has not worked?

Figure 7.3 (*Continued*)

GOAL ATTAINMENT CHART

22. To keep track of your long-term treatment goals, in Column I, generally describe goal and check whether you have negotiated this goal with client or whether it is your own. In Column II, write behaviorally specific definition of this goal. In Column III, rank importance of all goals for case. In Column IV, since the most important goals are not always addressed first, rank sequence of how you will address goals. In Column V, rate status of work on goal using (1) goal accomplished, (2) work in progress, (3) failed to accomplish goal, (4) haven't addressed goal yet.

Long-Term Goals

I. Goal	II. Operation-alization	III. Rank Importance	IV. Sequence in Therapy	V. Rate Success	VI. Other Comments
Negotiated with client?					
1 1) yes ____ 2) no ____					
2 1) yes ____ 2) no ____					
3 1) yes ____ 2) no ____					

*NOTE: Photocopy two copies of this chart. One should be given to your supervisor for his/her files; one is for your own use and file.

23. To keep track of your short-term treatment goals, in Column I, generally describe goal and check whether you have negotiated this goal with client or whether it is your own. In Column II, write behaviorally specific definition of this goal. In Column III, rank importance of all goals for case. In Column IV since the most important goals are not always addressed first, rank sequence of how you will address goals. In Column V, rate status of work on goal using (1) goal accomplished, (2) work in progress, (3) failed to accomplish goal, (4) haven't addressed goal yet.

(Continued)

Figure 7.3 (*Continued*)

Short-Term Goals

I. Goal	II. Operation-alization	III. Rank Importance	IV. Sequence in Therapy	V. Rate Success	VI. Other Comments
Negotiated with client?					
1 1) yes ____ 2) no ____					
2 1) yes ____ 2) no ____					
3 1) yes ____ 2) no ____					

*NOTE: Photocopy two copies of this chart. One should be given to your supervisor for his/her files; one is for your own use and file.

CHOICE OF TREATMENT MODEL

24. Given your observations of family structure and process, your systemic hypothesis, and your goal, what family therapy method or school are you planning to use with family member(s)? 1) ____ Structural 2) ____ Milan Systemic 3) ____ Strategic 4) ____ Structural Dynamic 5) ____ Transgenerational 6) ____ Symbolic/Existential 7) ____ I don't know 8) ____ Other (describe briefly):

*25. a. Briefly explain why you have chosen this family therapy method or school.
b. What is the role of children as defined by this school or implied in this method? Does your method or school adhere to or contain a stage theory of child and/or family development?

SELF-REFERENCE

*(SO) 26. Is there something about this family that feels familiar to you given your own family of origin? 1) yes ____ 2) no ____ If so, what is it?

*(SO) 27. Given your family of origin, what about this family feels as if it will be easiest for you to understand and/or treat?

Figure 7.3 (*Continued*)

*(SO) 28. a. Given your family of origin, what about this family feels as if it will be hardest for you to understand and/or to treat?
b. How are your conceptions of what it means to be a child and what it means to be a parent similar to or different from the family's conceptions? How may this match (or mismatch) affect the course of therapy?

*(SO) 29. What about you and your interpersonal style will most help your clinical work with this family?

*(SO) 30. What about you and your interpersonal style may hinder your clinical work with this family?

(SO) 31. List any questions you have for your supervisor.

match between the particular family in treatment and their own professional orientation or method of choice.

We encourage therapists to complete a supplementary Blue Form when they gather and use new diagnostic information in the course of therapy. From the supervisor's perspective, the appearance of none, some, several, or many Blue Forms spliced between the clusters of other Rainbow Forms is an immediate color-coded indicator that "something" is taking place between the client and the therapist in connection with the assessment or diagnostic process. To one supervisor, the appearance of many Blue Forms may suggest "drifting" or "unfocused therapy"; to another supervisor, the presence of numerous Blue Forms may suggest thoughtful revision (close attention to the appearance of new clinical information), and may seem quite appropriate. The process of reviewing the Rainbow Forms goes beyond the differential meanings and clinical interpretations that various supervisors ascribe to the presence of some, none, or many Blue Forms; it requires supervisors to reflect on their own therapy and supervisor model, and to distinguish between these and the therapist's method and model.

Case Summary and Presentation: The White Form

The information in the Blue Form is distilled on the White Form, which resembles a traditional case summary (see Figure 7.4). The White Form serves two basic purposes: case presentations in supervision and responses to requests for information from other treatment agencies. The form is a consolidated descriptive case summary, culminating in a systems diagnosis and a systemic hypothesis that specifically identifies the therapist's views on what structures need change, as well as the projected appearance of these structures following therapy.

Figure 7.4
White Form

CASE SUMMARY AND PRESENTATION

Therapist ______________________ Case #/Client Last Name ______________
Supervisor ______________________ Date of Service ______________________
Date of Form Completion ____________

1. What is the *context* of the referral (e.g., external factors that may impinge on the therapy system)?
2. What is the present family context?
   a) Genogram?
   b) Members involved in the crisis (immediate and remote)?
   c) Relevant social context?
   d) Which (if any) of the following may occur: physical abuse; suicidal behavior; homicidal behavior; excessive use of drugs; acute psychosis; etc.?
3. What is "The Problem"?
   a) according to the referring agent or agency?
   b) family's definition?
   c) therapist's *re*definition?
4. What is the (system) diagnosis?
   a) What is the system's developmental crisis?
   b) What is the system's key *counterproductive* strategy?
   c) Identify, if possible, the pattern or sequence that maintains the primarily ineffective or problematic structure.
   d) Indicate the results of your attempt to *test* this structure.
   e) Describe the system's impact on you as you attempt to enter.
   f) What is your (system) diagnostic formulation?
5. Develop a systemic hypothesis (the part that every member plays).
6. What is your program of change?
7. *Systems Diagnostic Map*
   Utilizing your chosen theoretical orientation and the preceding diagnosis, conceptualize the client system in spatial terms. Think about what the system looks like now and how you would eventually like it to look. Diagram the "MAIN PROBLEM STRUCTURE" (that is, what the system looks like now) and the "DESIRED OUTCOME STRUCTURE" (that is, what you want the system to look like). See the following example—"PROBLEM STRUCTURE" is drawn in solid lines, "OUTCOME" in dotted lines.

   Between each element in the "PROBLEM STRUCTURE" and the corresponding element in the "DESIRED OUTCOME STRUCTURE" draw 10 crossing lines dividing the distance into 10 "Units of Change." Indicate the amount (degree) of change necessary.

   Example:

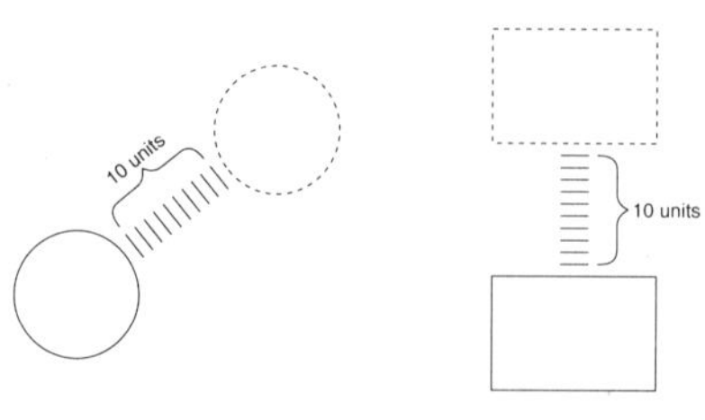

In contrast to items on other Rainbow Forms, those on the White Form do not have (with one exception) built-in sensor, assessment, or flag messages. This single exception involves the form's last item—the systems diagnosis map. In designing such a map, the therapist is asked to use his or her theoretical orientation and chosen method to conceptualize the client system in spatial terms and to diagram the structures that he or she proposes for change. The message conveyed in this task is simply that, if the theory is systems oriented, then the structures that it identifies can be represented in relationship terms.

The systems mapping carries both educative and clinical messages. It requires therapists to conceptualize the structure proposed for change and to think about the import of their predictions. It forces the articulation of an important issue underlying all therapy process and outcome: whether the therapist's chosen family method proposes an ideal for healthy family functioning. Furthermore, therapists must determine whether the proposed after-treatment structure represents their own or the theory's model. These questions help therapists to test their theories and methods, and to organize and formulate their working therapeutic processes. Most therapists operate with a desired outcome structure as a guide, but few ask what the cost is of having one, not having one, or having one that is discrepant with their personal model or that of the client family. For example, the therapist can compare his or her system diagnosis (structural map) with the family's Network Drawings (their structural map) to detect the presence of model differences. This comparison of perspectives can be made either at the beginning of therapy or periodically throughout therapy as "process measures." This is another illustration of the ways the Child-Centered Family Activities can be coordinated and integrated into therapy process to enhance self-supervision, professional training, and continued personal development as well as to help produce an informed, multidimensional evaluation of outcome.

The White Form asks therapists to make one other distinction in examining the change process. Figure 7.4 shows that therapists are directed to specify the Units of Change from 1 to 10, for each element (e.g., child, parent, couple system) represented in the before-and-after system maps. This item helps to make therapists aware that their model for change may contain within it rather specific statements on how mothers, fathers, spouses, and children are "supposed to be" in relation to one another, and that their own bias against one or another of these system components may be implicitly operating. In this way, the Rainbow Forms draw attention to the subtle influence of cultural differences and sensitivity to diverse family forms.

In requesting therapists' quantification of estimated change, the model once again is playing it "both ways." Looking outward, it reminds therapists that any evaluation of change that fails on some level, either to quantify or to standardize between-method measurements, is dealing in estimates so gross or global and subjective that comparisons across studies and therapy approaches are meaningless. Looking inward, it suggests that these quantifications are not to be taken too seriously; they represent analogues of biases and the judgments that therapists are always making (although they are often unaware of the impact of such judgments on practice). By quantifying these judgments on the White Form, therapists may develop a greater sense of responsibility for such clinical estimations and, ultimately, outcome decisions.

THERAPY PROCESS LONG FORM: THE BEIGE FORM

The Beige Form documents the therapy process, posing those questions that any good supervisor would ask. Form items ask the therapist to consider whether he or she had a plan for the session, how the plan worked, what techniques were used, and whether "anything happened" during the session that caused the therapist to change his or her plan or develop alternative techniques. The Beige Form not only draws the therapist's attention to structural features of the family system, but equally considers evolving relationship structures and involvement of the therapist. In this light, the Beige Form also poses questions that few supervisors would ask, unless they had been alerted to a problem by some revelation during a supervisory hour. For example, the therapist is asked about personal reactions to the client family: whether he or she likes or dislikes, feels close to or distant from, sexy or unsexy toward some family members more than others; whether events in the therapy hour felt similar to (reminiscent of) the therapist's childhood or current family experience. Form items alert the therapist to interpersonal problems on the horizon due to out of awareness experience; when events in therapy signal that the therapist may have "some growing up to do."

The final series of items on the Beige Form, comprised of sensor items and flag items, are designed to elicit and heighten the therapist's awareness of the influence of his or her persona, including possible effects on and involvements in forming structures. Collectively, these items invite therapists who detect problems arising from the therapist's personal (family/relationship) history in specific family therapy cases to ask for help and/or clarification from appropriate sources (e.g., supervisors, other therapists, self-reflection on the Rainbow Forms). Through the routine repetition of supervisorlike questions, each designed to give as well as to get information, items on the Beige Form encourage self-supervision (self-regulation) in the therapist (see Figure 7.5). By dividing and, therefore, alternating references to the therapist with references to the technology (i.e., therapy method), this research form and format unmistakably shows that the therapist and technology invariably interact.

Figure 7.5
Beige Form

THERAPY PROCESS LONG FORM

Therapist ______________________ Case #/Client Last Name ______________
Supervisor ______________________ Date of Service ______________________
Date of Form Completion __________ Planned Contact Unit _________________
Contact Unit Seen _______________ Focal Unit __________________________

NOTE: Items marked with * are Personal Model Clarification questions. Beginning therapists are usually not aware of their models, but are encouraged to try answering these questions and to talk them over with supervisors. Intermediate trainees should try to complete these items, and if you cannot, to think about what you need to learn to answer them. Advanced trainees should fill out all questions. Staff are not required to complete items marked with (SO) (Staff Optional), but are urged to do so.

COMPLETE QUESTIONS 1–6 BEFORE THE SESSION:

1. Go back to the process form of your last meeting. Briefly summarize the most important family structure you were working on.
2. Recall the end of your last meeting. Given the response to your most important intervention, think of where you would have gone if the meeting had lasted another ½ hour. With that in mind, briefly describe your specific plan for today's meeting.
3. What is your current hypothesis or formulation?
4. Does your hypothesis relate to your overall treatment plan?
   1) yes ____ 2) no ____

(SO) 5. Do you have a strategy for changing the family structure or testing your hypothesis? 1) yes ____ 2)no ____

If yes, describe briefly:

(SO) 6. Do you have a specific technique in mind? 1) yes ____ 2) no ____

If yes, describe briefly:

FILL OUT THE FOLLOWING QUESTIONS AFTER SESSION:

7. If you DID have a presession strategy:

Did you work on the structure you had identified?	1) Yes ____	2) No ____
Was your work on the structure successful?	1) Yes ____	2) No ____
Did you follow your strategy?	1) Yes ____	2) No ____
Did you alter your strategy?	1) Yes ____	2) No ____
Did you reach your goal?	1) Yes ____	2) No ____
Did you use your planned techniques?	1) Yes ____	2) No ____
Did you use any other non-presession planned techniques?	1) Yes ____	2) No ____
Did you design any new techniques during the session, whether or not you used them?	1) Yes ____	2) No ____

(Continued)

Figure 7.5 (*Continued*)

8. If you did NOT have a presession strategy:

Did you work on the structure you had identified?	1) Yes ____	2) No ____
Was your work on the structure successful?	1) Yes ____	2) No ____
Did you formulate a strategy during the session?	1) Yes ____	2) No ____
If yes, when? (Check one): 1st half ____ 2nd half ____		
Did you alter your strategy?	1) Yes ____	2) No ____
Did you formulate a specific goal?	1) Yes ____	2) No ____
If so, did you reach it?	1) Yes ____	2) No ____
Did you design and use any techniques during this session?	1) Yes ____	2) No ____
Did you design any techniques, whether or not you used them?	1) Yes ____	2) No ____

BRIEF SUMMARY OF SESSION:

9. Briefly describe what happened today (key content, highlights, etc.) in your own words.

10. Describe briefly today's session in structural terms.

11. Fill in identity of all those present and any significant reactions you had to each during the present session.

List All Present (by family membership)	(1) Distant From (2) Close to	(1) Dislike (2) Like	(1) Unsexy (2) Sexy
____________	____________	____________	____________
____________	____________	____________	____________
____________	____________	____________	____________
____________	____________	____________	____________
____________	____________	____________	____________

12. What subsystem(s) did you focus on most in this session? (Check all applicable): 1) marital ____ 2) parental ____ 3) sibling ____ 4) family ____ 5) identified patient ____ 6) other ____ (describe)

*13. In this session, I tried to effect change in: (rank order)
1) behaviors ____ 2) emotions ____ 3) meanings ____
4) no changes attempted ____

14. Did you observe something interesting in the clients' emotions, perceptions, or behaviors? 1) yes ____ 2) no ____

If so, rank order those applicable: 1) behavior ____
2) emotions ____ 3) perception of problem ____

If so, who changed?

(SO) 15. Were there any unsolicited reports relative to the presenting problem? If so, who said them and what were they?

16. Did you develop any new hypotheses as a result of this session? If so, briefly list them:

Figure 7.5 (*Continued*)

(SO) 17. Given the structure in mind that you were working on today, what was the most important thing you did to change it?

(SO) 18. Keeping in mind that structure, what you tried to change, and the client's response to your most important intervention, what should you do next time?

TECHNIQUES:

19. What school of family therapy are you employing with this family? (Check one):
    ____ Structural
    ____ Milan Systemic
    ____ Strategic
    ____ Structural Dynamic
    ____ Transgenerational
    ____ Symbolic/Existential
    ____ Unsure
    ____ Other (please specify): ___________

20. Check off any techniques you used in the session:

Systemic Techniques:

	Yes	No
a. restraint of change	1) ____	2) ____
b. get family history	1) ____	2) ____
b.1 genogram	1) ____	2) ____
c. urging change/restraining	1) ____	2) ____
c.1 split treatment team	1) ____	2) ____
d. observe sequences	1) ____	2) ____
e. reframing	1) ____	2) ____
f. circular questioning	1) ____	2) ____
g. use of metaphor	1) ____	2) ____
h. paradox	1) ____	2) ____
h.1 take one-down position	1) ____	2) ____
h.2 prescribe the symptom	1) ____	2) ____
h.3 symptom scheduling	1) ____	2) ____
i. elicit critical images	1) ____	2) ____
j. sculpture	1) ____	2) ____
k. mapping structures	1) ____	2) ____
k.1 testing the structure	1) ____	2) ____
k.2 restructuring	1) ____	2) ____
k.3 enactment/role playing	1) ____	2) ____
l. induce therapeutic crisis	1) ____	2) ____
m. preliminary change in psychopolitics	1) ____	2) ____
n. confusion techniques	1) ____	2) ____
n.1 escalate conflict	1) ____	2) ____
n.2 escalate runaway	1) ____	2) ____
o. give homework/tasks	1) ____	2) ____
p. coaching	1) ____	2) ____
q. isomorphic repatterning	1) ____	2) ____
q.1 therapeutic triangling	1) ____	2) ____

(*Continued*)

Figure 7.5 (*Continued*)

r. describe systemic hypothesis to family	1) ____	2) ____
s. engage family in documenting sequences	1) ____	2) ____
t. change family structures	1) ____	2) ____
t.1 change hierarchy	1) ____	2) ____
t.2 split coalitions	1) ____	2) ____
t.3 clarify boundaries	1) ____	2) ____
t.4 establish new alliances	1) ____	2) ____
u. prescribe ritual	1) ____	2) ____
v. change behavior sequence	1) ____	2) ____
w. promote differentiation	1) ____	2) ____
x. correct faulty communication	1) ____	2) ____
y. other (describe briefly):	1) ____	2) ____
________________	1) ____	2) ____
________________	1) ____	2) ____
________________	1) ____	2) ____

Nonsystemic Techniques:

	Yes	No
aa. supporting	1) ____	2) ____
bb. advice	1) ____	2) ____
cc. interpretation	1) ____	2) ____
dd. self-disclosure	1) ____	2) ____
ee. psychodramatic techniques	1) ____	2) ____
ff. facilitate expression of emotion	1) ____	2) ____
gg. education	1) ____	2) ____
hh. reflective listening	1) ____	2) ____
ii. behavior modification	1) ____	2) ____
jj. hypnosis	1) ____	2) ____
kk. gestalt techniques	1) ____	2) ____
ll. modeling	1) ____	2) ____
mm. other (describe briefly):	1) ____	2) ____
________________	1) ____	2) ____
________________	1) ____	2) ____
________________	1) ____	2) ____

HOMEWORK:

21. Did you assign homework last time? (If not, go to question 29) 1) Yes ____ 2) No ____
22. Did you ask today whether the client/family had done it? 1) Yes ____ 2) No ____
23. Was it done by client/family? 1) Yes ____ 2) No ____
24. Did the client follow the directions? 1) Yes ____ 2) No ____
25. If you assigned homework and the client did not complete it, did you respond to this in some way? 1) Yes ____ 2) No ____

Figure 7.5 (*Continued*)

26. Did the homework achieve the changes you were trying to accomplish?
1) Yes ____ 2) No ____

27. If the homework didn't succeed, was this because of a mismatch between the family and the homework? 1) Yes ____ 2) No ____

28. Did you give homework this time? 1) Yes ____ 2) No ____
If so, describe briefly:

PERSONAL AND PROFESSIONAL DEVELOPMENT:
TRACKING SELF-REFERENCE

*(SO) 29. What forming structure were you involved in today? (Check all applicable):
____ 1) The structure felt familiar, as if it were from my personal relationships
____ 2) I didn't feel fully in control in this structure
____ 3) I have some growing up to do in this structure
____ 4) I felt in control in this structure
____ 5) I don't know what forming structure I was in

30. Did you get stuck today? 1) yes ____ 2) no ____

If so, describe how:

31. If you were stuck, did you get unstuck? 1) yes ____ 2) no ____

If yes, describe how:

If no, describe why not?

*(SO) 32. What was the most important thing you learned in this session about being a therapist?

33. As you remember this session, rate yourself on the following using this scale: 1 = strongly disagree; 2 = disagree; 3 = neutral; 4 = agree; 5 = strongly agree
____ 1) Satisfied with this session
____ 2) Strategy was well planned and well carried out
____ 3) I felt powerful
____ 4) I felt in charge

*34. Did this session in any way remind you of a person and/or of an experience in your own family? 1) yes ____ 2) no ____

If so, what was it?

*35. Did you use this awareness? 1) yes ____ 2) no ____

If so, how?

If not, why not?

(SO) 36. What question(s), if any, do you have for your supervisor? Please list them.

THERAPY PROCESS SHORT FORM: THE YELLOW FORM

The Yellow Form, referred to as the "Therapy Process Short Form," reviews and organizes information from a different perspective. This Form is not necessarily shorter in length than its companion, "Therapy Process Long Form" (Beige). The difference lies in the type of response elicited. On one level, the Yellow Form is quicker to complete because its answers reflect the frame of reference used by the therapist to formulate his or her evaluations and observations of the events of therapy. It asks the therapist to make quantitative estimates and judgments on therapy process. In contrast to the Beige Form, the Yellow Form encourages the therapist to quantify his or her evaluations of process events (see Figure 7.6). The Yellow Form asks the therapist to think in terms of "discrete units" and rate his or her performance on key clinical dimensions—technical competence and personal model (informed use of self). On a scale from 1 (not at all) to 5 (very much), the therapist evaluates the extent to which he or she worked on the appropriate family structure; accomplished his or her clinical objective; whether he or she will continue to pursue this clinical strategy or, based on what the therapist now knows, will develop a new strategy for working with this family. In effect, the therapist is asked: Given your observations, will you continue to use the same techniques? Or, will you incorporate and apply new techniques (systemic, nonsystemic, "homework")?

Before the session, the therapist is expected to address questions that relate to planning and preparation. In general, the therapist is asked to identify (name) the structure that he or she expects to be working on; where the therapist wants to intervene; what techniques the therapist expects to use. After the session, the therapist faces a similar line of questions that focus on the relationship between the actual structure the therapist worked on and the therapist's diagnostic map (the structure identified for change). The therapist is asked to consider what changes have taken place, positive or negative; how long it will take to complete this stage of therapy; what systemic orientation the therapist is using; and whether the therapist's chosen techniques are appropriate for this family. The before and after session assessments available on the Yellow Form alert the therapist to broader, underlying recurrent themes. Items sensitize the therapist to the therapy time frame and signal when the therapy may be veering off course. The form makes the therapist aware of "stages" in the therapy process, draws attention to what "stage" the therapist is in with this family, and the implications or consequences of "not having a stage theory" of his or her own.

The Yellow Form provides a quick and accessible quantitative frame of reference or shorthand statement on therapy events that complements and counterbalances the information contained on the Beige Form. The Yellow Form serves not only as a self-reflective tool on therapy progress and thought

Figure 7.6
Yellow Form

THERAPY PROCESS SHORT FORM

TO BE FILLED OUT ONLY BY SUPERVISORS, STAFF, AND TRAINEES WHO HAVE SUBMITTED THE REQUISITE NUMBER OF LONG FORMS.

Therapist ______________	Case #/Client Last Name ______________
Supervisor ______________	Date of Service ______________
Date of Form Completion ______________	Planned Contact Unit ______________
Contact Unit Seen ______________	Focal Unit ______________

NOTE: Items marked with * are Personal Model Clarification questions. Beginning therapists are usually not aware of their models, but are encouraged to try answering these questions and to talk them over with supervisors. Intermediate trainees should try to complete these items, and if you cannot, to think about what you need to learn to answer them. Advanced trainees should fill out all questions.

I. BEFORE SESSION QUESTIONS

Please answer the next four questions BEFORE the session begins.

1. Considering questions 9 and 10 from your last Therapy Process Long Form, what *structure* should you be working on?
2. What is your *clinical objective* in this session, that is, what specifically are you trying to change?
3. What is your *strategy* to attain your clinical objective, that is, how will you get there?
4. What *technique(s)* will you use to carry out your strategy?

II. AFTER SESSION QUESTIONS

Please answer the following questions as soon as possible AFTER your session.

5. a. On a scale of 1 to 5, please indicate the extent to which you *got stuck:*

1	2	3	4	5
NOT AT ALL				VERY MUCH

   b. If you did get stuck at all, briefly describe how you got stuck:

6. a. If you did get stuck today, to what extent were you able to get *unstuck?*

1	2	3	4	5
NOT AT ALL				VERY MUCH

   b. If you were able to get unstuck, briefly describe how:

*7. a. To what extent did you have a strong emotional reaction to anything during this session?

1	2	3	4	5
NOT AT ALL				VERY MUCH

(Continued)

Figure 7.6 (*Continued*)

b. Please briefly describe the nature and context of this reaction:

8. Based on where you were at the end of the session, where would you have gone if the meeting had lasted another ½ hour?
9. What questions, if any, do you have for your supervisor?

Take a few moments to reflect on your presession orientation as indicated in questions 1 through 4. On a scale of 1 to 5, please indicate the extent to which *you were able to stick with your presession plans* in terms of structure, clinical objective, strategy, and technique.

10. Structure:

1	2	3	4	5
DID NOT WORK ON *THAT STRUCTURE*				WORKED ON *THAT STRUCTURE*

11. Clinical Objective:

1	2	3	4	5
DID NOT WORK TOWARD *THAT CLINICAL OBJECTIVE*				WORKED TOWARD *THAT CLINICAL OBJECTIVE*

12. Strategy:

1	2	3	4	5
DID NOT USE *THAT STRATEGY*				USED *THAT STRATEGY*

13. Technique:

1	2	3	4	5
DID NOT USE *THOSE TECHNIQUES*				USED *THOSE TECHNIQUES*

Similarly, on a scale of 1 to 5, please indicate the extent to which you will revise your orientation toward this family in terms of structure, clinical objective, strategy, and technique as a result of this session.

14. Structure:

1	2	3	4	5
WILL CONTINUE TO WORK ON *THIS STRUCTURE*				WILL WORK ON A *DIFFERENT STRUCTURE*

15. Clinical Objective:

1	2	3	4	5
WILL KEEP *THIS CLINICAL OBJECTIVE* FOR NOW				WILL DEVELOP A *NEW CLINICAL OBJECTIVE*

16. Strategy:

1	2	3	4	5
WILL STICK WITH *THIS STRATEGY*				WILL DEVELOP A *NEW STRATEGY*

Figure 7.6 (*Continued*)

17. Technique:

1	2	3	4	5
WILL CONTINUE TO USE *THOSE TECHNIQUES*				WILL APPLY *NEW TECHNIQUES*

18. What *school* of family therapy are you using? (Check one):
    ____ Structural
    ____ Milan Systemic
    ____ Strategic
    ____ Structural Dynamic
    ____ Transgenerational
    ____ Symbolic/Existential
    ____ Unsure
    ____ Other (please specify): ________________

19. a. What *systemic techniques* did you use this session?

____	restraint of change	____	induce therapy crisis
____	get family history	____	change psychopolitics
____	genogram	____	confusion techniques
____	urge change/restraint	____	escalate conflict
____	split treatment team	____	escalate runaway
____	observe sequences	____	give homework/tasks
____	reframing	____	coaching
____	circular questioning	____	describe systemic hypothesis
____	use of metaphors	____	document sequences with family
____	paradox	____	change family structure
____	take one-down position	____	change hierarchy
____	prescribe the symptom	____	split coalitions
____	symptom scheduling	____	clarify boundaries
____	elicit critical images	____	establish new alliances
____	sculpture	____	prescribe ritual
____	mapping structures	____	change behavior sequences
____	testing the structure	____	promote differentiation
____	restructuring	____	correct faulty communication
____	enactment/role play	____	fix the image

b. What *nonsystemic techniques* did you use this session?

____	supporting	____	behavior modification	____	advice
____	facilitate emotion	____	hypnosis	____	interpretation
____	education	____	gestalt techniques	____	self-disclosure
____	reflective listening	____	modeling	____	psychodramatic techniques

20. Did you assign homework for this session? (If not, go to question 23)
    yes ____ no ____

21. a. If you assigned homework, on a scale of 1 to 5, please indicate how well your clients did it:

1	2	3	4	5
NOT AT ALL WELL				VERY WELL

(Continued)

Figure 7.6 (*Continued*)

b. Please indicate how successful this homework was:

1	2	3	4	5
NOT AT ALL SUCCESSFUL				VERY SUCCESSFUL

22. Did you assign homework at this time?
    1) yes ____ 2) no ____

*23. a. What forming structure were you involved in today?
b. How sure of this are you?

1	2	3	4	5
NOT AT ALL SURE		SOMEWHAT SURE		VERY SURE

*24. How familiar does this forming structure feel to you?

1	2	3	4	5
NOT AT ALL FAMILIAR		SOMEWHAT FAMILIAR		VERY FAMILIAR

*25. How in control do you feel in this forming structure?

1	2	3	4	5
NOT AT ALL IN CONTROL		SOMEWHAT		VERY MUCH

*26. Do you think you have growing up to do in this forming structure?

1	2	3	4	5
NOT AT ALL		SOMEWHAT		VERY MUCH

As you remember this session, to what extent do you agree with the following statements:

27. I was satisfied with this session:

1	2	3	4	5
STRONGLY DISAGREE		NEUTRAL		STRONGLY AGREE

28. I felt in charge during this session:

1	2	3	4	5
STRONGLY DISAGREE		NEUTRAL		STRONGLY AGREE

29. I was helpful:

1	2	3	4	5
STRONGLY DISAGREE		NEUTRAL		STRONGLY AGREE

30. I was connected with the clients:

1	2	3	4	5
STRONGLY DISAGREE		NEUTRAL		STRONGLY AGREE

Figure 7.6 (*Continued*)

31. This session made me feel competent as a therapist:

1	2	3	4	5
STRONGLY DISAGREE		NEUTRAL		STRONGLY AGREE

*32. Did this session in any way remind you of a person and/or an experience in your own family?

1	2	3	4	5
NOT AT ALL		SOMEWHAT		VERY MUCH

33. Of the questions on this form, which ones are useful to you and which ones do you feel could be dropped. Your opinions will shape the new forms, so speak up!!

34. What questions that are not on here now would you like to see?

*35. (To be completed on alternating weeks only after you have completed six cases.) Write a single paragraph summarizing the session. Include noteworthy issues, the manner in which you addressed them, and the outcomes.

THANKS FOR TAKING THE TIME TO DO THIS FORM.

If you would like, use this space to write down any notes for yourself that might help you prepare for next week's session.

Form serves not only as a self-reflective tool on therapy progress and thought process (i.e., decision making), but also offers an ongoing research measure. The Yellow Form elicits the therapist's "before-and-after session" assessment of technical skill and personal development. The Yellow Form challenges the therapist to consider the import and evaluate the emergence of forming structures and to review and appraise the course of therapy in light of evolving client-therapist structures, a dimension often overlooked in supervision.

For example, the therapist is asked to disclose, seriously consider, and consciously track the insights on therapy and self-improvement generated from such pointed questions as, "To what extent did you have a strong emotional reaction to anything in this session?" "Did the session in any way remind you of a person and/or an experience in your own family?" "What forming structures were you involved in today? How sure of this are you?" "How familiar does this forming structure feel to you?" "How in control do you feel in this forming structure?" "Do you think you have growing up to do in this structure?"

A third dimension addressed on the Yellow Form extends beyond evaluation of technique and the personal factors implicated in forming structures to a consideration of the therapist's perceptions vis-à-vis the family of self (therapist) as a competent professional. For example, the therapist is asked to evaluate (rate) the degree to which the therapist "was satisfied with the session," "felt helpful," "competent," "in charge," and "connected" with the family. A supervisor, trainee, therapist in private practice, or family researcher can, for example, compare the qualitative content on the Beige Form with the pattern of quantitative ratings (self-assessments) on the Yellow Form to observe trends across similar and different family types, system diagnoses, and presenting problems. From this clinical-research perspective on maximizing outcomes and personal/professional development, the Yellow Form, like all the Rainbow Forms, provides a running account and accountability of therapy.

REVIEWING THERAPY PROGRESS: A DECLARATION OF THERAPEUTIC INTENT: THE GREEN FORM

The Green Form, which must be filled out "no later than the fourth session," represents a kind of declaration of therapeutic intent. With the exception of those therapists in specific training programs, therapists do not, as a rule, put their treatment plans and forecasts in writing. On this form, however, therapists are asked to do so if they can (again, the question itself reveals its message value to the therapist). Therapists know that their declarations on the Green Form are not cast in stone; there are ample provisions for revising a plan if information obtained in treatment suggests it would be appropriate to expand or change original hypotheses. Therefore, the more tentative therapists proceed with less trepidation.

Completed after every fourth therapy session, the Green Form is a review of the events and progress of therapy (see Figure 7.7). It challenges therapists to crystallize their clinical formulations and to assess, integrate, and explain to others and themselves their therapy machinations. The Green Form asks the therapist to be accountable. In completing this form, therapists are asked to put their method not only on the table, but also on the line.

This form serves an important integrative function. The therapist is encouraged, through the organization of the question items and the progression of the form, itself, to review, synthesize, and articulate what may be regarded as his or her "ongoing thought process" and set of interventions in a given case and preferred orientation and method of therapy in general. The Green Form draws together the separate strands of the therapy process into a practice statement. The form blends evaluation and self-supervision of technical or professional skill development with the therapist's growing awareness of personal style and an informed use of self. For example, the reflections that the therapist encounters around the "use of self" are consolidated and interwoven into an overall picture of therapy progress. The therapist is specifically asked to consider the level of match between the therapist's own preferred style and relationship history with the client family's relationship style, dynamics, and system type.

For example, items such as "When you are angry, bored, frustrated, or anxious about your client(s), whom do you perceive as blocking therapy the most and what does this remind you of in your own family history?" and "What factors (in you, in the family, in the therapist/family interface) have kept you from accomplishing your major goal?" are varied with items on the technical mastery of therapy, including the assessment of primary treatment method and the effectiveness of the treatment plan and chosen techniques. In effect, the Green Form, "Reviewing Therapy Progress," which can only be completed after the fourth session, bridges and unites in a comprehensive review, discrete information on the Beige and Yellow Weekly Process Forms.

Like all the Rainbow Forms, the Green Form is designed to refocus the therapist toward the client-family context; it reminds the therapist continually to consider the interaction between models and methods and the match between therapist and family. Items on the form call attention to the following important issues: Given this family's form of distress, is the therapist's orientation (method) appropriate; given this family's paradigm or model of reality, as the therapist knows it, is the therapist's approach (model of change and therapy method) appropriate. Going a step further, clusters of items on the form extend to an examination and exploration of the therapist and his or her method, probing such issues as: from

Figure 7.7
Green Form
REVIEWING THERAPY PROGRESS

Therapist ______________ Case #/Client Last Name ______________
Supervisor ______________ Focal Unit ______________
Date of Form Completion ______________

To complete this form, review the 3 weekly process forms since your last Beige or Yellow Process Forms, or since your Blue Forms. The answers to all questions should summarize the information from those 3 sessions.

NOTE: Items marked with * are Personal Model Clarification questions. Beginning therapists are usually not aware of their models, but are encouraged to try answering these questions and to talk them over with supervisors. Intermediate trainees should try to complete these items, and if you cannot, to think about what you need to learn to answer them. Advanced trainees should fill out all questions.

I. ENGAGEMENT AS ONGOING PROCESS: IS THE FAMILY REALLY IN TREATMENT OR WHO'S RUNNING THE SHOW?

1. Are the family members you want to come in attending therapy?
   1) ____ yes 2) ____ no, individuals I want to see don't consistently attend
   3) ____ no, there are too many no shows

2. What have you done about this?

*3. What aspect of your personal background, relationship history, and style of interacting might be involved in this problem with engagement and/or commitment to therapy?

4. In your assessment, is the family:
   1) ____ committed to therapy and working appropriately
   2) ____ seemingly committed to therapy but not really working
   3) ____ some family members are engaged and working, others are not
   4) ____ this family is here because they have to be, but are not really working
   5) ____ this family is here because they have to be, and are working appropriately
   6) ____ I don't know

5. Are the children fully engaged in therapy? If not, have you considered age-appropriate and alternative developmentally focused techniques for drawing children in as full participants?

II. REVIEW OF SYSTEMIC HYPOTHESIS

Review your notes on hypotheses that you have made about the client(s).

6. Has your original hypothesis of the interactional sequence and its FUNCTION continued to hold up? 1) ____ yes 2) ____ no

   If yes, how many times have you changed it since your last monthly form (or if this is your first monthly form, since the beginning of treatment)? ____

   If no, what is your current hypothesis? (Include a description of the crucial interactional sequence and its function.)

Figure 7.7 (*Continued*)

III. STAGES OF TREATMENT

7. a. Does your primary treatment method identify stages for reaching treatment goals? 1) ____ yes 2) ____ no 3) ____ don't know
   b. If yes, list the names of the stages and circle the one you are currently in:

8. Considering this map of your stages of treatment from beginning to end, are you currently in the appropriate stage? 1) ____ yes 2) ____ no 3) ____ don't know

9. What is your assessment of the pace of therapy?

   1) ____ I feel impatient and prefer to move faster, but I think the pace is right for the family
   2) ____ I feel impatient and prefer to move faster, and the pace is too slow for the family as well
   3) ____ I feel rushed and prefer to move slower, but the pace is right for the family
   4) ____ I feel rushed and prefer to move slower, and the pace is too fast for the family as well
   5) ____ The pace is about right for me and for the family

IV. STRUCTURAL WORK WITH FAMILY

*10. In every session, you attend to certain kinds of clinical information. Your questions, your moves, or what you respond to are guided by something in particular that you are focusing on. Sometimes that "something" is clear to you, and other times we are unaware of exactly what we are trying to understand or to change in our client(s). But we are always working on a particular STRUCTURE, which can be described from a number of frames of reference. Depending on how you punctuate things, structures can be static or dynamic, can refer to (1) the internal world of individuals; (2) the interface of intrapsychic and interpersonal worlds; (3) sequences of observable transactional sequences; or (4) the belief systems or paradigms which help maintain a system. Each school of family therapy has a conceptual model that highlights certain structures as clinically important. If you are working within a particular school of family therapy and identify structures within the vocabulary of that school, describe the key structures of your last 3 meetings with your client(s). BE SURE TO NOTE THE MOST IMPORTANT STRUCTURE WITH**

*11. Sometimes we focus on structures that cannot easily be described in the preestablished conceptual framework of a given school of family therapy, or we lack the technical words, or we focus on special things not currently labeled by family systems vocabularies. If you could not complete the above question, IN YOUR OWN WORDS, describe the key structures of your last 3 meetings with your client(s). Depending on how you punctuate things, structures can be static or dynamic, can refer to (1) the internal world of individuals; (2) the interface of intrapsychic and interpersonal worlds; (3) sequences of observable transactional sequences; or (4) the belief systems or paradigms which help maintain a system. BE SURE TO NOTE THE MOST IMPORTANT STRUCTURE WITH **

(Continued)

Figure 7.7 (*Continued*)

*12. When you think about the SEQUENCE or order of structures that you have worked on over the last 3 meetings, what is your evaluation of how much control you have exerted over which structure you focus on at any given time?
1) ____ I planned this sequence systematically and am satisfied that I am on the right track
2) ____ This sequence just kind of happened but seems to be in the right direction
3) ____ I planned this sequence but am haunted by a concern that I am not on the right track
4) ____ This sequence just kind of happened and I am not sure it is in the right direction
5) ____ I am not clear enough about my Primary Treatment Model (PTM) to be able to make this assessment

V. THERAPIST/FAMILY INTERFACE

"Forming Structures" are the usually unnoticed patterns that emerge from the interaction of the therapist's personal background and style of relating with some element of the client(s) system (such as triangles, coalitions, and alliances).

*13. List what forming structures you are currently involved in, with whom, describe the pattern and the basic issue around which it revolves.

*14. Is this structure therapeutically useful? 1) ____ yes 2) ____ no 3) ____ don't know

*15. Now that you are aware of this structure, are you going to change it? 1) ____ yes 2) ____ no 3) ____ don't know

*16. When you are angry, bored, frustrated, or anxious about your client(s), whom do you perceive as blocking therapy the most and what does this remind you of in your own family history?

VI. REVIEW OF TECHNIQUES

17. If you are trying to stick faithfully to one method or family therapy school, what is it?

18. If you are using a number of schools, list them and place an asterisk by the school you are primarily using.

19. If you are using more than one school of family therapy, why are you doing this?

Review the variety of techniques that you have used over the last 3 meetings.

20. Do your techniques draw primarily from one school or method of family therapy? 1) ____ yes 2) ____ no 3) ____ don't know

21. List the techniques that have been most successful with this particular case.

22. List the techniques that have not worked well with this particular case.

*23. What techniques have you been most comfortable with, regardless of their success or failure with this particular case? Why?

*24. When you think about the patterns of techniques that you have employed, what factors have influenced you?

Figure 7.7 (*Continued*)

25. I think I have 1) ____ used too many techniques 2) ____ been too cautious to try anything new 3) ____ have carefully matched my techniques with this case and where it is in the process of therapy 4) ____ other (describe briefly):

26. I tend to 1) ____ plan carefully which techniques I will use 2) ____ do only techniques that I am very familiar with 3) ____ use techniques that I just recently learned in class 4) ____ other (describe briefly):

*27. What do you think may be getting in the way of your carrying out the proper technical solutions with this family? (Check all applicable):

1) ____ I don't know what I am doing as a family therapist yet
2) ____ my personal history and/or attributes
3) ____ a combination of the limits of my family therapy knowledge and personal history and/or attributes.

*28. If you have checked 2 or 3 above, would you like help 1) ____ from supervisor 2) ____ from group 3) ____ I am dealing with this in other places 4) ____ I don't think I need any help with it

*29. What is the most important thing that you have learned about yourself and how you use techniques?

VII. PROGRESS IN GOAL ATTAINMENT

The goals of your treatment may refer to content you want the client(s) to address, to changes in family structure, or to altering interactional sequences. Your goals can be short-term or long-term.

30. Think about your major goals in the last 3 meetings. Write down your most important goal.

31. Have you accomplished this goal yet? 1) ____ yes 2) ____ somewhat 3) ____ no

*32. What factors (in you, in the family, in the therapist/family interface) have kept you from accomplishing your major goal?

33. At this juncture, if you have any new goals, please describe them.

VIII. ASSESSMENT OF PRIMARY TREATMENT METHODS (PTM)

NOTE: In this section, you will review the match between this case, your treatment method (the school of family therapy you are using) and your own treatment model which is in the process of development and conscious definition. Level 3 trainees and staff should fill out all items. Beginning level trainees can try these questions, if you would like to push your thinking.

*34. How do you feel about the match between your method and your model and/or personal style? 1) ____ perfectly matched 2) ____ well matched 3) ____ neutral or don't know 4) ____ not well matched 5) ____ very poorly matched

(Continued)

Figure 7.7 (*Continued*)

*35. Briefly explain your feelings about the match:

36. Given your attempts to use a particular treatment method, how do you feel about how you are mastering it and about its success with this particular family?

1) ____ I am satisfied with my performance and with the family's progress
2) ____ I am satisfied with my performance but not with family progress
3) ____ I am dissatisfied with my performance but satisfied with family progress in spite of it
4) ____ I am dissatisfied with my performance and with family progress
5) ____ I don't know

*37. How is your assessment of method and family progress related to your personal history and/or attributes?

*38. Take a crack at constructing a better question for getting at your personal history, experience, and/or attributes and their relationship to your model and assessment of progress, and answer it:

Question:

Answer:

IX. ASSESSMENT OF OVERALL TREATMENT PLAN

39. a. Concerning your method or approach, should you 1) ____ continue as is 2) ____ consider a new approach 3) ____ definitely change approaches 4) ____ get consultation about current method

b. What new areas of inquiry should you follow up on in the future?

*40. Should you, and if so, how should you position yourself differently with the client(s) in the future (for example, in terms of your distance; your alliances; your focus on affect, meaning or power)?

*41. The most self-critical thing you can say about your work over the past three sessions is:

*42. What made you the most proud of yourself as a therapist over the past three sessions?

*43. What is the most important thing you have learned about your treatment plan as a result of filling out this form?

what therapeutic position is the therapist operating; given the therapist's understanding of his or her own background, experience, and relationship history, is the therapist mismatched with this family. The therapist is encouraged to provide his or her theory to account for the mismatch and to take appropriate measures to avert this problem.

Items on the Green Form, first having directed the therapist's reflective gaze retrospectively to the beginning phases of therapy, then deeply settling the therapist's attention within the here and now of the present case, finally prepare the therapist for the transitional phase and the eventual termination process. The Green Form may best be described as manifesting a type of relentless quality or "circular" questioning. It helps therapists determine whether their method is working to their satisfaction.

Transfer/Termination: The Gold Form

The Gold Form focuses on the last phase of therapy, the termination process. Most family therapy orientations pay little attention to termination issues, but believe that:

- The termination process should be addressed on some level.
- The level of attention should correspond to the given therapy method's position on this issue.
- The termination process should reflect the type of family served and the presenting problem. For example, an intact family with a difficult adolescent may respond readily to brief therapy, which may end abruptly; however, a multiproblem family with such problems as abuse or incest will ordinarily require more extended family therapy.

The Gold Form's focus, as is the case with all the Rainbow Forms, is systemic (see Figure 7.8). Its items highlight and clarify the interrelationships among therapist, client, and method. Clusters of items on the form call attention to such issues as: Given the therapist's treatment method, did the therapy end as the therapist expected; was the therapist surprised by the termination process and in what ways. The therapist is asked to describe the sequence of events, including who initiated termination, and what the therapist's professional orientation and personal style contributed to the way therapy ended. Attention is also drawn to the client's contribution to termination; the extent to which termination was abrupt, a one-sided decision (therapist's or client's), or a mutual agreement (collaborative process). In effect, the Gold Form, like all of the Rainbow Forms, serves a multilevel, self-supervisory or training function (depending on the professional context).

Figure 7.8
Gold Form

TERMINATION/TRANSFER

TOTAL # OF SESSIONS: ___________

Therapist ________________________ Case #/Client Last Name ______________
Supervisor _______________________ Date of Service ____________________
Date of Form Completion ___________ Planned Contact Unit _______________
Contact Unit Seen ________________ Focal Unit ________________________

NOTE: Items marked with * are Personal Model Clarification questions. Beginning therapists are usually not aware of their models, but are encouraged to try answering these questions and to talk them over with supervisors. Intermediate trainees should try to complete these items, and if you cannot, to think about what you need to learn to answer them. Advanced trainees should fill out all questions. Staff are not required to complete items marked with (SO) (Staff Optional), but are urged to do so.

1. Nature of termination or transfer:
   ____ 1) planned: initiated by therapist/client agreed
   ____ 2) planned: initiated by client/therapist agreed
   ____ 3) client wanted to terminate/therapist disagreed
   ____ 4) therapist suggested termination/client disagreed
   ____ 5) client abruptly ended treatment
   ____ 6) occurred gradually as client just stopped coming in

2. a. Treatment ended because (Rank all applicable):
   ____ 1) satisfied with change
   ____ 2) therapist/family mismatch
   ____ 3) scheduling problems
   ____ 4) treatment alliance never well-established
   ____ 5) some of the family did not want to continue
   ____ 6) dissatisfaction with progress
   ____ 7) insurance ran out
   ____ 8) training year ended
   ____ 9) I don't know
   ____ 10) other (describe briefly):

   b. If transferred, describe why, to whom, and response of family:

I. ASSESSMENT OF THERAPY

NOTE: Use previous Rainbow Forms for contrast and comparison

(SO) 3. a. Initially, how many sessions did you expect to see client(s)? How many sessions did you actually see them? ____
If more than 3 sessions' difference between planned/actual number of sessions, how do you account for this?

b. Length of therapy was ____ 1) too long ____ 2) about right ____ 3) too short

Briefly explain your answer:

Figure 7.8 (*Continued*)

(SO) 4. Original treatment unit ______

Ending treatment unit ______

If different, why? ______

(SO) 5. General course of therapy was (Rank all applicable):

____ 1) unpredictable ____ 4) cyclical ups and downs
____ 2) smooth ____ 5) explosive
____ 3) boring ____ 6) other (describe briefly):

*(SO) 6. Is structural change a component of your treatment model?

1) yes ____ 2) no ____

(If no, go to question 10)

7. Map early family structure; map ending family structure; use Blue Form (Figure 7.3).

*(SO) 8. Is this the change you hoped to achieve? 1) yes ____ 2) no ____

*(SO) 9. If not, what prevented the change you were seeking?

(SO) 10. Write down early circular hypothesis from Blue Form (Figure 7.3), including how often, when and with whom the problem occurs, what each family member does, how the problem ends, and then how it begins again.

11. Has this critical sequence changed over the course of therapy?

____ 1) Yes, because:
____ 2) No, because:

12. *Problem Summary:* For entire course of treatment, check all problems identified in family member(s), and whether identified during intake interviews or later in course of treatment. Rate current status of each problem using the following scale: (1) resolved; (2) somewhat better; (3) no change; (4) somewhat worse; (5) much worse.

Problem	Intake	Later	Who Involved	Status of Problem	Comments
wife abuse	____	____	____	____	____
incest/sexual abuse	____	____	____	____	____
eating disorder	____	____	____	____	____
peer problems	____	____	____	____	____
adoption issues	____	____	____	____	____
mental retardation	____	____	____	____	____
juvenile delinquency	____	____	____	____	____
discipline problems	____	____	____	____	____
school problems	____	____	____	____	____
court involvement	____	____	____	____	____
divorce/separation	____	____	____	____	____
child abuse/neglect	____	____	____	____	____
substance abuse	____	____	____	____	____
blended family	____	____	____	____	____

(Continued)

Figure 7.8 (*Continued*)

marital problems					
infertility					
psychosis					
runaway					
communication					
sexual problems					
DSS involvement					
parent/child fights					
other problems					

(describe briefly):

13. Review all your Goal Attainment Charts over the course of therapy. Write down all your short- and long-term goals below. Rate your perceptions of how successfully each goal was accomplished using the following scale: (1) goal accomplished; (2) goal partially accomplished; (3) failed to accomplish goal; (4) never addressed goal. Then rate how stable or lasting you anticipate the progress on each goal will be, using the following scale: (1) solid; (2) temporary; (3) don't know; (4) not applicable.

Short-Term Goals | Long-Term Goals

Goal Description	Success	Stability	Goal Description	Success	Stability
1			1		
2			2		
3			3		
4			4		
5			5		
6			6		
7			7		
8			8		
9			9		
10			10		

II. ASSESSMENT OF TREATMENT METHOD AND TECHNIQUES

14. What family therapy school(s) or theoretical framework(s) did you use with this case?

*(SO) If more than one, how do you explain this?

Figure 7.8 (*Continued*)

*(SO) 15. Do you feel the treatment method was a good one for this family?
1) yes ____ 2) no ____

If not, why not:

16. What techniques were most effective in working with this family?

*(SO) 17. What is the most important thing you learned about the theoretical model you employed?

III. TERMINATION AND THE THERAPIST/CLIENT SYSTEM

*(SO) 18. Reading over your Engagement Forms (see Figure 7.1 and 7.2) with this family, how did your way of engaging possibly influence the nature of the termination (for example, you can discuss your feelings about the family, how well connected you felt with each member, the nature of your forming structure with them).

*(SO) 19. How did your personal history and/or attributes contribute to how termination occurred? (Check all applicable):
____ 1) when people get distant, I pursue
____ 2) I need to process separations or endings in detail
____ 3) I feel angry, scared, anxious during separations
____ 4) I took personally the client(s) decision to leave therapy
____ 5) when I sense someone getting distant from me, I detach first
____ 6) I need to hear from clients that I have done a good job
____ 7) other (describe briefly):

*(SO) 20. What did you most learn about yourself through your work with this client system? Include statement about what you specifically learned about your clinical strengths and weaknesses.

IV. CLOSING THOUGHTS

21. Rate your assessment of treatment:
1) very successful ____ 2) successful ____ 3) neutral ____
4) unsuccessful ____ 5) dismal failure ____

22. What are the most important accomplishments of the therapy?

23. What are the most important pieces of work the family member(s) still need(s) to accomplish?

24. Where is/are the family member(s) still most vulnerable?

25. Did you do a piece of preventive work around this vulnerability or around the next predictable crisis? 1) yes ____ 2) no ____ If yes, what did you do and how did the family respond? If no, why not?

26. If you were to tell another clinician the single most important thing about this family and how to work with them, if they sought treatment in the future or accept a transfer in the present, what would that statement be?

Exits and entrances in family therapy, similar to exits and entrances in the developmental history of a family system, not only highlight structural change, but convey the depth and quality of the system's relatedness: patterns of joining and separation. Closure, as well as new beginnings, can arouse strong feelings (emotional reactions) for family and therapist, alike. Joining a group raises personal and interpersonal feelings of self-evaluation and reflection; separations or, in instances of ending family therapy, saying "goodbye" can raise feelings of loss and uncertainty for both. Family therapists can explore their style of joining and separating—what their personal experiences bring to their professional style of ending therapy—by reviewing family of origin patterns and experiences around exists and entrances. Through the Family Photograph Activity (described in Chapter 6), family therapists can gather and integrate important information on the quality, range, and style of joining (engagement) and separating (termination, closure) that they bring to the therapy process and to an informed use of self.

The Structure of Effective Therapy

The color-coding of the Rainbow Forms provides immediate information and feedback about the therapy process, quite apart from their content. For example, a qualified person who picked up a case folder that contained eleven Green Forms (review and assessment of therapy progress and revised plan), each one interspersed not only with the anticipated three Yellow or Beige Forms (therapy process), but also with a sprinkling of five Blue Forms (diagnostic process) and three White Forms (diagnostic map), would know without reading a word that the therapist is conducting an extended therapy (11×3 or 33 sessions) with this case. Too, the therapist adds new diagnostic information from time to time, resulting periodically in changes in the therapeutic focus and treatment plans. In such a pattern, certain critical questions arise that can be readily answered by turning to single items in the forms, all easily accessed.

Before each session, supervisors can review supervisees' most recent forms. Prior to the biannual evaluations that therapists receive from their supervisors and supervision group, therapists can also review all case folders, formulating their own analyses of patterns in their treatments within and across cases. Similarly, therapists in private practice or in other treatment and social service settings can use the Rainbow Forms as "self-guides" and "comprehensive organizers" that integrate practice across cases. The ultimate goal of the Rainbow Forms is to improve therapy in a twofold way: to name the ongoing events of therapy and promote conscious evaluation of process, and to elicit awareness of the unfinished puzzle pieces of self and their impact on the course of therapy.

Only the knowledge and imagination of the trainee, therapist, or supervisor will limit the number, depth, and range of questions that can be posed and readily answered. Moreover, when the forms do not answer a question that seems significant, the questioner may add relevant items, contextualizing the forms to fit the demands of clinical practice, setting, and family population.* Also, in light of the shifting trends in health care and growing emphasis and influence of managed care, time-limited treatments, as exemplified by the Child-Centered Model, are becoming more crucial. The Rainbow Forms help therapists formulate, focus, and refine their treatment plans. In addition, therapy forecast items on the forms help therapists think (predict and plan for child and family change) in terms of discrete "time units." The forms aid in shaping time-limited treatment plans and objectives. In this way, the forms fulfill a practical and, given today's predominance of managed care, a pragmatic purpose.

The Rainbow Forms provide an important, comprehensive framework for therapists to think about the process of their work, whether or not a therapist actually completes the forms (physically fills out written responses to items). The reason for developing the forms was not that we (Kantor & Andreozzi, 1985) believed or expected that clinicians would use (physically fill out) the forms forever, but rather that therapists would internalize the frame that the forms provide to guide their reflections and self-disclosure. The Rainbow Forms represent what we regard as the structure of thinking about therapy, including professional and personal development, self-reflection, and observation of the unfolding course of therapy. In effect, the structure of the Rainbow Forms is what we have used in training people as family therapists. The Rainbow Forms can be variously applied. We have three recommendations for supervisors, trainees, and practicing therapists:

1. Use the Rainbow Forms in "bits and pieces," focusing on specific phases or stages of therapy (e.g., the process of engagement or family systems diagnosis).
2. Use the forms as a whole—a comprehensive structure depicting the overall flow and outcome of the therapy process. Accordingly, the forms can serve as research measures to monitor and evaluate family change and the relationship of process to outcome.
3. Internalize the framework and become a better therapist.

*The Rainbow Forms represent an evolving set of instruments that are the outgrowth of ongoing clinical research and child-centered practice. Accordingly, the forms change and are modified as a result of clinical use. The Rainbow Forms are, thus, the active product and reflect the active process of continued revision, involving the contributions of the research teams and staff of family therapists at The Family Center of Somerville, Massachusetts and the Kantor Family Institute of Cambridge, Massachusetts.

The Rainbow Forms in Practice

In Chapter 8, four case illustrations of family crisis-resolution and change will be examined in depth. Each family vignette will depict a different clinical issue, concept of the Child-Centered Structural Dynamic Model, and phase of therapy. The separate strands of the model, including the strategic and implicit use of the Rainbow Forms as an internalized, self-reflective process and model of professional development and self-supervision, are integrated into a comprehensive picture of the overall Child-Centered Family Therapy process.

In the day-to-day work of clinical practice and psychological consultation, the Rainbow Forms serve a crucial function. The collective or strategic use of information on some or all of the forms can act as a stabilizer and provide a meta-analytic view of the therapy process. The Rainbow Forms frame events in therapy, allowing the therapist to observe patterns: to stand back and gain perspective. In this light, the therapist can take a long-range assessment and make informed judgments about the appropriateness of treatment plans. The Rainbow Forms, in many respects, can function as a "therapist-companion" to the therapist, putting events into larger contexts. Just as the therapist works to create and heighten observational skills (self-regulatory and self-reflective capacities) in families, the Rainbow Forms can create the broader conceptual and practical system context in which the therapist operates. The Rainbow Forms can become a metaphorical kind of "informed observer" to the therapist and clinical practice, offering conscious, useful system-level insights, feedback, and understanding.

Consider the following example of the Rainbow Forms in application. The setting is the Psychological Consultation Center and Clinic (graduate clinical and school psychology training site) at a large university. The system participants include the clinical director, therapy supervisor, trainee, client-family, and the referral agency (Academic Counseling Center). A crisis has developed, incited by the actions and behavior of the client-family seeking treatment.

Myra, age 48, the mother of three adolescent children, and her husband, Bill, initially sought help for marital problems related to intimacy and trust. Myra appears sad, forlorn, and quite guarded, childlike in mannerism, suggestive of a kind of preadolescent vulnerability, as if transfixed at the developmental stage of 16. Her movements seem slow, automatic, precise, in a way that suggests a fear of making mistakes and a chronic underlying depression. At first glance, her demeanor appears calm. However, on a deeper level, it suggests both emotional numbing and considerable effort in the service of taming (controlling) strong, overwhelming emotions just below the surface. Myra looks as if she does not want to make eye contact with the world or anything in it. Eye contact, she explains, makes her feel naked and "translucent," as if she can almost be "seen clear through" and there are no protective distinctions between self and others. Face-to-face social contact frightens her. It feels too overstimulating. She seems to want to mute the world, life, and normal interpersonal interactions.

A significant incident accompanied Myra's reentry into the mental health system. When asked by the referring agency to complete routine questionnaires, she refused, reacting explosively, flinging papers at the office secretary, using obscenities, and then storming out irate. (In this treatment setting, the Academic Counseling Center is designated as the first step, or initial screening mechanism and, hence, the gatekeeper to family therapy. Because Myra and Bill are students at the university, they are required to seek help from the Academic Counseling Center first to determine the extent and intensity of the problem.) This incident temporarily halted the process of referral and precipitated a crisis among the staff, sharply polarizing them into two camps—one, systems-oriented and protective of her; the other, clinically viewing the episode as diagnostically suggestive of deeper, individual pathology (possibly borderline).

The events of the family's outspoken entrance into the therapeutic community generated a series of meetings involving Clinic and Counseling Center directors, therapy supervisor, and the therapist assigned to the case. All participants held quite disparate views (interpretations of events) and, hence, supported and proposed qualitatively different "solutions" (strategies for resolving the crisis created by the client's behavior). From such solutions and interpretations, treatment plans naturally and logically flow. Implicit in the choice of treatment and in the therapist's formulation of a plan are the therapist's professional model of therapy and "model for living." In this case, all system participants expressed strong reactions to the stimulus-behavior and different views (concepts) of change.

Both directors construed the client's outburst as indicative of pathology, localizing the problem within her, specifically her "noncompliant attitude" toward rules. (It was an almost ironclad university policy and, therefore, necessary procedural route to therapy that all university student clients first be interviewed and screened at the Academic Counseling Center level before a referral for more intensive psychological treatment could occur. The client-family directly challenged the logic and purpose of this rule.) Both directors recommended that she be required to return to the Academic Counseling Center and fill out university questionnaires; they wanted her to fulfill the "letter of the law." They were operating primarily from a closed system position. However, the supervisor and staff psychologist, the therapist in the case, saw things differently. They viewed her actions as a behavioral statement and expressed the position that to withhold therapy or, more precisely, to delay therapy (demand that she comply before treatment was made available) appeared somewhat punitive. Supervisor and therapist were operating from an open system position.

The client-family's intense response had, in turn, generated an equally intense response in the team of helping professionals. These strong reactions are indicative of the interplay of model differences. Such phenomena of the therapy process can be and, in fact, were articulated and clarified through the kinds of issues raised (items posed) on the Rainbow Forms. The operation of "personal bias" and the influence of "subjective judgments" on treatment decisions, once out in the open, can lead to a modified plan.

A conjoint decision was reached that struck a balance between both views: The therapist would meet with the family for a short time period to work on issues of compliance and anger. Next, the therapist, as a show of support, would, if the clients so chose, accompany them to the Academic Counseling Center to "complete the referral paperwork."

When asked by the therapist why she had reacted so vehemently, Myra explained that in some way something the receptionist had done triggered a flash of remembrance that felt like the kind of humiliation and abuse she had experienced in childhood from unrelenting, critical parents. After several weeks of interim therapy, Myra consented to complete the information packet necessary for referral and the family began therapy. Myra had entered the therapy system with the same kind of crisis and emotionality reminiscent of her first family relationships and dysfunctional family system. She later revealed a childhood family history permeated by scenes of psychological violence, emotional indignation, and neglect.

The Rainbow Forms are extremely useful when multiple systems are involved (several agencies or professionals). The Rainbow Forms can clarify the multiple levels of perception and cognition occurring simultaneously, teasing out the subjective from the objective, the decidedly professional from the marginally to intimately personal. Another instance in clinical practice where the Rainbow Forms enhance and improve therapy occurs when the items on the forms identify and untangle the overlapping realities of therapist's and family's worldviews. This can unfold in one of two ways: either when the therapist experiences a strong reaction to the client, or when the family presents resistance. Both of these contexts often require rethinking; the Rainbow Forms provide the necessary "cognitive pause" for doing so.

Unarticulated worldviews and divergent concepts of change are often at the root or, at least, play some part in the overall interpersonal equation we call resistance. The therapist can learn much about "practice patterns" (especially when working with family populations of different cultural or life history backgrounds outside the therapist's personal experience) by tracking technical skills and style of relating across cases. What we discover when we peruse the themes and content depicted and clarified on the Rainbow Forms are our strengths as well as our vulnerabilities, the unfinished puzzle pieces of our personal and professional identity. Chapter 8 turns to the practice of Child-Centered Structural Dynamic Therapy as shown in a range of family cases. Implicit within the therapy process involving each family is the conscious thought process of the Rainbow Forms.

CHAPTER 8

The Staging of Change and Structure of Effective Therapy

Families in Child-Centered Therapy

THE WORLD OF CHILDHOOD—the thought processes and interpersonal/emotional life of children—has been explored developmentally throughout this book. The dynamics of children and parent-child relations have been examined both within the family and the special circumstances of therapy. Child development guidelines, the reciprocal links or bridges between child and family development have been shown, and the Child-Centered Family Activities (Andreozzi, 1977, 1978, 1979a, 1979b, 1979c) have been described and illustrated in depth. The activities are designed to promote child and family development, with each activity providing flexibility for the therapist around a "structure of application." The activities have been constructed to match or "meld" with stage- and age-appropriate developmental considerations: the cognitive, affective, psychosocial level, skills, and readiness of children.

The activities consciously weigh and equally balance the developmental needs and interests of adults in therapy. Optimal child development is the centerpiece of all three levels or tiers (prevention, early intervention, and crisis intervention) of this therapy. The activities (described and fully illustrated in Chapters 5 and 6) are, therefore, decidedly child centered; they are devised with the ultimate goal or aim in mind of nurturing children (Andreozzi, 1977, 1988). However, to achieve this objective, the activities simultaneously engage parents, recognizing that full family and parental involvement is the best and most durable (long-lasting) route to sustained gains and positive change. To involve parents cognitively and affectively, capturing the family's imagination and immanent sense of possibility and renewed purpose, is the equivalent of ensuring that symptomatic children in families in crisis will be "seen and heard," "known and found," a principle that has been shown in child-centered clinical practice (Andreozzi, 1988, 1993a) to be the sine qua non of effective therapy.

Child and family developmental principles and strategies, combined with specific activities and assessment and intervention strategies, have been integrated into the phases and steps of the Child-Centered Model of family therapy. The Kantor (1980) critical identity image concept has been fully examined and adapted (Andreozzi, 1985a, 1988) for effective family therapy with children. The concept, applied to the world of children, is depicted as threeway image scenes that evolve developmentally between parents and children. The critical identity image represents the central explanatory principle—practical tool and conceptual lens—for promoting family growth and crisis resolution.

The therapist begins the process of change on a concrete behavioral level, structuring meaningful and observable changes in family patterns (transactions). Next, as the family experiences some relief from its entrenched state of crisis (ritual impasse) and is buoyed up by positive signs of change, the therapist proceeds to a deeper self and family understanding of the family conflict—critical identity struggle—on cognitive, behavioral, and affective or emotional levels. This is where the image exploration begins. Therapist and family fill in the details, emotional nuances, tacit unmet needs, and misunderstood personal and interpersonal expectations that surround and underlie each individual's critical identity image scene. The work of therapy is to integrate the puzzle parts—all the bits and pieces of image scenes—into a full picture of the family's developmental crisis and identity struggle. The therapist's work on structuring family change is, therefore, always focused on indicants (identification) of how these compressed, highly charged, emotionally arousing image scenes play into the family conflict and what part each family member's individual image contributes to the family struggle.

As we have seen, critical identity images are different for adults and children. The therapist accesses these images differently. As has been shown clinically and empirically (Andreozzi, 1985a, 1988, 1993a) children act out their critical identity images and use their behavior as a form of highly condensed statements about relationships (the self vis-à-vis significant others). Inroads to children's images often occur through fantasy and the symbolic world of play. Adults can talk about their critical identity images, the crucial interpersonal blueprints (scripts) that they use to guide their behavior with intimate others. Another salient difference with strong therapeutic implications is that children's critical identity images are in process. These images are forming and are the active work of childhood. Whereas we cannot and should not attempt to contradict or replace an adult's fundamental set of critical identity images (for these images are the essence of selfhood and cannot be eradicated), children's images are more pliant and, therefore, subject to primary prevention, greater influence, and significant change. With adults, it is not the foundation of the critical identity image that changes, but the meanings, behaviors, and expectations associated with the image that change and are the focus of therapy. For children, the critical identity image (worldview and palpable sense of self-in-relation to intimate others) can change in decisive ways. This makes the work of Child-Centered Therapy, the third tier of the model, preventive and compelling.

The building blocks of family process and the five Child-Centered Family Activities have been explored and illustrated in depth throughout the book. Three tiers of the model from primary prevention to therapy and crisis intervention, have been examined. Family vignettes and excerpts of therapy hours have been provided to illuminate developmental and clinical concepts and the phases of therapy. Both the differences and similarities in the therapist's application of techniques (the five activities) and method of assessment have been highlighted. This chapter draws the separate concepts and practice of Child-Centered Therapy into an integrated whole, a complete picture of the model. The practice of Child-Centered Therapy (its structure, thought process, and practical methods) come alive in the form of four family cases. Each family vignette represents a different family problem and developmental crisis and illuminates a different key clinical concept. The Brimmers are a multiproblem family; the Greens depict an extended, multigenerational family; the Clarke-Harrises represent a blended family; and the Stones reveal a nuclear family in the throes of domestic violence and at risk for escalating child abuse. Although each family problem and pathway of change emphasizes one clinical concept more than others—the Brimmers highlight the diagnostic importance of "family type"; the Greens, the salience of "player parts" in the ritualized, developmental impasse and crisis resolution; the Clarke-Harris family, the crucial assessment of current "family organization" on all four meaning, model, action, and pattern levels in relation to "image exploration"; and the Stones, the primacy and power of "family critical identity images" out of control—all four family cases illustrate how the model's network of concepts work in synthesis to influence and structure positive child and family development, practice, and change.

The Brimmers

The Brimmers call themselves the "Tons of Fun." The family is headed by Gail, the mother, age forty-seven, who was widowed at thirty-five. There are seven children, ranging in age from 12 to 22. All the family members are overweight. It seems as if they wrap themselves around and away from each other through food. Over the years the family has become a revolving door of "exits" and "re-entrances" with most of the children at one time or another leaving for foster care, only to return home again. The mother, overwhelmed with bouts of chronic depression, cannot cope with all that "horse-play, explosive energy, and disrespect."

The Brimmers reflect the problem-chronicity and history of a multiproblem family. They fall into Level Three on the Problem Level/Intensity assessment framework described in Chapter 3. The name that the Brimmers give themselves, "Tons of Fun," is a wry and ironic statement on the experience of their family life and the vantage point from which they view the world. The name conveys a central family image (how the Brimmers see themselves as a group). It also draws attention to what the family is not; its losses, what it senses is absent, its collective unspoken claims. *"Living in this family is not fun,"* the children describe in the second therapy session. The name "Tons of Fun," and my reason for dwelling on it, also reveals one of the family's strengths. The Brimmers, or the "Tons of Fun," are a creative, although at times misguided family who have survived much and can still talk about their lives and vulnerabilities with humor. As the first image introduction the family offered me, this particular name figured centrally in the image work in therapy.

The Brimmers have been through many social welfare agencies, mental health programs, and intervention plans. They now find themselves once again in a crisis at an outpatient pediatric unit in a large general hospital. They say they feel like veterans at this—experts in the knowledge of predictable cycles of stability and crisis, coping and chaos. However, while being able to predict it, *"seeing the train wreck coming once more for the 'Tons of Fun,'"* as Larry the oldest son put it, they feel powerless and helpless to change it. The train wreck is coming at them and they feel they cannot stop it; there is nothing that they think they can do about it.

Humor is an invaluable ally, therapeutic technique, and assessment index. What I found striking about the Brimmers was their capacity to view their life and circumstances humorously, as an antidote to despair and as a sign of some element of control over circumstances. This is not to say that at times their humor was a defense. The Brimmer's humor was often double-edged. Still, it was their humor that conveyed the family's capacity to look at themselves and gain perspective, providing a bridge and therapeutic inroad to change.

What system type are the Brimmers? And how does this relate to crisis resolution and joining with the family to form the working therapeutic system? The Brimmers represent, for the most part, a random system type for a variety of reasons that will become clear. Because no system type is a pure type, I found that the Brimmers functioned as a closed system as well. The reasons accounting for differences in behavior were contextual. The Brimmers were a random, flawed system among themselves. Family interaction revolved around struggles over individuals' rights versus the group as a whole, with individuals' winning out in a chaotic, unproductive way. When a random family system goes too far, there is interpersonal and emotional anarchy. The Brimmers had stood on this brink many times, stepping almost to the edge and then, for some reason or another, pulling back to avoid total chaos and dissolution of the family.

In other instances, the Brimmers showed the transactional signs of a closed system type. This orientation and behavior style was, however, seen primarily in the Brimmer's interaction with the outside world. Given their experience and history with social service agencies, there were good reasons for their closed, collective position. When a family feels threatened and its integrity feels fragile, with its dignity being usurped or misread, the system will act closed to protect its semblance of integration. The Brimmers act cautiously when it comes to the prospect of "letting in" authority figures, social workers, medical doctors, even therapists. This, to me, was a positive, not a negative sign: an indication that, on some level, the Brimmers held a collective identity.

What about the ritualized, developmental impasse and the critical identity struggle? The question around which the current crisis swirls is whether or not John, the youngest child and identified patient should be sent home to live while he recuperates from surgery. The courts and social workers are undecided (it has been my experience that when the courts or other social institutions are part of a family's life, and influence its developmental course, they become symbolically part of the "family in therapy"). John, who is 12 years old, is at the center of this developmental story. He has just had heart surgery and his weight problem poses a definite health risk. Should he be returned home? Would he heal there? Was the family an emotional risk? Or could it be a safe holding environment for him?

The first task ahead of the therapist is to identify the key elements of the developmental impasse as a prelude to understanding the critical identity image struggle. This involves pinpointing the family's unresolved developmental dilemma, the themes around which the crisis revolves, and the transactional parts that each individual plays in the conflict. I will turn first to the theme and developmental dilemma. The myth and subtext around the Brimmers' developmental story are that John's father died during Gail's pregnancy with John. John was born 2 months after his father's funeral. In our first session, John sits together with his worried family. He rarely and reluctantly speaks. This is partly a function of his age (the monosyllabic "Yes," "No," "I don't know" world of preadolescent boys), and partly a reflection of his quietly oppositional transactional stance. If he is silent, then family members, especially his mother, will entreat him. If he is aloof, then family members will pursue him. The game? Find me. At first, John resists offering an opinion on where he wants or wishes to live, foster family or home. Initially, he says he does not care. Later, his view changes. John's indifference is a required and necessary ingredient fueling the developmental impasse and struggle. On the front of John's T-shirt, the phrase "It's my life" (a developmentally appropriate assertion) is printed, in big bold black letters; on the reverse side, "Truth or dare!" (a reality claim—companion to John's critical identity image, which later emerges as central to the unresolved family conflict).

Everyone in the family has said that they love John and want him home. They also have said that they are sick and tired of strangers always butting into their family business, poking and prodding at them, always telling them what to do. They feel like a family without borders or walls or, on the worst days, like a family living in a fishbowl. John is theirs and theirs alone, so they want him home with them where he belongs. Yet prior to one therapy session, four out of the seven family members had telephoned me individually, offering their own private piece of contradictory or ambivalent information. For instance, Gail, the mother, (our first telephone contact) said: *"I'll tell you some things but not everything. There's a line I draw and a line I won't pass and a secret I will never tell, not to anyone, no matter what!"* (as if issuing me an old familiar battle cry or, on a deeper level, a challenge to be found).

Family myths fall within the interior life of family beliefs. Family secrets can be compelling motivators that direct and influence the outcome of family transactions, including ritualized struggles as in the Brimmers' situation. The secret that held the Brimmers as emotional hostages, providing more heat than light in their chronic struggles, surrounded the death of John's father. John had never been told the actual circumstances surrounding his father's death. Instead the family, mainly under the mother's direction and bidding, spun a glowing and ideal myth about the father's virtues. (John's father, who was, in many respects, a rough and unsavory character, had—after a night of drinking—been killed in a knife fight that grew out of an argument over a card game. This story, the truth about the details of John's father's death, Gail eventually told directly to John in a therapy hour.)

However, while the myth persisted, or, I should say, the illusion of the myth continued, instead of uplifting John's spirit (the family's original good intention), this myth had the opposite effect, depressing and angering John who felt emotionally alienated from his family (left out of the family's collective knowledge and history). But, as is often the case with myths and in families with secrets, John knew the truth (or at least he knew "bits and pieces" of the truth). Families talk and children overhear and "absorb" even when adults do not think they are listening. John's apathy and indifference, masking deeper anger, were not about the family "lie"—that his father was "wonderful and perfect"—for John knew otherwise through family conversations and collusive alliances *("I'll tell you if you don't tell Mom that I told you,"* or, *"Don't let on. It's just between you and me")*. In the end, "nobody" and "everybody" in the family knew. Note, also, the repetition of this pattern as seen before in the Brimmer's attempts to hold a series of individual and private conversations with me through telephone calls early in therapy. John's anger and apathy had to do with the persistence of the lie. Until family members communicated openly with each other, the tenacious influence of the myth and its underlying "secret" would continue to have a life and energy of its own.

Often the best route to change is the one most straightforward and simple. With multiproblem families such as the Brimmers, it is easy to become seduced by the exotic and unusual in their lives. For example, in the Brimmers' situation, there is the family pattern of living on the edge, the noise and chaos in the home, their chronic, troubled history, and their impoverishment. There was even the excitement that gripped the family early in therapy—a story that they were so anxious to open with—revolving around what Benny, (John's 18-year-old brother) had done. Racing down the stairs in the dark to answer the doorbell, he had somehow stepped on and (so everyone thought) killed the family cat. To be drawn in by the exotic and unusual is a mistake. These are distractions that obscure the commonplace and ordinary—the events and activities that connect the Brimmers to common, normalizing family process.

When I think of the Brimmers and other families like them, who are undergoing the process of assessment, therapy, and change, I think of E. A. Robinson's (1916) poem, *The Man Against the Sky.* In the poem, a "man" symbolizing all of us, stands alone, atop a hill, "amid the chaos and the glare." Following the logic and the metaphor in E. A. Robinson's depicted human journey, the Brimmers seemed to me like a family "against the sky, . . . alone amid the chaos and the glare." Central to the progress of therapy, the task at hand is to identify the "quiet, calm, ordinary center" amid the chaos and glare of family distractions and social service involvement. What is the family struggling with? What ordinary and normal life cycle task is the family trying to handle? The Brimmers were struggling between two unresolved family stages—Disengagement (death of the father) and Inclusion (the family's physical, psychological, and emotional incorporation of its members)—and the overlap and intersection of family life cycle tasks with child development stages, specifically autonomy and independence—a psychological "letting go."

The developmental aspect of the ritual impasse was confirmed through the image exploration. At the core of the struggle, each member, in turn, produced individual variations on a common image scene. The image scene involved separations: transactional scripts and emotionally charged, vivid scenes about "being taken away from family," or "having family members walk out or leave." The obvious and most painfully wrenching separation for the family, a potent unresolved issue resurfacing around John, was that mentioned before: his father's death. The themes and mood climate, if summarized across individual family member critical identity images, reflect various degrees and amounts of bereft affect, usurped power (e.g., power to guide and protect children and family, as in Gail's image), and lost or unvalidated identity. The individual and collective family imagery was best revealed and distilled through the sensitively timed clinical use of the Family Photograph Activity (Andreozzi, 1977, 1979c). The Family Photograph Activity was an appropriate choice given the family's struggle between overemotionality (too much affect) and underemotionality (blunted affect) associated with unresolved emotional loss. The Family Photograph Activity opened up pathways of communication and appropriate means to express, validate, and subsequently contain their loss.

Looking next to the key elements of player parts and the contribution of each family member's transactions to the crisis-conflict, the pattern that emerged was one of a family of ineffective movers. Because of the energy and presence of the myth or, as John called it *"the lie,"* family members lost the capacity to be direct and open with each other. As a result, intimacy failed or was emotionally sabotaged. Combined with concrete behavioral change, as the image exploration progressed, mover-follower patterns became synchronized (no longer out of phase). Again, the Family Photograph Activity served to heighten and crystallize family system awareness in concrete, palpable ways for this family. Through the Family Photograph Activity, family members could visualize and experience the problems arising from transactional roles in conflict. With the "cat out of the bag" about John's father, guilt and responsibility for his death relieved, John eventually returned home and the crisis was resolved.

The Greens

The Greens provide an exquisite illustration of the sensitive ways a child can lead the way for a family toward increased mental health. Billy, who is 5, and an astute family system observer had the tendency to "spill the family beans." For example, in a therapy hour, he says to his grandmother, *"You have greedy love."* But, I am getting ahead of the unfolding family therapy process.

In Chapter 2, we were introduced to the Green family. Tara Green is in her early 20s. She is a thin, pale, anxious-looking woman, with waist-length, thick black hair. Two wan and fragile-looking children trail behind her: Billy who is about 5 and shows signs of some neurological problems, and Tanya, who is barely 4. Tara's mother, Florence Perkins, the maternal grandparent—a robust, ruddy-looking woman—follows behind her daughter and the children. The children stand sandwiched, almost huddled between the two women.

The Child-Centered Structural Dynamic Model and process of family therapy centers around the concept of "distance regulation" (Kantor & Lehr, 1986): how physical and metaphoric space (the actual and symbolic distances between individual(s)) conveys an important statement about the kind and quality of connection between and among family members. Because of the unfolding nature of child development and the tendency of children to "speak volumes" through their actions, I have found children's behavior toward family members can provide the therapist with powerful, concise, symbolic statements about the "felt distances" among family members. As the Greens arrive for our first therapy session, the manner in which they enter the room (introduce themselves) communicates a powerful statement in visual form which reflects the current nature of family relationships. (This dynamic needs to be further explored and confirmed through observation and interaction as similar transactions repeat over time, coalescing into a definite, discernible pattern.) This epitomized visual scene provides a view into family structure and an early (preliminary) working system diagnosis—a hypothesis about family structure and change.

I have described various techniques and activities that heighten family system awareness and graphically illuminate family patterns, process, and structures. For example, I examined the system consciousness that becomes accessible and often visually apparent through the Family Photograph Activity, Family Network Drawing, and Living Sculpture Technique: Further, these methodologies can organize and integrate the family's intuitive understanding of relationship patterns and structure into consciously expressed knowledge of how a family works. At the clinical level, the visualized relationship statements that families make as they introduce themselves and arrange their chairs or take seats in the therapy room convey important information to be considered and assessed by the therapist. When the Greens entered the therapy room, from my perspective, they offered vivid and compelling information about who they were and what the struggle might be, providing, in their style of interpersonal "distancing," a visual map of the family's developmental crisis.

Another visually apparent aspect of the Greens that I was immediately struck by was the disparity within the family. Tara, the mother, and her two children, Billy and Tanya, were pale, anxious, and withdrawn. Their energy levels seemed depleted or perhaps pent-up and constrained. On the other hand, Tara's mother, Florence, the maternal grandparent seemed energetic, almost effervescent. One way of locating a ritual impasse and the outcome and direction of a family sequence is for the therapist to identify and follow the source of energy. The "energy" in a family often centers around and points a direct path to the family's manifest mover. A manifest mover is often a family member who tacitly, rather than overtly, influences an interaction and ultimately shapes its outcome.

An example drawn from everyday life might unfold as follows: Family members are undecided about how to spend a Saturday afternoon. Father suggests a movie. The 11-year-old daughter suggests the mall. Their 8-year-old son votes for the park. The family has asked mother for her input. Up to this point, she has been silent and noncommittal. Finally pressed, the family, recognizing the tacit influence that mother has in making the family's "mind up," turns to mother and asks: "What do you think?" She replies, "Oh, it really doesn't matter to me. Why don't we visit my mother?" An hour later, the family is at grandmother's house. In the Green family, Florence, the maternal grandparent is the manifest mover. In the Green family, Florence's role is a problem, a critical part of the evolving ritual impasse and developmental struggle.

Developmentally, the Greens represent one family nested within another. Tara is a single mother working hard to make ends meet. She is in a vocational training program studying to be a court stenographer. *"This is a demanding task—to capture all that court testimony. I have to be very careful and alert to detail with all of those lives and legal outcomes depending on my accuracy. What if I make a mistake? That scares me,"* she explains. Tara has been divorced less than one year. Economic circumstances have forced her and the children to move back in with her mother in a small, two-bedroom urban apartment. The family living space is physically and psychologically cramped and, as the family explores later, the two women, mother (Florence) and daughter (Tara) have become locked in an unfinished parent-adult child identity struggle. The developmental crisis and ritual impasse resolved through therapy presented a variety of sides and intersecting dilemmas.

If we were to place the individuals in the family on the Child and Family Development Assessment Chart (Figure 3.5) in Chapter 3, then the following developmental paths and individual imperatives would converge into the current ritual impasse and family-level developmental crisis. Florence is negotiating the task of Inclusion. Florence has been asked (via her daughter's and grandchildren's return home) to open up her system boundaries, literally and figuratively, to include these individuals. In addition to expansion, the family developmental task of Inclusion involves a deepening of relationships (a qualitative, authentic commitment to willingly include others). On this issue, as the process of therapy revealed, Florence was both practically reluctant and psychologically ambivalent. Her reluctance and ambivalence can be traced directly to her critical identity image around the themes of responsibility (being accountable for one's mistakes) and betrayal.

Tara's developmental dilemma walks the line between two equally important, simultaneously occurring, interactive tasks. One involves the unfinished emotional and interpersonal work around the developmental dilemmas of Decentralization, Differentiation, and Disengagement stages associated with the loosening of ties (transformation of relationships and reorganization of boundaries) that accompanies the process of divorce. Tara is adjusting to the changes she is experiencing in family form: moving from a two-parent to a single or one-parent household. This is no easy task for anyone, especially a young women barely out of adolescence with the responsibility of two small children. Tara's marriage was tumultuous, filled with her husband, Brandon's drugs and violence and what she said felt like *"empty sex."* Both of these emotionally unprepared teen parents were wrestling prematurely with the problems of intimacy and commitment.

Another stage dilemma Tara faces involves Differentiation from her family of origin, which her relationship with her mother symbolically represents. Tara is still working to carve out her own sense of identity and adult autonomy. At the same time, Tara is also working on the joint task of Inclusion. The only difference between Tara and her mother has to do with separate vantage points: Tara is predominantly on the receiving end of Inclusion (Tara is the one who seeks access to her mother's house and generosity) while Florence, Tara's mother, is on the giving end, opening up her world and social space to Tara and her children.

When I characterize Tara as being on the "receiving end" and Florence on the "giving end," I do not mean to suggest that Tara's role is passive. To the contrary, Tara is an active participant influencing the process and developmental crisis of Inclusion. As for the children, they bring to this evolving picture of current family development their own child development tasks. The children together face the developmental milestones of industry, initiative, and independence. Ironically, although on different levels (adult and child), both Tara and her children are in crisis over the demands and requirements of autonomy.

The developmental crisis identified, what about the themes and transactional parts that each family member contributes to the crisis and conflict? Where do the children, Billy and Tanya, fit in? How do Billy and Tanya lead the way with their verbal and nonverbal breakthrough system comments? The family had been referred to therapy because of Billy's diagnosed learning disability and the recommendation for family involvement. Tara urgently blurts out in our second session. *"I don't know how to describe it. The guilt I feel is so big that if I let it go, if I let it out, it would fill this entire room and there would be no space, no room left for anything else . . ."* Her hands cover her eyes, rubbing them. She leans forward, her hair falling, covering her face so that there is even less of her to be seen. The grandmother (Florence) suddenly interrupts. *"I'm so concerned. There is a story going around in our neighborhood that the woman next door beats her kids. I don't mean to change the subject but isn't there something we can do, we should do? How can people do such things to their own flesh and blood?"*

The children, well behaved, sit quietly together, listening. They are almost too well behaved, and there seems to be no motion or energy within or between them. Sometimes, however, Billy tries to speak. His speech is hard to understand, partly because of his age, partly because he whispers so softly, and partly because of slurring or lisping. The children sit close together, their arms almost joined. Each time Billy tries to speak, to make his observations and experiences known, Tanya, his sister, like a Greek chorus, begins, barely audibly, to clap. The sound is so soft, and the gesture of her hands so slight, that it could be easily missed. But it is also distinctly there, accompanying every one of Billy's faltering and halting efforts. It is as if she is trying to italicize, to draw attention to the purpose and meaning of his actions and his role in the family in some important way. Her almost imperceptible gestures on behalf of the brother she loves are both brave and faint, wanting and at the same time not wanting (fearing) to be heard. These are some of the important ways children lead families and therapists. The phrase Billy was uttering—a condensed and vivid account punctuating the theme of the crisis—was *"greedy love."*

In the preceding transactional interchange, we view the behavioral foundation of the Greens' crisis. This dynamic (sequence of disjointed parts) is at the heart of the ritual impasse and image exploration, the transactional sequence that was resolved (changed positively) through therapy. The children's parts are both poignant and crucial. Tara begins to act as a mover as she initiates conversation, drawing and defining the action-center and context when she begins to talk about the guilt and anxiety that fill her. However, her mother's brief but potent interruption overshadows Tara's move, shifting the focus of conversation away, in a different direction. The grandmother's interruption, thus, works as a strategic distance regulator—an opposer to her daughter, Tara's, action.

Also, in the Green family the children play important, and initially disqualified bystander roles. As Billy tries to speak, to offer comments on the family, what he sees from his child's view, he, like his sister Tanya, is disqualified; his whispered comments go unnoticed by family (not by therapist).

Similarly, in this brief scenario, Tanya shifts and enacts two crucial transactional player parts. First she moves to support her brother, a caring follower to his plight. This is seen in her gesture—the way children often communicate these interpersonal strategies and clear system awareness—as she subtly and quietly claps. Her actions serve a twofold, multidimensional purpose. She follows her brother, supporting him, and also joins with him as behavioral bystander, commenting on both how the family organizes itself and the places it accords its members.

There are several pieces of information missing that make Billy's meaning and the full context of the crisis clear. The following issues became apparent in therapy: Tara's guilt related to her having taken drugs during her pregnancy with Billy. She felt responsible because of her infrequent drug use (something she reluctantly did to please her husband, in essence to "keep him company"). Another central issue dealt with in therapy was Florence's method of discipline: harsh and physical, tending toward eventual abuse. Her statement, *"The woman next door beats her kids"* and her worry, *"How can people do such things to their own flesh and blood?"* reflected and also opened up discussion around her "desire for help." Billy was the only "male" in this world of guilty, stern, and worried women. Tanya, who led the way for me, along with Billy, forced the family to face important truths.

The Greens are, in many respects, a tense and emotionally overwrought family who cannot effectively manage anger. Both Florence and Tara are burdened with guilt and, to some extent, share the common experience of "not having been allowed to be children." In this context, it is useful and quite liberating to call on "role play"—especially "role reversals" (adults "playing children"; children "acting" as the adult or parent) to highlight the problem. This "swapping roles" technique often vividly brings home the "message" and "experience" of "what it feels like" to be a "child" and "what it means" to be a "parent." Because of Billy's and Tanya's developmental stage and their tendency to communicate nonverbally, action-oriented role play was effective in freeing the family to realize new ways of relating.

The Clarke-Harris Family

Through the Clarke-Harris family, I will illustrate the concept of current family organization and development in relation to the therapy process, specifically image exploration. Families develop image hierarchies: images that are organized and build layer on layer. For example, an individual will hold images of the self (personal level), interpersonal imagery of various family relationships (interpersonal level), and images of the family as a whole (collective identity level). When a couple meets, makes a commitment, and begins to form their new family system, each member of the couple takes his or her model of family, including these individual image hierarchies, to the creation of the current family. The couple, tacitly or explicitly, sorts, reviews, revises, and integrates crucial images. What the couple is working on are the details of their "model of family life." One of the central, cornerstone tasks that a couple faces has to do with attachment and intimacy. This is the focal issue and developmental crisis confronting Rachel Clarke and Don Harris.

In Chapter 3, two views of development were explored: current organization and family life-cycle change. The Clarke-Harris family, who are starting out as a couple, face the normal, first stage in family development of bonding and commitment. How has a normal developmental crisis, which could have led to growth, caused an impasse and struggle in the family? Some answers, along with a therapeutic line of inquiry (plan for change) lie in a look into current family organization. Family organization (development) is expressed in four ways and on four different levels for the therapist to consider: meaning, action, pattern, and model. Images implicitly guide and influence various levels. This aspect of clinical practice explains why the critical identity image exploration around the crisis provides such a comprehensive and effective inroad to positive family change. In the ritual impasse (family conflict), we find elements of all four levels of the critical identity images of individual family members: meaning, action, pattern, and model. A family's meaning level of organization is the family's foundation and reflects the content of a family's symbolic image life. This tells us and the family who it is. At the meaning level, we find what a family selectively notices, talks about, and likes to do.

The action and pattern levels also involve imagery. People's actions flow from their images (perceptions) of self and others in the world. What we choose to do or decide not to do—how we behave and interact—reflects our image of self and what we expect will happen. In this way, images influence behavior. How people behave toward others and treat themselves tells us a great deal about their imagery. Looking at a child's actions and the language of his or her behavior will tell us something significant about the child's self-concept and interpersonal sense of the world. Critical identity images are grasped initially through a therapist's understanding of an individual's and family's actions and patterns. A therapist intervenes at the action and pattern levels.

Change a family's behaviors (how individuals relate) and you change the meaning of critical identity images and resolve the crisis. The conflict patterns families show in therapy through their behavior and interactions are the visible, outward signs (indications) of critical identity images at work. At the highest level of family organization, images at the action, pattern, and meaning levels are integrated into a collective image (model level) of the family. This family model serves as a compass for guiding family interactions. When individuals disagree about "what a family is" and "how it should work," a crisis can and often does arise. The intensity of the conflicts we see in therapy relates directly to the images at stake in the struggle. This is the situation with the Clarke-Harris family.

Rachel Clarke is 40 years old and has never been married. She has a master's degree in child development and teaches handicapped children. She is warm, quiet, and sympathetic. There is a childlike vulnerability about her. Her fiance, Don Harris is 64. He is divorced and the father of eight grown children. Don is a blend of Native American and African-American cultures. He sees time and meaning quite differently from Rachel. His emotions are deeply disciplined. He believes strongly in inner strength, and passionately demands the truth from those closest to him. He often seems a wary observer and reluctant participant in life.

Rachel is a doer; Don is a watcher. Each calls the other a paradox too difficult to figure out. Underneath it all (as their image exploration in therapy revealed), they are more alike than they think. Problems with Rachel's two adolescent sons, Ryan and Alan, are the reason the family is in therapy. The crisis in the family centers around sexual images. Where there are problems around sexual images, there are problems around intimacy and identity. The burgeoning sexuality of Ryan and Alan has stirred recurrent, unresolved issues for the couple around similar themes. Together, the convergence of child and adult stages have produced a family crisis. The conflict the family has been going through is a system way of demanding that the family, especially the couple, take notice: settle unresolved issues. How is the crisis reflected in current family organization? What are the elements of the sexual conflict?

At the couple level, images around intimacy are in conflict. Rachel and Don have an on-again, off-again relationship. For them, *"one relationship is too many and a thousand relationships are not enough."* Don and Rachel have been living together for 3 years, unable to make a commitment. Yearning, and at the same time fearing genuine intimacy, the couple goes through cycles of passionate emotional fusion, followed by estrangement, bitter conflict, and despair. Several weeks into therapy, Rachel and Don recognize that they are "stuck" in trouble spots coming from their own personal relationship histories. We have identified that apparently once every 6 months, like clockwork, either Don abandons Rachel in an hour of need or Rachel, in a ritual to declare her emotional independence, sends Don (bag and baggage) packing. This is part, but not all, of this couple's developmental crisis.

Rachel experienced childhood sexual abuse that started at age 5 and continued until almost age 12; she is an incest survivor. For her, sexuality, the act of sex, and intimacy are muddled, confused, tinged and equated with dominance, violation, and a guilty kind of erotic excitement. The perpetrator and assailant of her innocence was a trusted grandparent (a maternal grandparent who lived with the family when she was a child). As a result, Rachel has trouble trusting people and making social judgments when relationships "heat up." She has also developed reflex responses (seen in trauma survivors) in which the familiarity of a scene, in terms of its recollection (affect arousal), causes her to react with intensity and anger. These flashbacks and vivid responses have carried over into their bedroom. For example, in a therapy hour alone with the couple, Rachel describes how certain gestures remind her of the abuse. She does not like Don walking up behind her, approaching her when she is not looking.

Similarly, she feels awkward and insecure about her body (body image). One incident that the couple relates highlights this: Don gave Rachel lingerie. He coaxed her to put it on and model it for him. (Don likes and does not like overtly sexy women. This ties into his critical identity image of "being cheated on" and "made a fool of" by his ex-wife.) Rachel was reluctant (opposing him). He responded by pushing further, steadily demanding (a forceful initiator). She complied, her anger rising silently until, as she explains, she was *"flooded with shame."* She ran out of the room and hid. Unaware, Don focused only on his own anger and hurt; he was insulted that she rejected (him) his gift. Rachel's critical image around intimacy, commitment and sexual identity is all about shame; Don's corresponding image and developmental puzzle piece image is all about "being shamed."

It takes more to create a crisis that has the intensity of the Clarke-Harris family's, as seen in therapy: It extends beyond the couple, rippling imagistically through all family levels—meaning, action, pattern, and model. What else is occurring? On the face of it, there is also the developmental crisis for which they initially sought help. At their wits' end, they did not know what to do with Rachel's sons. Neither Rachel nor Don knew how to handle Ryan, on the brink of adolescence, and Alan, in full hormonal bloom. Don sees Rachel as too permissive; Rachel views Don as too stern and authoritarian. She is unclear either about the limits or entitlements of boundaries, and unsure about how to assert herself with each "man-child" living in her house—boys who are growing in leaps and bounds, now towering over her in height and strength. Rachel finds herself alternating between angry criticisms of herself and the boys. Not quite knowing where he fits in, or what role he should play, Don is trying to figure out his personal as well as his developmental place in this family. At this level, we see the overlapping conflicts of critical identity images between couple and parental roles.

The incendiary rocket that set this family off in frantic search of answers is Alan's sexual behavior and the resulting sexual confusion, which came together in a troubling incident that the boy had experienced at work after school. For Rachel, her son's troubles have a much deeper, reverberating meaning that extends far beyond the borders of his experience and enters her own. The incident involved Alan and an older man, someone Alan trusted, a father-figure who had befriended the boy. (Alan and Ryan had grown up seeing their biological father infrequently. When I first met Alan and Ryan, it was clear that below their cool, MTV wisecracks, and macho poses, they were, at times, vulnerable, bewildered boys. It also was quite apparent that Don was a positive and important influence in their lives and that the roller-coaster emotional separations and reunions between Don and Rachel affected them deeply.) Alan and Ryan were in search of male guidance, an example, and role model.

That week Alan was unusually quiet, unlike himself. To Rachel, he seemed withdrawn; she sensed something was bothering him. Rachel has an open, sensitive way with her children and they are basically close. Suddenly, one evening, ready to talk, Alan blurted out what had happened. He was pretty sure of his heterosexual orientation but confused (and feeling betrayed) about the sexual turn of events. Although sexual curiosity and sexual experimentation are part of adolescence, there remains a fine line between such ventures and violation, manipulation, or abuse, reflecting the uneven power between adolescent and adult. This is the telltale image that lingered, connecting in vivid ways with Rachel's own incest experience.

That evening, Rachel and Don telephoned me. Rachel, understandably unnerved by the revelation, upset and angry, was all fired up to take on the world: do battle. The task at hand was to calm Rachel down, separating her experience from her son Alan's and offer her emotional support (validation) for the relationship ghosts (trauma) that were emerging for her. In this context, Don was supportive, recognizing, perhaps for the first time, the extent of Rachel's vulnerability. Don and Rachel were entrusted with the protective parental task of "keeping it cool" while they observed (watched for) any changes in Alan's behavior (clinical sequelae that we talked over). Because of the family's deep sense of trauma and Rachel's emotional vulnerability, the Family Notebook Activity (Andreozzi, 1979b) was a useful tool, helping the family to manage its emotional intensity, giving both past and recent events a cognitive frame and perspective. This brought the couple together, joining them on an important task: Alan's well-being. In this way, the family crisis that emerged imagistically on all four developmental levels was, over time, resolved on the family's meaning (deepest, foundation level), action and pattern (behavior), and model level (the Clarke-Harris's sense of core purpose and identity).

The Stones

This book ends with the Stones, the first family we were introduced to in Chapter 2, involving the particularly poignant story of Keith, the Stone's 6-year-old son. Keith is an exuberant child who came to therapy announcing himself in costume. He is dressed in a medley of boldly clashing colors: brown cowboy boots, red pants, purple striped shirt, green Ninja Turtle suspenders, a tall black top hat that he has made out of construction paper, and an orange insulated winter vest, too warm for the summer day. To his parents, Lila and Ted, he proclaims, *"I am the ringmaster. Ruler of the universe . . ."*

The Stones are in a desperate and rageful fury over food and the deeper nurturance it signifies. A number of transactional scenes depicting the family's ritualized, developmental struggle revolve around food at the dinner table: what Keith does and does not eat, the way he eats (table manners), and the portion sizes of the food. The pattern that has arisen involves mutual opposition between father and son (with Ted, the father, initiating the opposition and Keith, who learned his part, following suit). Lila is the "go-between" who simultaneously opposes Ted, her husband, to protect Keith, to whom she is a follower and ally. Ted, the father, withholds food (nurturance) much in the same way as he withholds his emotions and, most importantly, himself. He doles out access *"in teaspoons,"* his wife Lila complains.

Keith's mother Lila, tends to overcompensate for Ted's frugal nature. She indulges Keith, disheartened by his father's (Ted's) exacting and often critical stance. She tells her husband, Ted, in a therapy hour, *"You make Keith squirm and beg for everything—every little crumb, you act like he is 16, not 6. Why can't you be a real father to him?"* She means this for herself as well, wishing Ted could be more generous with intimacy and nurturance in their marital relationship.

Lila and Ted are not simply split or even sharply divided over their parenting behaviors and beliefs; they are in earnest emotional war over them. Their differences run deep and are fundamental. They are not only in an intense struggle over how to parent but what it means to be a child. The couple is battling out their extreme personal differences through their competing views on how to be a family and how a family should work (Lila prefers an open family system of consensus, dialogue, and expressed affection; Ted prefers a closed system of order, clearly specified rules, and emotional reserve). Keith is painfully caught in the middle of this developmental crisis between his mother whom he loves and needs as an ally and protector and his father whom he does not want to lose. As we saw in Chapters 2 and 3, and as Kantor's (1980) theory of structural dynamics asserts and clinical practice and research on child-centered family therapy confirm (Andreozzi, 1985a, 1988, 1993a, 1993b), the vivid, emotional intensity and tenacity of the Stones' conflict flows directly from separate critical identity images. Each image, as the family image exploration progressed, revealed positive (although well-hidden) reality claims (positive values). Lila's critical identity image involves the following emotional and transactional content: An asthmatic and ill child, she often felt ignored and overlooked, emotionally unimportant and without influence in her family of origin. She felt as though, to be noticed or get the affection she wanted, she always had to placate and please others. As she explained, *"I feel like I've spent a lifetime on the 'grateful train.'"*

Lila's reality claim (positive value) that we find when we turn her negative critical identity image and corresponding behavior into a positive one (changing the meaning of the image) is an enabling image. She says in recognition of what she has learned through the image exploration: *"I want to come across as sensitive to the feelings of others. I see myself as an empathetic person. I want to bring my husband, Ted, and my son, Keith, closer together, not drive them farther apart."*

Ted's critical identity image comes from a different place. His image is about physical and emotional violence. He is a boy in his image scenes who is torn between a stern, punitive father and a frightened mother who abnegates parental responsibility. The message his family of origin has taught him, he discovers and explains, is *"be tough, never let your guard down, and be ready to fight back."*

Ted's experiences of being bullied (beaten up by older neighborhood boys) and also berated by an emotionally distant father make him a prime candidate for perpetuating abuse. Where is Ted's positive reality assertion and value for Keith and himself? What is the positive intention underlying Ted's behavior toward Keith? He explains in a therapy hour that he *"wants the best for Keith."* Ted believes stern discipline will give Keith (or any child) *"a firm foundation, character, and structure."* Good intention. Wrong method.

When the Stones began therapy the family's crisis had risen from ritualized violence to real aggression. Father and son erupted in fisticuffs that went well beyond ordinary father-son roughhousing. Ted was oppositional; Keith was alternately rebellious and sad; and Lila was a frightened, torn, and helpless onlooker. Her interventions, designed to protect Keith emotionally and physically only enraged her husband, Ted, more, making him feel powerless, humiliated, and defeated in his role as parent.

There are other ways that a child learns violence. The child may not always be the direct and immediate recipient of the parents' aggression. The child can also be a witness to it. The child can be repeatedly immersed in scenes of hostility (verbal aggression) and physical outbursts (physical aggression). This is also the situation for 6-year-old Keith. In this paradoxical form of observed aggression and lessons in violence, the experience can be more potent and compelling for several reasons. The most obvious one is that the child often feels that she or he cannot do anything about the violence; the child perceives him- or herself as helpless and disempowered. Children who are involved aggressively with the parent are at least doing something, however destructive and inappropriate those actions might be. The child is not ready emotionally to handle this kind of power, received by default. The child who witnesses someone hurting someone else has the added emotional burden of not perceiving him- or herself as able to help, to act, or effectively intervene. In not being able to stop people from getting hurt, the child can have the very notion of personal competence stripped away. This was the dilemma and double burden 6-year-old Keith experienced and acted out in therapy.

Aggression can be taught by osmosis. Children can learn aggression, absorbing and internalizing violent models, as they watch on the sidelines, as they overhear the sounds of angry physical and emotional confrontation from behind closed doors, or from their beds at night. In a therapy hour, Keith says: *"Sometimes the noise is so big and loud inside my head that my head feels like its going to break open and pow!—explode! It's like everything is racing round and round in my head."* Then, as he turns to face his mother, he raises both of his hands to cover his head in a protective gesture. Showing his mother what he does late at night in his bed, he continues, *"See, Mommy, I take the covers like this and put them all the way over my head. That keeps the bad sound away. I leave just a teeny tiny place open so I can breathe. You should try that, Mommy."*

When events are not seen, they can become more terrifying, as children's imaginations are left to fill in the details. As clinical practice and research on children and trauma consistently show, when there are no real eyes to record and judge an event, or when the event is veiled in emotional unclarity, the traumatic event grows and its experience magnifies. For example, to Keith, his father's hot temper that *"zoomed from zero to one hundred miles an hour in ten seconds flat"* had no reason or predictable pattern to it, as he explained, *"I never know what's gonna happen."* The surprise and assault of Ted's (Keith's father's) temper felt like murderous rage. Keith worried, *"Will Daddy get so mad that he will turn into a monster and kill us . . . stab me?"* By witnessing aggression, children can learn vicariously as they watch one spouse hit another, or a parent hit one of their siblings, or in short, through any of the ways they experience the cycles of hostility and reconciliation common in abusive relationships.

The therapy with the Stones took time. Keith had absorbed violent examples (models of behavior). Keith would pound two figures together, making the sound effects of physical blows. He often talked about stabbing *"bad guys."* He referred to the playhouse in the therapy room as a *"haunted house"* (symbolically expressing his current experience in the family). In his play, he told stories about a little boy (himself) and how he (the boy) wished he could return to the *"old house."* (The Stone family's troubles began shortly after Keith turned 3 and entered into full-bloom independence, coinciding with the family's move to their current home.)

During one therapy hour, as the couple argued, Keith began to pummel two wooden figures, smashing them together. *"I'll stab him in the heart. I'll set a trap for him. I'll . . ."* he stopped. When I asked him who the *"bad guy"* is: *"Is it Daddy?"* Keith began to cry. *"I don't want my daddy to leave."* Turning to his mother, he asks, *"Mommy, does Daddy have a good heart? Tell me?"* Lila, his mother, turns away. *"Mommy,"* Keith continues, *"will Daddy's heart ever change back to the good way he was at the old house? Tell me, Mommy?"*

At the end of therapy, as the meanings of images and the behaviors of family members changed, Keith stood up. No longer having the need for his odd and compelling mismatched clothing, he was dressed in jeans and an X-Men t-shirt: He says, *"Let's hug."* His father rises first, joined next by Lila. As the family embraces, Keith looks up at both parents and smiles. He says, *"When we hug, I feel all warm inside like I'm protecting you."* Keith hesitates, *"Oops! I mean, you're protecting me."* I close with the Stones and Keith's incisive observation because this book and the model are ultimately all about the *psychological voices and vocabularies* of children.

Conclusion

Almost 20 years have been devoted to the creation, practice, and research of the Child-Centered Structural Dynamic Model for prevention, early intervention, and therapy. The motive and the impetus underlying the model are uncomplicated: The future of our society rests in the way we nurture our children. The model you have just learned about provides just such nurturance through family development, growth, and change.

Children today, who stand at the center of the shifting landscapes of our culture, are often vulnerable and families, facing many demands, are at risk. We hear with increasing frequency about problematic trends such as abuse or violence in the home, or on the streets, committed to or by a child or adolescent. We need to stop this hostility and aggression, sense of anonymity, and lost meaning, and instill in our children a sense of their own worth, purpose, and direction. We need to preserve family relationships, in all the varied forms of "family," before they are in crisis and result in lost and squandered moments between parent and child. Today's interactions are tomorrow's memories. We need to look carefully at the image imprints, legacies, and kinds of heroes we, as a culture and community, are leaving our children.

Children learn about themselves and human relationships early, even before they encounter their peer group, the school, or the streets. They learn by osmosis, through the examples they experience and witness in the intimate interpersonal environment of the family. But beyond the need to curb violence or indifference, there is a need to teach children many other compelling image lessons of empathy, caring, and connection: lessons in family courage, creativity, and survival. And so we face a set of salient, future-oriented, developmentally focused issues. Our task and challenge is to impart these crucial lessons in ways compatible with child development and family dynamics; in effect, to build positive relationships and relationship moments. In this way, we can reverse the cycle of apathy and anger apparent and growing in some of our youth.

The answer lies in prevention and early intervention. The Child-Centered Structural Dynamic Model offers family growth and change on a variety of levels. The model meets families on their own turf; in their physical, sociological, and psychological neighborhoods. The model's aim is to help children by helping families. Positive child development outcomes are nested in the family's future: wider identity and interactions. The activities of the Child-Centered Structural Dynamic Model are concrete and the technique (overriding objective) of the model is to teach families to be system experts—to know self, the family world, how to change it, and when the family does not know how to change, that it is all right to ask for help.

The Child-Centered Structural Dynamic Model, which extends well beyond a middle-class oriented enrichment experience, has proven effective with urban families living in difficult economic straits, and also has been used by suburban families. The goal of the model, an orientation I have stressed in these pages, is the commitment to uniting families through the recognition of common normalizing experience. Families across socioeconomic strata, while experiencing different economic realities, do, in fact, share critical psychological and interpersonal tasks: family development and the growth, nurturance, and protection of their children.

References

ACHENBACH, T. M. (1982). *Developmental psychopathology* (2nd ed.). New York: Wiley.

ACHENBACH, T. M. (1985). *Assessment and taxonomy of child and adolescent psychopathology.* Beverly Hills, CA: Sage.

ACHENBACH, T. M. (1990). What is "developmental" about developmental psychopathology. In J. Rolf, A. S. Masten, D. Cicchetti, K. H. Nuechterlein, & S. Weintraub (Eds.), *Risk and protective factors in the development of psychopathology* (pp. 29–48). New York: Cambridge University Press.

ACHENBACH, T. M. (1993). Taxonomy and comorbidity of conduct problems: Evidence from empirically based approaches. *Development and Psychopathology, 5,* 51–64.

ACHENBACH, T. M. (1995). Diagnosis, assessment, and comorbidity in psychosocial treatment research. *Journal of Abnormal Child Psychology, 23,* 45–65.

ACHENBACH, T. M., & EDELBROCK, C. S. (1983). *Manual for the Child Behavior Checklist and Revised Child Behavior Profile.* Burlington: University of Vermont Department of Psychiatry.

ACHENBACH, T. M., & EDELBROCK, C. S. (1986). *Child Behavior Checklist and Profile for ages 2–3.* Burlington: University of Vermont Department of Psychiatry.

ACHENBACH, T. M., & EDELBROCK, C. S. (1987). *Manual for the Youth Self-Report and Profile.* Burlington: University of Vermont Department of Psychiatry.

ACHENBACH, T. M., & HOWELL, C. T. (1993). Are American children's problems getting worse? A 13-year comparison. *Journal of the American Academy of Child and Adolescent Psychiatry, 32*(6), 1145–1154.

ACHENBACH, T. M., & MCCONAUGHY, S. H. (1987). *Empirically-based assessment of child and adolescent psychopathology: Practical applications.* Burlington: University of Vermont Department of Psychiatry.

ACKERMAN, N. W. (1966). *Treating the troubled family.* New York: Basic Books.

ALEXANDER, J. F., HOLTZWORTH-MUNROE, A., & JAMESON, P. B. (1994). The process and outcome of marital and family therapy: Research review and evaluation. In A. E. Bergin & S. L. Garfield (Eds.), *Handbook of psychotherapy and behavior change* (4th ed., pp. 595–630). New York: Wiley.

AMERICAN PSYCHIATRIC ASSOCIATION. (1994). *Diagnostic and statistical manual of mental disorders* (4th ed.). Washington, DC: Author.

ANDERSON, H. (1994). Rethinking family therapy: A delicate balance. *Journal of Marital and Family Therapy, 20,* 145–149.

ANDREOZZI, L. L. (1976, April). *Family education and parent involvement: A community approach to early childhood education.* Paper presented at the meeting of the National Association of the Education of Young Children, Anaheim, CA.

ANDREOZZI, L. L. (1977, February). *Family potential program: A family systems model of family growth and change.* Paper presented at the national conference on "Toward the Competent Parent," Georgia State University, Atlanta.

ANDREOZZI, L. L. (1978). *On being born into a family: Parents as family system experts.* Paper presented at the Regional Head Start Conference, Newport, RI.

ANDREOZZI, L. L. (1979a, April). *The family network drawing: A living tree of people, relationships, and events.* Paper presented at the annual meeting of the Rhode Island Association for the Education of Young children, Warwick, RI.

ANDREOZZI, L. L. (1979b, April). *The family notebook activity: Increasing family system-consciousness and optimal child development.* Paper presented at the annual meeting of the Rhode Island Association of the Education of Young Children, Warwick, RI.

ANDREOZZI, L. L. (1979c, April). *The family photograph activity: Relationship patterns and interpersonal imagery in visual form.* Paper presented at the annual meeting of the Rhode Island Association of the Education of Young Children, Warwick, RI.

ANDREOZZI, L. L. (1979d, April). *Integrating child and family development: Three interactive modules for promoting family system change.* Paper presented at the annual meeting of the National Association of the Education of Young Children, Warwick, RI.

ANDREOZZI, L. L. (1979e, February). *Family potential versus parent training: A trilevel family outreach program that integrates family systems development and child development.* Paper presented at the Parent Training Conference at Rhode Island College, Providence.

ANDREOZZI, L. L. (1980, April). *Family passages: Blueprints for family success and survival along the family life cycle.* Paper presented at the annual meeting of the Coordinating Council of Community Services, Warwick, RI.

ANDREOZZI, L. L. (1985a). *The effects of short-term structural-analytic oriented family therapy on families with a presenting child problem.* (Doctoral dissertation, University of Massachusetts, 1984). *Dissertation Abstracts,* Vol. 45b, ACC 8500051.

ANDREOZZI, L. L. (1985b). *The family assessment of the problem questionnaire.* Amherst, MA: University of Massachusetts.

ANDREOZZI, L. L. (1985c). *The family counseling evaluation.* Amherst, MA: University of Massachusetts.

ANDREOZZI, L. L. (Ed.). (1985d). *Integrating research and clinical practice.* Rockville, MD: Aspen Systems.

ANDREOZZI, L. L. (1985e). Why outcome research fails the family therapist. In L. L. Andreozzi (Ed.), *Integrating research and clinical practice* (pp. 1–9). Rockville, MD: Aspen Systems.

ANDREOZZI, L. L. (1988, October). *Child-centered family therapy: Treating the child inside the family.* Paper presented at the national meeting of the American Association for Marriage and Family Therapy, New Orleans, LA.

ANDREOZZI, L. L. (1993a). *Child-centered family therapy: Testing a clinical model.* Paper presented at the national meeting of the American Association for Marriage and Family Therapy, Anaheim, CA.

ANDREOZZI, L. L. (1993b). *Structural equation modeling in family therapy theory building.* Paper presented at the national meeting of the American Association for Marriage and Family Therapy, Anaheim, CA.

ANGELOU, M. (1969). *I know why the caged bird sings.* New York: Random House.

ANTHONY, E. J. (1980). The family and the psychoanalytic process in children. In A. Solnit, R. Eissler, A. Freud, M. Kris, & P. Neubauer (Eds.), *The psychoanalytic study of the child* (pp. 3–34). New Haven, CT: Yale University Press.

ANTHONY, E. J., & KOUPERNIK, C. (Eds.). (1974). *The child in his family: Vol. 3. Children at risk.* New York: Wiley.

ANTHONY, E. J., KOUPERNIK, C., & CHILAND, C. (Eds.). (1978). *The child in his family: Vol. 4. Vulnerable children.* New York: Wiley.

ARNOLD, L. E. (1990). *Childhood stress.* New York: Wiley.

AZAR, S. T. (1991). Models of child abuse: A meta-theoretical analysis: Physical child abuse. *Criminal Justice and Behavior, 18,* 30–46.

AZAR, S. T., BARNES, K. T., & TWENTYMAN, C. T. (1988). Developmental outcomes in abused children: Consequences of parental abuse or a more general breakdown in care giver behavior? *Behavior Therapist, 11*(2), 27–32.

AZAR, S. T., & SIEGEL, B. R. (1990). Behavioral treatment of child abuse: A developmental perspective. *Behavior Modification, 14,* 279–300.

BANDURA, A. (1977). Self-efficacy: Toward a unifying theory of behavioral change. *Psychological Review, 84,* 191–215.

BANDURA, A. (1986). *Social foundations of thought and action: A social cognitive theory.* Englewood Cliffs, NJ: Prentice-Hall.

BARNARD, K. E., MORISSET, C. E., & SPIEKER, S. (1993). Preventative interventions: Enhancing parent-infant relationships. In C. H. Zeanah, Jr. (Ed.), *Handbook of infant mental health* (pp. 386–401). New York: Guilford.

Belsky, J. (1981). Early human experience: A family perspective. *Developmental Psychology, 17,* 2–12.

Benson, M. J., Schindler-Zimmerman, T., & Martin, D. (1991). Accessing children's perceptions of their family: Circular questioning revisited. *Journal of Marital and Family Therapy, 17,* 363–372.

Bergin, A. E., & Garfield, S. L. (Eds.). (1994). *Handbook of psychotherapy and behavior change* (4th ed.). New York: Wiley.

Block-Lewis, H. (Ed.). (1987). *The role of shame in symptom formation.* Hillsdale, NJ: Erlbaum.

Brazelton, T. B. (1992). *Touchpoints: Your child's emotional and behavioral development.* Reading, MA: Addison-Wesley.

Bronfenbrenner, U. (1974). Is early intervention effective? *Teachers College Record, Columbia University, 76,* 279–303.

Bronfenbrenner, U. (1975). *A report on longitudinal evaluation of preschool programs* (DHEW Monograph No. 75-25). Washington, DC: U.S. Government Printing Office.

Bronfenbrenner, U. (1976). [The ecology of human development: History and perspectives.] *Psychologia Wychowawzca, 19,* 537–549.

Bronfenbrenner, U. (1977). Toward an experimental ecology of human development. *American Psychologist, 32,* 513–531.

Burgess, R., & Conger, R. D. (1978). Family interaction in abusive, neglectful, and normal families. *Child Development, 49,* 1163–1173.

Carlson, N. R. (1991). *Physiology of behavior.* Boston: Allyn & Bacon.

Chase, M. (1944). *Harvey.* New York: Dramatists Play Service.

Chess, S., & Thomas, A. (1986). *Temperament in clinical practice.* New York: Guilford.

Chilman, C. S. (1973). Programs for disadvantaged parents: Some major trends and related research. In B. M. Caldwell & H. N. Ricciuti (Eds.), *Review of child development research: Vol. 3. Child development and social policy* (pp. 403–466). Chicago: University of Chicago Press.

Clarke-Stewart, K. A. (1977). *Child care in the family: A review of research and some propositions for policy.* New York: Academic Press.

Clarke-Stewart, K. A. (1978). And daddy makes three: The father's impact on mother and young child. *Child Development, 49,* 466–478.

Combrinck-Graham, L. (1991). On technique with children in family therapy: How calculated should it be? *Journal of Marital and Family Therapy, 17,* 373–377.

Combrinck-Graham, L., & Kerns, L. (1989). Intimacy in families with young children. In D. Kantor & B. F. Okun (Eds.), *Intimate environments: Sex, intimacy and gender in families* (pp. 74–92). New York: Guilford.

Denton, W. (1990). A family systems analysis of DSM-III-R. *Journal of Marital and Family Therapy, 16,* 113–125.

Eliot, T. S. (1962). The love song of J. Alfred Prufrock. In T. S. Eliot, *The waste land and other poems* (pp. 1–10). New York: Harcourt Brace. (Original work published 1930)

Erikson, E. H. (1963). *Childhood and society* (2nd ed.). New York: W.W. Norton.

Estrada, A. U., & Pinsof, W. M. (1995). The effectiveness of family therapies for selected behavioral disorders of childhood. *Journal of Marital and Family Therapy, 21,* 403–440.

Faulkner, W. (1931). *The sound and the fury* (1st ed.). New York: Jonathan Cape & Harrison Smith. (Original work published 1929)

Fishler, P. H., Sperling, M. B., & Carr, A. C. (1990). Assessment of adult relatedness: A review of empirical findings from object relations and attachment theories. *Journal of Personality Assessment, 55,* 499–520.

Flemons, D. (1989). Consensus/dissensus: A relational alternative to the metaphor of power. *Journal of Strategic and Systemic Therapies, 8,* 58–64.

Fonagy, P., Steele, M., Steele, H., Moran, G., & Higgitt, A. C. (1991). The capacity for understanding mental states: The reflective self in parent and child and its significance for security of attachment. *Infant Mental Health Journal, 12,* 201–218.

Fraiberg, S., Adelson, E., & Shapiro, V. (1975). Ghosts in the nursery: A psychoanalytic approach to the problems of impaired infant-mother relationships. *Journal of American Academy of Child Psychiatry, 14,* 387–421.

French, A. P. (1977). *Disturbed children and their families: Innovations in evaluation and treatment.* New York: Human Sciences Press.

Gaebel, W., & Pietzcher, A. (1987). Prospective study of the course of illness in schizophrenia: Part III. Treatment and outcome. *Schizophrenia Bulletin, 13,* 307–316.

Gilligan, C. (1982). *In a different voice: Psychological theory and women's development.* Cambridge, MA: Harvard University Press.

Goldstein, M. J., & Miklowitz, D. J. (1995). The effectiveness of psychoeducational family therapy in the treatment of schizophrenic disorders. *Journal of Marital and Family Therapy, 21,* 361–376.

Guerin, P. J. (1976). Family therapy: The first twenty-five years. In P. J. Guerin (Ed.), *Family therapy: Theory and practice* (pp. 2–22). New York: Gardner.

Gurman, A. S., & Kniskern, D. P. (Eds.). (1991). *Handbook of family therapy.* New York: Brunner/Mazel.

Gurman, A. S., Kniskern, D. P., & Pinsof, W. M. (1986). Research on the process and outcome of marital and family therapy. In S. L. Garfield & A. E. Bergin (Eds.), *Handbook of psychotherapy and behavior change* (3rd ed., pp. 565–624). New York: Wiley.

Hahlweg, K., & Markman, H. J. (1988). Effectiveness of behavioral marital therapy: Empirical status of behavioral techniques in preventing and alleviating marital distress. *Journal of Consulting and Clinical Psychology, 56,* 440–447.

Haley, J. (1962). Family experiments: A new type of experimentation. *Family Process, 1,* 265–293.

Haley, J. (1963). *Strategies of psychotherapy.* New York: Grune and Stratton.

Haley, J. (1970). Approaches to family therapy. *International Journal of Psychiatry, 9,* 233–242.

Haley, J. (1971a). A review of the family therapy field. In J. Haley (Ed.), *Changing families: A family therapy reader* (pp. 1–12). New York: Grune and Stratton.

Haley, J. (Ed.). (1971b). *Changing families: A family therapy reader.* New York: Grune and Stratton.

Haley, J. (1972). Family experiments: A new type of experimentation. *Family Process, 1,* 265–293.

Haley, J. (1973a). Strategic therapy when a child is presented as the problem. *Journal of the American Academy of Child Psychiatry, 12,* 641–659.

Haley, J. (1973b). *Uncommon therapy.* New York: W.W. Norton.

Haley, J. (1976). *Problem solving therapy.* San Francisco: Jossey-Bass.

Haley, J. (1978). Ideas which handicap therapists. In M. M. Berger (Ed.), *Beyond the double bind: Communication and family systems, theories, and techniques with schizophrenics* (pp. 65–82). New York: Brunner/Mazel.

Hardy, K. V. (1994). Marginalization or development?: A response to Shields, Wynne, McDaniel, and Gawinski. *Journal of Marital and Family Therapy, 20,* 139–143.

Hazelrigg, M. D., Cooper, H. M., & Borduin, C. M. (1987). Evaluating the effectiveness of family therapies: An integrative review and analysis. *Psychological Bulletin, 101,* 428–442.

Hersen, M., & Last, C. G. (Eds.). (1990). *Handbook of child and adult psychopathology: A longitudinal perspective.* New York: Pergamon.

Hoffman, L. (1981). *Foundations of family therapy: A conceptual framework for systems change.* New York: Basic Books.

Horowitz, F. D., & Paden, L. Y. (1973). The effectiveness of environmental intervention programs. In B. M. Caldwell & H. N. Ricciuti (Eds.), *Review of child development research: Vol. 3. Child development and social policy* (pp. 331–402). Chicago: University of Chicago Press.

Horton, A. D., & Retzlaff, P. D. (1991). Family assessment: Toward DSM-III-R relevancy. *Journal of Clinical Psychology, 47,* 94–99.

Kantor, D. (1980). The critical identity image: A concept linking individual, couple, and family development. In J. K. Pearce & L. J. Friedman (Eds.), *Family therapy: Combining psychodynamic and family systems approaches* (pp. 137–167). New York: Grune and Stratton.

Kantor, D. (1983). The structural-analytic approach to the treatment of family developmental crisis. In J. C. Hansen (Series Ed.). & H. A. Liddle (Vol. Ed.), *Family therapy collections: Vol. 7. Clinical implications of the family life cycle* (pp. 12–34). Rockville, MD: Aspen Systems.

Kantor, D., & Andreozzi, L. L. (1985). The cybernetics of family therapy and family research. In J. C. Hansen (Series Ed.) & L. L. Andreozzi (Vol. Ed.), *Family therapy collections: Vol. 15. Integrating research and clinical practice* (pp. 37–50). Rockville, MD: Aspen Systems.

Kantor, D., & Lehr, W. (1986). *Inside the family: Toward a theory of family process.* San Francisco: Jossey-Bass. (Original work published 1975)

Kantor, D., & Neal, J. (1985). Integrative shift for the theory and practice of family systems therapy. *Family Process, 24,* 13–30.

Kohlberg, L. (1981). *Essays on moral development: Vol. 1. The philosophy of moral development: Moral stages and the idea of justice* (1st ed.). San Francisco: Harper & Row.

Kohlberg, L. (1984). *Essays on moral development: Vol. 2. The psychology of moral development: The nature and validity of moral stages* (1st ed.). San Francisco: Harper & Row.

Korner, S., & Brown, B. (1990). Exclusion of children from family psychotherapy: Family therapists' beliefs and practices. *Journal of Family Psychology, 3*, 420–430.

L'Abate, L. (1981). Skill training programs for couples and families. In A. S. Gurman & D. P. Kniskern (Eds.), *Handbook of family therapy* (pp. 631–661). New York: Brunner/Mazel.

Lamb, M. E. (1977). Father-infant and mother-infant interaction in the first year of life. *Child Development, 48*, 167–181.

Lee, H. (1960). *To kill a mockingbird.* Philadelphia: Lippincott.

Lerner, R. M., & Lerner, J. V. (1987). Children in their contexts: A goodness of fit model. In J. B. Lancaster, J. Altmann, A. S. Rossi, & L. R. Sherrod (Eds.), *Parenting across the life span: Biosocial dimensions* (pp. 377–404). Chicago: Aldine.

Lerner, R. M., Lerner, J. V., Windle, M., Hooker, K., Lenerz, K., & East, P. P. (1986). Children and adolescents in their contexts: Tests of goodness of fit model. In R. Plomin & J. Dunn (Eds.), *The study of temperament: Changes, continuities, and challenges* (pp. 337–404). Hillsdale, NJ: Erlbaum.

Lerner, R. M., & Tubman, J. G. (1989). Conceptual issues in studying continuity and discontinuity in personality development across life. *Journal of Personality, 57*, 343–373.

Levenstein, P. (1970). Cognitive growth in preschoolers through stimulation of verbal interaction with mothers. *American Journal of Orthopsychiatry, 40*, 426–432.

Lewis, M., & Rosenblum, L. A. (Eds.). (1979). *The child and its family.* New York: Plenum.

Masten, A. S. (1979). Family therapy as a treatment for children: A critical review of outcome research. *Family Process, 18*, 323–336.

McDermott, J. F., & Char, A. F. (1974). The undeclared war between child and family therapy. *Journal of the American Academy of Child Psychiatry, 13*, 422–436.

Miller, R. (1989). Schizophrenia as a progressive disorder: Relations to EEG, CT, neuropathological and other evidence. *Progress in Neurobiology, 33*, 17–44.

Minuchin, S. (1970). The use of an ecological framework in the treatment of a child. In E. J. Anthony & C. Koupernik (Eds.), *The child in his family: Vol. 1. The international yearbook for child psychiatry and allied disciplines* (pp. 41–58). New York: Wiley.

Minuchin, S. (1974). *Families and family therapy.* Cambridge, MA: Harvard University Press.

Nitz, K., Lerner, R. M., Lerner, J. V., & Talwar, R. (1988). Parental and peer demands, temperament, and early adolescent adjustment. *Journal of Early Adolescence, 8*, 243–263.

Piaget, J. (1963). *The origins of intelligence in children* (M. Cook, Trans.). New York: W.W. Norton. (Original work published 1952)

Piaget, J., & Inhelder, B. (1956). *The child's conception of space* (F. J. Langdon & J. L. Lunzer, Trans.). New York: Humanities Press.

Plomin, R., & Daniels, D. (1987). Why are children in the same family so different from one another? *The Behavioral and Brain Sciences, 10*, 1–60.

Robinson, E. A. (1916). The man against the sky. In *The man against the sky: A book of poems* (pp. 130–149). New York: Macmillan.

Sameroff, A. J. (1975). Early influence on development: Fact or fancy? *Merrill-Palmer Quarterly, 21*, 267–294.

Sameroff, A. J. (1993). Models of development and developmental risk. In C. H. Zeanah, Jr. (Ed.), *Handbook of infant mental health* (pp. 3–13). New York: Guilford.

Sameroff, A. J., & Seifer, R. (1990). Early contributors to developmental risk. In J. E. Rolf, A. S. Masten, D. Cicchetti, K. H. Nuechterlein, & S. Weintraub (Eds.), *Risk and protective factors in the development of psychopathology* (pp. 52–66). New York: Cambridge University Press.

Sander, L. W. (1980). Investigation of the infant and its caregiving environment as a biological system. In S. I. Greenspan & G. H. Pollock (Eds.), *The course of life: Psychoanalytic contributions toward understanding personality development: Vol. 1. Infancy and early childhood* (pp. 177–201). Bethesda, MD: National Institute of Mental Health.

Schaeffer, E. S. (1972). Parents as educators: Evidence from cross-sectional, longitudinal, and intervention research. In W. H. Hartop (Ed.), *The young child: Reviews of research* (Vol. 2, pp. 184–201). Washington, DC: National Association for the Education of Young Children.

Shadish, W. R., Montgomery, L. M., Wilson, P., Wilson, M. R., Bright, I., & Okwumabua, T. (1993). Effects of family and marital psychotherapies: A meta-analysis. *Journal of Consulting and Clinical Psychology, 61*, 992–1002.

STANGER, C., ACHENBACH, T. M., & MCCONAUGHY, S. H. (1993). Three-year course of behavior/emotional problems in a national sample of 4- to 16-year olds: III. Predictors of signs of disturbance. *Journal of Consulting and Clinical Psychology, 61,* 839–848.

STATON, J. (1994, October). AAMFT Foundation receives $300,000 grant for Head Start training. *Family Therapy News, 25*(5), 1, 10.

STERN, D. (1985). *The interpersonal life of the infant.* New York: Basic Books.

STEVENSON-HINDE, J. (1990). Attachment within family systems: An overview. *Infant Mental Health Journal, 11,* 218–227.

SZAPOCZNIK, J., KURTINES, W., SANTISTEBAN, D. A., & RIO, A. T. (1990). Interplay of advances between theory, research, and application in treatment interventions aimed at behavior problem children and adolescents. *Journal of Consulting and Clinical Psychology, 58,* 696–703.

TALWAR, R., NITZ, K., & LERNER, R. M. (1990). Relations among early adolescent temperament, parent and peer demands, and adjustment: A test of the goodness-of-fit model. *Journal of Adolescence, 13,* 279–298.

THOMAS, A., & CHESS, S. (1977). *Temperament and development.* New York: Brunner/Mazel.

VYGOTSKY, L. S. (1978). *Mind in society.* Cambridge, MA: Harvard University Press.

WEISSBOURD, B. (1993). Family support programs. In C. H. Zeanah, Jr. (Ed.), *Handbook of infant mental health* (pp. 402–413). New York: Guilford.

WERTHHEIM, E. S. (1973). Family unit therapy: The science and typology of family systems. *Family Process, 17,* 361–376.

WERTHEIM, E. S. (1975a). The science and typology of family systems: II. Further theoretical and practical considerations. *Family Process, 14,* 285–309.

WERTHEIM, E. S. (1975b). Positive mental health, western society and the family. *International Journal of Social Psychiatry, 20,* 247–254.

WERTHEIM, E. S. (1978). Developmental genesis of human vulnerability: Conceptual reevaluations. In E. J. Anthony, C. Koupernik, & C. Chiland (Eds.), *The child in his family: Vol. 4. Vulnerable children* (pp. 17–36). New York: Wiley.

WYNNE, L. C. (1983). Family research and family therapy: A reunion? *Journal of Marital and Family Therapy, 9,* 113–118.

WYNNE, L. C. (1993). Evaluating the outcome of therapy: A dialogue about research priorities. Panel presentation at the national meeting of the American Association for Marriage and Family Therapy, Anaheim, CA.

ZIGLER, E., HOPPER, P., & HALL, N. W. (1993). Infant mental health and social policy. In C. H. Zeanah, Jr. (Ed.), *Handbook of infant mental health* (pp. 480–492). New York: Guilford.

ZILBACH, J. J. (1989). Introduction and overview. Special issue: Children and family therapy: Treatment and training. *Journal of Psychotherapy and the Family, 5,* 3–14.

ZILBACH, J. J., BERGEL, E., & GASS, C. (1972). The role of the child in family therapy. In C. J. Sager & H. S. Kaplan (Eds.), *Progress in group and family therapy* (pp. 385–399). New York: Brunner/Mazel.

Selected Bibliography

Ackerman, N. W. (1972). The growing edge of family therapy. In C. J. Sager & H. S. Kaplan (Eds.), *Progress in group and family therapy* (pp. 440–456). New York: Brunner/Mazel.

Alexander, J., & Barton, C. (1976). Behavioral systems therapy for families. In D. H. L. Olson (Ed.), *Treating relationships* (pp. 167–188). Lake Mills, IA: Graphic.

Allman, L. (1982). The aesthetic preference: Overcoming the pragmatic error. *Family Process, 21,* 43–56.

Allman, L. (1982). The poetic mind: Further thoughts on an 'aesthetic preference.' *Family Process, 21,* 415–428.

Andreozzi, L. L. (1973). Their nightly ritual. *The Providence Review, 11,* 13–14.

Andreozzi, L. L. (1973). With his father's blood. *Helcoal Fiction Series, Brown University Literary Board, 4,* 12–14.

Andreozzi, L. L. (1974). For all the killing. *Alderbaran, 3,* 31–37.

Andreozzi, L. L. (1974). The suicides of Eleanor's child. *Espontaneo, 2,* 12–14.

Barlow, D. H. (1981). On the relation of clinical research to clinical practice: Current issues, new directions. *Journal of Consulting and Clinical Psychology, 49,* 147–155.

Beels, C. C., & Ferber, A. (1969). Family therapy: A view. *Family Process, 9,* 280–318.

Bentovim, A., & Kinston, W. (1978). Brief focal therapy when the child is the referred patient: I. Clinical. *Journal of Child Psychology and Psychiatry, 19,* 1–12.

Bergen, M., & Fowlkes, M. A. (1980). Family intervention: A family network model for serving young handicapped children. *Young Children, 35,* 22–32.

Bergin, A. E., & Garfield, S. L. (Eds.). (1994). *Handbook of psychotherapy and behavior change* (4th ed.). New York: Wiley.

Beutler, L. E., Machado, P. P. P., & Neufeldt, S. A. (1994). Therapist variables. In A. E. Bergin & S. L. Garfield (Eds.), *Handbook of psychotherapy and behavior change* (4th ed., pp. 229–269). New York: Wiley.

Bodin, A. M. (1981). The interactional view: Family therapy approaches of the mental research institute. In A. S. Gurman & D. P. Kniskern (Eds.), *Handbook of family therapy* (pp. 267–309). New York: Brunner/Mazel.

Boss, P. G., Doherty, W. J., LaRossa, R., Schumm, W. R., & Steinmetz, S. K. (Eds.). (1993). *Sourcebook of family theories and methods: A contextual approach.* New York: Plenum.

Boszormenyi-Nagy, I., & Framo, J. (Eds.). (1965). *Intensive family therapy: Theoretical and practical aspects.* New York: Harper & Row.

Boszormenyi-Nagy, I., & Spark, G. (1973). *Invisible loyalties: Reciprocity in intergenerational family therapy.* New York: Harper & Row.

Boszormenyi-Nagy, I., & Ulrich, D. (1981). Contextual family therapy. In A. S. Gurman & D. P. Kniskern (Eds.), *Handbook of family therapy* (pp. 159–186). New York: Brunner/Mazel.

Bowen, M. (1978). *Family therapy in clinical practice.* New York: Jason Aronson.

Broderick, C. B., & Schrader, S. S. (1981). The history of professional marriage and family therapy. In A. S. Gurman & D. P. Kniskern (Eds.), *Handbook of family therapy* (pp. 5–35). New York: Brunner/Mazel.

Brodey, W. M. (1967). A cybernetic approach to family therapy. In G. H. Zuk & I. Boszormenyi-Nagy (Eds.), *Family therapy and disturbed families* (pp. 74–84). Palo Alto, CA: Science and Behavior Books.

Buckley, W. (1967). *Sociology and modern systems theory*. Englewood Cliffs, NJ: Prentice-Hall.

Buckley, W. (Ed.). (1968). *Modern systems research for the behavioral scientist: A sourcebook*. Chicago: Aldine.

Burr, W. R., Hill, R., Nye, F. I., & Reiss, I. L. (1979). *Contemporary theories about the family: Research-based theories* (Vol. 1). New York: Free Press.

Cambien, J. (1989). Reality in psychotherapy. *Journal of Family Psychology, 3*, 29–38.

Cochran, M. W., & Brassard, J. A. (1979). Child development and personal networks. *Child Development, 50*, 601–616.

Colapinto, G. (1979). The relative value of empirical evidence. *Family Process, 18*, 427–441.

Combrinck-Graham, L. (1989). The borderline syndrome in childhood: A family systems approach. *Journal of Psychotherapy and the Family, 5*, 31–54.

Crane, R. S. (1985). Single-case experimental designs in family therapy research. *Family Process, 24*, 69–77.

Crespi, T. (1988). Major American schools of family therapy: Comparisons and contrasts. *International Journal of Family Psychiatry, 9*, 295–311.

Cromwell, R. E., Olson, D. H., & Fournier, D. G. (1976). Diagnosis and evaluation in marital and family counseling. In D. H. L. Olson (Ed.), *Treating relationships* (pp. 517–562). Lake Mills, IA: Graphic.

Dare, C., & Lindsey, C. (1979). Children in family therapy. *Journal of Family Therapy, 1*, 253–269.

Dell, P. F. (1982). Beyond homeostasis: Toward a concept of coherence. *Family Process, 21*, 21–41.

Dell, P. F. (1982). In search of truth: On the way to clinical epistemiology. *Family Process, 21*, 407–414.

de Shazer, S. (1983). Diagnosing = researching + doing therapy. In J. C. Hansen (Series Ed.) & B. P. Keeney (Vol. Ed.), *Family therapy collections: Vol. 4. Diagnosis and assessment in family therapy* (pp. 123–132). Rockville, MD: Aspen Systems.

Dewitt, K. N. (1978). The effectiveness of family therapy: A review of outcome research. *Archives of General Psychiatry, 35*, 549–561.

During, S. M., & McMahon, R. J. (1991). Recognition of facial expressions by abusive mothers and their children. *Journal of Clinical Child Psychology, 20*(2), 132–139.

Fisher, L. (1982). Transactional theories but individual assessment: A frequent discrepancy in family research. *Family Process, 21*, 313–320.

Fisher, S. G. (1980). The use of time limits in brief psychotherapy: A comparison of six-session, twelve-session, and unlimited treatment with families. *Family Process, 19*, 377–392.

Fisher, S. G. (1984). Time-limited brief therapy with families: A one-year follow-up study. *Family Process, 23*, 101–106.

Fraiberg, S. (1959). *The magic years: Understanding and handling the problems of early childhood*. New York: Charles Schribner.

Framo, J. L. (1970). Symptoms from a family transactional viewpoint. In N. W. Ackerman (Ed.), *Family therapy in transition* (pp. 125–171). Boston: Little, Brown.

Framo, J. L. (1972). *Family interaction: A dialogue between family researchers and family therapists*. New York: Springer.

Framo, J. L. (1979). Family theory and therapy. *American Psychologist, 34*, 988–995.

Framo, J. L. (1981). The integration of marital therapy with sessions with family of origin. In A. S. Gurman & D. P. Kniskern (Eds.), *Handbook of family therapy* (pp. 133–158). New York: Brunner/Mazel.

Fristad, M. A. (1988). Assessing social desirability in family self reports. *Perceptual and Motor Skills, 66*, 131–137.

Gale, A. (1979). Problems of outcome research in family therapy. In S. Walrond-Skinner (Ed.), *Family and marital psychotherapy: A critical approach* (pp. 225–244). London: Routledge & Kegan Paul.

Garfield, S. L. (1994). Research on client variables on psychotherapy. In A. E. Bergin & S. L. Garfield (Eds.), *Handbook of psychotherapy and behavior change* (4th ed., pp. 190–228). New York: Wiley.

Gilbert, R., & Christensen, A. (1985). Observational assessment of marital and family interaction: Methodological considerations. In L. L'Abate (Ed.), *The handbook of family psychology and therapy* (Vol. 2, pp. 961–988). Homewood, IL: Dorsey.

Glanville, R. (1982). Inside every white box there are two black boxes trying to get out. *Behavioral Science, 27,* 1–11.

Glass, G. V., McGaw, B., & Smith, M. (1981). *Meta-analysis in social research.* Beverly Hills, CA: Sage.

Golann, S. (1989). The thinking albatross: A comment on Falzer. *Journal of Family Psychology, 2,* 466–472.

Goldberg, L. R. (1970). Man versus model of man: A rationale, plus some evidence, for a method of improving on clinical inferences. *Psychological Bulletin, 73,* 422–432.

Goldstein, M. (1993). Evaluating the outcome of therapy: A dialogue about research priorities. Panel presentation at the national meeting of the American Association for Marriage and Family Therapy, Anaheim, CA.

Gottman, J. M. (1973). N of 1 and N of 2 research in psychotherapy. *Psychological Bulletin, 80,* 93–105.

Gresham, F. M., & Noell, G. H. (1993). Issues in classification of childhood psychopathology. In T. R. Kratochwill & R. J. Morris (Eds.), *Handbook of psychotherapy with children and adolescents* (pp. 108–128). Boston: Allyn & Bacon.

Guerin, P. J. (Ed.). (1976). *Family therapy: Theory and practice.* New York: Gardner.

Guerin, P. J., & Pendagast, E. G. (1976). Evaluation of family system and genogram. In P. J. Guerin (Ed.), *Family therapy: Theory and practice* (pp. 450–464). New York: Gardner.

Gurman, A. S. (1971). Group marital therapy: Clinical and empirical implications for outcome research. *International Journal of Group Psychotherapy, 21,* 174–189.

Gurman, A. S. (1973). The effects and effectiveness of marital therapy: A review of outcome research. *Family Process, 12,* 145–170.

Gurman, A. S., & Kniskern, D. P. (1978). Behavioral marriage therapy: II. Empirical perspectives. *Family Process, 17,* 139–148.

Gurman, A. S., & Kniskern, D. P. (1978). Deterioration in marital and family therapy: Empirical, clinical, and conceptual issues. *Family Process, 17,* 3–20.

Gurman, A. S., & Kniskern, D. P. (1978). Research on marital and family therapy: Progress, perspective, and prospect. In S. L. Garfield & A. E. Bergin (Eds.), *Handbook of psychotherapy and behavior change: An empirical analysis* (2nd ed., pp. 817–902). New York: Wiley.

Gurman, A. S., & Kniskern, D. P. (1978). Technolatry, methodolatry, and the results of family therapy. *Family Process, 17,* 275–281.

Gurman, A. S., & Kniskern, D. P. (1981). Family therapy outcome research: Knowns and unknowns. In A. S. Gurman & D. P. Kniskern (Eds.), *Handbook of family therapy* (pp. 742–775). New York: Brunner/Mazel.

Guttman, H. A. (1989). The augmentation of creativity: Epistemological concerns and the excitement of innovation in family therapy. *Journal of Family Psychology, 2,* 473–476.

Haley, J. (1984). *Ordeal therapy.* San Francisco: Jossey-Bass.

Haley, J., & Hoffman, L. (1967). *Techniques of family therapy.* New York: Basic Books.

Hall, A. D., & Fagen, R. E. (1968). Definition of system. In W. Buckley (Ed.), *Modern systems research for the behavioral scientist* (pp. 81–92). Chicago: Aldine.

Handel, G. (Ed.). (1967). *The psychosocial interior of the family: A sourcebook for the study of whole families.* Chicago: Aldine.

Hansen, J. C. (Series Ed.), & Keeney, B. P. (Vol. Ed). (1983). *Family therapy collections: Vol. 4. Diagnosis and assessment in family therapy.* Rockville, MD: Aspen Systems.

Hartop, W. W. (1979). The social worlds of childhood. *American Psychologist, 34,* 944–950.

Henry, J. (1971). *Pathways to madness.* New York: Random House.

Hersen, M., & Barlow, D. (1976). *Single case experimental designs: Strategies for studying behavior change.* New York: Pergamon.

Hess, R. D., & Handel, G. (1974). *Family worlds: A psychosocial approach to family life.* Chicago: University of Chicago Press. (Original work published 1959)

Jackson, D. D. (1957). The question of family homeostasis. *The Psychiatric Quarterly Supplement, 31,* 79–90.

Jacobson, N. S. (1978). A review of the research on the effectiveness of marital therapy. In T. L. Paolino & B. S. McCrady (Eds.), *Marriage and marital therapy: Psychoanalytic, behavioral and systems theory perspectives* (pp. 395–444). New York: Brunner/Mazel.

Jacobson, N. S. (1979). Behavioral treatments for marital discord: A critical appraisal. *Progress in Behavior Modification, 8,* 169–205.

Jacobson, N. S., & Margolin, G. (1979). *Marital therapy: Strategies based on social learning and behavior exchange principles.* New York: Brunner/Mazel.

Jacobson, N. S., & Martin, B. (1976). Behavioral marriage therapy: Current status. *Psychological Bulletin, 83,* 540–556.

Jacobson, N. S., & Weiss, R. L. (1978). Behavioral marriage therapy: II. The contents of Gurman et al. may be hazardous to our health. *Family Process, 17,* 149–164.

Jessee, E., & L'Abate, L. (1981). Comments on Dell's paper. *Family Process, 20,* 42–44.

Kantor, D. (1985). "Circularity" in the management of a case. In J. C. Hansen (Series Ed.), L. L. Andreozzi, & R. F. Levant (Vol. Eds.), *Family therapy collections: Vol. 15. Integrating research and clinical practice* (pp. 51–70). Rockville, MD: Aspen Systems.

Kantor, D. (1985). Couples therapy, crisis induction, and change. In A. S. Gurman (Ed.), *Casebook of marital therapy* (pp. 21–72). New York: Guilford.

Kaslow, F. W. (1980). History of family therapy in the United States: A kaleidoscopic overview. *Marriage and Family Review, 3*(1/2), 79–110.

Kazdin, A. E. (1978). Methodological and interpretive problems of single-case experimental designs. *Journal of Consulting and Clinical Psychology, 46,* 629–642.

Kazdin, A. E. (1993). Research issues in child psychotherapy. In T. R. Kratochwill & R. J. Morris (Eds.), *Handbook of psychotherapy with children and adolescents* (pp. 541–565). Boston: Allyn & Bacon.

Kazdin, A. E. (1994). Methodology, design, and evaluation in psychotherapy research. In A. E. Bergin & S. L. Garfield (Eds.), *Handbook of psychotherapy and behavior* (4th ed., pp. 19–71). New York: Wiley.

Kazdin, A. E. (1994). Psychotherapy for children and adolescents. In A. E. Bergin & S. L. Garfield (Eds.), *Handbook of psychotherapy and behavior change* (4th ed., pp. 543–594). New York: Wiley.

Keeney, B. P. (1983). Ecological assessment. In J. C. Hansen (Series Ed.) & B. P. Keeney (Vol. Ed.), *Family therapy collections: Vol. 4. Diagnosis and assessment in family therapy* (pp. 156–170). Rockville, MD: Aspen Systems.

Kellam, S. G., Ensminger, M. E., & Turner, R. J. (1977). Family structure and the mental health of children. *Archives of General Psychiatry, 34,* 1012–1022.

Keniston, K. (1977). *All our children: The American family under pressure.* New York: Harcourt Brace Jovanovich.

Kerr, M. (1981). Family systems theory and therapy. In A. S. Gurman & D. P. Kniskern (Eds.), *Handbook of family therapy* (pp. 226–266). New York: Brunner/Mazel.

Kiesler, D. J. (1966). Some myths of psychotherapy research and the search for a paradigm. *Psychological Bulletin, 65,* 110–136.

Kiesler, D. J. (1973). *The process of psychotherapy: Empirical foundations and systems of analysis.* Chicago: Aldine.

Klein, M. H., & Gurman, A. S. (1981). Ritual and reality: Some clinical implications of experimental designs. In L. Rehm (Ed.), *Behavior therapy for depression* (pp. 337–364). New York: Academic Press.

Kniskern, D. P., & Gurman, A. S. (1979). Research on training in marriage and family therapy: Status, issues and directions. *Journal of Marital and Family Therapy, 5,* 83–94.

L'Abate, L., & Wagner, V. (1985). Theory-derived, family-oriented test batteries. In L. L'Abate (Ed.), *The handbook of family psychology and therapy* (Vol. 2, pp. 1006–1034). Homewood, IL: Dorsey.

Lambert, M. J., & Bergin, A. E. (1994). The effectiveness of psychotherapy. In A. E. Bergin & S. L. Garfield (Eds.), *Handbook of psychotherapy and behavior change* (4th ed., pp. 143–189). New York: Wiley.

Lambert, M. J., Bergin, A. E., & Collins, J. L. (1979). Therapist-induced deterioration in psychotherapy. In A. S. Gurman & A. M. Razin (Eds.), *Effective psychotherapy: A handbook of research* (pp. 452–481). New York: Pergamon.

Lebow, J. (1981). Issues in the assessment of outcome in family therapy. *Family Process, 20,* 167–188.

Lerner, R. M., & Spanier, G. B. (1978). A dynamic interactional view of child and family development. In R. M. Lerner & G. B. Spanier (Eds.), *Child influences on marital and family interaction: A life-span perspective* (pp. 1–22). New York: Academic Press.

Mahler, M. S., Pine, F., & Bergman, A. (1975). *The psychological birth of the human infant: Symbiosis and individuation.* New York: Basic Books.

Mahoney, M. J. (1978). Experimental methods and outcome evaluation. *Journal of Consulting and Clinical Psychology, 46,* 660–672.

Martin, B. (1975). Parent-child relations. In F. D. Horowitz (Ed.), *Review of child development research* (Vol. 4, pp. 463–540). Chicago: University of Chicago Press.

McGillicuddy-DeLisi, A. V., Siegel, I. E., & Johnson, J. E. (1979). The family as a system of mutual influences: Parental beliefs, distancing behaviors, and children's representational thinking. In M. Lewis & L. A. Rosenblum (Eds.), *Genesis of behavior: Vol. 2. The child and its family* (pp. 91–106). New York: Plenum.

McLemore, C. W., & Benjamin, L. S. (1979). Whatever happened to interpersonal diagnosis? A psychosocial alternative to DSM-III. *American Psychologist, 34,* 17–34.

Minuchin, S., Rosman, B., & Baker, L. (1978). *Psychosomatic families.* Cambridge, MA: Harvard University Press.

Moss-Kagel, C., Abramovitz, R., & Sager, C. J. (1989). Training therapists to treat the young child in the family and the family in the young child's treatment. *Journal of Psychotherapy and the Family, 5,* 117–144.

Napier, A. Y., & Whitaker, C. A. (1978). *The family crucible.* New York: Harper and Row.

Neimeyer, R. A. (1993). An appraisal of constructivist psychotherapies. *Journal of Consulting and Clinical Psychology, 61,* 221–234.

O'Leary, K. D., & Turkewitz, H. (1978). Methodological errors in marital and child treatment research. *Journal of Consulting and Clinical Psychology, 46,* 747–758.

Olson, D. H. (1970). Marital and family therapy: Integrative review and critique. *Journal of Marriage and the Family, 32,* 501–538.

Olson, D. H. (Ed.). (1976). *Treating relationships.* Lake Mills, IA: Graphic.

Olson, D. H., Russel, C. S., & Sprenkle, D. H. (1980). Marital and family therapy: A decade of review. *Journal of Marriage and the Family, 42,* 973–993.

Orlinsky, D. E., Grawe, K., & Parks, B. K. (1994). Process and outcome in psychotherapy—noch einmal. In A. E. Bergin & S. L. Garfield (Eds.), *Handbook of psychotherapy and behavior change* (4th ed., pp. 270–376). New York: Wiley.

Palazzoli-Selvini, M., Boscolo, L., Cecchin, G. F., & Prata, G. (1974). The treatment of children through brief therapy of their parents. *Family Process, 13,* 429–442.

Parloff, M. B., Waskow, I. E., & Wolfe, B. E. (1978). Research on therapist variables in relation to process and outcome. In S. L. Garfield & A. E. Bergin (Eds.), *Handbook of psychotherapy and behavior change* (2nd ed., pp. 233–282). New York: Wiley.

Penn, P. (1982). Circular questioning. *Family Process, 21,* 267–280.

Pinsof, W. M. (1981). Family therapy process research. In A. S. Gurman & D. P. Kniskern (Eds.), *Handbook of family therapy* (pp. 699–741). New York: Brunner/Mazel.

Rabin, C. (1981). The potential contribution of the single-case design in family therapy evaluation research. *Family Process, 20,* 351–366.

Sattler, J. M. (1990). *Assessment of children* (3rd ed.). San Diego, CA: Jerome M. Sattler.

Schaefer, E. S. (1965). A configurational analysis of children's reports of parent behavior. *Journal of Consulting Psychology, 29,* 552–557.

Sells, S. P., Smith, T. E., Coe, M. J., Yoshioka, M., & Robbins, J. (1994). An ethnography of couple and therapist experiences in reflecting team practice. *Journal of Marital and Family Therapy, 20,* 247–266.

Shapiro, R. J. (1974). Therapist attitudes and premature termination in family and individual therapy. *Journal of Nervous and Mental Disease, 159,* 101–107.

Shapiro, R. J., & Budman, S. H. (1973). Defection, termination, and continuation in family and individual therapy. *Family Process, 12,* 55–67.

Shields, C. G. (1986). Family therapy research and practice: Constructs, measurement, and testing. *Journal of Marital and Family Therapy, 12,* 379–382.

Shields, C. G., Wynne, L. C., McDaniel, S. H., & Gawinski, B. A. (1994). Conceptual and structural marginalization: Challenges and opportunities for the field of family therapy {a rejoinder to Hardy and Anderson}. *Journal of Marital and Family Therapy, 20,* 297–300.

Shields, C. G., Wynne, L. C., McDaniel, S. H., & Gawinski, B. A. (1994). The marginalization of family therapy: A historical and continuing problem. *Journal of Marital and Family Therapy, 20,* 117–138.

Sholevar, G. P. (1981). The emotional impact of family disruption on children. In G. P. Sholevar (Ed.), *The handbook of marriage and marital therapy* (pp. 461–474). Philadelphia: Spectrum Publications Medical and Scientific Books.

Sigal, J. J., Lasry, J. C., Guttman, H., Chagoya, L., & Pilon, R. (1977). Some stable characteristics of family therapists' interventions in real and simulated therapy sessions. *Journal of Consulting and Clinical Psychology, 45,* 23–26.

Simmons, D. S., & Doherty, W. J. (1995). Defining who we are and what we do: Clinical practice patterns of marital and family therapists in Minnesota. *Journal of Marital and Family Therapy, 21,* 3–16.

Smith, T. E., Sells, S. P., & Clevenger, T. (1994). Ethnographic content analysis of couple and therapist perceptions in a reflecting team setting. *Journal of Marital and Family Therapy, 20,* 267–286.

Stanton, M. D. (1981). An integrated structural/strategic approach to family therapy. *Journal of Marital and Family Therapy, 7,* 427–439.

Stanton, M. D. (1981). Marital therapy from a structural/strategic viewpoint. In G. P. Sholevar (Ed.), *The handbook of marriage and marital therapy* (pp. 303–334). Philadelphia: Spectrum Publications Medical and Scientific Books.

Stanton, M. D. (1981). Strategic approaches to family therapy. In A. S. Gurman & D. P. Kniskern (Eds.), *Handbook of family therapy* (pp. 361–402). New York: Brunner/Mazel.

Stanton, M. D., & Todd, T. C. (1980). A critique of the Wells and Denzen review of the results of non behavioral family therapy outcome studies. *Family Process, 19,* 169–176.

Stierlin, H. (1976). The dynamics of owning and disowning: Psychoanalytic and family perspectives. *Family Process, 15,* 277–288.

Stierlin, H. (1977). *Psychoanalysis and family therapy.* New York: Jason Aronson.

Stierlin, H. (1983). Family therapy—a science or an art? *Family Process, 22,* 413–424.

Stierlin, H., Levi, L. D., & Savard, R. J. (1973). Centrifugal versus centripetal separation in adolescence: Two patterns and some of their implications. In S. C. Feinstein & P. L. Giovacchini (Eds.), *Annals of the American Society for Adolescent Psychiatry: Vol. 2. Developmental and clinical studies* (pp. 211–239). New York: Basic Books.

Todd, T. C., & Stanton, M. D. (1983). Research on marital and family therapy: Answers, issues, and recommendations for the future. In B. Wolman & G. Striker (Eds.), *Handbook of family and marital therapy* (pp. 91–116). New York: Plenum.

von Foerster, H. (1981). *Observing systems.* Seaside, CA: Intersystems.

Wambolt, F. S., Wambolt, M. Z., & Gurman, A. S. (1985). Marital and family research: The meaning for the clinician. In J. C. Hansen (Series Ed.) & L. L. Andreozzi (Vol. Ed.), *Family therapy collections: Vol. 15. Integrating research and clinical practice* (pp. 11–26). Rockville, MD: Aspen Systems.

Wellisch, D. K., Vincent, J., & Ro-Trock, G. K. (1976). Family therapy versus individual therapy: A study of adolescents and their parents. In D. H. L. Olson (Ed.), *Treating relationships* (pp. 275–302). Lake Mills, IA: Graphic.

Wells, R. A. (1980). Tempests, teapots (and research design): Rejoinder to Stanton and Todd. *Family Process, 19,* 177–178.

Wells, R. A., & Dezen, A. E. (1978). The results of family therapy revisited: The nonbehavioral methods. *Family Process, 17,* 251–274.

Wells, R. A., Dilkes, T. C., & Trivelli, N. (1972). The results of family therapy: A critical review of the literature. *Family Process, 11,* 189–208.

Whitaker, C. A., & Keith, D. V. (1981). Symbolic-experiential family therapy. In A. S. Gurman & D. P. Kniskern (Eds.), *Handbook of family therapy* (pp. 187–225). New York: Brunner/Mazel.

Winter, W. D., & Ferreira, A. J. (Eds.). (1969). *Research in family interaction: Readings and commentary.* Palo Alto, CA: Science and Behavior Books.

Woodward, C. A., Santa-Barbara, J., Levin, S., & Epstein, N. B. (1978). Aspects of consumer satisfaction with brief family therapy. *Family Process, 17,* 399–407.

Woodward, C. A., Santa-Barbara, J., Streiner, D. L., Goodman, J. T., Levin, S., & Epstein, N. B. (1981). Client, treatment, and therapist variables related to outcome in brief, systems-oriented family therapy. *Family Process, 20,* 189–197.

Ziegler, R. G., & Musliner, P. J. (1977). Persistent themes: A naturalistic study of personality development in the family. *Family Process, 16,* 293–305.

Author Index

Subject Index